Penguin Books

# THE PENGUIN CRICKETER'S COMPANION

Alan Ross was born in Calcutta, educated at Haileybury
and St John's College, Oxford. He played cricket and
squash rackets for Oxford and the Royal Navy, in which
he served during the war. He was Cricket Correspondent
of the *Observer* from 1953 to 1972, during which time he
wrote a number of cricket books, among them *Australia 55*,
*Cape Summer* and *Through the Caribbean*. He is at present
Editor of *London Magazine*. He has published several
volumes of poetry and now writes on cricket for *The
Times*.

# The Penguin
# Cricketer's Companion

Edited by Alan Ross

PENGUIN BOOKS

Penguin Books Ltd, Harmondsworth, Middlesex, England
Penguin Books, 40 West 23rd Street, New York, New York 10010, U.S.A.
Penguin Books Australia Ltd, Ringwood, Victoria, Australia
Penguin Books Canada Ltd, 2801 John Street, Markham, Ontario, Canada L3R 1B4
Penguin Books (N.Z.) Ltd, 182–190 Wairau Road, Auckland 10, New Zealand

—

First published by Eyre & Spottiswoode 1960
This revised and expanded Second Edition first published
by Eyre Methuen 1979
Published in Penguin Books 1981
Reprinted 1981, 1982, 1984

—

—

Made and printed in Great Britain by
Richard Clay (The Chaucer Press) Ltd,
Bungay, Suffolk
Set in Monotype Garamond

## TO JEREMY HUTCHINSON

# Contents

## PART III: MEN AND MOMENTS

## PART IV: THE POETRY OF CRICKET

# CONTENTS

# PART V: NEW POETRY

# CONTENTS

## PART VI: NEW PROSE

# Notes on the Illustrations

Cricket at Fenner's from *A Cambridge Scrapbook* (1859)
*title page*

Two Cartoons of W. G. Grace by Harry Furniss from *A Century of Grace* (1895). *Courtesy M.C.C.*    *pages* 220, 226

Four studies by G. F. Watts, taken from lithographs drawn to illustrate the principles of correct batsmanship for the treatise *Felix on the bat* by Nicholas Felix (Nicholas Wanostrocht), originally published in 1845. The quotations from Shakespeare attached to each appear at the head of the author's own chapters. *Courtesy Parker Gallery.*    *pages* 8, 204, 326, 398

'Well may "One of the Olden Time" stare with astonishment at the leather casings, military gauntlets, India rubber paddings, cork and whalebone accoutrements of "One of the Modern Time".' 'Felix' was concerned at the effects of the introduction of overarm bowling. *Courtesy Parker Gallery.*    *pages* 58, 316

Five humorous drawings, also from *Felix on the bat*, that illustrate 'What you ought not to do'. *Courtesy Parker Gallery.*
*pages* 150, 202, 270, 324, 340

Cricket played by the Gentlemen's Club, White Conduit Field, Islington, 1788. *Courtesy M.C.C.*    *page* 190

The other drawings are taken from Specimens of Polytype Ornaments cast by J. and R. M. Wood, and from 'A Handbook of Electros and Casts' (Stephenson, Blake).

# The Cricketer's Companion

# Preface to the Second Edition

In the nineteen years since the first edition of *The Cricketer's Companion* was published the game has changed out of all recognition. It is now more prosperous, more commercial and possibly more lethal. I don't know whether it is actually more dangerous, or merely appears to be so. Certainly, defensive equipment – helmets with visors, for close fieldsmen as well as for batsmen – suggests a different sort of contest altogether. It may simply be a passing fad, as ephemeral as Packer's Circus. On the other hand, it may spread to village cricket, with bizarre results. Perhaps by the time these words appear the bouncer may have been more strictly controlled and the helmet have become a thing of the past. Sir Leonard Hutton, who faced more bouncers in his career than most, has remarked that he never expected to be hit and only once was. Whether the wearing of helmets – hideous objects that make batsmen almost unrecognizable as individuals – will further encourage the bowling of bouncers is debatable. What cannot be in dispute is that the bouncer, except as a rarely used, surprise weapon, is in every way bad for cricket. The thumping of balls at great pace halfway down the pitch is a monotonous spectacle, restrictive of every stroke except the half protective stab and the hook. It will produce no literature. Similarly, the commercialization of cricket – as opposed to cricketers being able to make a decent living out of it – can only result in deterioration. What Mary Russell Mitford wrote, in the opening words of this anthology, 'I doubt if there be any scene in the world more animating or delightful than a cricket match', will no longer be the case. Cricket will be a different game, less beautiful, less part of the social fabric, less an extension of landscape. It will become a business, not a sport.

In 1959, when I prepared the first edition of this book, there were comparatively few overseas players in county cricket. Now West Indians, South Africans, Pakistanis, Australians, New Zealanders and Indians are the stars of it. They have raised the standard, but not to our own advantage. This, again, may change. As I write, we seem to be at the start of a new era in English cricket, to which defections to Packer have unwittingly contributed. When, say in another 15 years or so, a new edition of *The Cricketer's Companion* is being got ready, players like Botham and Gower may find their places among the ranks of Sobers and Graveney.

I have included nothing new in this edition that was written before 1960. To avoid re-setting the whole book the new material has been printed in two sections at the end. To make room for it I have excluded from this edition a story by H. A. Vachell, the section Great Matches, and a piece on Ranji by Country Vicar. The most surprising thing, perhaps, is the number of good poems written about cricket in recent years. There have been no stories of any quality to my knowledge, but we print extracts from two immensely enjoyable novels that have a good deal of cricket in them. As far as Great Players are concerned, it was largely a question of finding writing that did justice to the players I wanted. Among the great ones of my time I am conscious of many omissions, particularly May, Dexter, Trueman, Lindwall, Tyson, Evans, Ramadhin, Worrell, Weekes and Walcott. One could extend the list indefinitely, up to Barry Richards, Graham Pollock and Vivian Richards. But I have gone rather for the writer than for the player.

I wish the new sections could have been twice as long. There have been several good anthologies in recent years, notably those made by Benny Green, Kenneth Gregory and Ron

Roberts; I have tried to avoid duplication. As far as possible, *The Cricketer's Companion* is to do with literature, rather than journalism, if one may make such a distinction.

Alan Ross

Clayton, 1978

# Introduction

Stories, matches, players, poems, more or less this is how I have grouped these writings about cricket. In the third section, *Men and Moments*, the emphasis is on the writer as much as on the subject. Here, Nyren, Pycroft, Andrew Lang, Neville Cardus, Edmund Blunden, and Robertson-Glasgow among others show their paces, though some of them also appear in more specific contexts elsewhere, as poets or describing great cricketers.

There have, over the years, been a number of cricket anthologies. Gerald Brodribb's *The Book of Cricket Verse* and *The English Game*, Eric Parker's *Between the Wickets*, E. W. Swanton's *Best Cricket Stories*, R. H. Lowe's *A Cricket Eleven* immediately come to mind. An initial difficulty, therefore, is to produce something fresh. Necessarily, a fair amount of this book will be familiar to the experts. That is unavoidable, though I have seen to it that there are certain items that will be unknown even to them; at the same time, the familiar can take on new life in a sympathetic context. In the last resort, however, a good anthology is a personal affair, and my pleasure in making this one has come from just that weighing and selecting that derives from reading with more than casual purpose.

I aimed at two things, the creating of a book that contained the most essential and enjoyable writing on the game, in whatever medium, and one that gave as inclusive a view as possible of the great landmarks. So that, if this book was all that a shipwrecked mariner was able to salvage, he would get from it both a feeling of how cricket developed and a reminder of its greatest ornaments, from the forerunners through the Golden Age to the present day. It was an ambitious scheme, and all along the line there are inevitable gaps, either through lack of space or simply because certain great players failed to find their literary equivalent. It is a fact, regrettably, that writers about cricket, however knowing as commentators, or skilled at reading a match, have rarely set themselves to create a stereoscopic image of individual players, bringing forward their methods and mannerisms for the scrutiny of later generations. E. W. Swanton's extract on Compton is a good example of this. Since Nyren there have been a bare half-dozen. We live in an age of increasing reportage and anecdote, in which a literate and informed prose style, as practised, for example, by Neville Cardus and Robertson-Glasgow, has less and less place. What is missing from most contemporary writing is the power to suggest an atmosphere, to define character, or produce the kind of telling image that will linger on in the mind long after scores and statistics have staled. The discursive port-and-cigars manner went out with cloche hats. So did the essay. Nevertheless, having set myself the task of re-reading the whole literature of cricket – not without apprehension – I must admit that what started out as a chore ended with sufficient feeling of reward. There is dead and slovenly writing galore: but, if one has any fever for cricket at all, there are moments of high drama and rich character. Often these are not, for one reason or another, translatable into anthology terms, since I have determined to avoid the scrappiness that plagues most anthologies, wherein no sooner have you got into the mood of something than it is over. There is little here for the grasshopper: this book is for the reader, not the skimmer, else it would not have been worth the doing.

A note about the various sections. Cricket in fiction, which Gerald Brodribb describes in an essay, is almost exclusively rural and comic in character. It is one of the genuine mysteries that English novelists and short story writers of quality, even when passionately interested in sport, have made virtually no use of it. What I have printed here seems to me about the best that can be done.

The chapters from Rex Warner's *Escapade* and L. P. Hartley's *The Go-Between*, both published in the last seven years, represent rare excursions into cricket by distinguished writers of prose, and they are, because of this, of unusual interest. Yet there has been no novel of county cricket, scarcely a credible character study of a first-class cricketer. Perhaps it is that real cricket offers more drama than fiction ever could. Certainly, year in, year out, things happen that novelists would scarcely dare invent. It may be, simply, that professional cricket is a specialized, exclusive world, with an idiom and a manner not easily accessible to anyone not professionally involved in it. Yet there are writers, H. E. Bates for example, or Brian Glanville, whom one can imagine as being capable of bringing off the authentic background without loss of dramatic irony and without brazen simplification. Cricket could have done with a Ring Lardner, even a Nat Gould.

However, Part I is fairly representative of the best that has been written so far.

Part II, *Great Players*, speaks for itself. Since I have imagined one kind of this book's potential readers as being the young unbored, eager to see their heroes in the round, I have gone for passages that do rather more than give plain facts.

Denzil Batchelor on Fry's Box at Lord's, for example, creates an era of vanished splendour as vividly as do the red roses that adorn the buttonholes of ancient M.C.C. members, elegant and martial, on Test Match days. Similarly, John Arlott on Tate suggests not only a fine bowler in action, but Hove in the marvellous Twenties, with Tate at one end, Gilligan at the other, and a sea-fret that spelt death and destruction to their enemies. In this, and the next section, *Men and Moments*, I have tried to focus a number of great players, from Grace and Ranji to Hutton and Miller, at the same time offering a selection of the most notable passages of cricket prose, so that some sort of development can be traced from Nyren and Pycroft, through Daft and Andrew Lang, to Cardus, Blunden, and Robertson-Glasgow. Arthur Mailey may seem a stranger in this company, though he could not but be a welcome addition to any. However, in his description of how he dismissed his hero, Victor Trumper,

'There was no triumph in me as I watched the receding figure. I felt like a boy who had killed a dove', he has achieved one of the most tender images in cricket literature.

*The poetry of cricket* is, with few exceptions, light verse. There is nothing surprising about this, since professional poets of quality are in any case few and far between, and those who could claim to have cricket in their blood, so that a poem on cricket would be part of their experience rather than an academic exercise, even rarer. There is not much about Test matches here, except Lord Beginner's triumphant Victory Calypso, rather more about county cricket, but again not much, a few tributes to cherished or legendary cricketers, most nostalgic. By and large, the affections have been aroused by humbler activities altogether, by country cricket grounds, village encounters, rural eccentrics. The atmosphere of these comes through persuasively and clearly, without fuss or strain, principally through the element of participation. English allegiances are notoriously local, though our pride may be justifiably national.

There remains a gap, nevertheless, the absence of 'portrait' poems that give a close-up of cricketers and transfer them in habit and stature from the field to the page. These, as I know from experience, are difficult to achieve; yet the modern idioms of both cricket and poetry demand something more stylistically attuned than the stock sentimentalities, however moving in their context, of the recognized anthology pieces. 'O my Hornby and my Barlow long ago' has lost nothing in evocativeness over the years, but a confusion between cricket, character and moral standards has resulted in too much glutinous piety in all forms of cricket writing. First-class cricketers are no more sober and righteous than other men, and they will thank no one for saying they are. What they often have is a downright earthiness, a view of one another that stops some way short of idolatory, a gift for understatement and epithet. The best of them have professional pride, a true concern for technique, integrity, robust wit and courage. Test cricket is as tough a game as they come, its beauty and fascination are essentially for the connoisseur, and no one should have it otherwise. Cricket, however, exists on a variety of levels, each with its own characteristics, and they have all, as far as possible, been represented here.

One relies in a book such as this on friends for advice and help. I would like particularly to record my debt to Handasyde Buchanan, whose assistance in choosing and collecting the material for section II has been invaluable. Gerald Brodribb has done much initial research into the fiction and poetry of the game and without the benefit of his work mine would have been that much harder. I must also thank L. E. S. Gutteridge, of Epworth Books, for chasing up wanted items, for his generosity in loaning me many books and for so patiently awaiting their return.

ALAN ROSS

CLAYTON,
SUSSEX

# PART I

# Cricket Stories

'Patient, dramatic, serious, genial
From over to over the game goes on
Weaving a pattern of hardy perennial
Civilization under the sun.'

*Gerald Bullett*
VILLAGE CRICKET

**PLAY!**

'The play's the thing!'
*Hamlet*

# A Country Cricket Match

## MARY RUSSELL MITFORD

I doubt if there be any scene in the world more animating or
delightful than a cricket-match – I do not mean a set match at
Lord's Ground, for money, hard money, between a certain number of gentlemen and players, as they are called – people who
make a trade of that noble sport, and degrade it into an affair of
bettings, and hedgings and cheatings, it may be, like boxing or
horse-racing; nor do I mean a pretty fête in a gentleman's park,
where one club of cricketing dandies encounter another such
club, and where they show off in graceful costume to a gay
marquee of admiring belles, who condescend so to purchase
admiration, and while away a long summer morning in par-
taking cold collations, conversing occasionally, and seeming to
understand the game – the whole being conducted according to
ball-room etiquette, so as to be exceedingly elegant and exceedingly dull. No! the cricket that I mean is a real solid old-
fashioned match between neighbouring parishes, where each
attacks the other for honour and a supper, glory and half-a-
crown a man. If there be any gentlemen amongst them, it is
well – if not, it is so much the better. Your gentleman cricketer
is in general rather an anomalous character. Elderly gentlemen
are obviously good for nothing; and your beaux are, for the
most part, hampered and trammelled by dress and habit; the stiff
cravat, the pinched-in-waist, the dandy-walk – oh, they will
never do for cricket! Now, our country lads, accustomed to the
flail or the hammer (your blacksmiths are capital hitters) have
the free use of their arms; they know how to move their
shoulders; and they can move their feet too – they can run; then
they are so much better made, so much more athletic, and yet so

9

much lissimer – to use a Hampshire phrase, which deserves at least to be good English. Here and there, indeed, one meets with an old Etonian, who retains his boyish love for that game which formed so considerable a branch of his education; some even preserve their boyish proficiency, but in general it wears away like the Greek, quite as certainly, and almost as fast; a few years of Oxford, or Cambridge, or the Continent, are sufficient to annihilate both the power and the inclination. No! a village match is the thing – where our highest officer – our conductor (to borrow a musical term) is but a little farmer's second son; where a day-labourer is our bowler, and a blacksmith our long-stop; where the spectators consist of the retired cricketers, the veterans of the green, the careful mothers, the girls, and all the boys of two parishes, together with a few amateurs, little above them in rank, and not at all in pretension; where laughing and shouting, and the very ecstasy of merriment and good-humour prevail: such a match, in short, as I attended yesterday, at the expense of getting twice wet through, and as I would attend tomorrow, at the certainty of having that ducking doubled.

For the last three weeks our village has been in a state of great excitement, occasioned by a challenge from our north-western neighbours, the men of B., to contend with us at cricket. Now, we have not been much in the habit of playing matches. Three or four years ago, indeed, we encountered the men of S., our neighbours south-by-east, with a sort of doubtful success, beating them on our own ground, whilst they in the second match returned the compliment on theirs. This discouraged us. Then an unnatural coalition between a high-church curate and an evangelical gentleman-farmer drove our lads from the Sunday-even practice, which, as it did not begin before both services were concluded, and as it tended to keep the young men from the ale-house, our magistrates had winked at if not encouraged. The sport, therefore, had languished until the present season, when under another change of circumstances the spirit began to revive. Half-a-dozen fine active lads, of influence amongst

their comrades, grew into men and yearned for cricket; an enterprising publican gave a set of ribands: his rival, mine host of the
Rose, and out-doer by profession, gave two; and the clergyman
and his lay ally, both well-disposed and good-natured men,
gratified by the submission to their authority, and finding, perhaps, that no great good resulted from the substitution of public
houses for out-of-doors diversions, relaxed. In short, the practice
re-commenced, and the hill was again alive with men and boys,
and innocent merriment; but farther than the riband matches
amongst ourselves nobody dreamed of going, till this challenge
– we were modest, and doubted our own strength. The B.
people, on the other hand, must have been braggers born, a
whole parish of gasconaders. Never was such boasting! such
crowing! such ostentatious display of practice! such mutual
compliments from man to man – bowler to batter, batter to
bowler! It was a wonder they did not challenge all England. It
must be confessed that we were a little astounded; yet we firmly
resolved not to decline the combat; and one of the most spirited
of the new growth, William Grey by name, took up the glove
in a style of manly courtesy, that would have done honour to a
knight in the days of chivalry – 'We were not professed players,'
he said, 'being little better than school-boys, and scarcely older;
but, since they have done us the honour to challenge us, we
would try our strength. It would be no discredit to be beaten by
such a field.'

Having accepted the wager of battle, our champion began
forthwith to collect his forces. William Grey is himself one of
the finest youths that one shall see – tall, active, slender and yet
strong, with a piercing eye full of sagacity, and a smile full of
good honour – a farmer's son by station, and used to hard work
as farmers' sons are now, liked by everybody, and admitted to be
an excellent cricketer. He immediately set forth to muster his
men, remembering with great complacency that Samuel Long,
a bowler *comme il y en a peu*, the very man who had knocked down
nine wickets, had beaten us, bowled us out at the fatal return
match some years ago at S., had luckily, in a remove of a quarter

of a mile last Ladyday, crossed the boundaries of his old parish, and actually belonged to us. Here was a stroke of good fortune! Our captain applied to him instantly; and he agreed at a word. Indeed, Samuel Long is a very civilized person. He is a middle-aged man, who looks rather old amongst our young lads, and whose thickness and breadth gave no token of remarkable activity, but he is very active, and so steady a player! so safe! We had half gained the match when we had secured him. He is a man of substance, too, in every way; owns one cow, two donkeys, six pigs, and geese and ducks beyond count – dresses like a farmer, and owes no man a shilling – and all this from pure industry, sheer day-labour. Note that your good cricketer is commonly the most industrious man in the parish; the habits that make him such are precisely those which make a good workman – steadiness, sobriety, and activity – Samuel Long might pass for the beau ideal of the two characters. Happy were we to possess him! Then we had another piece of good luck. James Brown, a journeyman blacksmith and a native, who, being of a rambling disposition, had roamed from place to place for half-a-dozen years, had just returned to settle with his brother at another corner of our village, bringing with him a prodigious reputation in cricket and in gallantry – the gay Lothario of the neighbourhood. He is said to have made more conquests in love and in cricket than any blacksmith in the county. To him also went the indefatigable William Grey, and he also consented to play. No end to our good fortune! Another celebrated batter, called Joseph Hearne, had likewise recently married into the parish. He worked, it is true at the A. mills, but slept at the house of his wife's father in our territories. He also was sought and found by our leader. But he was grand and shy; made an immense favour of the thing; courted courting and then hung back – 'Did not know that he could be spared; had partly resolved not to play again – at least not this season; thought it rash to accept the challenge; thought they might do without him—' 'Truly I think so too,' said our spirited champion; 'we will not trouble you, Mr Hearne.'

Having thus secured two powerful auxiliaries and rejected a third, we began to reckon and select the regular native forces. Thus ran our list: William Grey, 1 – Samuel Long, 2 – James Brown, 3 – George and John Simmons, one capital the other so-so – an uncertain hitter, but a good fieldsman, 5 – Joel Brent, excellent, 6 – Ben Appleton – here was a little pause – Ben's abilities at cricket was not completely ascertained; but then he was so good a fellow, so full of fun and waggery! no doing without Ben. So he figured in the list, 7 – George Harris – a short halt there too! Slowish – slow but sure. I think the proverb brought him in, 8 – Tom Coper – Oh, beyond the world, Tom Coper! the red-headed gardening lad, whose left-handed strokes send *her* (a cricket-ball, like that other moving thing, a ship, is always of the feminine gender), send her spinning a mile, 9 – Harry Willis, another blacksmith, 10.

We had now ten of our eleven, but the choice of the last occasioned some demur. Three young Martins, rich farmers of the neighbourhood, successively presented themselves, and were all rejected by our independent and impartial general for want of merit – cricketal merit. 'Not good enough,' was his pithy answer. Then our worthy neighbour, the half-pay lieutenant, offered his services – he, too, though with some hesitation and modesty, was refused – 'Not quite young enough' was his sentence. John Strong, the exceeding long son of our dwarfish mason, was the next candidate – a nice youth – everybody likes John Strong – and a willing, but so tall and so limp, bent in the middle – a threadpaper, six feet high! We were all afraid that, in spite of his name, his strength would never hold out. 'Wait till next year, John,' quoth William Grey, with all the dignified seniority of twenty speaking to eighteen. 'Coper's a year younger,' said John. 'Coper's a foot shorter,' replied William: so John retired: and the eleventh man remained unchosen, almost to the eleventh hour. The eve of the match arrived, and the post was still vacant, when a little boy of fifteen, David Willis, brother to Harry, admitted by accident to the last practice, saw eight of them out, and was voted in by acclamation.

That Sunday evening's practice (for Monday was the important day) was a period of great anxiety, and, to say the truth, of great pleasure. There is something strangely delightful in the innocent spirit of party. To be one of a numerous body, to be authorized to say *we*, to have a rightful interest in triumph or defeat, is gratifying at once to social feeling and to personal pride. There was not a ten-year-old urchin, or a septuagenary woman in the parish who did not feel an additional importance, a reflected consequence, in speaking of 'our side'. An election interests in the same way; but that feeling is less pure. Money is there, and hatred, and politics, and lies. Oh, to be a voter, or a voter's wife, comes nothing near the genuine and hearty sympathy of belonging to a parish, breathing the same air, looking on the same trees, listening to the same nightingales! Talk of a patriotic elector! Give me a parochial patriot, a man who loves his parish. Even we, the female partisans, may partake the common ardour. I am sure I did. I never, though tolerably eager and enthusiastic at all times, remember being in a more delicious state of excitement than on the eve of that battle. Our hopes waxed stronger and stronger. Those of our players who were present were excellent. William Grey got forty notches off his own bat, and that brilliant hitter, Tom Coper, gained eight from two successive balls. As the evening advanced, too, we had encouragement of another sort. A spy, who had been despatched to reconnoitre the enemy's quarters, returned from their practising ground with a most consolatory report. 'Really,' said Charles Grover, our intelligence – a fine old steady judge, one who had played well in his day – 'they are no better than so many old women. Any five of ours would beat their eleven.' This sent us to bed in high spirits.

Morning dawned less favourably. The sky promised a series of deluging showers, and kept its word as English skies are wont to do on such occasions; and a lamentable message arrived at the head-quarters from our trusty comrade Joel Brent. His master, a great farmer, had begun the hay-harvest that very morning, and Joel, being as eminent in one field as in another, could not be spared. Imagine Joel's plight! the most ardent of all our eleven! a knight held back from the tourney! a soldier from the battle! The poor swain was inconsolable. At last, one who is always ready to do a good-natured action, great or little, set forth to back his petition; and, by dint of appealing to the public spirit of our worthy neighbour and the state of the barometer, talking alternately of the parish honour and thunder showers, of last matches and sopped hay, he carried his point, and returned triumphantly with the delighted Joel.

In the meantime, we became sensible of another defalcation. On calling over our roll, Brown was missing; and the spy of the preceding night, Charles Grover – the universal scout and messenger of the village, a man who will run half-a-dozen miles for a pint of beer, who does errands for the very love of the trade, who, if he had been a lord, would have been an ambassador – was instantly despatched to summon the truant. His report spread general consternation. Brown had set off at four o'clock in the morning to play in a cricket-match at M., a little town twelve miles off, which had been his last residence. Here was desertion! Here was treachery! Here was treachery against that goodly state, our parish! To send James Brown to Coventry was the immediate resolution; but even that seemed too light a punishment for such delinquency! Then how we cried him down! At ten on Sunday night (for the rascal had actually practised with us, and never said a word of his intended disloyalty) he was our faithful mate, and the best player (take him all in all) of the eleven. At ten in the morning he had run away, and we were well rid of him; he was no batter compared with William Grey or Tom Coper; not fit to wipe the shoes of Samuel Long, as a bowler; nothing of a scout to John Simmons; the boy David Willis was worth fifty of him –

> I trust we have within our realm
> Five hundred good as he

was the universal sentiment. So we took tall John Strong, who, with an incurable hankering after the honour of being admitted had kept constantly with the players, to take the chance of some such accident – we took John for our *pis aller*. I never saw anyone prouder than the good-humoured lad was of this not very flattering piece of preferment.

John Strong was elected, and Brown sent to Coventry; and when I first heard of his delinquency, I thought the punishment only too mild for the crime. But I have since learned the secret history of the offence (if we could know the secret histories of all offences, how much better the world would seem than it does now!) and really my wrath is much abated. It was a piece of gallantry, of devotion to the sex, or rather a chivalrous obedience to one chosen fair. I must tell my readers the story. Mary Allen, the prettiest girl of M., had, it seems, revenged upon our blacksmith the numberless inconsistencies of which he stood accused. He was in love over head and ears, but the nymph was cruel. She said no, and no, and no, and poor Brown, three times rejected, at last resolved to leave the place, partly in despair, and partly in the hope which often mingles strangely with a lover's despair, the hope that when he was gone he should be missed. He came home to his brother's accordingly, but for five weeks he heard nothing from or of the inexorable Mary, and was glad to beguile his own 'vexing thoughts' by endeavouring to create in his mind an artificial and factitious interest in our cricket-match – all unimportant as such a trifle must have seemed to a man in love. Poor James, however, is a social and warm-hearted person, not likely to resist a contagious sympathy. As the time for the play advanced, the interest which he had at first affected became genuine and sincere: and he was really, when he left the ground on Sunday night, almost as enthusiastically absorbed in the event of the next day, as Joel Brent himself. He little foresaw the new and delightful interest which awaited him at home, where, on the moment of his arrival, his sister-in-law and confidante presented him with a billet from the lady of his heart. It had, with the usual delay of letters sent by private hands in that rank of life, loitered on the road, in a degree inconceivable to those who are accustomed to the punctual speed of the post, and had taken ten days for its twelve miles' journey. Have my readers any wish to see this *billet-doux*? I can show them (but in strict confidence) a literal copy. It was addressed,

For mistur jem browne
'blaxmith by
'S'.

The inside ran thus:

'Mistur browne this is to Inform you that oure parish plays bramley men next monty is a week, i think we shall lose without yew, from your humbell servant to command

'Mary Allen.'

Was there ever a prettier relenting? a summons more flattering, more delicate, more irresistible? The precious epistle was undated; but, having ascertained who brought it, and found, by cross-examining the messenger, that the Monday in question was the very next day, we were not surprised to find that Mistur browne forgot his engagement to us, forgot all but Mary and Mary's letter, and set off at four o'clock the next morning to walk twelve miles, and to play for her parish, and in her sight. Really we must not send James Brown to Coventry – must we? Though if, as his sister-in-law tells our damsel Harriet he hopes to do, he should bring the fair Mary home as his bride, he will not greatly care how little we say to him. But he must not be sent to Coventry – True-love forbid!

At last we were all assembled, and marched down to H. common, the appointed ground, which, though in our dominions according to the maps, was the constant practising place of our opponents, and *terra incognita* to us. We found our adversaries on the ground as we expected, for our various delays had hindered us from taking the field so early as we wished; and as soon as we had settled all preliminaries, the match began.

But, alas! I have been so long settling my preliminaries, that

I have left myself no room for the detail of our victory, and must squeeze the account of our grand achievements into as little compass as Cowley, when he crammed the names of eleven of his mistresses into the narrow space of four eight-syllable lines. *They* began the warfare – those boastful men of B. And what think you, gentle reader, was the amount of their innings? These challengers – the famous eleven – how many did they get? Think! imagine! guess! – You cannot? – Well! – they got twenty-two, or rather, they got twenty; for two of theirs were short notches, and would never have been allowed, only that, seeing what they were made of, we and our umpires were not particular – They should have had twenty more if they had chosen to claim them. Oh, how well we fielded! and how well we bowled! our good play had quite as much to do with their miserable failure as their bad. Samuel Long is a slow bowler, George Simmons a fast one, and the change from Long's lobbing to Simmons's fast balls posed them completed. Poor simpletons! they were always wrong, expecting the slow for the quick, and the quick for the slow. Well, we went in. And what were our innings? Guess again! – guess! A hundred and sixty-nine! in spite of soaking showers, and wretched ground, where the ball would not run a yard, we headed them by a hundred and forty-seven; and then they gave in, as well they might. William Grey pressed them much to try another innings. 'There was so much chance,' as he courteously observed, 'in cricket, that advantageous as our position seemed, we might, very possibly, be overtaken. The B. men had better try.' But they were beaten sulky and would not move – to my great disappointment; I wanted to prolong the pleasure of success. What a glorious sensation it is to be for five hours together – winning –winning! always feeling what a whist-player feels when he takes up four honours, seven trumps! Who would think that a little bit of leather and two pieces of wood, had such a delightful and delighting power!

The only drawback on my enjoyment was the failure of the pretty boy, David Willis, who, injudiciously put in first, and playing for the first time in a match amongst men and strangers, who talked to him, and stared at him, was seized with such a fit of shamefaced shyness, that he could scarcely hold his bat, and was bowled out without a stroke, from actual nervousness. 'He will come off that,' Tom Coper says – I am afraid he will. I wonder whether Tom had ever any modesty to lose. Our other modest lad, John Strong, did very well; his length told in fielding and he got good fame. He ran out his mate, Samuel Long; who, I do believe, but for the excess of Joel's eagerness, would have stayed in till this time, by which exploit he got into sad disgrace; and then he himself got thirty-seven runs, which redeemed his reputation. William Grey made a hit which actually lost the cricket-ball. We think she lodged in a hedge, a quarter of a mile off, but nobody could find her. And George Simmons had nearly lost his shoe, which he tossed away in a passion, for having been caught out, owing to the ball glancing against it. These, together with a very complete somerset of Ben Appleton, our long-stop, who floundered about in the mud, making faces and attitudes as laughable as Grimaldi, none could tell whether by accident or design, were the chief incidents of the scene of action. Amongst the spectators nothing remarkable occurred, beyond the general calamity of two or three drenchings, except that a form, placed by the side of a hedge, under a very insufficient shelter, was knocked into the ditch in a sudden rush of the cricketers to escape a pelting shower, by which means all parties shared the fate of Ben Appleton, some on land and some by water; and that, amidst the scramble, a saucy gipsy of a girl contrived to steal from the knee of the demure and well-apparelled Samuel Long, a smart handkerchief which his careful dame had tied round it to preserve his new (what is the mincing feminine word?) – his new – inexpressibles, thus reversing the story of Desdemona, and causing the new Othello to call aloud for his handkerchief, to the great diversion of the company. And so we parted; the players retired to their supper, and we to our homes; all wet through, all good-humoured and happy – except the losers.

Today we are happy too. Hats, with ribands in them, go glancing up and down; and William Grey says, with a proud humility, 'We do not challenge any parish; but if we be challenged we are ready.'

*from* OUR VILLAGE *1832*

# *Dingley Dell v. All Muggleton*

## CHARLES DICKENS

The wickets were pitched, and so were a couple of marquees for the rest and refreshment of the contending parties. The game had not yet commenced. Two or three Dingley Dellers, and All-Muggletonians, were amusing themselves with a majestic air by throwing the ball carelessly from hand to hand; and several other gentlemen dressed like them, in straw hats, flannel jackets, and white trousers – a costume in which they looked very much like amateur stone-masons – were sprinkled about the tents, towards one of which Mr Wardle conducted the party.

Several dozen of 'How-are-you's?' hailed the old gentleman's arrival; and a general raising of the straw hats, and bending forward of the flannel jackets, followed his introduction of his guests as gentlemen from London, who were extremely anxious to witness the proceedings of the day, with which, he had no doubt, they would be greatly delighted.

'You had better step into the marquee, I think, sir,' said one very stout gentleman, whose body and legs looked like half a gigantic roll of flannel, elevated on a couple of inflated pillow-cases.

'You'll find it much pleasanter, sir,' urged another stout gentleman, who strongly resembled the other half of the roll of flannel aforesaid.

'You're very good,' said Mr Pickwick.

'This way,' said the first speaker; 'they notch in here – it's the best place in the whole field'; and the cricketer, panting on before, preceded them to the tent.

'Capital game – smart sport – fine exercise – very,' were the words which fell upon Mr Pickwick's ear as he entered the tent; and the first object that met his eyes was his green-coated friend of the Rochester coach, holding forth, to the no small delight and edification of a select circle of the chosen of All-Muggleton. His dress was slightly improved, and he wore boots; but there was no mistaking him.

The stranger recognized his friends immediately; and, darting forward and seizing Mr Pickwick by the hand, dragged him to a seat with his usual impetuosity, talking all the while as if the whole of the arrangements were under his especial patronage and direction.

'This way – this way – capital fun – lots of beer – hogsheads; rounds of beef – bullocks; mustard – cart loads; glorious day – down with you – make yourself at home – glad to see you – very.'

Mr Pickwick sat down as he was bid, and Mr Winkle and Mr Snodgrass also complied with the directions of their mysterious friend. Mr Wardle looked on, in silent wonder.

'Mr Wardle – a friend of mine,' said Mr Pickwick.

'Friend of yours! – My dear sir, how are you? – Friend of *my* friend's – give me your hand, sir' – and the stranger grasped Mr Wardle's hand with all the fervour of a close intimacy of many years, and then stepped back a pace or two as if to take a full survey of his face and figure, and then shook hands with him again, if possible, more warmly than before.

'Well; and how came you here?' said Mr Pickwick, with a smile, in which benevolence struggled with surprise.

'Come,' replied the stranger – 'stopping at Crown – Crown at Muggleton – met a party – flannel jackets – white trousers – anchovy sandwiches – devilled kidneys – splendid fellows – glorious.'

Mr Pickwick was sufficiently versed in the stranger's system of stenography to infer from this rapid and disjointed communication that he had, somehow or other, contracted an acquaintance with the All-Muggletons, which he had converted, by a process peculiar to himself, into that extent of good fellowship on which a general invitation may be easily founded. His curiosity was therefore satisfied, and putting on his spectacles he prepared himself to watch the play which was just commencing.

All-Muggleton had the first innings; and the interest became intense when Mr Dumkins and Mr Podder, two of the most renowned members of that most distinguished club, walked, bat in hand, to their respective wickets. Mr Luffey, the highest ornament of Dingley Dell, was pitched to bowl against the redoubtable Dumkins, and Mr Struggles was selected to do the same kind office for the hitherto unconquered Podder. Several players were stationed, to 'look out', in different parts of the field, and each fixed himself into the proper attitude by placing one hand on each knee, and stooping very much as if he were 'making a back' for some beginner at leap-frog. All the regular players do this sort of thing: indeed it's generally supposed that it is quite impossible to look out properly in any other position.

The umpires were stationed behind the wickets; the scorers were prepared to notch the runs; a breathless silence ensued. Mr Luffey retired a few paces behind the wicket of the passive Podder, and applied the ball to his right eye for several seconds. Dumkins confidently awaited its coming with his eyes fixed on the motions of Luffey.

'Play!' suddenly cried the bowler. The ball flew from his hand straight and swift towards the centre stump of the wicket. The wary Dumkins was on the alert; it fell upon the tip of the bat, and bounded far away over the heads of the scouts, who had just stooped low enough to let it fly over them.

'Run – run – another. – Now, then throw her up – up with her – stop there – another – no – yes – no – throw her up, throw her up!' – Such were the shouts which followed the stroke; and, at the conclusion of which All-Muggleton had scored two. Nor was Podder behindhand in earning laurels wherewith to garnish himself and Muggleton. He blocked the doubtful balls, missed the bad ones, took the good ones, and sent them flying to all parts of the field. The scouts were hot and tired; the bowlers were changed and bowled till their arms ached; but Dumkins and Podder remained unconquered. Did an elderly gentleman essay to stop the progress of the ball, it rolled between his legs or slipped between his fingers. Did a slim gentleman try to catch it, it struck him on the nose, and bounded pleasantly off with redoubled violence, while the slim gentleman's eye filled with water, and his form writhed with anguish. Was it thrown straight up to the wicket, Dumkins had reached it before the ball. In short, when Dumkins was caught out, and Podder stumped out, All-Muggleton had notched some fifty-four while the score of the Dingley Dellers was as blank as their faces. The advantage was too great to be recovered. In vain did the eager Luffey, and the enthusiastic Struggles, do all that skill and experience could suggest, to regain the ground Dingley Dell had lost in the contest – it was of no avail; and in an early period of the winning game Dingley Dell gave in, and allowed the superior prowess of All-Muggleton.

The stranger, meanwhile, had been eating, drinking, and talking, without cessation. At every good stroke he expressed his satisfaction and approval of the player in a most condescending and patronizing manner, which could not fail to have been highly gratifying to the party concerned; while at every bad attempt at a catch and every failure to stop the ball, he launched his personal displeasure at the head of the devoted individual in such denunciations as – 'Ah, ah! – stupid' – 'Now, butter-fingers' – 'Muff' – 'Humbug' – and so forth – ejaculations which seemed to establish him in the opinion of all around, as a most excellent and undeniable judge of the whole part and mystery of the noble game of cricket.

'Capital game – well played – some strokes admirable,' said

the stranger, as both sides crowded into the tent, at the conclusion of the game.

'You have played it, sir?' enquired Mr Wardle, who had been much amused by his loquacity.

'Played it! Think I have – thousands of times – not here – West Indies – exciting thing – hot work – very.'

'It must be rather a warm pursuit in such a climate,' observed Mr Pickwick.

'Warm! – red hot – scorching – glowing. Played a match once – single wicket – friend the Colonel Sir Thomas Blazo – who should get the greatest number of runs. – Won the toss – first innings – seven o'clock A.M. – six natives to look out – went in; kept in – heat intense – natives all fainted – taken away – fresh half-dozen ordered – fainted also – Blazo bowling – supported by two natives – couldn't bowl me out – fainted too – cleared away the Colonel – wouldn't give in – faithful attendant – Quanko Samba – last man left – sun so hot, bat in blisters, ball scorched brown – five hundred and seventy runs – rather exhausted – Quanko mustered up last remaining strength – bowled me out – had a bath, and went out to dinner.'

'And what became of what's-his-name, sir?' enquired an old gentleman.

'Blazo?'

'No – the other gentleman.'

'Quanko Samba?'

'Yes, sir.'

'Poor Quanko – never recovered it – bowled on, on my account – bowled off, on his own – died, sir.' Here the stranger buried his countenance in a brown jug, but whether to hide his emotion or imbibe its contents, we cannot distinctly affirm. We only know that he paused suddenly, drew a long and deep breath, and looked anxiously on, as two of the principal members of the Dingley Dell club approached Mr Pickwick, and said—

'We are about to partake of a plain dinner at the Blue Lion, sir; we hope you and your friends will join us.'

'Of course,' said Mr Wardle, 'among our friends, we include Mr —'; and he looked towards the stranger.

'Jingle,' said that versatile gentleman, taking the hint at once. 'Jingle – Alfred Jingle, Esq., of No Hall, Nowhere.'

'I shall be very happy, I am sure,' said Mr Pickwick.

'So shall I,' said Mr Alfred Jingle, drawing one arm through Mr Pickwick's, and another through Mr Wardle's, as he whispered confidentially in the ear of the former gentleman:

'Devilish good dinner – cold, but capital – peeped into the room this morning – fowls and pies, and all that sort of thing – pleasant fellows these – well behaved, too – very.'

There being no further preliminaries to arrange, the company straggled into the town in little knots of twos and threes; and within a quarter of an hour were all seated in the great room of the Blue Lion Inn, Muggleton – Mr Dumkins acting as chairman, and Mr Luffey officiating as vice.

There was a vast deal of talking and rattling of knives and forks, and plates: a great running about of three ponderous headed waiters, and a rapid disappearance of the substantial viands on the table; to each and every of which item of confusion, the facetious Mr Jingle lent the aid of half-a-dozen ordinary men at least. When everybody had eaten as much as possible, the cloth was removed, bottles, glasses, and dessert were placed on the table; and the waiters withdrew to 'clear away', or in other words, to appropriate to their own private use and emolument whatever remnants of the eatables and drinkables they could contrive to lay their hands on.

Amidst the general hum of mirth and conversation that ensued, there was a little man with a puffy Say-nothing-to-me, – or-I'll-contradict-you sort of countenance, who remained very quiet; occasionally looking round him when the conversation slackened, as if he contemplated putting in something very weighty; and now and then bursting into a short cough of inexpressible grandeur. At length, during a moment of comparative silence, the little man called out in a very loud, solemn voice, –

'Mr Luffey!'

Everybody was hushed into a profound stillness; as the individual addressed, replied –

'Sir!'

'I wish to address a few words to you, sir, if you will entreat the gentlemen to fill their glasses.'

Mr Jingle uttered a patronizing 'hear, hear', which was responded to by the remainder of the company; and the glasses having been filled the Vice-President assumed an air of wisdom in a state of profound attention, and said –

'Mr Staple.'

'Sir,' said the little man, rising, 'I wish to address what I have to say to *you* and not to our worthy chairman, because our worthy chairman is in some measure – I may say in a great degree – the subject of what I have to say, or I may say – to – '

'State,' suggested Mr Jingle.

—'Yes, to state,' said the little man. 'I think my honourable friend, if he will allow me to call him so (four "hears" and one certainly from Mr Jingle) – for the suggestion. Sir, I am a Deller – a Dingley Deller (cheers). I cannot lay claim to the honour of forming an item in the population of Muggleton; nor, sir, I will frankly admit, do I covet that honour; and I will tell you why, sir – (hear); to Muggleton I will readily concede all those honours and distinctions to which it can fairly lay claim – they are too numerous and too well known to require aid or recapitulation from me. But, sir, while we remember that Muggleton has given birth to a Dumkins and a Podder, let us never forget that Dingley Dell can boast a Luffey and a Struggles. (Vociferous cheering.) Let me not be considered as wishing to detract from the merits of the former gentlemen. Sir, I envy them the luxury of their own feelings on this occasion. (Cheers.) Every gentleman who hears me, is probably acquainted with the reply made by an individual, who – to use an ordinary figure of speech – "hung out" in a tub, to the emperor Alexander: "If I were not Diogenes," said he, "I would be Alexander." I can well imagine these gentlemen to say, "If I were not Dumkins

I would be Luffey; if I were not Podder I would be Struggles."
(Enthusiasm.) But, gentlemen of Muggleton, is it in cricket
alone that your fellowtownsmen stand pre-eminent? Have you
never heard ⌒f Dumkins and determination? Have you never
been taught to associate Podder with property? (Great applause.)
Have you never, when struggling for your rights, your liberties,
and your privileges, been reduced, if only for an instant, to
misgiving and despair? And when you have been thus depressed,
has not the name of Dumkins laid afresh within your breast the
figure which had just gone out; and has not a word from that
man lighted it again as brightly as if it had never expired?
(Great cheering.) Gentlemen, I beg to surround with a rich
halo of enthusiastic cheering, the united names of "Dumkins
and Podder".'

Here the little man ceased, and here the company commenced
a raising of voices, and thumping of tables, which lasted with
little intermission during the remainder of the evening. Other
toasts were drunk. Mr Luffey and Mr Struggles, Mr Pickwick
and Mr Jingle, were, each in his turn, the subject of unqualified
eulogium; and each in due course returned thanks for the
honour.

Enthusiastic as we are in the noble cause to which we have
devoted ourselves, we should have felt a sensation of pride
which we cannot express and a consciousness of having done
something to merit immortality of which we are now deprived,
could we have laid the faintest outline of these addresses before
our ardent readers. Mr Snodgrass, as usual, took a great mass
of notes, which would no doubt have afforded most useful and
valuable information, had not the burning eloquence of the
words or the feverish influence of the wine made that gentleman's hand so extremely unsteady, as to render his writing
nearly unintelligible, and his style wholly so. By dint of patient
investigation, we have been enabled to trace some characters
bearing a faint resemblance to the names of the speakers; and
we can also discern an entry of a song (supposed to have been
sung by Mr Jingle), in which the words 'bowl', 'sparkling',

'ruby', 'bright', and 'wine' are frequently repeated at short intervals. We fancy too, that we can discern at the very end of the notes, some indistinct reference to 'broiled bones'; and then the words 'cold' 'without' occur; but as any hypothesis we could found upon them must necessarily rest upon mere conjecture, we are not disposed to indulge in any of the speculations to which they may give rise.

We will therefore return to Mr Tupman: merely adding that within some few minutes before twelve o'clock that night, the convocation of worthies of Dingley Dell and Muggleton were heard to sing, with great feeling and emphasis, the beautiful and pathetic national air of

> We won't go home 'till morning,
> We won't go home 'till morning,
> We won't go home 'till morning,
> 'Till daylight doth appear.

*from* THE PICKWICK PAPERS *1837*

# Tom Brown's Last Match

## THOMAS HUGHES

Another two years have passed, and it is again the end of the summer half-year at Rugby; in fact, the school has broken up. The fifth-form examinations were over last week, and upon them have followed the speeches and the sixth-form examinations for exhibitions; and they too are over now. The boys have gone to all the winds of heaven, except the town boys and the eleven, and the few enthusiasts besides who have asked leave to stay in their houses to see the result of the cricket matches. For this year the Wellesburn return match and the Marylebone match are played at Rugby, to the great delight of the town and neighbourhood, and the sorrow of those aspiring young cricketers who have been reckoning for the last three months on showing off at Lord's ground.

The Doctor started for the Lakes yesterday morning, after an interview with the captain of the eleven, in the presence of Thomas, at which he arranged in what school the cricket dinners were to be, and all other matters necessary for the satisfactory carrying out of the festivities; and warned them as to keeping all spirituous liquors out of the close, and having the gates closed by nine o'clock.

The Wellesburn match was played out with great success yesterday, the School winning by three wickets; and today the great event of the cricketing year, the Marylebone match, is being played. What a match it has been! The London eleven came down by an afternoon train yesterday, in time to see the end of the Wellesburn match; and as soon as it was over, their leading men and umpire inspected the ground, criticizing it rather unmercifully. The captain of the School eleven, and one or two others, who had played the Lord's match before, and knew old Mr Aislabie and several of the Lord's men, accompanied them; while the rest of the eleven looked on from under the Three Trees with admiring eyes, and asked one another the name of the illustrious strangers, and recounted how many runs each of them had made in the late matches in 'Bell's Life'. They looked such hard-bitten, wiry whiskered fellows, that their young adversaries felt rather desponding as to the result of the morrow's match. The ground was at last chosen, and two men set to work upon it to water and roll; and then, there being yet some half-hour of daylight, someone had suggested a dance on the turf. The close was half-full of citizens and their families, and the idea was hailed with enthusiasm. The cornopean player was still on the ground; in five minutes the eleven and half a dozen of the Wellesburn and Marylebone men got partners somehow or another and a merry country dance was going on, to which everyone flocked, and new couples joined in every minute, till there were a hundred of them going down the middle and up again – and the long line of school buildings looked gravely down on them, every window glowing with the last rays of the western sun, and the rooks clanged about in the tops of the old elms, greatly excited, and resolved on having their country dance too, and the great flag flapped lazily in the gentle western breeze. Altogether it was a sight which would have made glad the heart of our brave old founder, Lawrence Sheriff, if he were half as good a fellow as I take him to have been. It was a cheerful sight to see; but what made it so valuable in the sight of the captain of the School eleven was that he there saw his young hands shaking off their shyness and awe of the Lord's men, as they crossed hands and capered about on the grass together; for the strangers entered into it all, and threw away their cigars, and danced and shouted like boys; while old Mr Aislabie stood by looking on in his white hat, leaning on a bat, in benevolent enjoyment. 'This hop will be worth thirty runs to us tomorrow, and will be the making of Raggles and Johnson', thinks the young leader, as he revolves many things in his mind, standing by the side of Mr Aislabie, whom he will not leave for a minute, for he feels that the character of the school for courtesy is resting on his shoulders.

But when a quarter to nine struck, and he saw old Thomas beginning to fidget about with the keys in his hand, he thought of the Doctor's parting monition, and stopped the cornopean at once, notwithstanding the loud-voiced remonstrances from all sides; and the crowd scattered away from the close, the eleven all going into the School-house, where supper and beds were provided for them by the Doctor's orders.

Deep had been the consultations at supper as to the ordeal of going in, who should bowl the first over, whether it would be best to play steady or freely; and the youngest hands declared that they shouldn't be a bit nervous, and praised their opponents as the jolliest fellows in the world, except perhaps their old friends the Wellesburn men. How far a little good-nature from their elders will go with the right sort of boys!

The morning had dawned bright and warm, to the intense relief of many an anxious youngster, up betimes to mark the signs of the weather. The eleven went down in a body before breakfast, for a plunge in the cold bath in the corner of the close. The ground was in splendid order, and soon after ten o'clock, before spectators had arrived, all was ready, and two of the Lord's men took their places at the wicket; the School, with the usual liberality of young hands, having put their adversaries in first. Old Bailey stepped up to the wicket, and called play, and the match has begun.

'Oh well bowled! well bowled, Johnson!' cries the captain, catching up the ball, and sending it high above the rook trees, while the third Marylebone man walks away from the wicket, and old Bailey gravely sets up the middle stump again and puts the bails on.

'How many runs?' Away scamper three boys to the scoring-table, and are back again in a minute amongst the rest of the eleven, who are collected together in a knot between wicket. 'Only eighteen runs, and three wickets down!' 'Huzza, for old Rugby!' sings out Jack Raggles, the long-stop, toughest, and burliest of boys, commonly called 'Swiper Jack'; and forthwith stands on his head, and brandishes his legs in the air in triumph, till the next boy catches hold of his heels and throws him over on to his back.

'Steady there, don't be such an ass, Jack,' says the captain, 'we haven't got the best wicket yet. Ah, look out now at cover-point,' adds he, as he sees a long-armed, bare-headed, slashing-looking player coming to the wicket. 'And, Jack, mind your hits; he steals more runs than any man in England.'

And they all find that they have got their work to do now; the new-comer's off-hitting is tremendous and his running like a flash of lightning. He is never in his ground, except when his wicket is down. Nothing in the whole game so trying to boys; he has stolen three byes in the first ten minutes, and Jack Raggles is furious, and begins throwing over savagely to the farther wicket, until he is sternly stopped by the captain. It is all that young gentleman can do to keep his team steady, but he knows that everything depends on it, and faces his work bravely. The score creeps up to fifty, the boys begin to look black, and the spectators, who are now mustering strong, are very silent. The ball flies off his bat to all parts of the field, and he gives no rest and no catches to anyone. But cricket is full of glorious chances, and the goddess who presides over it loves to bring down the most skilful players. Johnson, the young bowler, is getting wild, and bowls a ball almost wide to the off; the batter steps out and cuts it beautifully to where cover-point is standing very deep, in fact, almost off the ground. The ball comes skimming and twisting along about three feet from the ground; he rushes at it, and it sticks somehow or other in the fingers of his left hand, to the utter astonishment of himself and the whole field. Such a catch hasn't been made in the close for years, and the cheering is maddening. 'Pretty cricket,' says the captain, throwing himself on the ground by the deserted wicket with a long breath; he feels that a crisis has passed.

I wish I had space to describe the whole match; how the captain stumped the next man off a leg-shooter, and bowled slow cobs to old Mr Aislabie who came in for the last wicket. How the Lord's men were out by half-past twelve o'clock for nine-eight runs. How the captain of the School eleven went in first to give his men pluck, and scored twenty-five in beautiful style; how Rugby was only four behind in the first innings. What a glorious dinner they had in the fourth-form school, and how the cover-point hitter sang the most topping comic songs, and old Mr Aislabie made the best speeches that ever were heard, afterwards. But I haven't space, that's the fact, and so you must fancy it all, and carry yourselves on to half-past seven o'clock, when the School are again in, with five wickets down and only thirty-two runs to make to win. The Marylebone men played carelessly in their second innings, but they are working like horses now to save the match.

There is much healthy, hearty, happy life scattered up and down the close; but the group to which I beg to call your especial attention is there, on the slope of the island, which looks towards the cricket-ground. It consists of three figures; two are seated on a bench, and one on the ground at their feet. The first, a tall, slight, and rather gaunt man, with a bushy eyebrow, and a dry humorous smile, is evidently a clergyman. He is carelessly dressed, and looks rather used up, which isn't much to be wondered at, seeing that he has just finished six weeks of examination work; but there he basks, and spreads himself out in the evening sun, bent on enjoying life, though he doesn't quite know what to do with his arms and legs. Surely it is our friend the young master, whom we have had glimpses of before, but his face has gained a great deal since we last came across him.

And by his side, in white flannel shirt and trousers, straw hat, the captain's belt, and the untanned, yellow cricket shoes, which all the eleven wear, sits a strapping figure, near six feet high, with ruddy, tanned face and whiskers, curly brown hair, and a laughing, dancing eye. He is leaning forward with his elbows resting on his knees, and dandling his favourite bat, with which he has made thirty or forty runs today, in his strong brown hands. It is Tom Brown, grown into a young man nineteen years old, a praepostor and captain of the eleven, spending his last day as a Rugby boy, and let us hope as much wiser as he is bigger, since we last had the pleasure of coming across him.

And at their feet on the warm dry ground, similarly dressed, sits Arthur, Turkish fashion, with his bat across his knees. He too is no longer a boy, less of a boy in fact than Tom, if one may judge from the thoughtfulness of his face, which is somewhat paler too than one could wish; but his figure, though slight, is well knit and active, and all his old timidity has disappeared, and is replaced by silent, quaint fun with which his face twinkles all over, as he listens to the broken talk between the other two, in which he joins every now and then.

All three are watching the game eagerly, and joining in the cheering which follows every good hit. It is pleasing to see the easy, friendly footing which the pupils are on with their master, perfectly respectful, yet with no reserve and nothing forced in their intercourse. Tom has clearly abandoned the old theory of 'natural enemies', in this case at any rate.

But it is time to listen to what they are saying, and see what we can gather out of it.

'I don't object to your theory,' says the master, 'and I allow you have made a fair case for yourself. But now, in such books as Aristophanes, for instance, you've been reading a play this half with the Doctor, haven't you?'

'Yes, "The Knights",' answered Tom.

'Well, I'm sure you would have enjoyed the wonderful humour of it twice as much if you had taken more pains with your scholarship.'

'Well, sir, I don't believe any boy in the form enjoyed the sets-to between Cleon and the Sausage-seller more than I did – eh Arthur?' said Tom, giving him a stir with his foot.

'Yes, I must say he did,' said Arthur. 'I think, sir, you've hit upon the wrong book there.'

'Not a bit of it,' said the master. 'Why, in those very passages of arms, how can you thoroughly appreciate them unless you are master of the weapons? and the weapons are the language which you, Brown, have never half worked at; and so, as I say, you must have lost all the delicate shades of meaning which make the best part of the fun.'

'Oh! well played – bravo, Johnson!' shouted Arthur, dropping his bat and clapping furiously, and Tom joined in with a 'Bravo, Johnson!' which might have been heard at the chapel.

'Eh! what was it? I didn't see,' enquired the master; 'they only got one run, I thought?'

'No, but such a ball, three-quarters length and coming straight for his leg bail. Nothing but that turn of the wrist could have saved him, and he drew it away to leg for a safe one. Bravo, Johnson!'

'How well they are bowling, though,' said Arthur, 'they don't mean to be beat, I can see.'

'There now,' struck in the master, 'you see that's just what I have been preaching this half-hour. The delicate play is the true thing. I don't understand cricket, so I don't enjoy those fine draws which you tell me are the best play, though when you or Raggles hit a ball hard away for six I am as delighted as anyone. Don't you see the analogy?'

'Yes, sir,' answered Tom, looking up, roguishly, 'I see; only the question remains whether I should have got most good by understanding Greek particles or cricket thoroughly. I'm such a thick, I never should have had time for both.'

'I see you are an incorrigible,' said the master, with a chuckle, 'but I refute you by an example. Arthur there has taken in Greek and cricket too.'

'Yes, but no thanks to him; Greek came natural to him. Why, when he first came I remember he used to read *Herodotus* for pleasure as I did *Don Quixote*, and couldn't have made a false concord if he'd tried ever so hard – and then I looked after his cricket.'

'Out! Bailey has given him out – do you see, Tom?' cries Arthur. 'How foolish of them to run so hard.'

'Well, it can't be helped, he has played very well. Whose turn is it to go in?'

'I don't know; they've got your list in the tent.'

'Let's go and see,' said Tom, rising; but at this moment Jack Raggles and two or three more come running to the island moat.

'Oh, Brown, mayn't I go in next?' shouts the Swiper.

'Whose name is next on the list?' says the captain.

'Winter's, and then Arthur's,' answers the boy who carries it; 'but there are only twenty-six runs to get, and no time to lose. I heard Mr Aislabie say that the stumps must be drawn at a quarter past eight exactly.'

'Oh, do let the Swiper go in,' chorus the boys; so Tom yields against his better judgment.

'I daresay now I've lost the match by this nonsense,' he says, as he sits down again; 'they'll be sure to get Jack's wicket in three or four minutes; however, you'll have the chance, sir, of seeing a hard hit or two,' adds he, smiling, and turning to the master.

'Come, none of your irony, Brown,' answers the master. 'I'm beginning to understand the game scientifically. What a noble game it is, too!'

'Isn't it? But it's more than a game. It's an institution,' said Tom.

'Yes,' said Arthur, 'the birthright of British boys old and young, as habeas corpus and trial by jury are of British men.'

'The discipline and reliance on one another which it teaches is so valuable, I think,' went on the master, 'it ought to be such an unselfish game. It merges the individual in the eleven; he doesn't play that he may win, but that his side may.'

'That's very true,' said Tom, 'and that's why football and cricket, now one comes to think of it, are so much better games than fives or Hare and Hounds, or any others where the object is to come in first or to win for oneself, and not that one's side may win.'

'And then the captain of the eleven!' said the master. 'What a post is his in our school-world! almost as hard as the Doctor's, requiring skill and gentleness and firmness, and I know not what other rare qualities.'

'Which don't he may wish he may get!' said Tom, laughing; 'at any rate he hasn't got them yet, or he wouldn't have been such a flat tonight as to let Jack Raggles go in out of his turn.'

'Ah! the Doctor never would have done that,' said Arthur demurely. 'Tom, you've a great deal to learn yet in the art of ruling.'

'Well, I wish you'd tell the Doctor so, then, and get him to let me stop till I'm twenty. I don't want to leave, I'm sure.'

'What a sight it is,' broke in the master, 'the Doctor as a ruler. Perhaps ours is the only little corner of the British Empire which is thoroughly, wisely, and strongly ruled just now. I'm more and more thankful every day of my life that I came here to be under him.'

'So am I, I'm sure,' said Tom; 'and more and more sorry that I've got to leave.'

'Every place and thing one sees here reminds one of some

wise act of his,' went on the master. 'This island now – you remember the time, Brown, when it was laid out in small gardens, and cultivated by frost-bitten fags in February and March?'

'Of course I do,' said Tom; 'didn't I hate spending two hours in the afternoons grubbing in the tough dirt with the stump of a fives-bat? But turf-cart was good fun enough.'

'I daresay it was, but it was always leading to fights with the townspeople; and then the stealing of flowers out of all the gardens in Rugby for the Easter show was abominable.'

'Well, so it was,' said Tom, looking down, 'but we fags couldn't help ourselves. But what has that to do with the Doctor's ruling?'

'A great deal, I think,' said the master; 'what brought island-fagging to an end?'

'Why, the Easter Speeches were put off till Midsummer,' said Tom, 'and the sixth had the gymnastic poles put up there.'

'Well, and who changed the time of the speeches, and put the idea of gymnastic poles into the heads of their worships the sixth form?' said the master.

'The Doctor, I suppose,' said Tom. 'I never thought of that.'

'Of course you didn't,' said the master, 'or else, fag as you were, you would have shouted with the whole school against putting down old customs. And that's the way that all the Doctor's reforms have been carried out when he has been left to himself – quietly and naturally, putting a good thing in the place of a bad, and letting the bad die out; no wavering and no hurry – the best thing that could be done for the time being, and patience for the rest.'

'Just Tom's own way,' chimed in Arthur, nudging Tom with his elbow, 'driving a nail where it will go;' to which allusion Tom answered by a sly kick.

'Exactly so,' said the master, innocent of the allusion and by-play.

Meantime Jack Raggles, with his sleeves tucked up above his great brown elbows, scorning pads and gloves, has presented

himself at the wicket; and having run one for a forward drive of
Johnson's, is about to receive his first ball. There are only
twenty-four runs to make, and four wickets to go down, a
winning match if they play decently steady. The ball is a very
swift one, and rises fast, catching Jack on the outside of the
thigh, and bounding away as if from indiarubber, while they
run two for a leg-bye amidst great applause, and shouts from
Jack's many admirers. The next ball is a beautifully pitched ball
for the outer stump, which the reckless and unfeeling Jack
catches hold of, and hits right round to leg for five, while the
applause becomes deafening; only seventeen runs to get with
four wickets – the game is all but ours!

It is over now, and Jack walks swaggering about his wicket,
with the bat over his shoulder, while Mr Aislabie holds a short
parley with his men. Then the cover-point hitter, that cunning
man, goes on to bowl slow twisters. Jack waves his hand
triumphantly towards the tent, as much as to say, 'See if I don't
finish it all off now in three hits.'

Alas, my son Jack! the enemy is too old for thee. The first
ball of the over Jack steps out and meets, swiping with all his
force. If he had only allowed for the twist! but he hasn't, and so
the ball goes spinning up straight into the air, as if it would
never come down again. Away runs Jack, shouting and trusting
to the chapter of accidents, but the bowler runs steadily under
it, judging every spin, and calling out 'I have it,' catches it, and
playfully pitches it on to the back of the stalwart Jack, who is
departing with a rueful countenance.

'I knew how it would be,' says Tom, rising. 'Come along, the
game's getting very serious.'

So they leave the island and go to the tent, and after deep consultation Arthur is sent in, and goes off to the wicket with a last
exhortation from Tom to play steady and keep his bat straight.
To the suggestions that Winter is the best bat left, Tom only
replies, 'Arthur is the steadiest, and Johnson will make the runs
if the wicket is only kept on.'

'I'm surprised to see Arthur in the eleven,' said the master, as they stood together in front of the dense crowd, which was now closing in round the ground.

'Well, I'm not quite sure that he ought to be in for his play,' said Tom, 'but I couldn't help putting him in. It will do him so much good, and you can't think what I owe him.'

The master smiled. The clock strikes eight and the whole field becomes fevered with excitement. Arthur, after two narrow escapes, scores one; and Johnson gets the ball. The bowling and fielding are superb, and Johnson's batting worthy the occasion. He makes here a two, and there a one, managing to keep the ball to himself, and Arthur backs up and runs perfectly: only eleven runs to make now, and the crowd scarcely breathe. At last Arthur gets the ball again, and actually drives it forward for two, and feels prouder than when he got the three best prizes, at hearing Tom's shout of joy, 'Well played, well played, young 'un!'

But the next ball is too much for a young hand, and his bails fly different ways. Nine runs to make, and two wickets to go down – it is too much for human nerves.

Before Winter can get in, the omnibus which is to take the Lord's men to the train pulls up at the side of the close, and Mr Aislabie and Tom consult, and give out that the stumps will be drawn after the next over. And so ends the great match. Winter and Johnson carry out their bats, and, it being a one day's match, the Lord's men are declared the winners, they having scored the most in the first innings.

But such a defeat is a victory; so think Tom and all the School eleven, as they accompany their conquerors to the omnibus, and send them off with three ringing cheers, after Mr Aislabie has shaken hands all round, saying to Tom, 'I must compliment you, sir, on your eleven, and I hope we shall have you for a member if you come up to town.'

*from* TOM BROWN'S SCHOOLDAYS *1857*

# Chrystal's Century

## E. W. HORNUNG

It really began in the pavilion up at Lord's, since it was off Tuthill that most of the runs were made, and during an Eton and Harrow match that the little parson begged him to play. They had been in the same Harrow eleven some eighteen years before. The Reverend Gerald Osborne had afterwards touched the hem of first-class cricket, while Tuthill, who captained a minor county, was still the very finest second-class bowler in England.

'Who's it against?' asked Tuthill, with a suspicious glint in his clear eye; for if he was not good enough for first-class cricket, third-class was not good enough for him.

'A man who's made his pile and bought himself a place near Elstree; they let him have a week in August on the school ground, and I ran the side against him for the last match.'

'Decent wicket, then,' said Tuthill, with a critical eye upon the Eton bowling.

'I shouldn't wonder if you found it a bit fiery,' said the crafty priest, with a timely memory of Tuthill's happiest hunting-ground. 'And they'll put you up and do you like a Coronation guest.'

'I don't care twopence about that,' said Tuthill. 'Will they keep my analysis?'

'I'll guarantee it, Tuttles,' said the little parson.

And Tuttles consulted the diary of a conscientious cricketer.

'I can,' said he, 'and I don't see why I shouldn't. I was coming up for the Oval Test in any case. It will only mean taking another day or two while I am about it. You can put me down.'

'And rely on you?' added the other, as one whose fortune was too good to be true.

'My dear Jerry,' cried Tuttles, with characteristic emphasis, 'I never chucked a match in all my life! It's a promise, and I'll be there if no one else is. But who is this sporting pal of yours? I suppose he has a name?'

Osborne went out of his way to applaud a somewhat inferior stroke by the Harrow boy who was making all the runs.

'As a matter of fact,' he finally confessed, 'he was at school with us, though you probably don't remember him. His name's Chrystal.'

'Not old Ginger Chrystal, surely?'

'I believe they did call him Ginger. I don't remember him at school.'

'But I do! He was in our house, and super'd, poor beast! Ginger Chrystal! Why on earth didn't you tell me who it was before?'

'You've named one of my reasons, Tuttles. He's a bit shy about his Harrow days. Then he says himself that he was no more use at cricket than he was at work, and I thought it might put you off.'

'No more he was,' said Tuttles reflectively. 'Do you mean to say he's any good now?'

'No earthly,' replied the little parson, with his cherub's smile; 'only just about the keenest rabbit in the whole cricket warren!'

The finest second-class bowler in England displayed a readiness of appreciation doubly refreshing in an obviously critical temperament.

'And yet you say he has done himself well!' he added incredulously, as his mirth subsided.

'Only made a hundred thousand in South America, Tuttles.'

'Nonsense!'

'It might be double by the way he does things.'

'That utter rabbit at every mortal thing?'

'He's not one now, Tuttles, at anything but cricket. That's his only weak point. At everything else Chrystal's one of the smartest chaps you ever met, though he does weigh you and me put together, and quite one of the best. But he's so mad-keen on cricket that he keeps a pro. for himself and his son of seven, and by practising more than any man in England he scores his ten runs in all matches every season. However, when this boy runs into three figures, or gets out, you must come and meet the modern Chrystal in the flesh; there's plenty of it, though not too much for the heart inside, and at the present moment he's spreading every ounce of himself in a coach he's got here in my name.'

It was a fair enough picture that the parson drew, for Chrystal was really corpulent, though tall and finely built. He wore a stubby moustache of the hue which had earned him his school nickname, but underneath were the mouth of a strong man and the smile of a sweet woman. It was a beaming, honest unassuming face; but the womanly quality reappeared in a pair of very shapely, well-kept hands, one of which could come down with virile force on Tuthill's shoulder, while the other injured the most cunning bunch of fingers in second-class cricket. Then a shyness overcame the great fellow, and the others all saw that he was thinking of the one inglorious stage of his career. And his wife, a beautiful woman, took charge of little Osborne; and Tuthill, who had sense and tact, congratulated Chrystal point-blank and at once upon his great success in life.

But for an instant Chrystal looked quite depressed, as though success at school was the only sort worth achieving; then his smile came out like the sun, and his big body began to shake.

'Yes,' he whispered, 'they promised me a dog's life and a felon's death because I couldn't make Latin verses! Do you remember my second half of a pentameter?'

'Laomedontiaden!' cried Tuthill, convulsed with laughter at the sudden reminiscence.

'I never could see where the laugh came in,' confessed Chrystal, like the man he was. 'But I've no doubt that was what cooked my goose.'

Tuthill was much impressed.

'And he never said it didn't matter,' as he afterwards put it to the parson, 'or changed the subject to the things he has done, or took out a big gold watch, or drowned us in champagne, or did or said a single thing that wouldn't have done honour to the bluest blood on the ground. All he did say, at the end of the innings, was that he'd give half he'd got to have been in the eleven himself! Oh, yes, I've promised to play in his all right; who could refuse a chap like that? I'm going for the whole week; let's only hope he won't drop all his catches off my stuff.'

'You must forgive him his trespasses, Tuttles,' the clergyman said, with some gravity, and no irreverence at all.

'I can't forgive that one,' replied the candid demon of second-class cricket. 'I never could, and never shall.'

But it was not for Tuthill to forgive when the great week came, or at all events, before the week was at an end. It is true that the catches followed the non-cricketer to every position in the field, as catches will, and equally true that a large majority of them were duly 'put on the floor'. But, as good luck and his own accuracy would have it, the great bowler was not usually the sufferer. Once, indeed, when it was otherwise, he did tell his host, with unpremeditated emphasis, that the ball wouldn't bite him; but that was the only contretemps of the kind, and an ample apology followed when the wicket fell. But a more ample revenge was in store for the moving spirit of the week.

It had gone like wedding-bells from the first over of the first match; even the most hardened country-house cricketer of the party could not look back upon a better time. Mrs Chrystal proved a charming hostess, and Chrystal 'heavenly host' according to one of the many mushroom humorists who shot up in the genial atmosphere of his house. The house itself was old and red and mellow, but none the worse for the electric light and the porcelain baths which Chrystal had put in. The place, like so many in that neighbourhood was a mass of roses, and a stroll in the garden after dinner was like swimming in scent. There was a waggonette to take the players to the ground, a daily sweepstake on the highest scorer, a billiard handicap for the evenings. Creature comforts were provided on a scale which fell deliberately short of plutocratic display, but of no other standard applicable to the case. Finally, the weather was such as an English summer can still produce in penitent mood; and the only cloud of any sort that brooded over the week was the secret cloud in Robert Chrystal's heart; for it was half-broken by a sequence of failures most abject even for him.

'Four runs all the week, and they were an overthrow,' said he, with a rueful humour which but partially disguised the tremendous tragedy of the thing. 'Three times first ball! I'll tell you what I'll do before next August: I'll lay out a ground of my own, and it shall have a subterranean passage from the wicket to the pavilion. Either that, or let me be translated like Enoch when it happens to me again!'

There was one who whispered that it would be the first translation he had ever achieved; but, even that wag would have made Chrystal a present of his highest score, and they all felt the same. None more sympathetic than Tuttles when it was merely a batting misfortune; up to the Friday night he had twenty-nine for two hundred and thirty-one, and but for Chrystal it would have been twenty-eight for two hundred and thirty. Little Jerry Osborne was also full of sympathy, though he expressed it rather often, and gave Chrystal more advice than he was likely to have the least opportunity of following. One excellent fellow happened to have played in a match, some seasons before, in which Chrystal had actually made runs; and he talked about that. He reminded Chrystal of it every day. 'They were all from the middle of the bat. The man who took thirty-six like that may take a century any day. You've struck a bad patch, as we all do, and you've lost confidence; you shouldn't take it so seriously.' A tall Quidnunc, who said little but made his hundred most days, did declare after Chrystal's congratulations (in the hour of his own disaster) upon one of them, that he was 'Absolutely the best sportsman in Europe'; the grave Indian major treated him with silent respect; and the young schoolmasters, who made up the team and did the deep-field business, agreed most piously with the Quidnunc.

The poor devil was a cricketer at the core. That was the hard part. And he knew the game as many a real cricketer does not; you never heard Chrystal disparage the ball that had just bowled him; neither was it ever 'a ball that might have beaten Charles Fry.' He always knew, none better, exactly what he had done, and (which was more galling) precisely what he ought to have done. If he had made a half-volley into a yorker, he was the first to tell you so. He knew when he had played across a plain straight one, when he had failed to swing his left foot far enough over, or played at the pitch of a long-hop. Even as the wicket rattled he was playing the stroke again, and with academic correctness, in his own mind. That was Chrystal's cricket. Then he would walk back swinging his glove, and beginning to smile when the maker of centuries begins to run – to smile all over a face that felt like a death's head. And that was the stuff of which the man was made.

It was the Friday night, and all the others were so pleased with themselves! Everybody else had at least one little achievement of his own to form a gratifying reflection, and to justify his place in the team. Chrystal could hear them in the billiard room, and at the piano, as for a few minutes he walked up and down outside, with the wife from whom even he could not conceal his consuming chagrin.

'They're in great spirits!' Chrystal had exclaimed, with no bitterness in his voice, but with a whole tome of mortification. And his wife had pressed his arm; she had not made the mistake of going on to remind him that cricket was only a game, and that he could afford to fail at games.

'I believe you'll do better tomorrow,' was what she did say, with a quiet conviction not unjustified by the doctrine of chances in the mind of a lady who declined to regard cricket as a game of skill.

'Tomorrow!' Chrystal laughed outright. 'Why, if one could score a minus, that's what I should make tomorrow!'

'Is there any special reason for saying that?'

'There is,' said Chrystal grimly. 'There's good old Tuttles against us, for a change. He'll bowl me neck and crop first ball!'

They took another turn in silence.

'I'm not sure,' said Mrs Chrystal, 'that I quite like Mr Tuttles.'

'Not like old Tuttles? Why on earth not?'

'He has such a good opinion of himself.'

'He has reason!' cried Chrystal, with hardly ten per cent of envy in his loyal tone.

'Then I do think he's rather spiteful. To go and bowl you out first ball – if he did.'

'He'd bowl me out if I was his long-lost brother! He's so keen; and quite right, too. You've got to play the game, dear.'

If it had been the game of battle, murder, and sudden death, Chrystal's manner could not possibly have been more serious.

But a silence had fallen on piano and billiard-table; and Chrystal hurried indoors, as he said, 'to keep the ball rolling if I can't hit it.' They were only talking about the final match, however, in which Chrystal played his gardeners and grooms while little Osborne took the field against him with the like raw material from his own parish near Ware.

'It's all very well,' said Chrystal, joining in the cricket talk that was beginning to get on his nerves; 'but I ought really to object to Tuttles, you know. He has neither the birth qualification nor the residential; he isn't even your deputy-assistant-secretary, Jerry!'

'I suppose you really don't object?' said Tuttles himself, in the nicest way, the first time he and Chrystal were more or less alone.

'My dear fellow!' was all Chrystal said in reply, 'I want to see you take all the wickets,' he added; 'I promise you mine.'

Tuthill smiled at the superfluous concession.

'I'll have to do my best,' said he, as the hangman might of his painful duty. 'But, as a matter of fact, I'm not sure that my best will amount to much tomorrow. I've been bowling a bit too much, and a bit too well. My off day's about due, and on my off day I'm a penny treat. Full-pitches to leg and long-hops into the slips!'

Chrystal's mouth watered! The second sort of ball was often fatal to him, but the first was the one delivery with which he was almost as much at home in practice as in theory. He had seldom run into double figures without the aid of the repeated full-pitch to leg.

It so happened that there was rain in the night, but only enough to improve a pitch which had quite fulfilled little Osborne's promise of fire; and an absence of sun next day averted an even more insidious state of things. The last match was thus played on the worst day and the best wicket of the week. The ball came along stump-high without any tricks at all. Yet Osborne's side was out shortly after lunch for something under a hundred runs, of which Osborne himself made more than half. Tuthill, who did not take his batting seriously, but hit hard and clean as long as he was there, was beginning to look as though he never need get out when Chrystal, of all people, held him low down at point. It was a noble effort in a stout, slow man, but Tuthill walked away without a word. He was keen enough on his innings as long as he was in; but at luncheon he was the first to compliment Chrystal, who had not been so happy all that week. Chrystal had written himself last in the order, but, thus encouraged, he was persuaded to give himself one more chance, and finally went in fourth wicket down.

It was then 3.20 by the clock on the little pavilion, and one of those grey, mild days which are neither close nor cold, and far from unpleasant on the cricket field. The four wickets had fallen for less than forty runs, but Tuthill had only one victim, and it really did appear to be his off day; but he looked grim and inexorable enough as he waited by the umpire while Chrystal took centre and noted that it was now 3.21; at 3.22 he would be safe back in the pavilion, and his cricket troubles would be over for the season, if not for his life.

But the first ball was that wide long-hop of which Tuthill himself had spoken; down it skimmed, small as a racket-ball to Chrystal's miserable eye; he felt for it with half his heart, but luckily heard nothing before the dull impact of the ball in the gloves of an agile wicket-keeper standing back.

'No!' cried the tall Quidnunc at the opposite end; and Chrystal began to feel that he was playing an innings.

The second ball was the other infallible sign of Tuthill's off-day; it was a knee-high full-pitch just wide of Chrystal's pads; and he succeeded in flicking it late and fine, so that it skimmed to the boundary at its own pace. For one wretched moment Chrystal watched the umpire, who happened to be the man who had advised him not to take his cricket so seriously, and who now read his anxiety in a flash.

'That was a hit!' the unorthodox official shouted towards the scorers' table.

'And a jolly good one!' added the tall Quidnunc, while more distant applause reached the striker's trembling ears, and the ardent Tuttles waited for the ball with the face of a handsome fiend. Yet his next was nothing deadlier than a slow half-volley outside the off-stump, which Chrystal played gently but firmly as a delicate stroke at billiards, but with the air of Greek meeting Greek. Already the ball was growing larger and the time was 3.25.

Osborne was bowling at the other end; he always was either batting, bowling, or keeping wicket; but the bowler's was the only department of the game at which he exposed a definite inferiority. He was, however, very fond of bowling, and as he could claim two of the four wickets which had already fallen (one having been run out) it was extremely unlikely that he would spare himself until the tenth one fell. Osborne's first over after Chrystal's arrival was one of his least expensive. The Quid drove him for a languid single while Chrystal, after keeping out of mischief for four balls, sent the fifth high and dry through the slips for three. The stroke was a possible chance to none other than Tuthill, but it was not off his own bowling, and the impression upon the observant spectator must have been a bad one.

'Don't begin by running yourself off your legs,' Chrystal's partner crossed over to advise him between the overs. 'There's the whole afternoon before us, and you won't have many to run for me. I'm as limp as a wet rag, and my only chance of staying here is to sit on the splice while you punch 'em. But don't you be in any hurry; play yourself in.'

If Chrystal had made a respectable score every day, the tone of the best batsman on the side could not have betrayed more confidence in him; he began to feel confidence; the ball swelled to its normal size, and Tuttles' next long-hop went to third man for another sharp single. Chrystal apologized, but his partner had called him in response to an appealing look; evidently he was not too limp to run his captain's hits; it was only Chrystal himself who puffed and blew and leant upon his bat.

And even by the half-hour he was within a run of that two-figure rubicon which he had not passed for two seasons; his face showed the pale determination of a grave endeavour; in fact, it would hurt him more to get out now than to fall as usual to his only ball.

Yet what did happen? It was Tuthill's slow yorker, and Chrystal was in many minds from the time it left the bowler's hand; his good blade wagged irresolutely and the odious projectile was under it in a twinkling. But at the instant the umpire threw up his arm with a yell, and Chrystal never heard the havoc behind him; he was only instinctively aware of it as he watched Tuthill turn upon a comrade who had donned the long white coat over his flannels.

'No *what*?' demanded the best bowler in second-class cricket. 'I said "no ball"!'

'You're the first man who ever said it to me in my life,' remarked Tuttles, deadly calm, while he looked the other up and down as a new species of cricket curiosity. Then he held up his hands for the ball. 'There's a man still in,' he cried; and proceeded to send down a perfectly vicious full-pitcher upon Chrystal's legs, which the captain, who had the single virtue of never running away, promptly despatched for another four.

He had now made thirteen runs in less than thirteen minutes, and already the whole world was a different place, and that part of it a part of Paradise. He was emboldened to glance towards the seats: there was his dear wife strolling restlessly with her parasol, and their tiny boy clapping his hands. Chrystal could see how excited they were at a hundred yards; it only had the effect of making him perversely calm. 'I'm all right – I've got going at last!' he felt tempted to sing out to them; for he felt all right. He had even passed the stage of anticipating the imminent delivery and playing at the ball he expected instead of at the ball that came along. This had been one of Chrystal's many methods of getting rid of himself in the first over. And he had more suicidal strokes than an Indian Prince has scoring ones. But now he looked from his family in the long-field to the noble trees to square-leg, and from the trees down-hill to the reservoir gleaming through third-man's legs; it was hardly credible that he had wished to drown himself in its depths both yesterday and the day before.

The worst player in the world, with his eye in, may resist indefinitely the attack of the best bowler; after all, a ball is a ball and a bat is a bat; and if you once begin getting the one continually in the middle of the other, and keeping it out of harm's way, there is no more to be said and but little to be done. Chrystal was soon meeting every ball in the middle of a bat which responded to the unparalleled experience by driving deliciously. The majority of his strokes were not ideal, though even a critical Cambridge Quid was able to add a stimulating 'good shot!' to not a few, while some were really quite hard and clean. Never before had this batsman felt the bat leap in his hands, and the ball spring from the blade beyond the confines of his wildest hopes, at an unimagined velocity, half so often as he experienced these great sensations now. Great! What is there in the sensual world to put on the same page with them? And let your real batsman bear in mind that these divine moments, and their blessed memory, are greatest of all where they are most rare; in his heart who never had the makings of a real batsman, but who once in his life had played a decent game.

Chrystal was in heaven. No small boy succeeding in his first little match, no international paragon compiling his cool hundred before fifty thousand eyes, was ever granted the joy of the game in fuller or sweeter or more delirious measure than was Robert Chrystal that afternoon. Think of his failures. Think of his years. Think of his unathletic figure. Think of ball after ball – big as a football to him now – yet diminishing into thin air or down the hill or under the trees. 'Thank God there's a boundary!' murmured Chrystal, wiping his face while they fetched it. Yet he was cool enough in the way that mattered. He had lost all thought of his score. His mind was entirely concentrated on the coming ball; but it was an open mind until the ball arrived. If his thoughts wandered between the overs, it was back to Harrow, and to the pleasing persuasion that he might have been in the eleven but for his infernal ineptitude for Latin verses. Meanwhile, every ball brought its own anxiety and delight. And for several overs there was really very little to criticize except his style; then came an awful moment.

It was a half-volley on his legs, and Chrystal hit it even higher than he intended, but not quite so hard. One of those vigorous young schoolmasters was keeping himself hard and fit at deep mid-on; he had to run like a greyhound, and to judge a cross flight as he ran; but the apparent impossibility of the catch was simply a challenge to the young schoolmaster's calibre as a field; the ground was just covered, and the ball just held with extended hand. It was a supreme effort – or would have been. There are those catches which are held almost, but not quite, long enough to count. This was an exaggerated instance. Unable to check himself, the young schoolmaster must have covered at least a yard with the ball in his hand. Then it rolled out, and he even kicked it far in front of him in his headlong stride.

'Got him! No, he hasn't. Put him on the floor!' Chrystal heard the little parson say, as he himself charged down the pitch in his second run. He saw nothing. His partner was calling him for a third, and Tuttles was stamping and raving at the bowler's end.

'Was that a chance?' gasped Chrystal, as he grounded his bat.

'A chance?' snorted Tuttles. 'My dear fellow, he only held it about twenty minutes!'

'Am I out, then?' asked Chrystal of the umpire, his hot blood running cold.

'Not out!' declared that friendly functionary without an

instant's indecision. 'But I wouldn't appeal against myself, old chap! It's sporting, but it isn't war.'

The incident, however, had a disturbing effect upon Chrystal's nerves. He shuddered to think of his escape. He became self-conscious, and began to think about his score. It was quite a long time since they clapped him for his fifty. He must be in the eighties at the very least. On his own ground he would have the public scoring apparatus that they have at Lord's; then you would always know when you were near your century. Chrystal, however, was well aware that he must be pretty near his. He had hit another four, not one of his best, and given a stumping chance to little Osborne, who had more than once exchanged the ball for the gloves during the past two hours.

Yes, it was a quarter past five. Chrystal saw that, and pulled himself together, for his passive experience of the game reminded him that the average century is scored in a couple of hours. No doubt he must be somewhere about the nineties. Everybody seemed very still in the pavilion. The scorers' table was certainly surrounded. Chrystal set his teeth, and smothered a half-volley in his earlier no-you-don't manner. But the next ball could only have bowled him round his legs, and Tuttles hardly ever broke that way, besides which, this one was too fast, and, in short, away it went skimming towards the trees. And there and then arose the sweetest uproar that Robert Chrystal had ever heard in all his life.

They were shouting themselves hoarse in front of the little pavilion. The group about the scoring table was dispersing with much hat-waving. The scorer might have been seen leaning back in his chair like a man who had been given air at last. Mrs Chrystal was embracing the boy, probably (and in fact) to hide her joyous tears. Chrystal himself felt almost overcome, and quite abashed. Should he take his cap off or should he not? He would know better another time; meanwhile he meant to look modest, and did look depressed; and half the field closed in upon him, clapping their unselfish hands, while a pair of wicket-keeping gloves belaboured his back with ostentatious thuds.

More magnanimous than the rest, Tuttles had been the first to clap, but he was also the first to stop clapping, and there was a business air about the way in which he signalled for the ball. He carried it back to the spot where he started his run with as much deliberation as though measuring the distance for an opening over. There was peculiar care also in the way in which he grasped the leather, rolling it affectionately in his hand, as though wiping off the sawdust which it had not been necessary to use since the morning. There was a grim light in his eye as he stood waiting to begin his run, a subtle something in the run itself, the whole reminding one, with a sudden and characteristic emphasis, that this really was the first bowler in second-class cricket. A few quick steps firm and precise; a couple of long ones, a beautiful swing, a lovely length, and Chrystal's middle stump lay stretched upon the grass.

It was a great ending to a great innings, a magnificent finale to a week of weeks; but on the charming excesses on the field I shall touch no more than on the inevitable speeches that night at dinner. Field and house alike were full of good hearts, of hearts good enough to appreciate a still better one. Tuthill's was the least expansive; but he had the critical temperament, and he had been hit for many fours, and his week's analysis had been ruined in an afternoon.

'I wasn't worth a sick headache,' he told Chrystal himself, with his own delightful mixture of frankness and contempt. 'I couldn't have outed the biggest sitter in Christendom.'

'But you did send down some pretty good ones, you know!' replied Chrystal, with a rather wistful intonation.

'A few,' Tuttles allowed charily. 'The one that bowled you was all right. But it was a very good innings, and I congratulate you again.'

Now Chrystal had some marvellous old brandy; how it had come into his possession, and how much it was worth, were, respectively, a very long and rather a tall story. He only broached a bottle upon very great occasions; but this was obviously one, even though the bottle had been the last in the cellar, and its contents liquid gold. The only question was whether they should have it on the table with dessert or with their coffee in the study.

Chrystal debated the point with some verbosity; the fact was that he had been put to shame by hearing and speaking of nothing but his century from the soup to the speeches; and he resolutely introduced and conscientiously enlarged upon the topic of the brandy in order to throw a deliberate haze over his own lustre. His character shone the more brilliantly through it; but that could be said of each successive incident since his great achievement. He beamed more than ever. In a sudden silence you would have expected to catch him purring. And Mrs Chrystal had at last agreed to his giving her those particular diamonds which she had over and over again dissuaded him from buying: if he must make some offering to his earthly gods it might as well be to the goddess on the hearth. But none of themselves knew of this, and it was of the Chrystal known to men as well that all sat talking when he had left the dining-room with his bunch of keys. Mrs Chrystal felt the tears coming back into her eyes; they were every one so fond of him, and yet he was all and only hers! It was she who made the move, and for this reason, though she said she fancied he must be expecting them to follow him to the study, for he had been several minutes gone. But Mrs Chrystal led the other ladies to the drawing-room, merely pausing to say generally to the men:

'If you don't find him there he must have gone to the cellar himself, and I'm afraid he's having a hunt.'

Now the Chrystals, like a sensible couple, never meddled with each other's definite departments in the house, and of course Mrs Chrystal knew no more about her husband's cellar arrangements than he did of the inside of her store-room. Otherwise she would have known that he very seldom entered his own cellar, and that he did not require to go there for his precious brandy.

Yet he did seem to have gone there now, for there was no sign of him in the study when the cricketers trooped in. Osborne was saying something in a lowered voice to Tuthill, who, looking round the empty room, replied as emphatically as usual.

'I'm glad you think I did it well. Man and boy, I never took on such a job in all my days, and I never will another. The old sitter!'

And he chuckled good-humouredly enough.

'It's all right, he's down in the cellar,' the little clergyman explained. 'Trust us not to give the show away.'

'And me,' nodded the scholastic hero of the all-but-gallery-catch.

'You precious near did!' Osborne remonstrated. 'You held it just two seconds too long.'

'But fancy holding it at all! I never thought I could get near the thing. I thought a bit of a dash would contribute to the general verisimilitude. Then to make the catch of a lifetime and to have to drop it like a hot potato!'

'It showed the promising quality of self-restraint,' the clerical humourist allowed. 'You will be an upper usher yet.'

'Or a husher upper?' suggested a wag of baser mould, to wit, the sympathetic umpire of the afternoon. 'But your side-show wasn't a patch on mine. Even Osborne admits that you had two seconds to think about it. I hadn't the fifth of one. Tuttles, old man, I thought you were going to knock me down!'

'I very nearly did,' the candid bowler owned. 'I never was no-balled in my life before, and for the moment I forgot.'

'Then it wasn't all acting?'

'Half and half.'

'I thought it was too good to be untrue.'

'But,' continued Tuttles with his virile vanity, 'you fellows buck about what you did, as though you'd done, between you, a thousandth part of what I did. You had your moment apiece. I had one every ball of every over. Great Lord! if I'd known how hard it would be to bowl tosh. Full-pitches on the pads! That's a nice length to have to live up to through a summer afternoon. I wouldn't do it again for five-and-twenty golden sovereigns!'

'And I,' put in the quiet Quidnunc. 'It's the first time I ever sat on the splice while the other man punched them, and I hope it's the last.'

He had been tried as a bat for an exceptionally strong Cambridge eleven.

'Come, come,' said the grave major. 'I wasn't in this myself. I distinctly disapproved. But he played quite well when he got his eye in. I don't believe you could have bowled him then if you'd tried.'

'My good sir,' said he, 'what about the ball after the one which ran him into three figures?'

'Where *is* the dear old rabbit?' the ex-umpire exclaimed.

'Well, not in the hutch,' said the little parson. 'He's come right out of that, and I shouldn't be surprised if he stopped out. I only wish it was the beginning of the week.'

'I'm going to look for him,' the other rejoined, with the blank eye that has not seen a point. He stepped through a French window out into the night. The young schoolmasters followed him. The Indian major detained Osborne.

'We ought to make a rule not to speak of this again. It would be too horrible if it leaked out!'

'I suppose it would.' The little parson had become more like one. Though full of cricket and of chaff, and gifted with a peculiarly lay vocabulary for the due ventilation of his favourite topic, he was yet no discredit to the cloth. A certain superficial insincerity was his worst fault; the conspiracy, indeed, had originated in his nimble mind; but its execution had far exceeded his conception. On the deeper issues the man was sound.

'Can there be any doubt?' the major pursued.

'About the momentary bitter disappointment, no, I'm afraid not; about the ultimate good all round no again; but there I don't fear, I hope.'

'I don't quite follow you,' said the major.

'Old Bob Chrystal,' continued Osborne, 'is absolutely the best sportsman in the world, and absolutely the dearest good chap. But until this afternoon I never thought he would get within a hundred miles of decent cricket; and now I almost think he might, even at his age. He has had the best practice he ever had in his life. His shots improved as he went on. You saw for yourself how he put on the wood. It is a liberal cricket education to make runs, even against the worst bowling in the world. Like most other feats, once you get going, every ten runs come easier than the last. Chrystal got a hundred this afternoon because we let him. I said just now I wished it was the beginning of the week. Don't you see my point?'

The major looked a brighter man.

'You think he might get another?'

'I don't mind betting he does,' said the little parson, 'if he sticks to the country cricket long enough. *Possunt quia posse videntur*!'

They went out in their turn; and Chrystal himself at last stole forth from the deep cupboard in which he kept his cigars and his priceless brandy. An aged bottle still trembled in his hand; but a little while ago his lip had been trembling also, and now it was not. Of course he had not understood a word of the little clergyman's classical tag; but all that immediately preceded it had made, or may make, nearly all the difference to the rest of even his successful life.

His character had been in the balance during much of what had passed in his hearing, and yet behind his back; whether it would have emerged triumphant, even without Gerald Osborne's final pronouncement, is for others to judge from what they have seen of it in this little record.

'It was most awfully awkward,' so Chrystal told his wife. 'I was in there getting at the brandy – I'd gone and crowded it up with all sorts of tackle – when you let all those fellows into the study, and they began talking about me before I could give the alarm. Then it was too late. It would have made them so uncomfortable, and I should have looked so mean.'

'I hope they were saying nice things?'

'Oh, rather; but don't you let them know I overheard them, mind.'

Mrs Chrystal seemed the least suspicious.

'About your century, darling?'

'Well, partly. It was little Osborne, you know. He knows

more about cricket than any of them. Tuttles is only a bowler.'

'I *don't* like him,' said Mrs Chrystal. 'I've quite made up my mind. He was trying to bowl you out the whole time.'

'Little Osborne,' her husband continued, rather hastily, 'says I ought to make a hundred – another hundred – if I stick to it.'

'But of course you will,' said Mrs Chrystal, who just then would have taken Chrystal's selection for England as a matter of course.

Her husband was blushing a little, but glowing more. It was one of those moments when you would have understood his making so much money and winning such. Never was a mouth so determined, and yet so good.

'I don't know about that, dear,' he opened it to say, 'but I mean to try!'

*from* OLD OFFENDERS AND A FEW OLD SCORES *1923*

"ONE OF THE OLDEN TIME."

# Linden Lea

## EDWARD BUCKNELL

It was a glorious afternoon, after a dull morning, when George made his way, in flannels and a brand new pair of cricket boots, towards Ewe Lease. He had resisted, for some time, the solicitations of the Squire to turn out for Norton, representing that he had played his last game at Oxford, ten years before, and that on that occasion his contribution to the gaiety of the afternoon had been a nought, and a dropped catch; but he had been forced to admit, under a searching cross-examination, that he had played for Winchester as a slow bowler, and taken wickets against Eton: and in the end he had capitulated. An evening's practice against the local talent had demonstrated that he could still turn the ball, and that in itself was enough to put him in a class by himself among the Norton bowlers; it had, moreover, awakened in him something of his old enthusiasm for the art, which even the state of his shoulder next morning could not damp. Today, however, he understood that he would have to face an opposition more sophisticated than Bill Toller and the rest of the sturdy optimists who had fallen such easy prey at the nets. Wendlebury were a strong side, as things went in the neighbourhood, and Norton had not beaten them since the War; since, in fact, the Squire had been a young man, and, with the help of the then doctor, had won the match off his own bat.

As he crossed the Park, on his way to the ground, he saw several small parties converging upon Ewe Lease. Cricket was a great institution at Norton, and the Squire's hospitality was famous. Ahead of him were the young doctor and Gomer, carrying a cricket bag between them, the former in flannels, the latter in a pair of white duck trousers that had belonged to General Pilsdon (a tall man and broad in proportion) and George's golf coat, with his head encased in a broad-brimmed hat of a kind of basket-work. Away to his right, coming from the direction of the church, was Bill Toller, with his celebrated four-pound bat over his shoulder; while behind him he could hear the voices of Timothy Clote and a group of friends uplifted in animated conversation.

'I went fur to drive the barl, when er curled round the bat – '

'That'd be one o' they gogglies, I count, Timothy.'

'Well, whether or no, I were teaken my pad off, when up came Harry Moxon. " 'Twould ha' gone a tarrible long way if you'd ha' hit 'un, Timothy!" he says. "Ar!" I says, "an' you'd be a wise man this day, Harry, if so be you hadn't been barn a fule," I says.'

Here George came to the gate, and surveyed the field of action. Ewe Lease was a level stretch of grass – the only flat piece of its size in Norton – with a view of the Hall nestling among ancient trees, and an abundance of shade for the spectators from other trees along one hedge. An open pavilion commanded the ground from one corner, and another, sacred to the Squire's wife and her friends, was ensconced under a huge elm hard by. Seated in garden chairs near the latter could be distinguished Lady Pilsdon, the Vicar, Mrs Tudstock, and a couple of unfamiliar feminine figures, who had, no doubt, come over with the Wendlebury team. A brake was just moving away, having unloaded its freight, and a strange two-seater was parked near the pavilion, in the shade. The Squire, in a faded Forester blazer, was the centre of a group of visitors, while two or three of the more serious-minded were out in the middle of the ground, shaking their heads over the wicket.

George went across to pay his respects to the ladies, and was immediately hailed by Lady Pilsdon.

'Come here, Mr Mordyn,' cried the old lady, 'I want to introduce you to my cousin, Miss Dering! Her brother's on the wrong side this afternoon, but I hope you'll preserve an armed neutrality.'

A pretty girl at her side laughed pleasantly.

'I hear you're expected to tie us up, Mr Mordyn,' she said, looking up at George with frank eyes. 'I'm looking forward to it, for some of our people have had things too much their own way the last year or two.'

'I'm afraid I shall disappoint you,' he said. 'I'm only a very moderate performer.'

'Well, we shall see,' said Miss Dering, unconvinced. 'It would really be a kindness to deal with my brother Toby; he made a hundred last week, against the feeblest bowling, at Durnton, and he's been very hard to live with since!'

Before George could reply to this unexpected remark, the Squire bore down upon him with the information that they had lost the toss, and were in the field; and which end would suit him best? George chose that which gave him the longest boundary on the leg side, and got his field placed, with some difficulty, for the greater part of the Norton side had never seen leg-break bowling before, and viewed his dispositions with misgivings.

'What! furder still!' murmured Timothy Clote, as he was waved back on to the square-leg boundary. 'I rackon they'll run a pair while I be throwen in!' He looked round the outfield critically. There was Gomer, with his knees slightly bent in an attitude of intense watchfulness, in front of the ladies' pavilion, and, almost behind the bowler, young Peter Vince, taking up his braces another hole. Timothy shook his head forebodingly. Only one slip, and no long-stop. It might be all right, but it wasn't what he was accustomed to, and he feared the worst. In any case, time would show.

As it turned out, he had not long to wait, for no sooner had old George Vince settled his spectacles, after giving Guard, and called 'Play!' than the batsman, mistaking George's first delivery for a half-volley, which it certainly resembled very closely, ballooned the ball straight into the hands of the sceptic at deep square-leg. Straight, that is to say, to the place where his hands would have been if he had stood still and waited for it. But Timothy's temperament was too much for him, under the shock of his undreamt-of-opening, and, running in towards the ball, he realized too late that he ought to have stayed where he was, tried to retreat again, sat down heavily, and heard it plump into the ground behind him. Rising, in a passion of remorse, he hurled the ball in, but three runs had been scored in the meanwhile, and a chance missed which would probably not occur again for some time.

George was now faced by young Dering, a cool youth with a Woolwich cap and a hint of swagger, who showed at once that he was not going to be caught napping. Watching the ball with the eye of a hawk, he played solidly back to the first two, declined to nibble at the going-away one, pulled a shorter one for two, and drove the last of the over, a genuine half-volley this time, for four of the best. George looked thoughtful as he threw the ball to Eli, who was bowling at the other end.

However, when, after an over of very varied merit from him, he found that his first victim was batting again, he set to work on him with some confidence. The ball was biting well on the rather mossy turf, and the batsman, having suffered a loss of morale already, saw snares on all sides, and finally was clean bowled playing back to a half-volley. By this time the field had woken up to the possibilities of this form of bowling, and for the next hour-and-a-half George enjoyed himself thoroughly taking seven wickets, of which two were bowled and the remainder caught; one, a brilliant effort by the Squire at backward point, and one by Gomer, who lost sight of the ball, saw it again, fell over his feet, recovered himself, and brought off an amazing fluke with one hand, holding up his trousers with the other. At the other end, a succession of bowlers had taken one wicket between them, and one man had been run out. The score was 136 for 9, and young Dering, who was still in, and seeing the ball like a balloon, was bagging the bowling with considerable skill. George had succeeded in keeping him quiet, and there had been one difficult chance of stumping him which had been beyond the doctor at the wicket.

Once more he took the ball. He would dearly like to get the fellow out, and he had spent the preceding over thinking hard. Toby Dering waited for the field to settle down in an attitude of easy confidence, and then took his stance. The first ball was outside the off-stump, a little over-pitched, and flashed past Gomer to the boundary, amidst rapturous applause. The second was on the stump and a good length. Dering stepped across and let it break away with a smile. The doctor gathered the ball and returned it to George, who retired for his short run with a determined expression on his face. Could he reproduce that overspin, which had come off at the nets all right the other evening, *and* keep his length? It was now or never. He advanced to the wicket and delivered the ball. In flight and length it exactly resembled the one before, and once more the batsman moved across and lifted his bat. The ball pitched, took a little divot out of the wicket, and went straight on, keeping rather low. There was a thud, and a little cloud of pipeclay from Dering's pad.

'How's that?' asked George quietly.

'The gentleman be Out!' replied old Vince, lifting his hand in the Scotch fashion.

'Oh! well bowled, well bowled!' said the Squire; and then the cheering started.

Toby Dering, however, was obviously dissatisfied with the decision, and as the Norton side came over to the ladies' pavilion for tea, he was still standing at his sister's side, grumbling in a low voice.

'Don't be an ass, Toby,' she said, as George approached. 'You were plumb out. I could see it from here! . . . Congratulations, Mr Mordyn,' she went on, as her brother withdrew sulkily; 'I enjoyed watching you bowl immensely. It's a pleasure to see anyone using his head, after the stuff we're accustomed to, isn't it, Cousin Eleanor?'

'Don't ask me!' said Lady Pilsdon. 'I haven't the most elementary knowledge of the game; but I've had a very pleasant afternoon, my dear, and I hope we shall see Norton win.'

'Cousin Eleanor's like my Aunt Mildred,' said Miss Dering to George. 'Somebody was talking about cricket in her presence, and she said, "Oh! I know all about cricket. You throw the ball and then you run!"'

George smiled at her approvingly. She was fair, with good

features and periwinkle-blue eyes, that looked at one with perfect frankness and self-possession, and her sensitive mouth was made for laughter. He brought his cup and a chair, and sat down at her side.

'You seem to know local form better than I do,' he said. 'Do you think we're good for a hundred and forty-one?'

'How many are you good for yourself?' she inquired.

'Oh, I?' George laughed. 'I'm hopeless. The Squire insists on my going in Number Nine, but that's two too high.'

'In that case,' she said, 'I don't really fancy your chances. Our bowling's nothing very wonderful but neither, I believe, is your batting, unless the first wicket does wonders.'

As she spoke, the Squire and the doctor walked out, and the innings started. Toby Dering opened the bowling, and looked rather formidable, keeping a length and maintaining a fine pace. The doctor was early in difficulties with him, and even the Squire, though he had evidently been a batsman of real class in his time, found his work cut out to play him. The other bowling was ordinary enough, and both players scored freely from it, the Squire bringing off some beautiful strokes of the old-fashioned style; but at twenty-five the doctor's fall, postponed by luck, came at last, and Jesse Jupp, who succeeded him, never looked like staying.

'This is serious!' said George. 'Holloa! What's the Squire coming in for?'

'I shouldn't be surprised if he's sending in your blacksmith – what's his name – oh, yes, Toller – out of his turn. That's very good tactics, you know. Toby'll get his tail down in no time if he's hit.'

Miss Dering's prognostication turned out to be correct, for at that moment Bill Toller made his appearance, with his mighty bat on his shoulder, turning up his sleeves from his knotted arms. Years of ecclesiastical office had added a decent solemnity to his walk, but there was no doubt about his determination as he spat on his hands and lifted his weapon in the air in readiness for action.

'Now then!' said Miss Dering . . . 'Oh! good, good!' as Bill Toller swept a good-length ball unconcernedly out of the ground over long-on's head. 'Just look at Toby! He is annoyed! One more like that, and he'll go to pieces!'

Young Dering was, in fact, showing signs of temper, and when, after missing the wicket by a hair's breadth with his second ball, he saw the third follow the first into the next field, he lost his poise altogether, and finished the over with a succession of long hops. The Wendlebury captain, rather injudiciously, took him off at once, and Bill Toller and the Squire played havoc with the substitute, to such effect that when at last Dering came on again, and knocked the smith's middle-stump out of the ground with his first ball, the score was 105 for 2.

'It looks like providing a finish, after all,' observed George, when the applause which greeted Bill Toller's return from the wicket had died down.

'I think the score-board flatters your prospects a bit,' said Miss Dering. 'Toby's recovered his tone again now, and your batting won't put up much of a show, I'm afraid – unless you've been too modest about your own form.'

'No,' said George, 'that's the one stable factor in the uncertainty of cricket!'

It certainly looked as though young Dering would carry all before him – always excepting the Squire, who had really got going, and was batting in a masterly style. Three more wickets fell to him in rapid succession, to the dismay of the spectators, the batsman being completely nonplussed in each case. When the sixth fell, George put on his pads and prepared for imminent execution. But, by one of those curious patches of luck which add so much to the fascination of the game, the newcomer – it was Peter Vince – proved unexpectedly difficult to dislodge. Time after time the ball beat him completely, and grazed the wicket, but still he remained, sweating with excitement, and tying himself into knots in his endeavours to score, without so much success as might have got him out. As the score crept up to 120, the excitement round the ground became painful, every run being rapturously applauded, and when, at 123, Peter Vince at length touched the ball, and was immediately caught at third-man, the groan which ran round the circle of onlookers was tragic.

George stood up and took off his coat.

'This is the end!' he said grimly.

'Oh! nonsense,' she replied. 'If you only keep your end up, Mr Sanderstead will get the runs.'

'There is much virtue in that "if"!' said George, setting out for the wicket with a sinking feeling in his heart.

As he got near the wicket, the Squire came to meet him.

'Look out for the good-length ball on the off-stump!' he said. 'There's a bit of a spot there, and they're coming back like lightning.'

George smiled. 'I've never yet recognized a good-length ball when I've seen it,' he said, 'but I'll do my best.'

Old Vince was trembling with emotion, and had to take off and polish his glasses before he could give him guard, but at last that formality was observed and he settled himself to face the worst. Young Dering ran up to the wicket, swung himself through an easy action and delivered the ball. It flashed through the air, pitched on the 'spot' the squire had warned him of, and came back fast and low. George, who had felt a momentary impulse to play forward, pulled himself up just in time, and clapped his bat down on the ball as it shot towards his leg-stump.

'Well played, indeed!' said the Squire fervently.

The next was outside the off-stump and could safely be left alone, and then it was over, and he could relax again for a moment. In the next over the Squire hit a couple of fours, and they managed to steal a single from the last ball, to George's heartfelt relief, and then a tragedy occurred. Off Dering's first ball, a shortish one on the leg side, the Squire turned to bring off his favourite glance, failed to get over it, and was caught by the wicket-keeper standing back. A delighted chorus arose from the Wendlebury team, followed by many hearty congratulations on a fine innings; but George's heart sank into his boots.

Nine runs to win, and two wickets to go, but what was to be expected from Timothy Clote and Gomer, who had not been thought worthy to precede him in the batting order? And Dering had still five balls to finish the over. A glance at Timothy, who had arrived at this juncture, shaking like an aspen leaf, did nothing to reassure him, nor did his reception of his first ball, at which he waved his bat wildly, promise any better. If only he could get down to that end himself! George laughed at the idea of his being the hope of the side, and the next moment he was running for his life, shouting to Timothy, who was rooted to the ground, to get a move on. The ball had somehow touched his bat and glanced off towards third-man who was even now hurling it furiously at the wicket-keeper's end. The latter ran up to the wicket, too late to save the mischief, and three runs were added to Timothy's score.

Six to win and three more balls in the over.

Toby Dering, rising to the occasion, bowled three of his best, and George, though he concentrated on keeping them out of his wicket, and made no attempt to score, had hard work to deal with them, particularly the last, which was the 'spot-ball' in its most virulent form. He succeeded, however, by the skin of his teeth; there was no chance of bagging the bowling, and he could only pray that Timothy, at the other end, would survive his less exacting test and give him an opportunity of running. A kind of exaltation had descended on the field, the wicket-keeper changed over talking excitedly to himself, the bowler was in a pitiable state of nervousness, and all round the ground the tension was tremendous.

At last the field was set, and the bowler delivered the ball – a deplorable long-hop. George was half-way down the wicket as it pitched, ready to run if Clote so much as touched it. The latter, inspired by a vision of victory and fame, turned to cart it out of the ground, swung his bat with all the strength of his body, missed it completely, and was cleaned bowled on the second hop. For a moment he stood aghast, contemplating the ruin of his wicket; then, with a gesture of despair, turned and ran for the pavilion. George watched him go with a set face. All seemed to be over, but he would go down fighting, and, going to meet Gomer, who now made his appearance, with his basket hat crammed over his eyes and a resolute bearing, he besought him to stop the straight ones, if possible, and stand by to run for anything he played.

'Never you fear, sir,' said Gomer, touching his hat politely; 'us'll beat yet. I count I'll never hear the last of it from my Polly, else!'

Somewhat reassured, George returned to his crease, but, to his horror, Gomer, attacking his first ball with a windmill motion of his bat, skied it above the wicket, and then remained thunder-struck, watching the wicket-keeper stepping back leisurely to take it.

'*Run!*' shouted George desperately, and Gomer, coming to himself with a start, ran.

Meanwhile, the whole Wendlebury side watched the ball with fascinated eyes; none more so than first slip, who, convinced that the catch concerned himself only, moved forward as the wicket-keeper moved back, and finally crashed into the latter's back, just as he was on the point of securing the ball, and tumbled him over, amidst a tempest of cheers from the crowd. George was contemplating their recumbent figures with much satisfaction when he heard a roar behind him, and discovered, with stupefaction, that Gomer was under way for a second run. A spirited scene followed; George sending Gomer back, that infatuate blind and deaf to everything; the pair on the ground, their recriminations put aside, struggling for the ball to run one of the batsmen out, and the spectators wailing in an agony of apprehension.

At any other stage of the game the mistake would have been fatal. As it was, the general demoralization had become so great that the chance was fumbled, and once again a grain of hope sprang up in George's heart.

A profound silence ensued, as he faced the bowler again. Five to win, now! . . . The first was so wide that he left it alone; the second was straight and looked a fair length – he decided not to risk anything, and contented himself with stopping it. The third – oh, joy! – was the one ball he was sure of recognizing, a half-volley outside the leg-stump. Throwing caution and style to the winds he wound his bat round his neck and hit hard and high. There was a breathless pause, while everyone watched the ball mounting and gathering flight; then, as it descended well outside the boundary hedge, the dams were burst, and pande-monium broke loose.

The excitement had hardly subsided when Gomer was bowled by Toby Dering with the first ball of the next over and both teams received an ovation when they came in.

'Best finish I can remember,' said the Wendlebury captain to the Squire, cordially, among the babel of voices.

'When I see thic barl drop over-right th' hedge,' said Bill Toller, 'I took an' shook Timothy here by the hand – didn't I so, Timothy?'

'Ar! I believe,' said Timothy, with a pale smile, nursing the injured member.

'An' I says to un, "That be *cricket*," I says. " 'Tis a gift," I sayd, "same as swingen my tenpund hammer be!" '

'I really believe I've been crying with excitement, Alice, my dear,' said Lady Pilsdon, wiping her eyes. 'Mr Mordyn, you've given us a memorable afternoon!'

'I wish you could have heard Mr Dacres yelping like a terrier when you and Gomer were pursuing each other up and down the wicket,' said Miss Dering. 'I'm afraid we've all disgraced ourselves in the last quarter of an hour! ... I see Toby's fuming to get away. It's done *him* no harm, anyway. Good-bye, Cousin Eleanor. Good-bye, Mr Mordyn; you mustn't fail to come over to us for the return! Coming, Toby, coming!'

*from* LINDEN LEA *1925*

# The Flower Show Match

## SIEGFRIED SASSOON

Ten minutes late, in the hot evening sunshine, my train bustled contentedly along between orchards and hop-gardens, jolted past the signal-box puffed importantly under the bridge, and slowed up at Baldock Wood. The Station was exactly the same as usual, and I was very pleased to see it again. I was back from Ballboro' for the summer holidays. As I was going forward to the guard's van to identify my trunk and my wooden play-box, the station-master (who, in those days, wore a top-hat and baggy black frock coat) saluted me respectfully. Aunt Evelyn always sent him a turkey at Christmas.

Having claimed my luggage, I crossed the bridge, surrendered my ticket to a red-nosed and bearded collector, who greeted me good-naturedly, and emerged from the station, with my cricket bat (which was wrapped in my cricket pads) under my arm. Dixon was waiting outside with a smart pony and trap. Grinning at me with restrained delight, he instructed my luggage-trundling porter to put it on the village omnibus and I gave the man the last sixpence of my journey-money. As we rattled up the road the unpunctual train with a series of snorts and a streamer of smoke, sauntered sedately away into the calm agricultural valley of its vocation.

How jolly to be home for the holidays, I thought to myself. So far neither of us had said a word; but as soon as we were out of the village street (it wasn't our own village) he gave the pony a playful flick of the whip and made the following remark, 'I've got a place for you in tomorrow's team,' subdued triumph was in his voice and his face.

'What, for the Flower Show Match!' I exclaimed, scarcely able to believe my ears. He nodded.

Now the Flower Show Match was the match of the year, and to play in it for the first time in my life was an outstanding event:

words were inadequate. We mutually decided not to gush about it.

'Of course, you're playing, too?' I enquired. He nodded again. Dixon was one of the mainstays of the village team – a dashing left-hand bat and a steady right-arm bowler. I drew a deep breath of our local air. I was indeed home for the holidays! Expert discussion of tomorrow's prospects occupied the remaining mile and a half to the house.

'Miss Sherston won't half be pleased to see you,' he said as we turned briskly in at the white gate. 'She misses you no end, sir.'

Aunt Evelyn heard us coming up the drive, and she hurried across the lawn in her white dress. Her exuberant welcome ended with, 'But you're looking rather thin in the face, dear ... Don't you think Master George is looking rather thin, Dixon? ... We must feed him up well before he goes back.' Dixon smiled and led the pony and cart round to the stable-yard.

'And now, dear, whatever do you think has happened? I've been asked to help judge the vegetables at the Flower Show tomorrow. Really, I feel quite nervous! I've never judged anything except the sweet peas before. Of course I'm doing them as well.' With great restraint I said that I was sure the vegetables would be very interesting and difficult.

'I'm playing in the match,' I added, with casual intensity. Aunt Evelyn was overjoyed at the news, and she pretended to be astonished. No doubt she had known about it all the time. The roast chicken at dinner tasted delicious and my bed felt ever so much more comfortable than the one at school.

My window was wide open when I went to bed, and I had left the curtains half drawn. I woke out of my deep and dreamless sleep to a gradual recognition that I was at home and not in the cubicled dormitory at Ballboro'. Drowsily grateful for this, I lay and listened. A cock was crowing from a neighbouring farm; his shrill challenge was faintly echoed by another cock a long way off.

I loved the early morning; it was luxurious to lie there, half awake, and half aware that there was a pleasantly eventful day in front of me ... Presently I would get up and lean on the window-ledge to see what was happening in the world outside ... There was a starling's nest under the window where the jasmine grew thickest, and all of a sudden I heard one of the birds dart away with a soft flurry of wings. Hearing it go, I imagined how it would fly boldly across the garden. Soon I was up and staring at the tree-tops which loomed motionless against a flushed and brightening sky. Slipping into some clothes, I opened my door very quietly and tiptoed along the passage and down the stairs. There was no sound except the first chirping of the sparrows in the ivy. I felt as if I had changed since the Easter Holidays. The drawing-room door creaked as I went softly in and crept across the beeswaxed parquet floor. Last night's half-consumed candles and the cat's half-empty bowl of milk under the gate-legged table seemed to belong neither here nor there, and my own silent face looked queerly at me out of the mirror. And there was the familiar photograph of 'Love and Death', by Watts, with its secret meaning which I could never quite formulate in a thought, though it often touched me with a vague emotion of pathos. When I unlocked the door into the garden the early-morning air met me with its cold purity; on the stone step were the bowls of roses and delphiniums and sweet peas which Aunt Evelyn had carried out there before she went to bed; the scarlet disc of the sun had climbed an inch above the hills. Thrushes and blackbirds hopped and pecked busily on the dew-soaked lawn, and a pigeon was cooing monotonously from the belt of woodland which sloped from the garden towards the Weald. Down there in the belt of river-mist a goods train whistled as it puffed steadily away from the station with a distinctly heard clanking of buffers. How little I knew of the enormous world beyond that valley and those low green hills.

From over the fields and orchards Butley Church struck five in mellow tones. Then the clock indoors whizzed and confirmed it with a less resonant tongue. The Flower Show Match was hours away yet – more than six hours, in fact. Suppose I'd better go back to bed again, I thought, or I'll be feeling tired out before the match begins. Soon the maids would be stirring overhead, padding about the floor and talking in muffled voices. Meanwhile I stole down to the pantry to cut myself a piece of cake. What a stuffy-smelling place it was, with the taps dripping into the sink and a blue-bottle fly buzzing sleepily on the ceiling. I inspected the village grocer's calendar which was hanging from a nail. On it there was a picture of 'The Relief of Ladysmith' . . . Old Kruger and the Boers. I never could make up my mind what it was all about, that Boer War, and it seemed such a long way off . . . Yawning and munching, I went creaking up to my room. It was broad daylight out of doors, but I was soon asleep again.

2

After breakfast there was no time to be wasted. First of all I had to rummage about for the tin of 'Blanco', which was nowhere to be found. Probably the parlourmaid had bagged it. Why on earth couldn't they leave things alone? I knew exactly where I'd left the tin at the end of last Holidays – on the shelf in the schoolroom, standing on an old case of beetles (of which, for a short time, I had been a collector). And now, unless I could find the tin quickly, there'd never be time for me to 'Blanco' my pads, for they took ever so long to dry in the sun, even on a blazing hot day like this one –

'Really, it's a bit thick, Aunt Evelyn; someone's taken my tin of "Blanco",' I grumbled. But she was already rather fussed, and was at that moment preoccupied in a serious discussion with Mabb, the gardener, about the transportation of the crockery which she was lending for the Cricket Tea.

In a hasty parenthesis she confessed that she had given the tin to Dixon only a week or two ago, so I transferred myself and my grimy pads to the harness room, where I discovered Dixon putting the finishing touches to his white cricket boots; he had already cleaned mine, and he apologized for not having done my pads, as he had been unable to find them. While I busied myself with dabbing and smearing the pads we had a nice chat about county cricket; he also told me how he had taken a 'highly commended' at the Crystal Palace Dog Show with one of the smooth-haired collies which he had recently begun breeding. There had been a lull in his horse-buying activities after I went to school; since then I had given up my riding, as my aunt could not afford to keep a cob specially for me to ride in the holidays. So Dixon had consoled himself with his collies and village cricket; and the saddles were only used when he was exercising the sedate horse which now shared the carriage work with the smart little pony Rocket.

Leaving my pads to dry in the sun, I sauntered contentedly back to the house to have a squint at the morning paper, which never arrived until after breakfast. I had a private reason for wanting to look at the *Morning Post*. I was a firm believer in predestination, and I used to improvise superstitions of my own in connection with the cricket matches I played in. Aunt Evelyn was rustling the newspaper in the drawing-room, where she was having a short spell of inactivity before setting forth to judge the vegetables and sweet peas. Evidently she was reading about politics (she was a staunch Tory).

'I can't understand what that miserable Campbell-Bannerman is up to; but thank heaven the Radicals will never get in again!' she exclaimed, handing me the sheet with the cricket news on it.

Carrying this into the garden I set about consulting the omens for my success in the match. I searched assiduously through the first-class scores, picking out the amateurs whose names, like my own, began with S, and whose initial was G. There were only two that day: the result was most unsatisfactory. G. Shaw run out, 1; G. Smith, c. Lilley, b. Field, 0. According to that I should score half a run. So I called in professional assistance, and was rewarded with: Shrewsbury, not out, 127. This left me in a very awkward position. The average now worked out at 64. The highest score I had ever made was 51, and that was only in a practice game at Ballboro'. Besides, 51 from 64 left 13, an unlucky number. It was absurd even to dally with the idea of my making 64 in the Butley Flower Show Match. Anything between

20 and 30 would have been encouraging. But Aunt Evelyn's voice from the drawing-room window informed me that she would be starting in less than ten minutes, so I ran upstairs to change into my flannels. And, anyhow, the weather couldn't have been better . . . While we were walking across the fields Aunt Evelyn paused on the top of a stile to remark that she felt sure Mr Balfour would be a splendid Prime Minister. But I was meditating about Shrewsbury's innings. How I wished I could bat like him, if only for one day!

The village of Butley contained, as one of its chief characters, a portly and prosperous saddler named William Dodd who now greeted us at the field-gate and ushered Aunt Evelyn into the large, tropical-temperatured tent where the judges had already begun their expert scrutiny of the competing vegetables.

In the minds of most of the inhabitants of Butley, William Dodd was an immemorial institution, and no village affairs could properly be transacted without his sanction and assistance. As a churchwarden on Sundays his impressive demeanour led us to suppose that, if he was not yet on hat-raising terms with the Almighty, he at any moment expected to be. During a Parliamentary Election he was equally indispensable, as he supervised the balloting in the village schoolroom; and the sanguine solemnity with which he welcomed the Conservative candidate left no doubt at all as to his own political opinions. He was a man much respected by the local gentry, and was on free and easy terms with the farmers of the neighbourhood. In fact, he was a sort of unofficial Mayor of the village, and would have worn his robes, had they existed, with dignity and decorum. Though nearer fifty than forty, he was still one of the most vigorous run-getters in the Butley eleven, and his crafty underarm bowling worked havoc with the tail-end of many an opposing team. On Flower Show day he was in all his glory as captain of the cricket team and secretary and treasurer of the Horticultural Society and his manner of receiving my aunt and myself was an epitome of his urbane and appreciative attitude towards the universe with which the parish of Butley was discreetly associated. Waggish persons in the village had given him the nickname 'Did-I-say-Myself'. Anyone who wanted to discover the origin of this witticism could do so by stopping outside the saddler's shop on a summer morning for a few minutes of gentle gossip. Laying aside whatever implement of his craft he happened to be using, he would get up and come to the door in his protuberant apron, and when interrogated about 'the team for tomorrow', 'Let me see,' he would reply in a gravely complacent voice, 'let me see, there's Mr Richard Puttridge; and Myself; my brother Alfred; Tom Dixon; Mr Jack Barchard; young Bob Ellis 9 and did I say Myself?' – and so on, counting the names on his stubby fingers, and sometimes inserting 'and I think I said Myself' again towards the end of the recital. But his sense of his own importance was justified when he had a bat in his hand. No one could gainsay that.

Having, so to speak, received the freedom of the Flower Show from this worthy man, there was nothing more for me to do until the rest of the players had arrived. At present there wasn't a cricketer to be seen on the small but well-kept ground, and it seemed unlikely that the match would begin before noon. It was now a little after eleven and a cloudless day. Sitting in the shadow of a chestnut tree I watched the exertions of a muscular man with a mallet. He was putting up a 'coconut shy' in the adjoining meadow, where a steam roundabout, some boat swings, a shooting gallery, and other recreative facilities were in readiness for the afternoon. On the opposite side of the cricket field had been erected a Tea Tent, which would contain such spectators as were prevented by their social status from shying at coconuts or turning almost upside-down in a boat-swing. The ground sloped from the Tea Tent to the side where I was sitting (twenty-five summers ago), so that genteel onlookers were enabled to feel themselves perceptibly above the rest of the proceedings.

Behind the tent was a thick thorn hedge; beyond the hedge ran the dusty high road to the village. In the late afternoon of a cricket match there would be several dilatory vehicles drawn up on the other side of the hedge, and the drivers would watch the game in Olympian detachment. There would be the carrier's van, and the brewer's dray, and the baker's cart, and the doctor's gig, and sometimes even a wagon-load of hay. None of them ever seemed to be pressed for time, and once they were there they were likely to stay till the end of the innings. Rooks would be cawing in the vicarage elms, and Butley, with its huddle of red roofs and square church tower, was a contented-looking place.

In my retrospect the players are now beginning to appear in ones and twos. Some skim easily across the greensward on bicycles; others arrive philosophically on foot, pausing to inspect the wicket, which has a nasty habit of causing fast bowling to 'bump' after a spell of dry weather.

Dixon and I were having a little practice up against the fence, when Aunt Evelyn emerged from the Flower Show Tent with a bevy of head-gardeners. She signalled to me, so I clambered over the palings and went up to her. She only wanted to tell me that she would be back again after lunch and did so hope she wouldn't miss my innings.

'I'm feeling quite proud that Master George is playing in the match,' she exclaimed, turning to a short clean-shaven small-eyed man in a square bowler hat and his dark Sunday suit, who was standing near her. And then, to me, she added, 'I was just congratulating Mr Bathwick on his wonderful vegetables. We've given him the first prize and he thoroughly deserves it. You never saw such tomatoes and cucumbers! I've been telling Mr Bathwick that he's a positive example to us all!'

Sam Bathwick, who had a very large mouth, grinned bashfully, though his heavy sallow face had an irrepressibly artful look about it. He farmed a little bit of land in an out-of-the-way corner of the parish, and was reputed to have put by more money than he admitted.

Climbing over the fence again, I became aware of the arrival of the Rotherden eleven in a two-horse brake. It was close on twelve o'clock, but they'd had a fourteen mile drive and the road was up and down hill all the way. How enormous they looked as they sauntered across the ground – several of them carrying cricket bags. I should be lucky if I made any runs at all against such men as they were!

Butley Church clock was tolling twelve while our opponents were bearing down on us from the other side of the field, with William Dodd already half-way across to meet them. But the Rotherden men appeared to be in no great hurry to begin the game as they stopped to have a look at the wicket. Meanwhile Butley bells chimed sedately to the close of the mellow extra celebration which Providence allowed them every three hours without fail.

'I suppose they've got their best team?' I faltered to Dixon, whose keen gaze was identifying the still distant stalwarts.

'You bet they have!' he replied with a grim smile.

Two of the tallest men had detached themselves from the others and were now pacing importantly down the pitch, with Dodd between them. Dixon indicated this group. 'They've got Crump and Bishop, anyhow,' he remarked . . . Crump and Bishop! The names had a profound significance for me. For many years I had heard Dixon speak of them, and I had even watched them playing in a few Flower Show Matches. Heavily built men in dark blue caps, with large drooping moustaches, one of them bowling vindictively at each end and Butley wickets falling fast; or else one of them batting at each end and Butley bowling being scored off with masterful severity.

But they had also produced a less localized effect on me. Rotherden was on the 'unhunted' side of our district; it was in a part of the county which I somehow associated with cherry-blossom and black-and-white timbered cottages. Also it had the charm of remoteness, and whenever I thought of Crump and Bishop I comprehensively visualized the whole fourteen miles of more or less unfamiliar landscape which lay between Butley and Rotherden. For me the names meant certain lovely glimpses of the Weald, and the smell of mown hayfields, and the noise of a shallow river flowing under a bridge. Yet Crump was an ordinary auctioneer who sold sheep and cattle on market days, and Bishop kept the Rose and Crown at Rotherden.

### 3

Butley had lost the toss. As we went on to the field I tightened the black and yellow scarf which I wore round my waist; the scarf proved that I had won a place in my house eleven at school, and it was my sole credential as a cricketer. But today was more exciting and important than any house-match, and my sense of my own inferiority did not prevent me from observing every detail of the proceedings which I am now able to visualize so clearly across the intervening years.

The umpires in their long white coats have placed the bails on the stumps, each at his own end, and they are still satisfying themselves that the stumps are in the requisite state of exact uprightness. Tom Seamark, the Rotherden umpire, is a red-faced sporting publican who bulks as large as a lighthouse. As an umpire he has certain emphatic mannerisms. When appealed to he expresses a negative decision with a severe and stentorian 'Not out'; but when adjudicating that the batsman is out he silently shoots his right arm towards the sky – an impressive and irrevocable gesture which effectively quells all adverse criticism. He is, of course, a tremendous judge of the game, and when not absorbed by his grave responsibilities he is one of the most jovial men you could meet with.

Bill Sutler, our umpire, is totally different. To begin with, he has a wooden leg. Nobody knows how he lost his leg; he does not deny the local tradition that he was once a soldier, but even in his cups he has never been heard to claim that he gave the limb for Queen and Country. It is, however, quite certain that he is now a cobbler (with a heavily waxed moustache), and Butley has ceased to deny that he is a grossly partisan umpire. In direct contrast to Tom Seamark, he invariably signifies 'not out' by a sour shake of the head; when the answer is an affirmative one he bawls 'Hout' as if he'd been stung by a wasp. It is reputed that (after giving the enemy's last man out leg-before in a closely fought finish) he was once heard to add, in an exultant undertone: 'And I've won my five bob.' He has also been accused of making holes in the pitch with his wooden leg in order to facilitate the efforts of the Butley bowlers.

The umpires are in their places. But it is in the sunshine of my own clarified retrospection that they are wearing their white coats. While I was describing them I had forgotten that they have both of them been dead for many years. Nevertheless their voices are distinctly audible to me. 'Same boundaries as usual, Bill?' shouts Seamark, as loudly as if he was talking to a deaf customer in his tap-room. 'Same as usual Muster Seamark; three all round and four over the fence. Draw at six-thirty, and seven if there's anything in it,' says Sutler. And so, with an intensified detachment, I look round me at the Butley Players, who are now safely distributed in the positions which an omniscient Dodd has decreed for them.

I see myself, an awkward overgrown boy, fielding anxiously at mid-on. And there's Ned Noakes, the whiskered and one-eyed wicketkeeper, alert and active, though he's forty-five if he's a day. With his one eye (and a glass one) he sees more than most of us do, and his enthusiasm for the game is apparent in every attitude. Alongside of him lounges big Will Picksett, a taciturn good-natured young yokel; though over-deliberate in his move-ments. Will is a tower of strength in the team, and he sweeps half-volleys to the boundary with his enormous brown arms as though he were scything a hayfield. But there is no more time to describe the fielders, for Dodd has thrown a bright-red ball to Frank Peckham, who is to begin the bowling from the top end. While Crump and Bishop are still on their way to the wickets I cannot help wondering whether, to modern eyes, the Butley team would not seem just a little unorthodox. William Dodd, for example, comfortably dressed in a pale-pink shirt and grey trousers; and Peter Baitup, the groundsman (whose face is framed in a 'Newgate fringe') wearing dingy white trousers with thin green stripes, and carrying his cap in his belt while he bowls his tempting left-hand slows. But things were different in those days.

In the meantime Bill Crump has taken guard and is waiting with watchful ease to subjugate the first ball of the match, while Peckham, a stalwart fierce-browed farmer, takes a final look round the field. Peckham is a fast bowler with an eccentric style. Like most fast bowlers, he starts about fifteen paces from the wicket, but instead of running he walks the whole way to the crease, very much on his heels, breaking his aggressive stride with a couple of systematic hops when about halfway to his destination. Now he is ready. Seamark pronounces the word 'Play!' and off he goes, walking for all he is worth, gripping the ball ferociously, and eyeing the batsmen as if he intended to murder him if he can't bowl him neck and crop. On the ultimate stride his arm swings over, and a short-pitched ball pops up and whizzes alarmingly near Crump's magnificent moustache. Ned Noakes receives it rapturously with an adroit snap of his gauntlets. Unperturbed, and with immense deliberation, Crump strolls up the pitch and prods with his bat the spot where he had to make up his mind that the ball hit the ground on its way towards his head. 'Don't drop 'em too short, Frank,' says Dodd mildly, with an expostulatory shake of his bristly grey cranium. Thus the match proceeds until, twenty-five years ago, it is lunch time, and Rotherden has made seventy runs with three wickets down. And since both Crump and Bishop have been got rid of, Butley thinks it hasn't done badly.

The Luncheon Tent stood on that part of the field where the Flower Show ended and the swings and roundabouts began. Although the meal was an informal affair, there was shy solemnity in the faces of most of the players as they filtered out of the bright sunshine into the sultry half-lit interior, where the perspiring landlord of the Chequers and his buxom wife were bustling about at the climax of their preparations. While the cricketers were shuffling themselves awkwardly into their places, the brawny barman (who seemed to take catering less seriously than his employers) sharpened the carving-knife on a steel prong with a rasping sound that set one's teeth on edge while predicting satisfactory slices of lamb and beef, to say nothing of veal and ham pie and a nice bit of gammon of bacon.

As soon as all were seated Dodd created silence by rapping the table; he then put on his churchwarden face and looked towards Parson Yalden, who was in readiness to take his cue. He enunciated the grace in slightly unparsonic tones, which implied that he was not only Rector of Rotherden but also a full member of the M.C.C. and first cousin once removed to Lord Chatwynd. Parson Yalden's parishioners occasionally complained that he paid more attention to cricket and pheasant-shooting than was fit and proper. But as long as he could afford to keep a hard-working curate he rightly considered it his own affair if he chose to spend three days a week playing in club and country-house matches all over the county. His demeanour when keeping wicket for his own parish was both jaunty and magisterial, and he was renowned for the strident and obstreperous bellow to which he gave vent when he was trying to bluff a village umpire into giving a batsman out 'caught behind.' He was also known for his habit of genially engaging the batsman in conversation while the bowler was intent on getting him out, and I have heard of at least one occasion when he tried this little trick on the wrong man. The pestered batsman rounded on the rather foxy-faced clergyman with, 'I bin playing cricket nigh on thirty years, and, parson or no parson, I take the liberty of telling you to hold your blasted gab.'

But I hurriedly dismissed this almost unthinkable anecdote when he turned his greenish eyes in my direction and hoped, in hearty and ingratiating tones, that I was 'going to show them a little crisp Ballboro' batting'.

The brisk clatter of knives and forks is now well started, and the barman is busy at his barrel. Conversation, however, is scanty, until Tom Seamark, who is always glad of a chance to favour the company with a sentiment, clears his throat impressively, elevates his tankard, fixes Jack Barchard with his gregarious regard and remarks, 'I should like to say, sir, how very pleased and proud we are to see you safe 'ome again in our midst.' Jack Barchard had recently returned from the Boer War, where he served with the Yeomanry. The 'sentiment' is echoed from all parts of the table, and glasses are raised to him with a gruff 'Good 'ealth, sir', or 'Right glad to see you back, Mr Barchard'. The returned warrior receives their congratulations with the utmost embarrassment. Taking a shy sip at my ginger-beer, I think how extraordinary it is to be sitting next to a man who has really been 'out in South Africa'. Barchard is a fair-haired young gentleman farmer. When the parson suggests that 'it must have been pretty tough work out there', he replies that he is thundering glad to be back among his fruit trees again, and this, apparently, is about all he has to say about the Boer War.

But when the meal was drawing to an end and I had finished my helping of cold cherry-tart, and the barman began to circulate with a wooden platter for collecting the half-crowns, I became agonizingly aware that I had come to the match without any money. I was getting into a panic while the plate came clinking along the table, but quiet Jack Barchard unconsciously saved the situation by putting down five shillings and saying, 'All right, old chap, I'll stump up for both.' Mumbling, 'Oh, that's jolly decent of you', I wished I could have followed him up a hill in a 'forlorn hope'. . . He told me, later on, that he never set eyes on a Boer the whole time he was in South Africa.

The clock struck three, and the Reverend Yalden's leg stump had just been knocked out of the ground by a vicious yorker from Frank Peckham. 'Hundred and seventeen. Five. Nought,' shouted the Butley scorer, popping his head out of the little flat-roofed shanty which was known as 'the pavilion'. The battered tin number-plates were rattled on to their nails on the scoring-board by a zealous young hobbledehoy who had under-taken the job for the day.

'*Wodger* say last man made?' he bawled, though the scorer was only a few feet away from him.

'Last man, *blob*.'

The parson was unbuckling his pads on a bench near by, and I was close enough to observe the unevangelical expression on his face as he looked up from under the brim of his panama hat with the M.C.C. ribbon round it. Mr Yalden was not a popular character on the Butley ground, and the Hobbledehoy had made the most of a heaven-sent opportunity.

From an undersized platform in front of the Horticultural Tent the Butley brass band now struck up 'The Soldiers of the Queen'. It's quite like playing in a county match, I thought, as I scanned the spectators, who were lining the fence on two sides of the field. Several easily recognizable figures from among the local gentry were already sauntering towards the Tea Tent, after a gossiping inspection of the Flower Show. I could see slow-moving Major Carmine, the best dressed man in Butley, with his white spats and a carnation in his buttonhole; and the enthusiastic curate, known as 'Hard Luck' on account of his habit of exclaiming, 'Oh, hard luck!' when watching or taking part in games of cricket, lawn tennis, or hockey. He was escorting the Misses Patton, two elderly sisters who always dressed alike. And there was Aunt Evelyn, with her red sunshade up, walking between rosy-faced old Captain Huxtable and his clucking, oddly dressed wife. It was quite a brilliant scene which the Butley Band was doing its utmost to sustain with experimental and unconvincing tootles and drum-beatings.

Soon afterwards, however, the 'Soldiers of the Queen' were overwhelmed by the steam-organ, which, after a warning hoot, began to accompany the revolving wooden horses of the gilded roundabout with a strident and blaring fanfaronade. For a minute or two the contest of cacophonies continued. But in spite of a tempestuous effort the band was completely outplayed by its automatic and inexhaustible adversary. The discord becoming intolerable, it seemed possible that the batsmen would 'appeal against the music' in the same way that they sometimes 'appeal against the light' when they consider it inadequate. But William Dodd was equal to the emergency; with an ample gesture he conveyed himself across the ground and prohibited the activity of the steam-organ until the match was finished. The flitting steeds now revolved and undulated noiselessly beneath their gilded canopy, while the Butley Band palavered peacefully onwards into the unclouded jollity of the afternoon.

The clock struck four. Rotherden were all out for 183, and Tom Dixon had finished the innings with a confident catch on the boundary off one of Dodd's artfully innocent lobs. No catches had come my way, so my part in the game had been an unobtrusive one. When Dodd and Picksett went out to open our innings it was a matter of general opinion in the Beer Tent that the home team had a sporting chance to make the runs by seven o'clock, although there were some misgivings about the wicket, and it was anticipated that Crump and Bishop would make the ball fly about a bit when they got to work.

Having ascertained that I was last but one on the list in the score-book, I made my way slowly round the field to have a look at the Flower Show. As I went along the boundary in front of the spectators who were leaning their elbows on the fence I felt quite an important public character. And as I shouldn't have to go in for a long while yet, there was no need to feel nervous. The batsmen, too, were shaping confidently, and there was a shout of 'Good ole Bill! That's the way to keep 'em on the carpet!' when Dodd brought off one of his celebrated square-cuts to the hedge off Bishop's easy-actioned fast bowling. Picksett followed this up with an audacious pull which sent a straight one from Crump skimming first bounce into the Tea Tent, where it missed the short-sighted doctor's new straw hat by half an inch and caused quite a flutter among the tea-sipping ladies.

'Twenty up,' announced the scorer, and the attendant hobbledehoy nearly fell over himself in his eagerness to get the numbers up on the board. A stupendous appeal for a catch at the wicket by the Reverend Yalden was countered by Sutler with his surliest shake of the head, and the peg-supported umpire was the most popular man on the field as he ferried himself to his square leg location at the end of the over. Forty up; then Dodd was clean bowled by Crump.

'Ow's that?' bawled a ribald Rotherden partisan from a cart in the road, as the rotund batsman retreated; warm but majestic, he acknowledged the applause of the onlookers by a slight lifting of his close-fitting cap. Everybody was delighted that he had done so well, and it was agreed that he was (in the Beer Tent) 'a regular chronic old sport' and (in the Tea Tent) 'a wonderful man for his age'. Modest Jack Barchard then made his appearance and received a Boer War ovation.

Leaving the game in this prosperous condition, I plunged into the odoriferous twilight of the Horticultural Tent. I had no intention of staying there long, but I felt that I owed it to Aunt Evelyn to have a look at the sweet peas and vegetables, at any rate. In the warm muffled air the delicate aroma of the elegant sweet peas was getting much the worst of it in an encounter with the more agressive smell of highly polished onions. Except for a couple of bearded gardeners who were conferring in professional undertones, I had the tent to myself. Once I was inside I felt glad to be loitering in there, alone and away from the optical delirium of cricket. The brass band had paused to take breath; now and again the brittle thud of a batsman's stroke seemed to intensify the quiescence of the floralized interior.

As I sniffed my way round I paid little attention to card-inscribed names of the competitors (though I observed that the Miss Pattons had got second prize for a tasteful table decoration): I found many of the flowers tedious and unpleasing – more especially the bulbous and freckled varieties with th, unpronounceable names – the kind of flowers which my aunt always referred to as 'gardeners' greenhouseries'. On the whole the fruit and vegetables gave me the most enjoyment. The black cherries looked delicious, and some of the green gooseberries were as large as small hen's eggs. The two gardeners were concentrating on Sam Bathwick's first-prize vegetables, and as they seemed to grudge making way for me I contented myself with a glimpse of an immense marrow and some very pretty pink potatoes. As I passed, one of the gardeners was saying something about 'copped 'im a fair treat this time', and I absent-mindedly wondered who had been copped. When I emerged, the home team had lost two more wickets and the condition of the game was causing grave anxiety. Reluctantly I drifted towards the Tea Tent for a period of social victimization.

The Tea Tent was overcrowded and I found Aunt Evelyn sitting a little way outside it in comparative seclusion. She was in earnest communication with Miss Clara Maskall, a remarkable old lady who had been born in the year of the Battle of Waterloo and had been stone-deaf for more than sixty years.

My aunt was one of the few people in the neighbourhood who enjoyed meeting Miss Maskall. For the old lady had a way of forgetting that the rest of the world could hear better than she could, and her quavering comments on some of the local gentle-folk, made in their presence, were often too caustic to be easily forgotten. She was reputed to have been kissed by King George the Fourth. She was wearing a bunched-up black silk dress, and her delicately withered face was framed in a black poke-bonnet, tied under the chin with a white lace scarf. With her piercingly alert eyes and beaky nose she looked like some ancient and intelligent bird. Altogether she was an old person of great dis-tinction, and I approached her with an awful timidity. She had old-fashioned ideas about education, and she usually inquired of me, in creaking tones, whether I had recently been flogged by my schoolmaster.

But the menace of Roman Catholicism was her most sub-stantial and engrossing theme; and up to the age of ninety she continued to paste on the walls of her bedroom every article on the subject which she could find in *The Times* and the *Morning Post*. Aunt Evelyn told me that the walls were almost entirely papered with printing matter, and that she had more than once found Miss Maskall sitting on the top step of a library ladder reading some altitudinous article on this momentous question of 'the Scarlet Woman'. To the day of her death she never so much as trifled with a pair of spectacles. But she was still very much alive when I saw her at the Flower Show Match. Sitting bolt upright in a wicker-chair, she scrutinized me keenly and then favoured me with a friendly little nod without losing touch with what my aunt was engaged in telling her by 'finger-talk'.

'What is it the man has been doing, Evelyn?' she asked, her queer, uncontrolled voice quavering up to a bird-like shrillness. There was something rather frightening about her defective intonation.

'Write it down; write it down,' she screeched, clawing a tablet and pencil out of her lap and consigning them to Aunt Evelyn, who hurriedly scribbled two or three lines and returned the tablet for her to read aloud; 'such a dreadful thing, the judges have found out that Bathwick has been cheating with his prize vegetables'. She passed it back with a tremulous cackle.

'How did he do it?' More scribbling, and then she read out, 'He bought all the vegetables at Ashbridge. The judges suspected him, so they went to his garden in a pony trap and found that he has no glass – not even a cucumber frame.' Miss Maskall chuckled delightedly at this, and said that he ought to be given a special prize.

'I call it downright dishonest. Almost as bad as embezzlement,' wrote Aunt Evelyn, who, as one of the judges, could scarcely be expected to treat the offence in a spirit of levity.

Miss Clara now insisted that she must herself inspect the fraudulent vegetables. Rising energetically from her chair, she grasped her ebony stick with an ivory knuckled hand, and shaped an uncompromising course for the Horticultural Tent, with Aunt Evelyn and myself in tow. The villagers at the gate made way for her with alacrity, as though it dawned on them that she was not only the most ancient, but by far the most interesting object to be seen at the Flower Show Match.

Miss Maskall had made the game seem rather remote. She cared nothing for cricket, and had only come there for an afternoon spree. But she was taciturn during her tour of the Flower

Show: when we tucked her into her shabby old victoria she leant back and closed her eyes. Years ago she must have had a lovely face. While we watched her carriage turn the corner I wondered what it felt like to be eighty-seven; but I did not connect such antiquity with my own future. Long before I was born she had seen gentlemen playing cricket in queer whiskers and tall hats.

Next moment I was safely back in the present, and craning my neck for a glimpse of the score-board as I hustled Aunt Evelyn along to the Tea Tent. There had been a Tea Interval during our absence, so we hadn't missed so very much. Five wickets were down for ninety and the shadows of the cricketers were growing longer in the warm glare which slanted down the field. A sense of my own share in the game invaded me and it was uncomfortable to imagine that I might soon be walking out into the middle to be bowled at by Crump and Bishop, who now seemed gigantic and forbidding. And then impetuous Ned Noakes must needs call Frank Peckham for an impossibly short run, and his partner retreated with a wrathful shake of his head. Everything now depended on Dixon, who was always as cool as a cucumber in a crisis.

'Give 'em a bit of the long handle, Tom!' bawled someone in the Beer Tent, while he marched serenely towards the wicket, pausing for a confidential word with Noakes, who was still looking a bit crestfallen after the recent catastrophe. Dixon was a stylish left-hander and never worried much about playing himself in. Bishop was well aware of this, and he at once arranged an extra man in the outfield for him. Sure enough, the second ball he received was lifted straight into the long-off's hands. But the sun was in the fielder's eyes and he misjudged the flight of the catch. The Beer Tent exulted vociferously. Dixon then set about the bowling and the score mounted merrily. He was energetically supported by Ned Noakes. But when their partnership had added over fifty, and they looked like knocking off the runs, Noakes was caught in the slips off a bumping ball and the situation instantly became serious again.

Realizing that I was next in but one, I went off in a fluster to put my pads on, disregarding Aunt Evelyn's tremulous 'I do so hope you'll do well, dear'. By the time I had arrived on the other side of the ground, Amos Hickmott, the wheelwright's son, had already caused acute anxiety. After surviving a tigerish appeal for 'leg-before', he had as near as a toucher run Dixon out in a half-witted endeavour to escape from the bowling. My palsied fingers were still busy with straps and buckles, when what sounded to me like a deafening crash warned me that it was all over with Hickmott. We still wanted seven runs to win when I wandered weakly in the direction of the wicket. But it was the end of an over, and Dixon had the bowling. When I arrived the Reverend Yalden was dawdling up the pitch in his usual duck-footed progress when crossing from one wicket to the other.

'Well, young man, you've got to look lively this time,' he observed with intimidating jocosity. But there seemed to be a twinkle of encouragement in Seamark's light-blue eye as I established myself in his shadow.

Dixon played the first three balls carefully. The fourth he smote clean out of the ground. The hit was worth six, but 'three all round and four over' was an immemorial rule at Butley. Unfortunately, he tried to repeat the stroke, and the fifth ball shattered his stumps. In those days there were only five balls to an over.

Peter Baitup now rolled up with a wide grin on his fringed face, but it was no grinning moment for me at the bottom end when Sutler gave me 'middle-and-leg' and I confronted impending disaster from Crump with the sun in my eyes. The first ball (which I lost sight of) missed my wicket by 'a coat of varnish' and travelled swiftly to the boundary for two byes, leaving Mr Yalden with his huge gauntlets above his head in an attitude of aggrieved astonishment. The game was now a tie. Through some obscure psychological process my whole being now became clarified. I remembered Shrewsbury's century and became as bold as brass. There was the enormous auctioneer with the ball in his hand. And there I, calmly resolved to look lively and defeat his destructive aim. The ball hit my bat and trickled slowly up the pitch. 'Come on!' I shouted and Peter came gallantly on. Crump was so taken by surprise that we were safe home before he'd picked up the ball. And that was the end of the Flower Show Match.

*from* MEMOIRS OF A FOX-HUNTING MAN *1928*

# Fincham v. Besterton

## J. C. MASTERMAN

Saturday was fine, as fine and gorgeous as an English August day could be, and Monty, having breakfasted both late and well, felt superbly and gloriously happy. A perfect day for cricket in company which he enjoyed and surroundings which he loved – he could ask no more. Ignoring his host's advice to get some practice before the game, he played a game of golf croquet with Cynthia, and then strolled down to the ground.

There by an act of almost criminal carelessness he allowed himself to be button-holed by Colonel Murcher-Pringle, who had just arrived. Criminal carelessness, for among all those who played on the Fincham ground the Colonel was by common consent the one whom the judicious would always avoid. Many vocabularies had been exhausted in the attempt to do justice to his unpopularity, and many attempts had been made to induce George Appleby to drop him from his side, but without success. He had come to live in the neighbourhood eight years before, and had spent an entire winter talking cricket with George, who had asked him to play in the week in the summer following. Once invited, he had regarded himself as a permanent member of the side, and good-nature, weakness or just innate conservatism had prevented George from discarding him. In appearance he looked exactly what he was; his face was red, his hair of a ginger shade, speckled with grey; he was small but self-assertive, with unquenchable pugnacity written on every feature. 'Always looking for a row, and invariably finding it,' as Basil had once said. Monty, searching his more obscure eighteenth-century authors for an apt description, had called him a 'nasty little stiff-rumped fellow', and so in appearance he was. He was angular and self-opinionated, dogmatic and fussy at the same time, selfish and conceited. George, feebly trying to defend him, was fond of declaring that he had his good points; pressed for details, he would say that the Colonel was really keen on the game and must have been a very good bat once. With characteristic effrontery he seemed to regard the Fincham week as run for his special benefit, and was loudly critical of everything and everybody. In the first match in which he had played he had declared that he always fielded at point and was with difficulty persuaded that most modern bowlers had come to dispense with a point altogether. Always protesting, he had been induced to stand in the gully as being the nearest approach to his favourite position. In that place, which to satisfy his scruples he always referred to as backward-point, he was accustomed to drop catches at critical moments – a habit which never prevented him from animadverting bitterly on the fielding of the rest of the side. But it was when his turn came to bat that the Colonel showed his worst side. On his first appearance he had explained that a loose cartilage made it necessary for him to be allowed a runner. That he was able-bodied and perfectly competent to run for himself was clear to everyone, but no captain had yet had the courage to refuse him his demand. To escape the hated duty of running for the Colonel became the primary object of all the other players, for no one had ever succeeded in carrying it out satisfactorily. Objurgations to back up, criticism of the calling and running, and a stream of comment from the Colonel, who grew more and more peppery as he became heated with his efforts, invariably reduced the unfortunate runner to a state either of intense irritation or of complete bewilderment. Only the impossibility of refusing George Appleby could induce most of his side to undertake the task at all. Monty's great triumph had occurred some years before. He had organized a ten-shilling sweep among the eight junior members of the side, winner – or loser, as he preferred to call it – to take the lot and to run for the Colonel. He had himself drawn the fatal ticket, and he still remembered with undiminished pleasure the indignation among the contributors when he had succeeded, owing to a pardonable misunderstanding, in running out the Colonel before he had scored. His cheerful 'Sorry, Colonel, wanted to get you off the mark', and the outburst which it brought forth had done something to satisfy the others that they had had value for their money, but some of them still felt that he had been overpaid for two minutes' work.

If, then, Monty had not been criminally careless he would have avoided the Colonel; but his mind was elsewhere, and he was button-holed before he realized his danger.

'Good morning, Renshaw. So you're here again. I'm bound to confess that I don't believe in changing the side in the middle of the week, but I suppose you couldn't get here before.'

'No. I've been too busy.'

'The cricket has been bad, definitely bad, this year. Appleby seems to have no idea whatever of getting his side together. Yesterday he had one of the bowlers fielding for an hour in the deep. Everyone ought to have his fixed position in the field and stick to it. And if I've told him once, I've told him a hundred times, not to keep Slingsby on so long; he's bowling the other side in all the time on these wickets. No element of surprise about him. And Hawes – an absurd bowler to my mind. Fast, of course, and swings the new ball, but far too erratic for this class of cricket. No idea of the value of length. When I was young every side had four bowlers at least who could keep a length – an immaculate length – for the whole day if necessary. Yet nowadays we must open our bowling with a wild tearaway brainless slinger like Hawes. It's all wrong. Of course, Appleby ought to get a fast bowler who can keep a length all the time to start the bowling.'

'Don't you think a bowler like that tends to play the other side in?' suggested Monty a little maliciously.

An angry gleam lighted up the Colonel's eye. 'Play them in! Nonsense. Get them *out*, sir. I said a *fast* bowler; it's *slow* length bowling, like Slingsby's, that plays them in. But it's no good preaching ordinary common sense to Appleby. He never does what I suggest – and what's the result? Look at this week's matches! We beat the Hunt, but then they're no sort of a side; we can only just draw with the Old Uptonians, although half of them have only just left school; and we get thrashed, yes thrashed, by a most mediocre Forester side. And half of it's captaincy. Of course, Appleby is an excellent fellow – I'd never say a word against him – but it's pitiable to see him let his side go to pieces. We collapsed yesterday, positively collapsed, and I don't believe he gave any orders whatever to the batsmen. That conceited puppy Paraday-Royne, for example, got out trying to hook a long-hop before he'd had a look at the bowling. If I'd been captain he'd have had the most emphatic orders to take no risks of that kind at all until he was thoroughly set. And though I don't like saying it, Appleby made the greatest possible mistake in putting me in so late. Number nine, and just when an experienced player was wanted to go in early and keep the side together. I was not out at the finish – a waste of a wicket.'

Monty was a good-natured man, but his patience was being rapidly exhausted.

'Look at those ducks coming over to the pond,' he said; and then as the Colonel turned his head away from the pavilion, 'But surely that's Oliver arriving; I must go and say how-do-you-do to him.'

It was not Sir Anstruther, as Monty very well knew, but he was away from the seat before the Colonel could start another sentence.

A few minutes later the cars bringing the Besterton side arrived at the pavilion. That was always an exciting moment, for Sir Anstruther, with the cunning born of long experience of these encounters, would never disclose the composition of his side until the day of the match. Nothing gave him greater pleasure than to spring a surprise upon the enemy – some new batsman of impregnable defence or some new bowler of irresistible attack. Like the Duke of Wellington in the Peninsula, Sir Anstruther liked to keep his reserves out of sight until the last moment; only when the battle was about to be joined and when it was too late to counter them would the full strength of his dispositions be revealed. So there was a lively and almost fearful interest in the moment of arrival. Old opponents were being hilariously greeted, and it seemed to Monty as he joined the group that this year there were no new faces. But the last car was now unloading and from it appeared two young men whom he did not at first recognize.

'Ah, Appleby,' said Sir Anstruther, with elaborate unconcern, 'here are my two new recruits – let me introduce them to you; Mr Colquhoun, Mr Lees.'

Monty chuckled appreciatively. So Oliver had done it again, the crafty old dog! Colquhoun had batted number one for Cambridge that year, and Lees had been the most successful bowler in the same side. 'That'll shift the betting,' he murmured to himself, as he watched the captains toss.

You could see from a hundred yards away whether George Appleby had called right or not, for his cheerful face was an open book. On this occasion he registered disappointment so obviously that Monty did not trouble to wait to hear Sir Anstruther announce his intention to bat. Ten minutes later the Fincham side were ready to take the field, and the two umpires were on their way to the wicket.

They, of course, had their place in the ritual of the Saturday match. Boone, who always 'stood umpire' for Sir Anstruther, was groundsman at Besterton, whither he had migrated when passing years and even more quickly increasing weight had terminated his engagement with the Hampshire County Club. To him the appearance of George Appleby's umpire offered a surprising contrast, for on the Saturday Merton the butler always officiated. Tall and cadaverous, he was as much a contrast to Boone in appearance as he was an equal in dignity. How he contrived, amidst all his multifarious duties, to umpire was known only to himself; the fact remained that once a year on the second Saturday in August he put on the white coat of authority. It would, indeed, have seemed incredible to the Fincham side had he not done so. That Boone and Merton were strictly impartial at eleven-thirty in the morning was undeniable – that they remained so throughout the afternoon was open to question; that towards evening they watched one another as rivals rather than colleagues was certain. Merton had on one occasion admitted that he thought it right, occasion having offered, to correct a slight injustice for which Boone had been earlier responsible. In the long run, no doubt, justice was done. Monty could recall a specially tight finish when Merton, rejecting the evidence of eye and ear alike, had given him 'not out' in face of a triumphant appeal for a catch at the wicket. A short-lived triumph! He could have sworn in the next over he had passed the second crease when the wicket was broken, but Boone, with the countenance of a High Court Judge, had given him run out. Basil's comment, 'What you gain on the swings you lose on the roundabouts', had not unfairly summed up the situation. Privately each captain thought his own umpire impeccable, and his rival's something not far removed from a common cheat; but more light-hearted cricketers, such as Monty, regarded both as a good though dangerous joke, and reminded themselves to position their legs somewhat differently for defensive purposes according to which end they were batting.

The start of the Besterton innings was sensational. It was opened by Colquhoun and Railton, the latter of whom was probably the soundest, if not the most brilliant batsman on the side. He had played for many years in the Saturday match, and had the reputation of never failing to get runs; if he was dismissed for less than fifty Fincham supporters considered that they had done well. Bobby Hawes opened the bowling. It was perhaps true, as Colonel Murcher-Pringle had pointed out, that Bobby's direction and length were alike untrustworthy but he was undeniably fast, and, like all fast bowlers, he had his moments. His first ball might almost have been signalled as a wide, and would have been had he been bowling from Boone's end, but his second was of perfect length and pitched on the middle and leg. It swung late and just little enough for Railton to get a touch; the next moment Monty, very much to his surprise, found that he had contrived to hang on to the ball at first slip, though to tell the truth it had come so quickly that he had hardly seen it. George, full of jubilation, was patting him on the back, and reminding him of a similar catch 'in the year that Rawstone got two hundreds in the week'. 'And that year we had them all out for 93,' he ended triumphantly, as the next Besterton batsman reached his wicket. Elated by success, Bobby Hawes discharged the four remaining balls of the over at his fastest pace; one, a full-pitch to leg, was diverted to the boundary for four, the others, all wide on the off side, were left severely alone. At the other end Colquhoun played the second over with quiet efficiency. Of the first four balls, all of good length, he left one alone, and played three back to the bowler; he pushed the fifth for two square of mid-on, and took an easy single to third man off the sixth. Thus he faced Bobby at the beginning of the latter's second over.

The first ball was pitched just, but only just, outside the off stump. Perhaps it lifted a little, perhaps it was not quite so fast as it seemed to be, perhaps Colquhoun's eye had not quite recovered from the motor drive, perhaps he was not quite determined as to whether he should play it or leave it alone. Whatever the cause may have been, he played a shot unworthy of himself – a half-hearted, indeterminate, bat-hanging-out shot which had its inevitable result. The ball struck the edge of his bat, and fell thence in a gentle parabola into the hands of gully. Into the Colonel's hands, but not to stay there. The stubby fingers grabbed convulsively but too late; the ball hit them and bounced, hit the Colonel's chest and bounced again, hit his clutching hands once more, and fell miserably to earth.

'Damn!' grunted the Colonel. 'Sorry, Appleby, sorry. Never

remember dropping a catch like that before; sun in my eyes.'
George Appleby prided himself on his behaviour in the field,
and he was incapable of rudeness, but, even so, he was unable to
summon to his lips the conventional 'bad luck' with which to
disguise the Colonel's blunder. It was indeed too flagrant and
too obviously destructive to the Fincham chances to be lightly
pardoned. A drawling but very audible comment from Basil,
which announced to the world in general that that day the sun
seemed to have risen in the west, did something to satisfy the
almost murderous feelings of the rest of the side towards the
culprit, and drew from him a scowl of annoyance. It did not take
long to prove that the missed catch had turned the fortune of the
game. Colquhoun was good enough player to take every advantage of his luck, and soon he had obtained a mastery over all the
bowlers alike. Bobby Hawes pounded up to the wicket with
undiminished zeal, but his length became more and more
erratic, as Colquhoun with a fine impartiality glided him to fine-
leg or slashed him for four behind cover-point. When at length
he varied the programme by hitting him twice in the same over
for four over mid-on's head it became obvious that the fast
bowler's bolt was shot. Slingsby, too, he played like a master;
always quick on his feet, he was out to the pitch of the ball whenever that was possible and cracking it through the covers.
Mid-off was soon nursing a pair of bruised hands, and extra-
cover on the boundary was hard put to it to turn fours into
singles. When again Slingsby tried to drop them a bit shorter he
was dealt with even more drastically; the batsman seemed to be
back and shaped for his hook with all the time he needed.
Slingsby was always a good-length bowler, but on that wicket,
when the ball would not turn, Colquhoun's footwork was too
much for him. The other Fincham bowlers were equally powerless; before the morning ended seven of them had tried their
skill, and even Monty, by dint of swinging his right arm
vigorously at the end of every over, had secured the privilege of
bowling a couple of overs before lunch. He bowled so-called
leg-breaks, and relied for success on what he called bluff, but

Colquhoun had passed the stage when he was likely to fall to such wiles, and Monty's two overs, though he enjoyed bowling them, added 31 to the Besterton score. At half-past one, when lunch came, the telegraph showed 204 runs for two wickets, and Colquhoun was 126 not out.

George Appleby was almost tearful. 'I never remember 200 being scored against us before lunch before. What the devil am I to do Monty? They'll get 400 if this goes on.'

Monty, busily engaged in the difficult choice between lobster and salmon, was inclined to take things more philosophically.

'Put on your slow bowlers, George; they're sure to get careless after lunch. Slow bowlers with plenty of men out. You might persevere with me, you know. I thought I had Colquhoun in two minds once or twice before lunch.'

George snorted. 'In two minds! What about? Whether to hit you for four or six, I suppose. You've had *your* bowl for the day. Still, there's the new ball that we can take now, and that may help a bit.'

'That's right – look on the bright side,' replied Monty, as he beckoned to a footman for a second shandy. 'At the worst common decency will compel them to declare the slaughter over at about half-past three, and we can then bat. Meantime it would give me the greatest pleasure in the world if you could make that damned Colonel man field in the deep for a change and do some of the running.'

'Cricket is a funny game.' How is it possible to describe a match without using that odious remark, or to discuss a match without dragging it in? Colonel Murcher-Pringle said that cricket was a funny game; who would have thought it possible that he of all men would have missed a catch? – an offensive weapon which was greeted with a cold and hostile silence. Sir Anstruther Oliver said that cricket was a funny game – look, said he, how the match had suddenly turned in favour of the visiting side, which looked like having a disastrous start – but this patronizing and false bonhomie further exacerbated George

Appleby's feelings. Monty said cricket seemed to him an extraordinarily funny game, when he reflected that George Appleby had taken a wicket and he had not – a remark which George did not consider funny at all. And Cynthia Hetherington said that cricket was the funniest game of all to watch when Colonel Murcher-Pringle or Admiral Findon-Duff had to chase the ball – a remark which was fortunately drowned in the general conversation. And George, who was always a good host, refrained from saying that cricket was in no sense of the term a funny game at all; it was a great game, and exciting and dramatic and even at times tragic – but funny it emphatically was not.

And yet the hour's play after lunch went far to prove that the ancient and banal remark was true after all. The bare facts were these; at lunch-time Besterton had made 204 for two wickets, the wicket was perfect and the batsmen had laid bare in the most convincing fashion the weakness of the Fincham bowling. Yet at half-past three the whole side was out for 276, and no one quite knew how it happened. Lunch helped, no doubt; Colquhoun, replete with food and drink made a lethargic shot in the first over after lunch and was caught at the wicket; two batsmen trying to score too quickly were caught in the deep off George Appleby, and Merton, in response to a couple of very half-hearted appeals for leg-before-wicket, had taken the responsibility of dismissing two men. ('A mistake, Merton,' thought Monty, 'to play your trumps so early, when Boone has got three and a half hours to get even with you.') Yet even so it was difficult to explain why the Besterton side made only 70 odd runs after luncheon, and lost eight wickets in doing so. Fincham supporters, however, observed with distress that no bowler on their side had taken more than three wickets.

George Appleby's dejection had changed to the wildest optimism.

'I really believe we ought to win this match, Monty; if we can only get a decent start. We must watch that fellow Lees while the shine's still on the ball. Now, look here, about the order. Rawstone hasn't been in luck this week, and wants to go in late,

so I'm going to put him down to number seven – he knows then
whether he's got to get them quickly or sit on the splice. I shall
start with you and Clark; the boy's batted very consistently and
well all the week – and, of course, Johnny Rashwood goes
number three. Then I'm going to put in the Colonel; he owes us
runs, God knows, and he's more likely to make them going in
high up, than lower down; then the Admiral. I've never seen
him bat, but I believe he used to play for the Navy and I must
give him a chance. After him Basil at six; he always gets them
quickly, and it's just the sort of wicket for him to make runs on –
he's too impatient if the ball's turning. Then Rawstone, and then
Bobby and Slingsby and Tom and myself to finish with – but
really we haven't got a tail at all. We've got lots of time – I don't
see a bit why we shouldn't get the runs. But don't you flick at
that off-ball.'

Privately Monty considered that the morale of the side would
have been improved if the Colonel had been firmly relegated to
number eleven, and the Admiral – whose weight and bulk had
proved unequal to the task of fielding for nearly 300 runs – to
number ten, but it was not for him to say so. He nodded agreement and went to put on his pads.

As he played Lees' opening over his first sensation was one of
impotence and irritation. He was out of practice; the fellow
swung the ball late and had a damnably deceptive flight; he
would be out any ball and poor old George would be sick as
muck. But after a couple of overs his mood changed. He was
still there, and what damned good fun it was, anyhow – yorker,
but still alive! That was better! After ten minutes he had passed
into a mood of almost reckless exhilaration. A half-volley went
racing to the boundary – batting was sheer pleasure when shots
were timed like that! And it would be ridiculous to waste time;
his eye was in, he was on top of the bowling, and he *would* make
runs. The score mounted with gratifying rapidity, and then,
suddenly, came the catastrophe. Lees had bowled him a ball just
outside the off stump, and almost but not quite a half-volley.
Monty had jumped out, got well across and hit it in the middle of

the bat. A spectator picked the ball out of the long grass behind extra-cover and threw it back to the bowler. The next ball was a shade wider, and a little shorter – the very bait which Monty had never been able to resist. He flicked at it – he had to flick at it! Colquhoun, at second slip, took the catch with the easy confidence of a good fieldsman in full practice, and Monty, kicking himself, walked back to the pavilion. The score was 44, of which he had made 36.

Johnny Rashwood took his place. He was a stylish and quick-scoring batsman, and he did not suffer from nerves. But though he was not nervous, he was temperamental, and ill-chance had arranged that he had sat next to the Colonel as he waited for his innings. An innocent shout of 'Good shot' from him during Monty's innings had elicited some pungent criticism from his companion.

'I don't call that a good shot at this stage in the innings. Renshaw is always absurdly reckless. He ought to be consolidating the position for later batsmen, not taking risks when we need so many runs. He doesn't watch the ball long enough, or know when he ought to leave the off ball alone. He's –'

'Good shot,' broke in Johnny in a possibly unduly aggressive tone, as Monty scored another boundary.

The Colonel flushed angrily.

'Reckless, reckless,' he observed. 'Renshaw's utterly lacking in judgment and patience. Ah! I told you so' – for Colquhoun had just caught Monty in the slips. 'Just what he deserved, and what I expected. Now don't you do anything foolish, young man. You've got to play very steadily for half an hour or so – there are plenty of us to get runs quickly if need be later on. Go slow, and watch the ball.'

No advice could have been more certain to rouse Johnny's worst instincts.

'I'll teach that bloody old man to lecture me on cricket,' he murmured as he walked to the wicket. 'Why the hell can't he keep quiet – after fielding worse than anyone on God's earth too.' No doubt after a couple of overs he would have recovered his equanimity, but that breathing-space was not allowed him. His first ball was a half-volley, and Johnny, jumping in to hit, put into his shot all the irritation which he had bottled up during his conversation with the Colonel. He hit it full in the middle of the bat, and it looked a six all the way. Looked good for six, and deserved to be six, but was not – for Lees' long-field moving about five yards caught the ball with one hand high above his head just inside the boundary.

'Bad luck,' said Basil as he came into the pavilion, 'but what a magnificent catch.'

Johnny grinned a little sheepishly; fortunately he had humour enough to laugh at himself.

'Yes, grand catch,' he said; 'the hands were the hands of Esau, but the voice, if you follow me, was the voice of Murcher-Pringle.' The Colonel meantime had marched to the wicket attended by Tom Appleby, who was to run for him. Having by now recovered from the exertions of fielding, and having forgotten his own errors in the field, he was again at the height of his form, for it had pleased him to see the two previous batsmen prove the accuracy of his forebodings. He lectured Tom, as they walked out, on the necessity of smart backing up, he told Clark at the other end to be careful not to run on the wicket, he took guard with elaborate fussiness, and then instructed the fielding side, quite unnecessarily, to shift the screen a couple of yards to the right. Most of his own side would cheerfully have drowned him, had opportunity offered, before he went in to bat; by the time that he prepared to take his first ball the visiting side, though not so actively hostile, would certainly not have pulled him out of the water had he chanced to fall in. But the Colonel, as George always said, was still a difficult man to dislodge; he had a disconcerting habit of stopping the ball somehow, and of scoring an occasional single off the edge of his bat. Scoring at the rate of about a run a minute he and Clark rather laboriously added 20 to the score; at half-past four, with a quarter of an hour still to go to tea-time, the total was 65, and the bowling was beginning to lose its sting.

'Game seems to have got into a flat spin,' suggested Bails sitting in the pavilion; but he had hardly spoken before, in the current phrase, things began to happen.

Clark had batted very steadily, but slowly, for an hour, and he knew that he must begin to take risks if his side was not to get behind the clock. He therefore swung round at a shortish ball and tried to take four off it on the leg side. Unfortunately he hit it on the upper edge of the bat, and the ball soared up in the direction of square-leg. Even so, he seemed safe enough, for there was no one fielding there – but mid-on thought otherwise. He was very fast and he had started as the shot was made. Making a great deal of ground he just reached the catch, going at full speed. But Boone, the square-leg umpire, had not observed his approach, and the fieldsman, clutching the ball, crashed into him, head against head, as the catch was made. Clark was out, but so, in a slightly different sense, were both umpire and mid-on. The heads of both were cut, and it was obvious that they would have to go in for repairs. George Appleby came hurrying out with offers of assistance.

'I'm terribly sorry, Oliver,' he said; 'what can we do about this?'

'Oh – a bit of sticking-plaster will put them right, Appleby, and it's only ten minutes to tea-time. If you don't mind, send out a substitute to field, and perhaps you wouldn't mind taking over the umpire's job yourself till the tea interval.'

'Of course I will. But, by the way, I'm afraid I've got to ask you to allow my next batsman to have a runner as well – the Admiral's leg has gone.'

'Naturally, Appleby. Let him have a runner by all means, and we'll get on with the game.'

By the time that the game was restarted there were, therefore, no less than six of the batting side (not counting Merton) on the field of play. George was acting as temporary umpire, Johnny Rashwood was fielding as substitute, the Colonel was batting at one end with Tom as his runner, and the Admiral was at the other end with Clark in attendance. Monty noticed with amusement that Sir Anstruther, who never gave anything away, had reorganized his field in order to put Johnny at cover-point.

He turned to Cynthia, who was sitting by him.

'This is really a fine sight, Cynthia,' he remarked; 'observe the chivalry of both sides, each anxious to assist the other, and watch the gallant Admiral determined to do his best, in spite of all physical handicaps. What does he remind you of?'

'A battleship, heavily damaged by enemy fire,' suggested Cynthia.

'Not bad. But I suggest a wooden ship; the *Fighting Téméraire* or something of that sort:

"Round the world if need be, and round the world again,
With the lame duck lagging, lagging all the way."'

The Admiral was indeed in a somewhat battered condition, though his enthusiasm was undiminished. In the field he had pursued the ball with praiseworthy zeal, but as he was a heavy man and carried a good deal of fat he had rapidly become distressed. It was some time since he had taken violent exercise, and his muscles were unequal to the strain put upon them. He had mopped his brow with a large bandana handkerchief, he had creaked in every joint as he lumbered across the field, and, shortly after lunch, in attempting to intercept a ball at mid-on, he had pulled a muscle in his thigh. Through the rest of the Besterton innings he had hobbled gallantly, but now, after he had sat still for an hour, his leg had stiffened, and his movements were slow and cumbrous in the extreme. However, he waved his bat cheerfully to the Colonel as he passed him on his progress to the wicket.

'We're a couple of old crocks, Colonel,' he remarked, 'but we'll show them how to bat, what?'

'I can look after *my* end,' replied the Colonel with a scowl, and prepared to receive the bowling, for his runner and Clark had crossed while the catch was in the air.

Lees delivered the next ball – a ball which was destined to

become famous in the annals of Fincham cricket. It was just outside the off stump, and the Colonel succeeded in hitting it, for the first time in his innings, with the middle or almost the middle of his bat, into the gap between cover and extra. A certain one or two runs, possibly four if extra-cover could not cut it off on the boundary. But the Colonel had forgotten Johnny Rashwood at cover. In that position Johnny was, so all the critics said, about as good as Jessop had been at his best. He moved swiftly and low over the ground (as in the case of all the great cover-points, his centre of gravity seemed to be low), his anticipation was uncanny, and, above all, he had the perfect throw for a cover-point, with elbow and hand both apparently below the shoulder, and the flick of the wrist which returned the ball at lightning speed to the wicket. As the Colonel played his shot Johnny moved like a panther to the right, swooped on to the ball with no inch to spare, picked it cleanly off the grass, and was in the same movement poised to hurl it at the wicket. Meantime a confused shout had arisen from the batsmen and their runners. At the post-mortem afterwards no one agreed exactly as to the responsibility of the protagonists. Monty's account was as likely to be correct as that of anyone else. Let it be stated, then, without comment. The fierce 'Run' must have come from the Colonel's throat, the thunderous 'No' from the Admiral's. 'Come on' was probably Clark's contribution, and the anxious 'Wait' was that of Tom Appleby. Whosesoever the fault, both runners charged up the pitch, and met just in time to realize that Johnny had intercepted the ball; they hesitated and were lost.

'Run, sir!' screamed the Colonel.

'Come back!' bellowed the Admiral.

Caught in a common panic, both runners charged madly down the pitch, but both, unfortunately, in the same direction. They arrived neck and neck at the Admiral's end. A roar of delight from the crowd warned them of their situation; as though governed by some higher power, both raced side by side back to the middle of the pitch. Still the Admiral thundered instructions from one end, while the Colonel trumpeted inarticulate wrath from the other. The runners had both entirely lost grip of the situation; they stood helpless side by side in the middle of the pitch.

Meantime Johnny Rashwood hesitated. It was his moment, and well he knew it! All day he had suffered from the Colonel, but the time for revenge had come; he had only to flick the ball to the wicket-keeper and the Colonel was out. But was he? Just as he prepared to throw he realized that the two runners were side by side, and it was not at all clear to him which batsman would be out if he threw to the wicket-keeper's end. And so as they raced together to the bowler's end and then back to the middle he still held his fire; finally he could hesitate no longer; he flung the ball to the wicket-keeper, who gently removed the bails, and George Appleby's finger went up.

'Out!' he said – rather unnecessarily.

Both the Colonel and the Admiral, however, stood firm, and each glared at the other. The Admiral spoke first.

'Bad luck, Colonel,' he said, 'I'm sorry you're out; that ends our little partnership.'

The reply was brusque and uncompromising.

'Rubbish, Admiral; it's you that has just been given out. Ridiculous how these young men lose their heads in a crisis.'

Admiral Findon-Duff was a good-tempered man, but he was unused to contradiction. Insensibly he assumed the manner of the quarter-deck.

'I understand, sir, that the umpire is there to decide such matters. Appleby, which batsman is out?'

'I don't know,' said George helplessly.

The Colonel snorted. 'When I was a boy we were accustomed to accept decisions in a sporting spirit; I'm surprised, Admiral, that you should hesitate to follow the spirit as well as the letter of the law.'

Many years spent in bullying his juniors had made the Colonel careless in his methods, but now he had fairly roused an opponent in every sense worthy of him. For the Admiral, once committed to the quarrel, was determined to see it through.

His chest swelled with indignation, and he hobbled down the pitch to confront his opponent

'Colonel Murcher-Pringle,' he said in a voice hoarse with indignation, 'I shall take no notice of that gratuitous insult. But I am the senior officer present, and as such I order you to leave the field. You are out, sir, and out you shall go.'

The red of the Colonel's face slowly acquired a purple hue.

'Seniority in the services has nothing whatsoever to do with the matter. I am the older man, and entitled to some consideration. And, sir, allow me to remind you that the good of the side must be taken into account. I am firmly set – you have not commenced your innings – it is obvious that, in the interests of the side, you should retire.'

In sober truth the Colonel had made 11 – a four to leg, which he had scored in protecting his body from a fast full pitch (bowled, perhaps, not without malice), and seven singles, all scored behind the wicket with the edge of his bat. But he produced his argument with conviction. The Admiral, however, was ready for him.

'Then, sir,' he snapped, 'as the older man you are probably already exhausted, and in the interests of the side you should make room for younger and fresher players – I feel fit to play a long innings.'

At this moment George Appleby approached the two angry men, in the manner of one anxious to put an end to a dog-fight, but uncertain of the best method to adopt to achieve that result.

'I am going to spin a coin,' he announced in a voice which he hoped sounded firmer to others than it did to himself, 'and the one who loses the toss must go.' He spun the coin high into the air before either had time to raise an objection.

'Tails,' shouted the Colonel.

'Tails,' roared the Admiral, a half-second after him. The coin fell to the ground, the head upwards.

'Aha, I'm afraid you've called wrong,' said the Admiral. 'Now I hope you will see the propriety of retiring.'

'What the devil do you mean, sir? You called "tails" yourself as well.'

'I was merely repeating your call to make sure that I had heard you correctly and that you would not attempt to alter it,' retorted the Admiral with barefaced effrontery.

Johnny Rashwood, convinced at last that the Colonel had met his match, could scarcely forbear to cheer, but George Appleby was making another effort to settle the dispute. He was about to suggest spinning his coin again when he noticed that Merton had left his end and come up beside him.

'Consult the other umpire, sir,' the butler whispered in his ear.

'Ah, yes,' George breathed a sigh of relief. 'Merton, are you able to give a decision?'

'Yes, sir. Colonel Murcher-Pringle is out, sir.' Like a wounded boar, struck by another spear from a fresh angle, the Colonel turned savagely to face his new enemy.

'What the devil do you mean, Merton, and what business is it of yours? Keep to your end of the ground. Out? How the devil do you mean, out?'

'Run out, sir,' replied Merton with icy composure. Supported by his butler's firmness, George Appleby made up his mind at last.

'I'm sorry, Colonel, you must go,' he said. 'You've been given out.'

No more could be said. Purple with rage and indignation, the Colonel abandoned the struggle and commenced his route march to the pavilion, pursued by the comments of his successful adversary, whose good humour had been wholly restored.

'Have a long whisky and soda ready for me at the end of my innings, Colonel,' he shouted. 'I shall get pretty hot out here.'

But the Colonel for once had no retort ready.

'I shall waive the two minutes' rule, Appleby,' said Sir Anstruther, with ponderous humour, as Basil Paraday-Royne walked out from the pavilion.

Basil was a beautiful bat to watch, especially on a hard wicket, and he was desperately keen to impress Cynthia. He met the bowling with the middle of the bat, and contrived not only to score three beautifully timed fours but also to keep the bowling to himself for the next two or three overs. It was not, therefore, until the last over before tea that the Admiral took his first ball. To the onlookers it was soon clear that he was a batsman of one shot, and one shot only. Heaving himself up, and advancing his left foot towards mid-on, he struck a mighty blow at each successive ball, irrespective of its length. The exertion was immense, the result incommensurate with the exertion. Three times he made his flail-like movement, three times he smote the air, and three times the ball missed the wicket and was taken by the wicket-keeper. Breathing more and more stertorously, the Admiral smote for the fourth time and over the leg boundary. A very short-lived triumph. At the fifth ball the Admiral slogged with even crookeder bat and even more mighty effort; he missed it, and all three stumps were spreadeagled.

'The glorious uncertainty of the game,' said the Admiral, entirely content with his four runs, though in point of fact nothing could have been more certain than his downfall. Together with the fielding side he hobbled in to tea. The score was 86 for five, and Basil had made 17 not out.

During the cricket week George Appleby always issued invitations broadcast throughout the neighbouring country-side, and there were in consequence sixty or seventy people gathered round the tea-tent as the players came in. Among them Monty noticed Lady Dormansland, who had driven over with her party from Critton Park; somewhat to his surprise, Robin Hedley was with her.

'That's new, isn't it?' he said to Cynthia, who was sitting by him. 'I didn't know that Robin was a friend of Lady D's.'

'Don't be silly, Monty; can you think of any really successful author who has not become a friend of hers? Don't you know that "Pertinacity" was the best of best-sellers this year? Be sensible and tell me about the game. Have we any chance of winning?'

'Just a hope, but hardly that. We're 190 behind and there'll be

just two hours' play after tea; that's not impossible by any
means, but it's quick. It really all depends on the next wicket;
Basil is as likely to make a quick hundred as anyone in England,
and Rawstone's a really good player – they might do it. After
them any of the rest are good for 20 or 30, but not much more.
It's a thin chance.'

Lady Dormansland approached them – even as a guest she
seemed the perfect hostess.

'Cynthia dear, how delightful to see you, and how nice to
think that you are coming to Critton next week. And Monty,
too. Remember I'm expecting you.'

'As if I should forget. Your invitations are always commands,
and I've been looking forward to my August visit for weeks.
In fact the thought of it is the only thing that has made London
bearable through July.'

Lady Dormansland purred.

'For a modern young man, Monty, you have very nice
manners,' she remarked archly, and then turned to greet Basil.

'Oh, Basil, I did hope that I should meet you today. I want to
persuade you to join my little party next week at Critton. All
sorts of delightful people, and if you can come it will be quite
perfect. Now you really must not disappoint me.'

Basil did not really like Lady Dormansland, whose kindness
of heart impressed him much less than her vulgarity. He had,
too, a shrewd suspicion that he was asked to Critton less because
of his social gifts than because his father sat in the House of
Lords. But he enjoyed comfort; and Lady Dormansland was a
born hostess – so he hesitated between acceptance and a refusal.

'Cynthia and Monty are both coming,' she continued,
'and –'

Basil's mind was made up at once.

'How too kind of you, Lady Dormansland. I should like it
above all things. I'll be driving down from town, so perhaps I
could give Cynthia a lift.'

'You kind man – do. Oh! and that charming man whom you
like so much, Robin Hedley – the man whose book you wrote,

you know (how nice and self-sacrificing of you, Basil) – he's coming again. He's with me now, and I like him so much that I made him promise to come again next week. That'll be another inducement, I know.'

Basil winced. So he would have to share Cynthia's company with Robin. Well, better so than to leave her to Robin alone.

'Now, Basil,' said Cynthia, 'you simply must make a hundred; Monty says we can't possibly win unless you do. Promise me to play your very best.'

'Of course I will. No efforts shall be spared to give you pleasure. A hundred and fifty if you like.'

'Splendid. I do like confident men, don't you, Monty? And I shall sit with Mr Hedley and watch you do it. What heaven!' She smiled in a manner a little reminiscent of the Mona Lisa, and followed Lady Dormansland towards the shade of the trees.

'Damn!' said Basil, picking up his gloves and bat.

Monty could not altogether repress a smile.

'And I suppose Cynthia had him asked to Critton,' added Basil thoughtfully.

George Appleby came fussing up to Monty as the Besterton side took the field.

'I can't make up my mind,' he said, 'what to tell Rawstone to do; it's just possible to win the game still, but only just. He's a fine player, you know, a very fine player, but not really a quick scorer. I've half a mind to tell him to put up the shutters right away and play for a draw.'

'I'd let him have his head if I were you. Better to have loved and lost, and all that, you know. Basil's in pretty good fettle, too, and mad keen to get runs.'

'Well, if you think so I daresay you're right. I won't give him any instructions for the present. I can always send out a message later on.'

The message was never sent. The real good player, having taken his guard and having made a careful survey of the dis-position of the field, faced the bowler with apparent confidence. It may have been, as George Appleby afterwards suggested, that he was wondering whether attack or defence was expected of him; it may have been more simply, as Monty declared, that he played back at a half-volley. In any case he was bowled neck and crop by the first ball he received and retired disconsolately to the pavilion.

Then in the very next over came the final catastrophe. Basil appeared to attempt to push a good-length off his legs; he missed it. There was a rather half-hearted appeal from the wicket-keeper, and Boone, who, covered in sticking-plaster, had returned to duty, held up his finger. Basil accepted the decision with the worst possible grace. At first he affected not to have heard the appeal or to have seen the decision. When the wicket-keeper pointed out to him that he was out, he advanced down the wicket and patted an imaginary spot a foot outside the leg stump. Then, with a face of thunder, he strode from the wicket and flung himself on the ground beside Cynthia and Robin Hedley.

'Bad luck,' said the latter a little maliciously, 'we were all looking forward to that hundred of yours, especially Cynthia.'

An almost murderous glance was the only reply he received, as Basil threw first his bat and then his gloves savagely away from him on the ground.

'He *has* got a streak,' thought Monty to himself. Aloud he said: 'Boone in form, what?'

'In form? The man's a damned disgrace; why the devil does George let him come on the ground? That ball pitched six inches outside the leg stump, and I left it alone on purpose. And that damned wicket-keeper? Why the bloody hell did he appeal when he was obviously unsighted?'

'Really, Basil,' said Cynthia, with a glance towards Lady Dormansland.

But Basil was much too angry to recover his usual smooth courtesy. Success was his métier, and to fail just when he wished to impress was more than he could bear. His pads were off now, and he flung them away on the grass as though he never wished to use them again.

'It's simply cheating – and nothing else. I'm damned if I play in this match again.'

He got up and stalked towards the pavilion, leaving bat and gloves and pads where they had fallen.

'British sportsman, not quite at his best,' remarked Monty with a smile, but Cynthia was too much annoyed to smile in return. She was accustomed to see Basil's best side, to watch him winning with grace and talking with intent to please. Basil in a bad temper, and behaving, as she was compelled to admit to herself, like a very complete cad, was new to her and she did not like it. Nor was she anxious to await his return.

She turned towards Lady Dormansland. 'Dear Lady Dormansland, don't you think we might collect your party and drive over to Critton; we should have time for some tennis before dinner, and your courts are so perfect that it's a shame not to use them. And really the cricket is a little dull. I can drive my car over and be back in time for dinner.'

'I was thinking just the same, my dear. Give me my parasol, Mr Hedley, and we'll go and find the others. Goodbye, Monty, and don't forget that I expect you for next week-end at Critton.'

Over the rest of the Fincham innings a veil should, in charity, be drawn. Merton stood firm against two confident appeals, but alone he could not stem the tide of disaster. Lees was bowling at his best, and at half-past five the last wicket fell, with the score-board showing the meagre total of 97.

George Appleby was almost in tears as he addressed his humiliated side.

'We've not lost a match by that margin as long as I can remember. A miserable show. Well, out we go to field again.'

In the view of some of his side the worst was still to come, for it was the best-established dogma of George's creed that cricket time should not be wasted, and that play, whatever the state of the game, should continue till seven. Nor did Sir Anstruther, who in the Saturday match neither asked nor expected quarter, show the least disposition to enforce the follow-on.

'I think we'll bat again, Appleby,' he remarked in a voice from which the tone of almost patronizing triumph was not entirely banished. 'My lads have bowled splendidly and deserve a rest. You'll find it very pleasant fielding in the cool of the evening.'

'Cool of the evening; it's still hot as hell,' groaned Bobby Hawes, as he and his disconsolate colleagues took the field and prepared to give the Besterton champions some batting practise. There till seven they remained. Some unexpected relief there was. The Admiral had insisted on fielding, but his journey from mid-on at one end to mid-on at the other was so laborious that the rest of the fieldsmen were able to rest a little between each over; the Colonel, partially tamed by annoyance and weariness, was almost silent, and Basil, sulking furiously, had been banished to the deep-field at the far end of the ground. Only George Appleby's enthusiasm and Monty's invincible optimism remained unimpaired. The latter indeed, having been allowed to bowl unchanged for almost half an hour – an exploit which had gained his side one wicket, and cost it an indecently large number of runs and a ball lost in the pond – was frankly happy. But as the players crowded round the drinking-tent when at length seven o'clock came, the disaster of the day began to appear less formidable. Forgetting the troubles of the later time, Bobby Hawes was explaining to Railton exactly how the ball which had dismissed him had swung away at the last moment, and Colquhoun and Johnny Rashwood were discussing the 'Varsity match as viewed from one side of the pavilion and the other. Above the din Sir Anstruther's voice, booming and resonant, was heard telling George Appleby of his own family affairs.

'I'm sending both my young nephews into the Air Force,' he declared. 'That's the service nowadays for young men of spirit and initiative. A grand service. They teach them manners there, too.'

An instinctive impulse caused the Admiral and the Colonel to turn towards one another, as though they had been challenged by a common foe. Characteristically it was the Admiral who took the initiative.

'Let me pour you out another whisky and soda, Colonel,' he said. 'By Gad, we've deserved a second drink after that spell of fielding; we older men, especially.'

For a moment the Colonel hesitated – then he accepted the proferred olive-branch.

'Quite right, quite right, Admiral,' he grunted. 'Deserved it more than some of these youngsters, what? I flatter myself we can still teach them something about cricket. When I was a subaltern we thought very little of fielding out all day in the sun – in India, too.'

He glared round pugnaciously as though expecting contradiction. 'Yes, the modern generation isn't as tough as we were,' agreed the Admiral, as he emptied a lump of ice into each glass.

'Here's fortune, Colonel. I hope to see you making many a big score on this ground.' The two long glasses were raised, and emptied.

'What about the other half of that drink?' said the Colonel, ignoring the fact that his third drink was already finished.

'I shan't say no,' replied the Admiral; 'this running about in the field does take it out of one nowadays.'

'Well, he *did* manage to cross after each over,' murmured Monty to himself, 'but running about is pitching it rather strong. Somehow I don't fancy that he gets his place next year.'

Afterwards Monty always said that it was Merton who saved the situation at dinner, but Merton, for his part, gave the credit to Monty. The party had hardly sat down when George Appleby noticed the champagne glasses on the tables.

'Merton,' he called out.

'Yes, sir?'

'Why are there champagne glasses on the table? You know the rules; we lost today – miserably – no one made 50 or took five wickets – or – did anything respectable at all.'

Merton was an old and trusted servant; he knew his place, and he knew just how far he could go.

'Yes, sir. I am aware that we were defeated today. But you remarked at tea-time, if you will allow me to remind you, sir, that you would never have Colonel Murcher-Pringle on your side again, and Mr Renshaw instructed me that that was worth a great many wins in the future – and that I was to serve champagne in consequence. I hope I have done right, sir.'

For a moment George Appleby hesitated, then he made up his mind.

'Perfectly right, Merton.'

Then he turned towards Monty.

'And I damned well *won't* ask him again, Monty. Though he *was* a good bat once, you know.'

*from* FATE CANNOT HARM ME *1935*

# The Cricket Match
## from 'England, Their England'
### A. G. MACDONELL

'Don't forget Saturday morning Charing Cross Underground Station,' ran the telegram which arrived at Royal Avenue during the week, 'at ten-fifteen sharp. Whatever you do don't be late. Hodge.'

Saturday morning was bright and sunny, and at ten minutes past ten Donald arrived at the Embankment entrance of Charing Cross Underground Station, carrying a small suitcase full of clothes suitable for outdoor sports and pastimes. He was glad that he had arrived too early, for it would have been a dreadful thing for a stranger and a foreigner to have kept such a distinguished man and his presumably distinguished colleagues even for an instant from their national game. Laying his bag down on the pavement and putting one foot upon it carefully, for Donald had heard stories of the surpassing dexterity of metropolitan thieves, he waited eagerly for the hands of a neighbouring clock to mark the quarter past. At twenty minutes to eleven an effeminate looking young man, carrying a a cricketing bag and wearing a pale blue silk jumper up to his ears, sauntered up, remarked casually, 'You playing?' and, on receiving an answer in the affirmative, dumped his bag at Donald's feet and said, 'Keep an eye on that like a good fellow. I'm going to get a shave,' and sauntered off round the corner.

At five minutes to eleven there was a respectable muster, six of the ten having assembled. But at five minutes past a disintegrating element was introduced by the arrival of Mr Harcourt with the news, which he announced with the air of a shipwrecked mariner who has, after twenty-five years of vigilance, seen a sail, that in the neighbourhood of Charing Cross the pubs opened at eleven o'clock. So that when Mr Hodge himself turned up at twenty-five minutes past eleven, resplendent in flannels, a red and white football shirt with a lace-up collar, and a blazer of purple and yellow stripes, each stripe being at least two inches across, and surmounted by a purple and yellow cap that made him somehow reminiscent of one of the Michelin twins, if not both, he was justly indignant at the slackness of his team.

'They've no sense of time,' he told Donald repeatedly. 'We're late as it is. The match is due to begin at half-past eleven, and it's fifty miles from here. I should have been here myself two hours ago, but I had my Sunday article to do. It really is too bad.'

When the team, now numbering nine men, had been extricated from the tavern and had been marshalled on the pavement, counted, recounted, and the missing pair identified, it was pointed out by the casual youth who had returned, shining and pomaded from the barber, that the char-à-banc had not yet arrived.

Mr Hodge's indignation became positively alarming and he

covered the twenty yards to the public telephone box almost as quickly as Mr Harcourt covered the forty yards back to the door of the pub. Donald remained on the pavement to guard the heap of suitcases, cricket bags and stray equipment – one player had arrived with a pair of flannels rolled in a tight ball under his arm and a left hand batting glove, while another had contributed a cardboard box which he had bought at Hamley's on the way down, and which contained six composite cricket balls, boys' size, and a pair of bails. It was just as well that Donald did remain on guard, partly because no one else seemed to care whether the luggage was stolen or not, partly because Mr Hodge emerged in a perfect frenzy a minute or two later from the telephone box to borrow two pennies to put in the slot, and partly because by the time the telephone call was at last in full swing and Mr Hodge's command over the byways of British invective was enjoying complete freedom of action, the char-à-banc rolled up beside the kerb.

At twelve-thirty it was decided not to wait for the missing pair, and the nine cricketers started off. At two-thirty, after halts at Catford, the White Hart at Sevenoaks, the Angel at Tunbridge Wells, and three smaller inns at tiny villages, the char-à-banc drew up triumphantly beside the cricket ground of the Kentish village of Fordenden.

Donald was enchanted at his first sight of rural England. And rural England is the real England, unspoilt by factories and financiers and tourists and hustle. He sprang out of the char-à-banc, in which he had been tightly wedged between a very stout publisher who had laughed all the way down and had quivered at each laugh like the needle of a seismograph during one of Japan's larger earthquakes, and a youngish and extremely learned professor of ballistics, and gazed eagerly round. The sight was worth an eager gaze or two. It was a hot summer's afternoon. There was no wind, and the smoke from the red-roofed cottages curled slowly up into the golden haze. The clock on the flint tower of the church struck the half-hour, and the vibrations spread slowly across the shimmering hedge rows, spangled with white blossom of the convolvulus, and lost themselves tremulously among the orchards. Bees lazily drifted. White butterflies flapped their aimless way among the gardens. Delphiniums, larkspur, tiger-lilies, evening primrose, monk's hood, sweet peas, swaggered brilliantly above the box hedges, the wooden palings and the rickety gates. The cricket field itself was a mass of daisies and buttercups and dandelions, tall grasses and purple vetches and thistledown, and great clumps of dark red sorrel, except, of course, for the oblong patch in the centre – mown, rolled, watered – a smooth, shining emerald of grass, the Pride of Fordenden, the Wicket.

The entire scene was perfect to the last detail. It was as if Mr Cochran had, with his spectacular genius, brought Ye Olde Englyshe Village straight down by special train from the London Pavilion, complete with synthetic cobwebs (from the Wigan factory), hand-made smocks for ye gaffers (called in the cabaret scenes and the North West Mounted Police scenes the Gentlemen of the Singing Ensemble), and aluminium EeziMilk stools for the dairymaids (or Ladies of the Dancing Ensemble). For there stood the vicar, beaming absent-mindedly at everyone. There was the forge, with the blacksmith, his hammer discarded, tightening his snake-buckled belt for the fray and loosening his braces to enable his terrific bowling arm to swing freely in its socket. There on a long bench outside the Three Horseshoes sat a row of elderly men, facing a row of pint tankards, and wearing either long beards or clean-shaven chins and long whiskers. Near them, holding pint tankards in their hands, was another group of men, clustered together and talking with intense animation. Donald thought that one or two of them seemed familiar, but it was not until he turned back to the char-à-banc to ask if he could help with the luggage that he realized that they were Mr Hodge and his team already sampling the proprietor's wares. (A notice above the door of the inn stated that the proprietor's name was A. Bason and that he was licensed to sell wines, spirits, beers, and tobacco.)

All round the cricket field small parties of villagers were

patiently waiting for the great match to begin; a match against gentlemen from London is an event in a village and some of them looked as if they had been waiting for a good long time. But they were not impatient. Village folk are very seldom impatient. Those whose lives are occupied in combating the eccentricities of God regard as very small beer the eccentricities of man.

Blue and green dragonflies played at hide and seek among the thistledown, and a pair of swans flew overhead. An ancient man leaned upon a scythe, his sharpening stone sticking out of a pocket in his velveteen waistcoat. A magpie flapped lazily across the meadows. The parson shook hands with the squire. Doves cooed. The haze flickered. The world stood still.

At twenty minutes to three Mr Hodge had completed his rather tricky negotiations with the Fordenden captain and had arranged that two substitutes should be lent by Fordenden in order that the visitors should field eleven men, and that nine men on each side should bat. But just as the two men on the Fordenden side, who had been detailed for the unpleasant duty of fielding for both sides and batting for neither, had gone off home in high dudgeon, a motor car arrived containing not only Mr Hodge's two defaulters but a third gentleman in flannels as well, who swore stoutly that he had been invited by Mr Hodge to play and affirmed that he was jolly well going to play. Whoever stood down, it wasn't going to be him. Negotiations therefore had to be reopened, the pair of local Achilles had to be recalled, and at ten minutes to three the match began upon a twelve-a-side basis.

Mr Hodge, having won the toss by a system of his own founded upon the differential calculus and the Copernican theory, sent in his opening pair to bat. One was James Livingstone, a very sound club cricketer, and the other one was called, simply, Boone. Boone was a huge, awe-inspiring colossus of a man, weighing at least eighteen stone and wearing all the majestic trappings of a Cambridge Blue. Donald felt that it was hardly fair to loose such cracks upon a humble English village until he fortunately remembered that he, of all people, a foreigner, admitted by courtesy to the National Game, ought not to set himself up to be a judge of what is, and what is not, cricket.

The Fordenden team ranged themselves at the bidding of their captain, the Fordenden baker, in various spots of vantage amid the daisies, buttercups, dandelions, vetches, thistledown and clumps of dark red sorrel; and the blacksmith, having taken in, just for luck as it were, yet another reef in his snake buckle belt, prepared to open the attack. It so happened that at the end at which he was to bowl the ground behind the wicket was level for a few yards and then sloped away rather abruptly, so that it was only during the last three of four intensive, galvanic yards of his run that the blacksmith, who took a long run, was visible to the batsman or indeed to anyone on the field of play except the man stationed in the deep field behind him. This man saw nothing of the game except the blacksmith walking back dourly and the blacksmith running up ferociously, and occasionally a ball driven smartly over the brow of the hill in his direction.

The sound club player having taken guard, having twiddled his bat round several times in a nonchalant manner, and having stared arrogantly at each fieldsman in turn, was somewhat surprised to find that, although the field was ready, no bowler was visible. His doubts, however, were resolved a second or two later, when the blacksmith came up, breasting the slope superbly like a mettlesome combination of Vulcan and Venus Anadyomene. The first ball which he delivered was a high full pitch to leg, of appalling velocity. It must have lighted upon a bare patch among the long grass near long leg, for it rocketed, first bounce, into the hedge and four byes were reluctantly signalled by the village umpire. The row of gaffers on the rustic bench shook their heads, agreed that it was many years since four byes had been signalled on that ground, and called for more pints of old and mild. The other members of Mr Hodge's team blanched visibly and called for more pints of bitter. The youngish professor of ballistics, who was in next, muttered something about muzzle velocities and started to do a sum on the back of an envelope.

The second ball went full pitch into the wicketkeeper's stomach and there was a delay while the deputy wicketkeeper was invested with the pads and gloves of office. The third ball, making a noise like a partridge, would have hummed past Mr Livingstone's left ear had he not dexterously struck it out of the ground for six and the fourth took his leg bail with a bullet-like full pitch. Ten runs for one wicket, last man 6. The professor got the fifth ball on the left ear and went back to the Three Horseshoes, while Mr Harcourt had the singular misfortune to hit his wicket before the sixth ball was even delivered. Ten runs for two wickets and one man retired hurt. A slow left hand bowler was on at the other end, the local rate collector, a man whose whole life was one of infinite patience and guile. Off his first ball the massive Cambridge Blue was easily stumped, having executed a movement that aroused the professional admiration of the Ancient who was leaning upon his scythe. Donald was puzzled that so famous a player should play so execrable a stroke until it transpired, later on, that a wrong impression had been created and that the portentous Boone had gained his Blue at Cambridge for rowing and not for cricket. Ten runs for three wickets and one man hurt.

The next player was a singular young man. He was small and quiet, and he wore perfectly creased white flannels, white silk socks, a pale pink shirt and a white cap. On the way down in the char-à-banc he had taken little part in the conversation and even less in the beer drinking. There was a retiring modesty about him that made him conspicuous in that cricket eleven, and there was a gentleness, an almost finicky gentleness about his movements which hardly seemed virile and athletic. He looked as if a fast ball would knock the bat out of his hands. Donald asked someone what his name was, and was astonished to learn that he was the famous novelist, Robert Southcott himself.

Just as this celebrity, holding his bat as delicately as if it was a flute or a fan, was picking his way through the daisies and thistledown towards the wicket, Mr Hodge rushed anxiously, tankard in hand, from the Three Horseshoes and bellowed in a most unpoetical voice: 'Play carefully, Bobby. Keep your end up. Runs don't matter.'

'Very well, Bill,' replied Mr Southcott sedately. Donald was interested by this little exchange. It was the Team Spirit at work – the captain instructing his man to play a type of game that was demanded by the state of the team's fortunes, and the individual loyally suppressing his instincts to play a different type of game.

Mr Southcott took guard modestly, glanced furtively round the field as if it was an impertinence to suggest that he would survive long enough to make a study of the fieldsmen's positions worth while and hit the rate collector's first ball over the Three Horseshoes into a hay field. The ball was retrieved by a mob of screaming urchins, handed back to the rate collector, who scratched his head and then bowled his fast yorker, which Mr Southcott hit into the saloon bar of the Shoes, giving Mr Harcourt such a fright that he required several pints before he fully recovered his nerve. The next ball was very slow and crafty, endowed as it was with every iota of fingerspin and brain power which a long-service rate collector could muster. In addition, it was delivered at the extreme end of the crease so as to secure a background of dark laurels instead of a dazzling white screen, and it swung a little in the air. A few moments later the urchins, by this time delirious with ecstasy, were fishing it out of the squire's trout stream with a bamboo pole and an old bucket.

The rate collector was bewildered. He had never known such a travesty of the game. It was not cricket. It was slogging; it was wild, unscientific bashing; and, furthermore, his reputation was in grave danger. The instalments would be harder than ever to collect, and heaven knew they were hard enough to collect as it was, what with bad times and all. His three famous deliveries had been treated with contempt – the leg break, the fast yorker, and the slow, swinging off break out of the laurel bushes. What on earth was he to try now? Another six and he would be laughed out of the parish. Fortunately the village umpire came out of a trance of consternation to the rescue. Thirty-eight years of umpiring for the Fordenden Cricket Club had taught him a thing or two and he called 'over' firmly and marched off to square leg. The rate collector was glad to give way to a Free Forester, who had been specially imported for this match. He was only a moderate bowler, but it was felt that it was worth while giving him a trial, if only for the sake of the scarf round his waist and his cap. At the other end the fast bowler pounded away grimly until an unfortunate accident occurred. Mr Southcott had been treating with apologetic contempt those of his deliveries which came within reach, and the blacksmith's temper had been rising for some time. An urchin had shouted, 'Take him orf!' and the other urchins, for whom Mr Southcott was by now a firmly established deity, had screamed with delight. The captain had held one or two ominous consultations with the wicketkeeper and other advisers, and the blacksmith knew that his dismissal was at hand unless he produced a supreme effort.

It was the last ball of the over. He halted at the wicket before going back for his run, glared at Mr Harcourt, who had been driven out to umpire by his colleagues – greatly to the regret of Mr Bason, the landlord of the Shoes – glared at Mr Southcott, took another reef in his belt, shook out another inch in his braces, spat on his hand, swung his arm three or four times in a meditative sort of way, grasped the ball tightly in his colossal palm, and then turned smartly about and marched off like a Pomeranian grenadier and vanished over the brow of the hill. Mr Southcott, during these proceedings, leant elegantly upon his bat and admired the view. At last, after a long stillness, the ground shook, the grasses waved violently, small birds arose with shrill clamours, a loud puffing sound alarmed the butterflies, and the blacksmith, looking more like Venus Anadyomene than ever, came thundering over the crest. The world held its breath. Among the spectators conversation was suddenly hushed. Even the urchins, understanding somehow that they were assisting at a crisis in affairs, were silent for a moment as the mighty figure swept up to the crease. It was the charge of Von Bredow's Dragoons at Gravelotte over again.

But alas for human ambitions! Mr Harcourt, swaying slightly from leg to leg, had understood the menacing glare of the bowler, had marked the preparation for a titanic effort, and, for he was not a poet for nothing, knew exactly what was going on. Mr Harcourt sober had a very pleasant sense of humour, but Mr Harcourt rather drunk was a perfect demon of impishness. Sober, he occasionally resisted a temptation to try to be funny. Rather drunk, never. As the giant whirlwind of vulcanic energy rushed past him to the crease, Mr Harcourt, quivering with excitement and internal laughter, and wobbling uncertainly upon his pins, took a deep breath and bellowed, 'No ball!'

It was too late for the unfortunate bowler to stop himself. The ball flew out of his hand like a bullet and hit third-slip, who was not looking, full pitch on the knee-cap. With a yell of agony third-slip began hopping about like a stork until he tripped over a tussock of grass and fell on his face in a bed of nettles, from which he sprang up again with another drum-splitting yell. The blacksmith himself was flung forward by his own irresistible momentum, startled out of his wits by Mr Harcourt's bellow in his ear, and thrown off his balance by his desperate effort to prevent himself from delivering the ball, and the result was that his gigantic feet got mixed up among each other and he fell heavily in the centre of the wicket, knocking up a cloud of dust and dandelion-seed and twisting his ankle. Rooks by hundreds arose in protest from the vicarage cedars. The urchins howled like intoxicated banshees. The gaffers gaped. Mr Southcott gazed modestly at the ground. Mr Harcourt gazed at the heavens. Mr Harcourt did not think the world had ever been, or could ever be again, quite such a capital place, even though he had laughed internally so much that he had got hiccups.

Mr Hodge, emerging at that moment from the Three Horseshoes, surveyed the scene and then the scoreboard with an imperial air. Then he roared in the same rustic voice as before.

'You needn't play safe any more, Bob. Play your own game.'

'Thank you, Bill,' replied Mr Southcott as sedately as ever, and, on the resumption of the game, he fell into a kind of cricketing trance, defending his wicket skilfully from straight balls, ignoring crooked ones, and scoring one more run in a quarter of an hour before he inadvertently allowed, for the first time during his innings, a ball to strike his person.

'Out!' shrieked the venerable umpire before anyone had time to appeal.

The score at this point was 69 for six, last man 52.

The only other incident in the innings was provided by an American journalist, by name Shakespeare Pollock, an intensely active, alert, on the spot young man. Mr Pollock had been roped in at the last moment to make up the eleven and Mr Hodge and Mr Harcourt had spent quite a lot of time on the way down trying to teach him the fundamental principles of the game. Donald had listened attentively and had been surprised that they made no reference to the Team Spirit. He decided in the end that the reason must have been simply that everyone knows all about it already, and that it is therefore taken for granted.

Mr Pollock stepped up to the wicket in the lively manner of his native mustang, refused to take guard, on the ground that he wouldn't know what to do with it when he had got it, and, striking the first ball he received towards square-leg, threw down his bat, and himself set off at a great rate in the direction of cover-point. There was a paralysed silence. The rustics on the bench rubbed their eyes. On the field no one moved. Mr Pollock stopped suddenly, looked round, and broke into a genial laugh.

'Darn me –' he began, and then he pulled himself up and went on in refined English, 'Well, well! I thought I was playing baseball.' He smiled disarmingly round.

'Baseball is a kind of rounders, isn't it, sir?' said cover-point sympathetically.

Donald thought he had never seen an expression change so suddenly as Mr Pollock's did at this harmless, and true, statement. A look of concentrated, ferocious venom obliterated the disarming smile. Cover-point, simple soul, noticed nothing, however, and Mr Pollock walked back to the wicket in silence and was out next ball.

The next two batsmen, Major Hawker, the team's fast bowler, and Mr Hodge himself, did not score, and the innings closed at 69, Donald not out nought. Opinion on the gaffers' bench, which corresponded in years and connoisseurship very closely with the Pavilion at Lord's, was sharply divided on the question whether 69 was, or was not, a winning score.

After a suitable interval for refreshment, Mr Hodge led his men, except Mr Harcourt, who was missing, out into the field and placed them at suitable positions in the hay.

The batsmen came in. The redoubtable Major Hawker, the fast bowler, thrust out his chin and prepared to bowl. In a quarter of an hour he had terrified seven batsmen, clean bowled six of them, and broken a stump. Eleven runs, six wickets, last man two.

After the fall of the sixth wicket there was a slight delay. The new batsman, the local rate collector, had arrived at the crease and was ready. But nothing happened. Suddenly the large publisher, who was acting as wicketkeeper, called out, 'Hi! Where's Hawker?'

The words galvanized Mr Hodge into portentous activity.

'Quick!' he shouted. 'Hurry, run, for God's sake! Bob, George, Percy, to the Shoes!' and he set off at a sort of gallop towards the inn, followed at intervals by the rest of the side except the pretty youth in the blue jumper, who lay down; the wicketkeeper, who did not move; and Mr Shakespeare Pollock, who had shot off the mark and was well ahead of the field.

But they were all too late, even Mr Pollock. The gallant Major, admitted by Mr Bason through the back door, had already lowered a quart and a half of mild and bitter, and his subsequent bowling was perfectly innocuous, consisting, as it did, mainly of slow, gentle full pitches to leg which the village baker and even, occasionally, the rate collector hit hard and high into the long grass. The score mounted steadily.

Disaster followed disaster. Mr Pollock, presented with an

easy chance of a run-out, instead of lobbing the ball back to the wicketkeeper, had another reversion to his college days and flung it with appalling velocity at the unfortunate rate collector and hit him in the small of the back, shouting triumphantly as he did so, 'Rah, rah, rah!' Mr Livingstone, good club player, missed two easy catches off successive balls. Mr Hodge allowed another easy catch to fall at his feet without attempting to catch it, and explained afterwards that he had been all the time admiring a particularly fine specimen of oak in the squire's garden. He seemed to think that this was a complete justification of his failure to attempt, let alone bring off, the catch. A black spot happened to cross the eye of the ancient umpire just as the baker put all his feet and legs and pads in front of a perfectly straight ball, and, as he plaintively remarked over and over again, he had to give the batsman the benefit of the doubt, hadn't he? It wasn't as if it was his fault that a black spot had crossed his eye just at the moment. And the stout publisher seemed to be suffering from the delusion that the way to make a catch at the wicket was to raise both hands high in the air, utter a piercing yell, and trust to an immense pair of pads to secure the ball. Repeated experiments proved that he was wrong.

The baker dashed away vigorously and the rate collector dabbed the ball hither and thither until the score – having once been 11 runs for six wickets – was marked up on the board at 50 runs for six wickets. Things were desperate. Twenty to win and five wickets – assuming that the blacksmith's ankle and third-slip's knee-cap would stand the strain – to fall. If the lines on Mr Hodge's face were deep, the lines on the faces of his team when he put himself on to bowl were like plasticine models of the Colorado Canyon. Mr Southcott, without any orders from his captain, discarded his silk sweater from the Rue de la Paix, and went away into the deep field, about a hundred and twenty yards from the wicket. His beautifully brushed head was hardly visible above the daisies. The professor of ballistics sighed deeply. Major Hawker grinned a colossal grin, right across his jolly red face, and edged off in the direction of the Shoes.

Livingstone, loyal to his captain, crouched alertly. Mr Shakespeare Pollock rushed about enthusiastically. The remainder of the team drooped.

But the remainder of the team was wrong. For a wicket, a crucial wicket, was secured off Mr Hodge's very first ball. It happened like this. Mr Hodge was a poet, and therefore a theorist and an idealist. If he was to win a victory at anything, he preferred to win by brains and not by muscle. He would far sooner have his best leg spinner miss the wicket by an eighth of an inch than dismiss a batsman with a fast, clumsy full-toss. Every ball that he bowled had brain behind it, if not exactness of pitch. And it so happened that he had recently watched a county cricket match between Lancashire, a county that he detested in theory, and Worcester, a county that he adored in fact. On the one side were factories and the late Mr Jimmy White; on the other, English apples and Mr Stanley Baldwin. And at this particular match, a Worcestershire bowler, by name Root, a deliciously agricultural name, had outed the tough nuts of the County Palatine by placing all his fieldsmen on the leg side and bowling what are technically known as 'in-swingers'.

Mr Hodge, at heart an agrarian, for all his book-learning and his cadences, was determined to do the same. The first part of the performance was easy. He placed all his men upon the leg side. The second part – the bowling of the 'in-swingers' – was more complicated, and Mr Hodge's first ball was a slow long-hop on the off side. The rate collector, metaphorically rubbing his eyes, felt that this was too good to be true, and he struck the ball sharply into the untenanted off side and ambled down the wicket with as near an approach to gaiety as a man can achieve who is cut off by the very nature of his profession from the companionship and goodwill of his fellows. He had hardly gone a yard or two when he was paralysed by a hideous yell from the long grass into which the ball had vanished, and still more by the sight of Mr Harcourt, who, aroused from a deep slumber amid a comfortable couch of grasses and daisies, sprang to his feet and, pulling himself together with miraculous rapidity after a lightning if somewhat bleary glance round the field, seized the ball and unerringly threw down the wicket. Fifty for seven, last man 22. Twenty to win, four wickets to fall.

Mr Hodge's next ball was his top-spinner, and it would have, or might have, come very quickly off the ground had it ever hit the ground; as it was, one of the short legs caught it dexterously and threw it back while the umpire signalled a wide. Mr Hodge then tried some more of Mr Root's stuff and was promptly hit for two sixes and a single. This brought the redoubtable baker to the batting end. Six runs to win and four wickets to fall.

Mr Hodge's fifth ball was not a good one, due mainly to the fact that it slipped out of his hand before he was ready, and it went up and came down in a slow, lazy parabola, about seven feet wide of the wicket on the leg side. The baker had plenty of time to make up his mind. He could either leave it alone and let it count one run as a wide; or he could spring upon it like a panther and, with a terrific six, finish the match sensationally. He could play the part either of a Quintus Fabius Maximus Cunctator or of a sort of Tarzan. The baker concealed beneath a modest and floury exterior a mounting ambition. Here was his chance to show the village. He chose the sort of Tarzan, sprang like a panther, whirled his bat cyclonically, and missed the ball by about a foot and a half. The wicketkeeping publisher had also had time in which to think and to move, and he also had covered the seven feet. True, his movements were less like the spring of a panther than the sideways waddle of an aldermanic penguin. But nevertheless he got there, and when the ball had passed the flashing blade of the baker, he launched a mighty kick at it, stooping to grab it was out of the question, and by an amazing fluke kicked it on to the wicket. Even the ancient umpire had to give the baker out, for the baker was still lying flat on his face outside the crease.

'I was bowling for that,' observed Mr Hodge modestly, strolling up the pitch.

'I had plenty of time to use my hands,' remarked the wicketkeeper to the world at large, 'but I preferred to kick it.'

Donald was impressed by the extraordinary subtlety of the game.

Six to win and three wickets to fall.

The next batsman was a schoolboy of about sixteen, an ingenuous youth with pink cheeks and a nervous smile, who quickly fell a victim to Mr Harcourt, now wideawake and beaming upon everyone. For Mr Harcourt, poet that he was, understood exactly what the poor, pink child was feeling, and he knew that if he played the ancient dodge and pretended to lose the ball in the long grass it was a hundred to one that the lad would lose his head. The batsman at the other end played the fourth ball of Mr Livingstone's next over hard in the direction of Mr Harcourt. Mr Harcourt rushed towards the spot where it had vanished in the jungle. He groped wildly for it, shouting as he did so, 'Come and help. It's lost.' The pink child scuttered nimbly down the pitch. Six runs to win and two wickets to fall. Mr Harcourt smiled demoniacally.

The crisis was now desperate. The fieldsmen drew nearer and nearer to the batsman, excepting the youth in the blue jumper. Livingstone balanced himself on his toes. Mr Shakespeare Pollock hopped about almost on top of the batsmen and breathed audibly. Even the imperturbable Mr Southcott discarded the piece of grass which he had been chewing so steadily. Mr Hodge took himself off and put on the Major, who had by now somewhat lived down the quart and a half.

The batsmen crouched down upon their bats and defended stubbornly. A snick through the slips brought a single. A ball which eluded the publisher's gigantic pads brought a bye. A desperate sweep at a straight half-volley sent the ball off the edge of the bat over third-man's head and in normal circumstances would have certainly scored one, and possibly two. But Mr Harcourt was on guard at third man, and the batsmen, by nature cautious men, one being old and the sexton, the other the postman and therefore a government official, were taking no risks. Then came another single off a mis-hit, and then an interminable period in which no wicket fell and no run was scored

It was broken at last disastrously, for the postman struck the ball sharply at Mr Pollock who picked it up and, in an ecstasy of zeal, flung it madly at the wicket. Two overthrows resulted.

The scores were level and there were two wickets to fall. Silence fell. The gaffers, victims simultaneously of excitement and senility, could hardly raise their pint pots for it was past six o'clock, and the front door of the Three Horseshoes was now as wide open officially as the back door had been unofficially all afternoon.

Then the Major, his red face redder than ever and his chin sticking out almost as far as the Napoleonic Mr Ogilvy's, bowled a fast half-volley on the leg-stump. The sexton, a man of iron muscle from much digging, hit it fair and square in the middle of the bat, and it flashed like a thunderbolt, waist-high, straight at the youth in the blue jumper. With a shrill scream the youth sprang backwards out of its way and fell over on his back. Immediately behind him, so close were the fieldsmen clustered, stood the mighty Boone. There was no escape for him. Even if he had possessed the figure and the agility to perform back-somersaults, he would have lacked the time. He had been un-sighted by the youth in the jumper. The thunderbolt struck him in the midriff like a red-hot cannonball upon a Spanish galleon and with the sound of a drumstick upon an insufficiently stretched drum. With a fearful oath, Boone clapped his hands to his outraged stomach and found that the ball was in the way. He looked at it for a moment in astonishment and then threw it down angrily and started to massage the injured spot while the field rang with applause at the brilliance of the catch.

Donald walked up and shyly added his congratulations. Boone scowled at him.

'I didn't want to catch the bloody thing,' he said sourly, massaging away like mad.

'But it may save the side,' ventured Donald.

'Blast the bloody side,' said Boone.

Donald went back to his place.

The scores were level and there was one wicket to fall. The

last man in was the blacksmith, leaning heavily upon the shoulder of the baker, who was going to run for him, and limping as if in great pain. He took guard and looked round savagely. He was clearly still in a great rage.

The first ball he received he lashed at wildly and hit straight up in the air to an enormous height. It went up and up and up, until it became difficult to focus it properly against the deep, cloudless blue of the sky, and it carried with it the hopes and fears of an English village. Up and up it went, and then at the top it seemed to hang motionless in the air, poised like a hawk, fighting, as it were, an heroic but forlorn battle against the chief invention of Sir Isaac Newton, and then it began its slow descent.

In the meanwhile things were happening below, on the terrestrial sphere. Indeed, the situation was rapidly becoming what the French call *mouvementé*. In the first place, the blacksmith forgot his sprained ankle and set out at a capital rate for the other end, roaring in a great voice as he went, 'Come on, Joe!' The baker, who was running on behalf of the invalid, also set out, and he also roared, 'Come on, Joe!' and side by side, like a pair of high-stepping hackneys, the pair cantered along. From the other end Joe set out on his mission, and he roared, 'Come on, Bill!' So all three came on. And everything would have been all right, so far as the running was concerned, had it not been for the fact that Joe, very naturally, ran with his head thrown back and his eyes goggling at the hawk-like cricket ball. And this in itself would not have mattered if it had not been for the fact that the blacksmith and the baker, also very naturally, ran with their heads turned not only upwards but also backwards as well, so that they too gazed at the ball, with an alarming sort of squint and truly terrific kink in their necks. Half-way down the pitch the three met with a magnificent clang, reminiscent of early, happy days in the tournament-ring at Ashby-de-la-Zouch, and the hopes of the village fell with the resounding fall of their three champions.

But what of the fielding side? Things were not so well with

them. If there was doubt and confusion among the warriors of Fordenden, there was also uncertainty and disorganization among the ranks of the invaders. Their main trouble was the excessive concentration of their forces in the neighbourhood of the wicket. Napoleon laid it down that it was impossible to have too many men upon a battlefield, and he used to do everything in his power to call up every available man for a battle. Mr Hodge, after a swift glance at the ascending ball and a swift glance at the disposition of his troops, disagreed profoundly with the Emperor's dictum. He had too many men, far too many. And all except the youth in the blue silk jumper, and the mighty Boone, were moving towards strategical positions underneath the ball, and not one of them appeared to be aware that any of the others existed. Boone had not moved because he was more or less in the right place, but then Boone was not likely to bring off the catch, especially after the episode of the last ball. Major Hawker, shouting 'Mine, mine!' in a magnificently self-confident voice, was coming up from the bowler's end like a battle-cruiser. Mr Harcourt had obviously lost sight of the ball altogether, if indeed he had ever seen it, for he was running round and round Boone and giggling foolishly. Livingstone and Southcott, the two cracks, were approaching competently. Either of them would catch it easily. Mr Hodge had only to choose between them, and, coming to a swift decision, he yelled above the din, 'Yours, Livingstone!' Southcott, disciplined cricketer, stopped dead. Then Mr Hodge made a fatal mistake. He remembered Livingstone's two missed sitters, and he reversed his decision and roared, 'Yours, Bobby!' Mr Southcott obediently started again while Livingstone, who had not heard the second order, went straight on. Captain Hodge had restored the *status quo*.

In the meantime the professor of ballistics had made a lightning calculation of angles, velocities, density of the air, barometer-readings and temperatures, and had arrived at the conclusion that the critical point, the spot which ought to be marked in the photographs with an X, was one yard to the north-east of Boone, and he proceeded to take up station there, colliding on the way with Donald and knocking him over. A moment later Bobby Southcott came racing up and tripped over the recumbent Donald and was shot head first into the Abraham-like bosom of Boone. Boone stepped back a yard under the impact and came down with his spiked boot, surmounted by a good eighteen stone of flesh and blood, upon the professor's toe. Almost simultaneously the portly wicketkeeper, whose move-ments were a positive triumph of the spirit over the body bumped the professor from behind. The learned man was thus neatly sandwiched between Tweedledum and Tweedledee, and the sandwich was instantly converted into a ragout by Living-stone, who made up for his lack of extra weight – for he was always in perfect training – by his extra momentum. And all the time Mr Shakespeare Pollock hovered alertly upon the outskirts like a rugby scrum-half, screaming American University cries in a piercingly high tenor voice.

At last the ball came down. To Mr Hodge it seemed a long time before the invention of Sir Isaac Newton finally triumphed. And it was a striking testimony to the mathematical and bal-listical skill of the professor that the ball landed with a sharp report upon the top of his head. Thence it leapt up into the air a foot or so, cannoned on to Boone's head, and then trickled slowly down the colossal expanse of the wicketkeeper's back, bouncing slightly as it reached the massive lower portions. It was only a foot from the ground when Mr Shakespeare Pollock sprang into the vortex with a last ear-splitting howl of victory and grabbed it off the seat of the wicketkeeper's trousers. The match was a tie. And hardly anyone on the field knew it except Mr Hodge, the youth in the blue jumper, and Mr Pollock him-self. For the two batsmen and the runner, undaunted to the last, had picked themselves up and were bent on completing the single that was to give Fordenden the crown of victory. Un-fortunately, dazed with their falls, with excitement, and with the noise, they all three ran for the same wicket, simultaneously realized their error, and all three turned and ran for the other –

the blacksmith, ankle and all, in the centre and leading by a yard, so that they looked like pictures of the Russian troika. But their effort was in vain, for Mr Pollock had grabbed the ball and the match was a tie.

And both teams spent the evening at the Three Horseshoes, and Mr Harcourt made a speech in Italian about the glories of England and afterwards fell asleep in a corner, and Donald got home to Royal Avenue at one o'clock in the morning, feeling that he had not learnt very much about the English from his experience of their national game.

*from* ENGLAND, THEIR ENGLAND *1933*

## *Tilling fold play Wilminghurst*

### HUGH DE SELINCOURT

Gauvinier's experience in running the Tillingfold side for some years had led him to pay small heed to any bad preliminary rumours as to the composition of the Saturday team. The list was posted in the village on Thursday evening and unless he had official information that a man could not turn out, he left it at that.

As in all clubs, of course, on some Saturdays eighteen Tillingfold men were keen for a game, on others eight: and on the latter occasions men who groused to the effect that they were never asked to play, invariably had a prior engagement or grumblingly consented to 'make one', inferring, as was often painfully true, that they would not have been asked if anyone else had been available. Getting up a side is no easier at Tillingfold than it is elsewhere, but the games which Tillingfold played were better games than he had ever played elsewhere.

The ride to the ground or to the conveyance that was to take the team from the village square to the opponents' ground was always an anxious ride for the good Gauvinier, skipper of the Tillingfold eleven.

The ride was more anxious than usual this Saturday, when Tillingfold were playing Wilminghurst, pet opponents, with whom many close battles had been fought in past seasons. Two good men were genuinely unable to play: the team's best bowler was seedy but would turn out if he could. Report credited Wilminghurst with a specially hot side.

No one was about in the square. The conveyance waited dolefully empty. Old John Meadows limping by to the 'pub' smiled to Gauvinier: 'Got to scratch the match, I hear.' He had played for Tillingford forty years ago and did not approve of the way young fellows went on nowadays, 'what with motor cycles, pickchers and sech'.

'Oh, I hope not!' Gauvinier answered.

'Can't raise a side, I'm told,' the old fellow continued gleefully.

'Oh, we'll do that all right if we have to rope in the chaps from the Union.'

'Ah, things ain't what they was: not by a long chalk.'

Gauvinier turned away to meet Tom Rutherford, slow bowler, staunch cricketer, who had spent many years in Tasmania and advocated in gentle undertones drastic measures with slackers and grousers.

'Got a side?' he asked.

'Don't know yet!'

'Not going to scratch?' he inquired.

'Scratch!' snapped Gauvinier.

They both laughed. Then went through the side: Eight men and a boy were certainties and among the men were two the mention of whose names caused bitter mirth to the friends.

'We're in for the deuce of a hiding.'

'Damn good job, too.'

Sam Bird, the umpire trod softly into the square, careful not to jolt himself or to stamp holes in the road with his bulk. He announced like a conspirator, smiling at a secret joke:

'I'm told Mr Marling is playing for Wilminghurst.' He surveyed the sky with beady eyes and addressed it. 'Saw he made ninety-one for 'Orsam against Littlehampton t'other day in twenty-three minutes.'

But Sam Bird could not remain disheartening: his devotion to Tillingfold cricket and the Tillingfold skipper was deep and unshakable.

'However,' he said slowly, tapping the words out with a fat finger on Gauvinier's coat, 'at cricket – you – never – know. Never.'

Eight men and a boy, Gauvinier was grimly thinking; it would be the first time in seven seasons he had come on the field without a full side. Nice thing, Tillingfold turning out short!

It was not a cheery team that left the village square-at 1.58 for their Saturday afternoon sport. 'A bloomin' funeral, more like,' as one man put it.

Arrived, they straggled sadly over the field to the pavilion in the far corner of the ground. It was obvious that Wilminghurst had got a hot side, even before their captain Southernhay's bright asseveration of the fact to Gauvinier, who was in the mood to find him disgustingly sympathetic. 'What a pity! It does spoil a game so, doesn't it, when one side is too vastly superior?'

'Oh, we're not beaten yet!' laughed Gauvinier.

'Marling's turned out for us. Hit up ninety-one –'

'Yes, I know. Let's toss.'

'Ninety-one in twenty-three minutes is pretty good going. And this ground's faster. You cry.'

'Heads.'

'It is.'

'You bat first.'

It was the first time Gauvinier had ever put opponents in as the result of sheer cowardice. In their present mood his men were not good for twenty runs. But he felt guilty and ashamed.

'Come on!' he told them in the visitors' room. 'I've put 'em in! We'll get 'em on the run! Then knock off the runs.'

'Some 'opes!' was chorused.

He did not stop to argue, but hurried out to tackle the unpleasant job of asking for a substitute. For two he could not bring himself to ask.

Hardly a catch was flung from one to another as the team (eight men, a boy, and a substitute) proceeded sadly into the field, followed closely by Marling, the cheeriest soul who ever gripped a bat handle, chatting and laughing with Southernhay, obviously awed at opening the innings in such brilliant company. Marling took middle and leg, made his block with two rapid little taps and stood up, twiddling his bat round, surveying the field with a confident beam that meant business.

Gauvinier took the first over; keen as Lucifer to get a quick wicket, knowing well how shaky Marling could be before he felt the ball clean and hard upon his bat. Gauvinier was made to begin the game; once in it, all odious preliminaries were immediately forgotten. There was something to bite into, something good and solid. But he was in for a penitential half-hour, which he vaguely sensed as he eyed his placed field for the last time – three men who were safe to hold a catch, two real good triers, the rest . . . oh, well, it was decent of them to turn out at all, especially when one remembered how devilishly hard a cricket ball must seem to them. Gauvinier bowled medium-fast, using his height well. His first ball Marling played out to freely and returned to him at a fair pace along the carpet; his second ball beat Marling and came within a couple of inches of the off bail. The wicket-keeper grinned cheerfully as he lobbed the ball back, wagging his head to one side knowingly. Gauvinier was so braced that he felt no annoyance to hear mid-off, whose fielding was a calamity, draw attention to his presence by remarking, 'That's the stuff to give the troops.'

The third ball struck the edge of Marling's bat and flew straight at short slip, who stumbled back as he saw it coming, stumbled forward as the ball smacked into his large hands, and fell, dropping as easy a catch as short slip will ever have in this wicked world where no catch at short slip is really easy. Gauvinier forced a grin upon his face, forced a shout of 'Bad luck' from his lips to the sorry fieldsman, and turned to deliver his next ball, with black fury boiling through his veins. A yorker: you could see the wicket shake as it shaved the leg stump and went for two byes, which Marling picked himself up to run, after his huge missed effort to wipe a full toss out of the ground.

Gauvinier was not consoled by Marling's kindly remark: 'A squeak, that! Your luck's well out!'

The gay batsman could stand no more of this nonsense: the next ball he drove hard – a lovely shot, bang against the wooden pavilion, terrifying mid-off by his proximity to its flight.

Gauvinier curbed his bitter wish to say how wise it was not to have put a hand out at that one: might possibly have stopped it. He listened without a word to mid-off's remark that he appreciated a good hit when an opponent made it; he was, at any rate, a true sportsman in speech, whatever his more practical deficiencies might be. The last ball of the over was a slower one, which Marling, slightly mistiming, lifted towards Jenkins in the deep. Gauvinier had a vivid imagination, but he never imagined for an instant that the good Jenkins would hold such a catch. He had to walk three steps forward and wait for the ball to fall into his hands: instead of which Jenkins, pleased with himself for noticing that it was a catch at all, ran back, shouting 'That's mine,' then, like a wounded bird, hurried to the right, then to the left, and finally dashing forward as the ball fell, stumbled on to his hands. He got up, walked leisurely after the ball, flipping his stung hand, found it and hurled it in, furious and convinced that the catch was well out of his reach.

During these manoeuvres, the batsmen had run three, and Marling with a laughing apology for bagging the bowling faced the fastish but erratic Longman, who took three little steps to the wicket and delivered the ball with the unexpected suddenness of a catapult. An early success inspired him. On his day he could be deadly, and Gauvinier hoped this might be his day: he hoped it very much, but Longman's first ball was a hot long hop, shoulder high, which Marling hit out of the ground for six.

'I like them,' he remarked to the wicketkeeper, while the wall was climbed and the ball retrieved.

Poor Longman found the wait of an inordinate length. He stood on fire with his blush, silently watching the man climb back over the wall to his place. Longman's second ball was also short, on the off, and beaten past cover to the boundary: his third was driven for two; his fourth went somewhere near the wicket; his fifth, a desperately fast one, was short on the leg, and effortlessly lifted over that accursed wall; his last was outside the batsman's reach on the off.

Runs were coming at a terrible pace; and the pace continued growing faster still when Gauvinier tried a double change. The hundred went up for no wickets. The wicketkeeper supposed grimly that they'd make about three hundred and declare.

'Oh, you never know your luck!' Gauvinier bravely answered. 'We've got ours. This time.'

Never had the Tillingfold team been seen with tails so lowly drooping or apparently with such good reason. Gauvinier put on his first bowlers again, changing their ends. Marling faced Longman, ran out and drove a good-length ball clean out of the ground – a huge hit. The bowler's face was a study. Marling must have decided where the next ball was going before it was delivered, for he was yards out of his ground to what luckily chanced to be a short long hop; he waved his bat at it, fell forward and was ignominiously stumped.

108 – 1 – 89, the score-board read.

A stranger came in, wearing a Sussex Martlet's cap.

'Lord! Look at this!' said Jenkins. 'I'm blowed if we've done with 'em yet.'

But the stranger, deceived no doubt by the queer suddenness of Longman's delivery, played across his first ball and retired, with his off stump leaning well back – a very pleasant sight to the Tillingfold team. No more wickets and no more runs that over. Gauvinier bowled a maiden, which was so refreshing after the orgy of runs that the tails of the Tillingfold team visibly rose; but they drooped during Longman's next, which he started with a juicy full toss and followed by a juicier long hop knee-high on the leg side – a gift of eight runs which was quietly taken; then he settled down and the last four balls were a good length.

Gauvinier is as likely to remember the next over as he is likely to remember that disastrous first. Southernhay, the Wilminghurst skipper, who was set, snicked his first ball and the wicket-keeper took a palpable catch, a good one too, on the leg side. Gauvinier's next ball shaved the new-comer's wicket, and his third, the new-comer being too anxious to emulate the happy Marling, hit the middle peg. Wilminghurst's chief hitter came in next, a familiar figure, obviously resolved to show the visitors what the home side could do in the way of hard hitting, but he, too, began too soon, and drove this first ball back to Gauvinier, who jumped to hold a nice catch. His last ball yorked Number seven.

119 – 6 – 0.

Tom Rutherford came up, quivering with excitement.

'One hundred and fifty on this ground means only ninety on ours. Easily. We're not done yet.'

Sam Bird backed him well up. 'That's right!' he slowly declared with immense emphasis. 'And they've not got one hundred and fifty, I may mention.'

'No. Nor will,' declared the wicketkeeper. 'Lord! what a lark to beat 'em with a side like this!'

'We'll make a show, anyhow,' Tom Rutherford remarked quietly, wisely fearful of over-confidence.

'Any of the new crowd bowlers?' he inquired of their umpire.

'Can't say.'

'Man in!'

They sprang to their places – a different side.

Seven runs came from the erratic Longman's first five, then a beauty knocked the off stump clean out of its hole.

A wily old man came in to bat, and, facing Gauvinier after a one to leg, played the last five balls like an ancient book. If only that beggar could keep a length, thought Gauvinier ardently of the solid, unsmiling Longman. But the beggar could not. Came a full toss that went for two byes, a long hop that went for two runs – the two balls would have been a gift of twelve runs to Marling – one that thumped the clumsy batsman on the chest woke him up, perhaps, for he hit the next one for four and the one after for three. One hundred and thirty was up on the score-board.

Gauvinier's unuttered curse was modified by hope at having a go at that batsman and not at the wily old man. 'He'll cow-shot a good length ball for four and hit across a half-volley.' He itched to have his chance; bet a hundred to one he'd get him. His chance came. He bowled the ball he wanted to – a half-volley slightly slower – round whirled the bat, well across, down went the wicket. Gauvinier purred to himself like a happy cat, or any bowler who has done precisely what he wanted to do, foreseeing the right ball, and bowling it. An absurd call ran the wily old man out. Longman knocked the last wicket down with a furious full toss. Tillingfold had one hundred and thirty-nine to make to win, after one hundred had been on the board for no wickets.

'That's about seventy-five on our ground,' Tom Rutherford kept quietly assuring every member of the team in turn. Gauvinier in sad silence pondered on the batting order. There was no doubt about Number one. Ernest Settatree was a good and careful bat, keen all through, and with any luck might stay there. Lord! how he missed old John McLeod and Trine and Dick Fanshawe and Sid Smith. Still, there were the two Carruthers – the wicketkeeper and his young brother Bill – strong as lions, and, when they got going, dangerous: very dangerous, when, oh! when, they got going! There was half-an-hour's play before tea. If four wickets fell . . . hence loathed melancholy.

'Bill,' he cried cheerfully, 'what about first knock?'

Bill blushed and laughed. 'May as well, first as last.'

'Watch the first few, you young fool,' said his brother severely, 'and you'll be right as rain.'

'Not 'alf. You bet. Not if it snows ink!' said Bill, too thrilled at the prospect of going out to bat first to talk perfect sense.

'You've only got to pat 'em to get four here,' said Jenkins, beaming encouragement.

'Oh, I'll pat 'em all right!' quoth Bill.

His elder brother vehemently begged him 'not to act silly' – a way with elder brothers – and Bill replied that he was as Gawd made him – or words to that effect – while he nervously buckled on his pads, and asked young Settatree to let him take first over that he might 'get his' as soon as possible; and again elder brother adjured him with savage vehemence 'not to act so damned silly.'

'The young blighter!' Ted Carruthers bitterly remarked as the batsmen walked out to the wicket. 'He'd be a decent bat if he wouldn't act silly.'

'Number Three, Ted; I'm four, Tom Rutherford five, Jenkins six –'

'Our tail ought to wag, I don't think!' began Ted with grim humour. 'Couldn't raise . . .' But he stopped. The first ball was being bowled. Eyes stared tensely, to see Bill lunge feebly at it, not a hit, not a shot, not even a cow-shot. The ball struck the edge of the bat and soared over slip's head. They ran two.

'Steady, Bill!' roared the enraged Ted, and muttered to his neighbours, 'You'd think he'd never held a bat in his hand before, the young turnip!'

Poor Ted, wounded in his family pride, could only groan as Bill met the next ball with the same futile half-hearted lunge, a shot he never indulged in at the nets, but kept exclusively for matches – hit the ball this time and lifted it high and straight and easy into the hands of deep mid-on.

He came in laughing loudly to hide his miserable discomfiture. 'Haven't kept you waiting long, Ted,' he breezily remarked, and then unable to keep it up, lamented: 'What I needs make that assish scoop for –'

'Yes, you wants a good slap behind yer ears,' growled his brother, choosing a batting-glove. Out he strode, chin forward to maintain the family honour.

Impatience, however, was a family failing, for, much to little brother's glee, Ted viciously lashed at the first ball he received and missed it apparently by feet.

'Look at that now! Look at that! And he tells me not to have a punch!' cried Bill convulsed.

But Gauvinier and Tom Rutherford were thankful to observe that he was steadier after that first absurdity, and he and Settatree settled down to play good, sound cricket, picking the right one to hit, and hitting it hard and clean. Every ball was watched with excitement; every run cheered.

Thirty-two was on the board when the teams came in for tea. Settatree, not out twelve; Ted Carruthers, not out fourteen.

Tensity relaxed during tea, which was taken on a long trestle-table under trees outside the pavilion: huge plates of bread and butter, piled slices of plum cake, tea from an enormous urn. Laughter and chat and vigorous munching; gulps of hot tea, cup after cup.

Tillingfold ate heartily, talked gaily; after the disastrous beginning they were making a good fight of it.

Gauvinier, lighting a cigarette, urged the reluctant umpires out into the sun. The tensity of the game was resumed. Both men went on batting like books, taking no risks, running well, hitting the loose ones hard and true. There was every sign of a stand. Forty went up on the board.

And then one cocked up at young Settatree, point fell forward, rolled over, held up the ball, shouting: 'How's that?' Young Settatree looked towards the bowler's umpire, who hesitated then half-raised a diffident finger; so he appealed to the other umpire, Sam Bird.

'Ah! I couldn't rightly see,' Sam Bird faltered and called out stoutly to the bowler's umpire: 'How was it?'

'Out!' he snapped, looking at no one, and young Settatree had to retire, a very disgruntled man.

'It hit the ground first, I'll swear,' said young Settatree, almost weeping, to Gauvinier, whom he passed on his way out to bat.

'Rotten luck, anyhow. You were batting better than I've ever seen you bat before.'

'Give it 'em, skipper, for the Lord's sake!'

Gauvinier went out, sincerely hoping that he would, and clearly praying in his own mind that the bowler might not find his blind spot on the leg stump – large and fatal always for his first few balls.

Providence and the bowler were kind, for down came a shortish good-length ball on the off, which went past cover to the boundary, his favourite shot. The next, pitched further up, he used his reach to drive pleasantly back to mid-off, who was glad to stop it, and retreated a few yards at the bowler's suggestion. Thank goodness he was seeing them! Thank goodness, too, it did not occur to the bowler to put a man at extra-cover.

Up to nine he kept count of his runs, though he had no wish to do so; it was unsettling; made him in a hurry. Quietly he stayed there; not feeling that each ball might be his last; not visualizing horrid mis-hits, silly mistakes that would be his undoing. The score was mounting; they were putting up seventy. Ted Carruthers was batting soundly, hitting the loose ball hard; two fours: ah! there was eight going up. No disgrace now. It would be fun to put the hundred up. Oh, here was a good one: shortish on the off, again. Full in the centre of the bat. And no extra-cover, he chuckled to himself, watching the ball thump against the wooden pavilion.

The bowler hopefully set mid-off wider and deeper: and forgetting Gauvinier's length and reach, bowled what would have been a good-length ball to a shorter man. The Tillingfold captain stepped out and hit a half-volley straight past where mid-off was standing before his hopeful shifting – a satisfactory drive to watch as it sped over the fast ground to the boundary.

Ninety went up on the score-board, and the fieldsmen looked at the figures with earnest faces. The Tillingfold team, too, excited to sit, kept hurrying to the score-box to see the exact score, cheering each run. Every now and then some supporter of the home team would utter a stentorian request to know what Wilminghurst were up to, now.

And the batsmen had that set, unhurried manner that is so depressing to a fielding side.

There came two maidens as the century approached – two maidens which put the field alert on their toes and dug the batsmen in. Why hurry? After the first three balls of the next over, played confidently back, the strain proved too great for the bowler; he sent his first bad ball for five overs, a full toss which Ted Carruthers swept out of the ground for six, and the hundred went up amid roars of delight. Then a long hop pulled fiercely against the wall. He must be nearing his fifty. But out he leapt and lashed viciously at the last ball; he might have been bowled, he might have been stumped, he might have been caught; but none of these sad things happened. He made a complete miss: the ball shaved the off stump; the wicketkeeper fumbled it. Ted scrambled back.

'Steady, Ted; steady!' came the shriek of his young brother, timid to death of the family impatience.

Gauvinier took two nice fours in the next over, and then for the first time the idea entered his mind, anxious till that moment merely to make a decent show and avert disgrace, that they were well on the way towards winning the match! Heavens! They must be near one hundred and twenty now – very near. Curse it! He wished he hadn't realized it, and could just have gone steadily batting on. He finished the over, nervous as when he came out to bat: superstitious really.

Ted hit another four. Shouts of joy acclaimed the fact of his fifty. Then he took another dip, oh! a wild one! There was a nasty snick, slip dived forward, tossed up the ball. 127 – 3 – 52.

'Well played, Ted!' shouted Gauvinier, with a sinking in the stomach at the thought of how long and thin was the tail. Twelve runs – three fours, twelve runs – three fours beat rhythmically through his brain.

Tom Rutherford walked in, his face set, a trier every inch of ₥im. Good man. But the sun on his glasses; his sight not so good as it was.

leg-bye. They ran an easy one.

Marling had been put on. Gauvinier, strung up, had hardly noticed the change of bowling, and had not noticed at all the change of field. Came a medium-fast short one on the off – 'Here's one of them,' he thought; 'a gift,' and hit it full and strong, to look up as he ran forward, to find it travelling straight into the hands of extra cover. He stopped dead in surprise to watch the catch, a good one at the pace the ball was travelling, then walked miserably back to the pavilion, cursing his idiocy. Marling frankly rejoiced. 128 – 4 – 46. Jenkins took his place. Marling sent him down a fast yorker on the leg stump, which the ball shaved. The wicketkeeper side-stepped too late, kicked it: two runs. Jenkins waved his bat at the next ball and was bowled. 130 – 5 – 0. Oh, Lord! To be so near! Well, anyhow it was a damned good game.

'Fancy being such a fool as to beat it straight into his hands!' Gauvinier spoke to Heaven.

Longman was walking in. He had one shot and one only. A little half-step forward, a mighty circular lurch to leg: a good-length ball on the middle or leg stump hit the bat and went for four. At everything else he pushed his bat daintily sideways slowly and cunningly and always ineffectually.

Marling was taking no risks. He bowled a good-length ball on the leg stump – right on to the swinging bat, and, with astonishment, saw it go for four. Gauvinier began to laugh, almost hysterical with amusement and the game's thrill. Wild cheers rent the air. Another good-length ball hit the lurching bat, but not quite full this time, so that it missed the fieldsman, brought up after the last shot. He saved the four, though; and they ran two. Only three more! Only three more! But shortish ones on the off followed, at which Longman dabbed warily, and luckily, failed to touch.

The first ball of the next over beat Tom Rutherford all ends up and passed not more than one inch over the bails. At the second, anxious to make sure of the game, he lunged gallantly out, hit, skied, and was caught and bowled.

136 – 6.

Followed the boy, and all the fieldsmen crowded cruelly near. But all four balls he gamely managed to stop.

'Will he now, oh, will he bowl on his bat?' Gauvinier ached to think, watching, with horror, Marling place another man on the leg side.

It is difficult for any bowler to realize that a man can have one shot and one only like a mechanical toy. Down came the good-length ball on the middle stump – hit the swinging bat, flew between the fieldsmen – struck the wall.

Too late Marling realized his mistake. He sent a slow, high full toss, an absolutely fatal ball to Longman, who tried to pat it with his bat as with a tennis racket, and was bowled.

But the impossible had happened. Tillingfold with eight men and a boy had beaten Wilminghurst, after a hundred had stood on the score-board, for the first time in the annals of Tillingfold cricket, for no wickets.

*from* THE GAME OF THE SEASON *1933*

# Herecombe v. Therecombe

## HERBERT FARJEON

Sharp practice in our national game is probably a good deal
more common than most Englishmen would care to admit.
Although it is true that the other side is seldom openly accused
of cheating, there can be hardly a pavilion in the country which
has not at some time in its existence creaked with dark whis-
perings against the impartiality of umpires from men who have
been given out lbw, or against the honour of wicket-keepers
from men who cannot bring themselves to believe that such a
ball could possibly have hit the stumps. League cricket in
particular produces complaints from batsmen who are convinced that they are not really so much bowled or caught or
stumped as tricked out. Yet I question whether any match has
ever been conducted in a more thoroughly unsportsmanlike
manner than a certain officially 'friendly' match between the old-
world villages of Herecombe and Therecombe. In the annals of
the game it will, I imagine, stand for all time as the only match
in which, although there was not a drop of rain, although play
continued uninterrupted through the whole afternoon, and
although both sides had a knock, only two balls were bowled.
That, I feel sure, must be one of the most remarkable of all the
records unchronicled in the pages of *Wisden*.

Herecombe and Therecombe were old antagonists. For some
reason, as irrelevant as it is mysterious, there was no love lost
between them. The Feud, I believe, went deeper (if anything
can) than cricket. But after the sensational tie in which a Herecombe batsman, backing up, was run out before the delivery of
the ball, and a Therecombe batsman, politely rolling the ball
back to the bowler, was successfully appealed against for
'handling', small wonder that each side vowed to win the next
encounter by hook or crook. And small wonder, perhaps, that

even the winning of the toss by Herecombe was viewed by Therecombe with deep suspicion.

The Herecombe captain elected to bat. Of course, he had no idea when he marched to the wicket to open the innings that it would be over in one ball. It was an astonishing ball, striking a flint – the ground was like that – and skidding at right angles to square leg.

The Herecome captain slashed at it, missed it, was dumb-founded, and audibly ejaculated 'Well, I declare!' Everybody on the ground heard him, including the Therecombe captain. And the Therecombe captain was not slow to sieze his oppor-tunity.

'Come along, boys!' shouted the Therecombe captain, and made for the pavilion. His boys followed him. Nobody, with the exception of the Therecombe captain knew quite what was happening. An explanation was demanded. The explanation was given.

'Didn't your captain say he declared?' asked the Therecombe captain. 'Very well, then. Us to bat, boys, and one run to win!'

A heated discussion ensued. Everybody called everybody else a dirty swindler. Threats were levelled, fists were shaken. The umpires read the Laws of Cricket through three times. In the end they decided that the Herecombe captain had in-escapably, if unintentionally, declared. The Herecombe team thereupon proposed to chuck it.

But suddenly the light of battle glinted in the eye of the Herecombe captain.

'All right,' he said to the Therecombe captain, 'we're game! You go in and win if you can!'

Then he led his men on to the field, handed the ball to little Smith, who had never bowled in a match in his life but who had once won a local Marathon race, and whispered a few words of command in his ear.

The Therecombe batsmen came out. The umpire called 'Play!' Little Smith began a long, zig-zag run up to the wicket. But before Little Smith reached the bowling-crease a queer thing happened. He doubled back. Then, like a dog after its tail, he began running in circles.

What, gasped the spectators, was up with little Smith? Had he gone stark, staring mad? There he was – turning and twisting – twisting and turning – darting this way and that – hopping, skipping, jumping – a most eccentric run, indeed – but never delivering the ball.

'Hi!' growled the Therecombe batsman, 'what's your bowler think he's doing?'

'Oh,' drawled the Herecombe captain, grinning, 'just playing out time, you know, playing out time –'

So that was it! Another heated discussion now arose. Crowds congregated round the umpires, who read the Laws of Cricket all over again, while little Smith kept on running. But they could find nothing in the Laws of Cricket limiting the length of a bowler's run. Apparently a bowler could run all day before delivering the ball, and apparently he meant to.

Hour after hour little Smith kept up his capering – a noble effort – the batsman sternly refusing to leave the wicket lest he should be bowled in his absence. The fieldsmen lay down at full length on the ground. Spectators went away and then came back again, to find little Smith still running. Longer and longer grew his shadow as the sun travelled into the west. The clock on the old church tower chimed five, then six, then seven.

And now a new point of discussion arose. It had been agreed that at seven o'clock stumps should be drawn. But was it legal to draw stumps in the middle of a ball? The umpires got together again and, after much cogitation, decided that it would not be legal.

Then things became really exciting.

Little Smith shouted that if that was so, then dang him if he would deliver the ball till it was pitch dark. Still the batsman stood grimly on guard, determined if possible to make a winning swipe when the chance came at last. Again the spectators departed – this time for supper. Again they returned – this time under a harvest moon.

And there were the fieldsmen still lying on the grass, there was the batsman still standing at the wicket, and there was little Smith, still running.

At ten o'clock came the climax. It was dark. The moon had disappeared behind a cloud. Half a dozen of the fieldsmen had taken up positions beside the wicket-keeper behind the stumps to prevent an untimely bye. Little Smith let fly.

The Therecombe batsman screwed up his eyes to pierce the gloom. He struck. He missed.

'Match drawn!' shouted the Herecombe captain.

It was not quite the end. During his long vigil, the batsman had been doing a bit of thinking. He now protested that if stumps could not be drawn in the middle of a ball neither could they be drawn in the middle of an over. The umpires started to consider the latest point. But while they were debating, the Herecombe captain put an end to doubt by appealing against the light – a rare thing indeed for a fielding side to do – the umpires allowed the appeal, and the game was over.

Whether the umpires were right in all their rulings may be open to question. I think they were. In any case, it must be conceded that they had some very knotty points to solve, and that on the whole they appear to have discharged their duties conscientiously.

*from* HERBERT FARJEON'S CRICKET BAG *1946*

# A Question of Policy

## IAN PEEBLES

Mr Dumble was seated comfortably on the heavy roller as the member came round the corner of the pavilion. If he had any qualms at being surprised in this attitude of repose he gave no sign. Having acquired several extra stones since his glorious days as England's and Loamshire's fast bowler, he was neither physically nor temperamentally prone to the guilty start.

'Evenin',' he said, affably, waving his pipe in answer to the member's greeting. 'Just havin' a look at things. Great mistake to overwork turf at this time o' year.'

It occurred to the member that as long as Mr Dumble was groundsman to Redthorne Cricket Club they should be fairly free from the fashionable accusation of over-prepared pitches. As it hardly seemed tactful to say so at this particular moment, he handed him his evening paper.

'I see they've made your old skipper President of the County,' he said.

'Aye,' said Mr Dumble, studying the announcement. 'He's a great man, is Mr Borrington. Though he were a rare green 'un when he coom to us first, straight from a fine public school and the University. You can guess he didn't know nowt, not t'in-swinger from leg-break.'

'He must have come on a lot since then,' said the member, thinking of the long list of honours and directorships which an admiring Press had printed in full.

'Aho aye,' replied Mr Dumble. 'It were wunnerful the way he coom on when he got in with us chaps. Very keen to learn he was, and though he were a bit younger than meself we were soon close friends. He learns so much about game and all, that when they makes me 'ead pro they makes 'im skipper.'

'He was a pretty good one, was he not?' the member asked.

'He were that' allowed the great man. 'Though he were a bit

full of 'igh falutin' notions and wot he calls strategy. I had to keep him straight most times, but when things came right he always thought he 'ad doon it, and of course I never let on.'

Mr Dumble relit his pipe and chuckled in such a satisfied manner that the fob on his ample paunch bobbled up and down like a dottle of cream on a jelly.

'I mind the time,' he said, 'when we takes Championship from Bailshire. We're neck and neck all season and when we coom to play them at 'ome everything depends on t'match; whoever wins that wins Championship. Unfortunately at same time theers Test Match and selectors take most of their batters, but all our regular bowlers, bar meself, so we're in a proper tangle.

'When team's announced I'm sitting in saloon bar of local with Mr Borrington, having an 'arf pint. Mr Borrington reads through list and works himself into a fine state.

' "Dick," he says, slapping t'paper. "It's plain barefaced robbery, that's wot it is. They've took all our bowlers and left me with a broken-down old cab 'orse, and a couple of school-boys."

' "Maybe you'll get a bowl yourself this match," I says.

' "This is no time for silly jokes," he says, very testy. "It'll cost us Championship."

' "Not if our skipper has one o' them brain waves," I says, soothin' him. "It'll coom right."

' "That it will," he says, brightening up a bit. "It's brains wot wins matches, Dick. You leave it to your old skipper, he'll get you through."

'He takes a pull at his tankard and sits looking so wise that at first I thinks beer must be a bit orf. I'm just finding out when he gives table such a thoomp that it takes me a couple o' minutes to cough my 'arf pint out of me loongs.

' "Pull yourself together, Doomble," he says, "and listen. Match is already in t'bag."

'I've heard this 'un afore so I just dries me eyes and says nowt.

' "You know this young Jack Castor who cooms in for Joe Blackburn," he says. "I hear he's best thrower in t'country."

' "Aye," I says, "he can throw, and, as a matter of fact, he's next door in t'four ale bar."

' "Then fetch him in," says skipper. "As he's my chosen instrument of victory he'd best be in at start."

'So I fetches Jack in and he says "Good evenin' " very polite and sits down.

' "Young man," says skipper, turning to 'im like he was his grandpa about to leave 'im a million quid, "you're going to win Championship for County."

' "Yessir," says young Jack, very confused. "Certainly, sir."

' "Now, gentlemen," says skipper, very solemn, "what is the chief problem what confronts us in this coming Bailshire match? I will tell you," he says. "It is Jim Buckle, a bit old for Test Match, but still best player they have got and maybe best in England. Get him out and with four of their regulars out of side there's only their skipper, old 'Shellback' Macsnayle, and we can keep him quiet."

' "Can our knock-kneed attack get Jim Buckle out?" he says. "No. Therefore we must apply strategy. So you, Jack will throw left-handed or lob underhand right through the match, until they takes one every time the ball is struck to you. But when I give you the pass-word 'Let her go' you whips her in like a bullet. This will likely be early in their second innings and with a bit of luck, Jim Buckle will be about half-way down pitch."

'Skipper looks so triumphant-like at this that I thinks he'll fall out of 'imself, but Jack is a bit took aback.

' "Wot will our chaps think about it, sir?" he says.

' "Tell 'em you've busted your arm," I says, "and you'll never throw again."

' "That's right," says skipper. "But if you breathe a word of wot's been said 'ere we'll saw your bat in two and sell you to Australia as practice bowler."

' "Yessir," says Jack, and off he goes looking as if he'd just been hit on't thumb by 'arold Larwood.

'I sits on talking to skipper and I says to 'im Jim Buckle is one of t'nicest, kindest men wot ever took middle and leg. But old Macsnayle's 'eart of stone has got hardened with ten years as local manager of the "Straight Bat" Insurance Company. Couldn't we roon him out instead?

' "No, Dick," says skipper. "We must be above sentiment in this case. Knock away keystone," he says, "and down cooms bridge."

'Well, match goes pretty normal until third day. We wins toss and makes 253 and they make 327. Second innings we makes 223 so its pretty critical when they start last innings just about midday. Jim Buckle, who's made hundred first innings, cooms in first with old "Shellback," and soon they've got 30 on't board, going very nice. Every time they 'its ball to Jack Castor at extra they takes one, and Jack lobs ball back very gentle. It's very hard on 'im with crowd jeering and he feels reet silly. Our captain's at short fine leg and he keps  shouting at 'im to keep up pretence and winking at 'im to keep up his spirits.

'Presently Mr Macsnayle pushes ball to Jack and says "Coom on, Jim, always one 'ere." He starts down pitch and skipper yells "Let er go."

'Jack picks 'er up and wot with rage and rest he surpasses himself. I hardly sees ball but I sees batsmen in't middle of pitch so I knows everything's going to be fine.

'And it would have been fine if skipper hadn't of forgot to warn wicket keeper. He, poor man, is on his 'eels, expecting another lob. He just sees ball in time to' give a yelp of 'orror and spring smartly to one side. But skipper just behind 'im is theer to stop it, which he does with 'is mid-rift. He makes a noise like someone treading on't bulb 'orn, and folds up like a jack knife.

'We roons to help 'im but he looks pretty bad so theer's nowt for it but to cart 'im off. He's had most of the breath knocked out of 'im but what's left is so 'ot that we have to warn him when we're passing Ladies' Stand.

'Dr Broom, one of our Committee, is in't dressing room and he chases everyone out except myself.

' "He's winded very bad," he says, when he's had a look.

"But there's nowt broke and he'll be all right. Still, we'd better get 'im off home."

'So we gets an old shutter and lays 'im on it and covers him with blanket. Meantime, I've doon a bit o' thinkin'.

'You know, Doctor,' I says, " I think it might be in't best interests of Club if you refused to make any statement for the present."

'He looks at me very sharp.

' "I think I knows my own business best," he says. Then he looks again.

' "Maybe you are right," he says.

'So we send for a couple of strong chaps to carry him out to President's car what's parked behind and starts out. They wants to take 'im out back way but I says stairs are a bit steep so it will be safer round front. To save him any embarrassment from vulgar spectators I pulls blanket over his 'ead and tells 'im to keep quiet. Then as it's a hot day I takes my cap off and walks behind with it in my hand.

'Theer's a terrible hush as we pass by and, wot with people in front getting up to have a look, soon everyone's on their feet and, may be because of the heat, most follow my example and take their 'ats off too. We gets 'im snug in't car and just before he goes off he pops his 'ead out of blanket, very depressed.

' "That's torn it proper," he says, "That ruddy Jim will get another oondred and win match, blast 'im."

'Well, I goes back on't field where play's been stopped and Jim Buckle cooms up to me.

' "We sees him carried orf?" he says, very white. "Did he – is he really –?"

'I just looks sad at ground.

' "Let's get on with match," I says.

' "I don't feel much like it," says Jim. "I think we should stop."

' "Jim," I says, putting my hand on his shoulder. "Just afore he was took orf he talked of you. He would like you to go on."

'Jim turns back to crease, wiping 'is eyes, and Mr Macsnayle cooms to me in a terrible state.

' "Wot's this about 'is being took orf?" he says, very agitated. "He's as strong as an 'orse, dammit."

' "Mr Macsnayle," I says to 'im, very stern, "this is no time for such words. Let us get on with game."

'But I'm baffled to see him so upset and feel sorry I've misjudged him in't past.

' "Give me the ball," I says to bowler. "I'm going on meself."

'Well, first straight ball hits Jim's middle stump and in cooms their last real hope, a good batter named Sams. He hits first ball to Jack Castor and starts to roon.

' "Get back, you stupid fool," yells Mr Macsnayle, beside 'imself. In his emotion he calls Sams every rogue he can lay his tongue to, and soon neither knows whether its leg stump or t'Oval pavilion. Sam 'its next ball to same place and this time he's too confused to hear Mr Macsnayle, and he's roon out by length of pitch.

'While he's waiting for t'next batter Mr Macsnayle's walking round in circles, laffing, and cursing and biting bat 'andle. Next over he's out to worst stroke of 'is life and there's an end on't. They make 74, and most of them is byes, as our wicket-keeper acts very apprehensive and starts dodgin' out of road of ball.

'When I changes and goes into Bailshire dressing room atmosphere seems very strained. Jim Buckle asks me wot about skipper, and I tells him that he's out of danger and like as not when he hears score he'll make a complete recovery. Wot with everyone opening 'is mouth to say summat that won't coom out, place looks like bowl of goldfish, but old "Shellback" Macsnayle cooms oop trumps.'

' "I'm delighted to 'ear it, Doomble," he says. "Please congratulate him from me."

'Well, I gets on't bicycle and goes up to skipper's house, where Mrs Borrington let's me in.

' "Wounded hero's sitting oop in't bed doing fine," she says "Go straight in."

' "Hullo, Dick," says skipper, as I cooms round door. "What happened, I suppose we lost?"

' "No, we did not," I says. "We woon. But first, how's yourself?"

' "We woon!" he says. "Well, I'm fine, just fine, but," he says, "I'll carry trade mark of Seam & Co., ball makers, on me tum for rest of me days. Tell us about match."

'So I tells 'im what happens and how some people seem to misunderstand, and think he must be worse than is the case.

' "But there's one thing baffles me," I says, "and that is why Mr Macsnayle was so upset at time, and so reet glad to hear you was all right."

' "I'm very touched indeed," says skipper.

' "Well," I says, "either he's had a change of 'eart or we've misjudged him cruel in't past."

' "You may be right," says skipper. "On t'other hand, it might be summat to do with my first born in March last."

' " 'Ow could that have anything to do with it?" I says. "D'ye mean he's that fond of children?"

' "No, not quite," says skipper. "But when young George is born old 'Shellback' writes me a nice letter congratulating me, and saying that as a family man I'll no doubt want to make provision for the future. The enclosed form, he says, will show that as a fit man of 29, for £100 a year the Straight Bat Insurance Company will insure me for £10,000 payable at my death. It seems so generous that, with the help of Aunt Aggie, I pays the first premium right away."

'He gives 'is tummy a rub.

' "Well, there you are," he says. "I told you your old skipper would get you through." ' '

*from* BATTER'S CASTLE *1957*

# The Average Match

## REX WARNER

The Average cricket eleven were to play that afternoon against their old rivals, the neighbouring village of Fancy-under-Edge, a solid enough combination of players who had in the past at least held their own among the village teams of the district. It was, indeed, said that Fancy-under-Edge owed much of its success to its own umpire, Mr Clear, whose decisions had often appeared unorthodox, but had always been to the benefit of his own side. Such a reputation had caused some pain on many occasions to Major Feather, the captain, but he was powerless to control Mr Clear, partly because he had always been umpire, partly because it was on Mr Clear that he himself relied for his supplies of unrationed meat. On this occasion he had, however, cautioned the umpire in the bus. 'For God's sake, Clear,' he had said, 'don't give young Average out l.b.w. It will look bad.' Mr Clear had replied noncommittally, 'When a man's in he's in, but after he's out, he's a goner.'

The bus arrived late, and now no time was wasted. Sir Fielding won the toss and sent his own side in to bat. First, however, he communicated to his two opening batsmen, Mr Darcy and Mr Lord, the instructions which he habitually gave to them and which were never obeyed. 'Just take the edge of the bowling,' said Sir Fielding, 'and then open out a bit.'

Mr Darcy and Mr Lord looked at each other. Their faces expressed both pity and insubordination. Neither Mr Darcy nor Mr Lord had ever 'opened out a bit' and neither was likely to do so. They had only one standard by which to measure the merit of an innings, and that was its actual duration in time. The scoring of runs was, to them, something wholly incidental and in fact often to be deplored. For when their eyes were 'in' they would meet each ball steadily with the centre of the bat and propel it gently back to the bowler. It was only when they had failed to master the attack that a ball might glance from the edge of the bat towards some unprotected portion of the field. They would then feel compelled to run, but as they ran, they were conscious that this was not what they had intended to do.

'You see,' said Sir Fielding, 'I can't possibly declare by five o'clock unless we've got 150 on the board.'

Mr Darcy and Mr Lord made no comment. In Sir Fielding's position they would never under any circumstances have declared an innings closed. Victory to them meant the denial of it to the other side.

Sir Fielding, though he knew that his words were in vain, repeated them once more and then made his way to the pavilion. As he approached it Mrs Helpless rose to intercept him, but he nimbly eluded her by stepping to the other side of his wife's chair. He then plunged through the door of the pavilion and locked himself in the scoring box. Mrs Helpless made as though to follow him but Lady Average laid a restraining hand upon her arm. 'Leave him alone now, dear,' she said. 'I think he's doing some sort of accounts.'

'But he will come back again, won't he?' said Mrs Helpless, staring about her wildly.

'He will have to come out,' said Lady Average, 'when it is his turn to go and hit the ball.'

'But will he be hitting it for a long time?'

'No, not for long,' said Lady Average.

Mrs Helpless sighed. 'Oh well!' she said, as she sat down again.

'Shall I go on?' said Lady Average.

'Oh, please do. You were just telling me about what he looked like in his sailor suit.'

The ladies resumed their conversation, which was interrupted from time to time by the appearances and disappearances of Miss Parkinson whose patrol had now taken the form of slow circlings of the pavilion.

Meanwhile, Sir Fielding and others were watching the opening over of the day. It was Mr Darcy who first confronted the fast bowling of Fancy-under-Edge. His stance might have reminded one of some great boulder which stands impervious to the motion of wind and water, and he made no move of any kind as the first two balls flashed past him, one outside his leg and one outside his off stump. The third ball pitched short and hit him violently on the shoulder. There was an immediate appeal from the bowler, an appeal which was somewhat embarrassing to Mr Clear, the umpire, who, as it happened, had not observed this ball, since his attention had been occupied with a cock pheasant under the trees at the further end of the ground. Mr Clear began automatically to raise his hand, but, unfortunately for the batsman, Major Feather was close enough to the umpire to make himself heard.

'I say, Clear,' he said, 'you know that one hit him on the shoulder.'

Mr Clear, with his gesture interrupted, stared fiercely at Mr Darcy, who glowered back at him. Finally, a gracious look appeared on the umpire's face. 'Not out,' he said and Mr Darcy defiantly replied: 'I should say not.'

The next ball hit Mr Darcy in about the same place and at about the same speed. There was another appeal, and this time even more hesitation from the umpire before he reached the conclusion that Mr Darcy was not out. However, he consoled the bowler by whispering to him: 'He's had two chances. Next time he's a goner.'

But Mr Clear did not have to redeem his pledge. Though Mr Darcy remained as immovable as ever when the next ball was bowled, the ball did not hit him. It hit his wicket and his brief innings was over.

His place was taken by Teddy Average, who played the first ball he received firmly past the bowler and called for a run. But here he was reckoning without Mr Lord, who was not used to taking runs in the first over of the day and, after the dismissal of his colleague, was even more averse from the idea of any kind of risk. Teddy was more than half-way down the pitch before he realized that Mr Lord would, under no circumstances, move. He hurried back to his own crease, just reaching it in time. It was fortunate for him that it was not Mr Clear who was called upon to decide whether or not he was run out.

After this unsteady opening, the fortunes of Average revived, and runs came quickly, except at the periods when Mr Lord was batting. At the end of half an hour Sir Fielding was looking complacently at the scoring book which read:

| | |
|---|---|
| Darcy, bowled Bragg | o |
| Lord, not out | o |
| Average, E., not out | 50 |
| Extras | 10 |

Sir Fielding cautiously descended the ladder that led from the scoring box to the interior of the pavilion. He wished to discuss with other members of the team the brilliant innings now being played by his son. He found, however, that he was still trapped. Mrs Helpless's chair was firmly planted in the doorway, and Mrs Helpless herself was still listening intently to the narrative of Lady Average, which had now reached the period of her husband's residence at the university. Beyond the two ladies' heads Sir Fielding could see at some distance away a group consisting of Bloom, Damp, Boo and Briggs. He looked in vain for Colonel Bracer and for the Canon and his nephew. It occurred to him that he might be able to climb out by a small back window, and he moved, again with great caution, in the direction of one of the two lower rooms into which the pavilion was divided.

The door of this room was open and facing the door was the small window through which Sir Fielding was minded to make his escape. Here too, however, he found himself thwarted, for, glued against the lower pane of the window and bearing a look of the most extreme concentration, was the face of Miss Parkinson. Sir Fielding, like one who has seen a snake in the grass before his feet, stepped back hurriedly, placing himself out of reach of those observant eyes. Now, sheltered from the view of Miss Parkinson by the half-open door, he was still able to see into the interior of the room and he was surprised at what he saw. Colonel Bracer was sitting stiffly on the top of a locker where the pads were kept. His face was extraordinarily grim as he stared at George Breather who stood rigidly to attention in front of him. What perplexed Sir Fielding even more than the unusual attitudes of the two men was the fact that they appeared to be speaking in some foreign language.

'Wieviel Buchstaben hat das Alphabet?' said George as though he was imparting a piece of information.

'Ausfahrt!' replied the Colonel contemptuously.

'Ihre Huhner waren drei,' George continued.

Sir Fielding was amazed to observe a look of extreme anger on the Colonel's face as he pounded the locker with one fist: 'Umleitung,' he shouted.

As though attempting patiently to explain George pronounced the words, 'jedes legt noch schnell ein Ei, und dann kommt der Tod herbei.'

The Colonel appeared slightly mollified. 'Willamovitz Moellendorf,' he replied.

'Zumpt,' said George and saluted.

'Look here,' said the Colonel in English. 'Zumpt is one of mine.'

At this point Sir Fielding, half in alarm and half in curiosity, entered the room. So startled had he been by the appearance and language of his two friends that for the moment he had forgotten about Miss Parkinson, but as he moved forward he saw that lady quickly remove her face from the window. His first impulse was to exclude the intruder and he crossed the room with the intention of shutting the upper pane of glass. As he reached the window he saw Miss Parkinson's figure bowed low, scuttling out of sight behind a corner of the pavilion. He saw that she was carrying a notebook in her hand.

In great bewilderment he turned back to the room and was the more bewildered to find George and the Colonel sitting together on the locker and laughing helplessly. Through his laughter the Colonel said, 'You had no right to say "Zumpt".'

'I'm sorry,' said George, 'but I thought it would go well with the salute.'

'What on earth were you doing?' said Sir Fielding.

'A conversation in German,' said George.

'Never knew you knew the lingo, Bracer,' said Sir Fielding.

'I know a few road signs,' said the Colonel modestly, 'and I can remember the names of some German scholars who used to come into textbooks at school. That's why George had no right to say "Zumpt".'

'Well,' said George, 'now for a spot of Russian. That's a good deal harder, because I don't know any at all.'

Sir Fielding was mystified, but he preferred to proceed slowly. 'Miss Parkinson,' he said, 'was listening to your conversation.'

His news was greeted with laughter. 'We know,' said the Colonel, and 'That was the point,' said George.

'You mean,' said Sir Fielding slowly, 'that this is some kind of a joke.'

'Would you mind,' George asked, 'being the Shah of Persia, if it was absolutely necessary?'

Sir Fielding, still mystified, was beginning to consider this proposition when they were disturbed by the noise of clapping from outside the pavilion. 'Good heavens!' said Sir Fielding, 'I hope that doesn't mean that Teddy's out. Go and find out, will you. You see, there's that woman outside.'

George left the room and soon returned with the news that Teddy was still in, having scored seventy runs by this time. It was Mr Lord who had been given out leg-before-wicket.

Colonel Bracer was next man in, but, in Sir Fielding's view, the Colonel, who was still chuckling to himself over this in-comprehensible joke, was not yet in a fit state of mind to go to the wicket. 'I think,' he said, 'that if you don't mind, Bracer, I'll take a knock myself now. What we want to do now is to push the score along.'

While Sir Fielding began to put on his pads George and the Colonel looked cautiously at each other. Their looks implied that in their opinion the desired end was most likely to be achieved by their captain. 'I'd better be getting my pads on, too,' said the Colonel. 'I mean just in case.'

'And I'd better start on the Russian,' said George, 'before it's my turn to go in.'

'I shall declare,' said Sir Fielding, 'at a hundred and fifty.' He then, after having rather scampered than walked past Mrs Helpless's chair, proceeded in a dignified way to the wicket. He would have been sorry to have known that his appearance was producing an excellent effect on the morale of Fancy-under-Edge. Indeed, his opponents had had little so far to encourage them. Teddy had been dealing with their bowling almost as he liked. Mr Lord, though he had only scored three runs, had appeared impregnably set in his position and would indeed still have been there had any other umpire except Mr Clear been called upon to answer the appeal for leg-before-wicket. Eighty-four runs for one wicket had looked bad, but it was now eighty-four for two, and, in the confident opinion of every player, it would soon be eighty-four for three. Major Feather spoke to the bowler Bragg. 'Just send him down a straight one,' he said. 'That's all you've got to do.' Bragg looked gleefully at the approaching victim. For nearly the entire innings he had been bowling maiden overs at Mr Lord. His average so far was good, and he saw every prospect of improving it.

Meanwhile Sir Fielding was entering into a short consultation with his son. 'Anything special about the bowling?' he enquired, and Teddy replied: 'Nothing special, but don't get hit anywhere or they'll give you out l.b.w.

'I shall play myself in,' said Sir Fielding gravely, 'for an over or two. Then I think we might open out.'

Teddy had himself, as the score showed, been 'opening out' ever since the beginning of his innings, but he made no comment other than a smile on his father's plan of campaign.

Sir Fielding took guard, looked slowly and deliberately round the field, and prepared to face the remaining balls of Bragg's over. He followed strictly the policy which he had laid down for himself and played a defensive stroke to the first ball. It was a stroke which, in all respects but one, might have served as a model for all young cricketers. The bat was perfectly straight, the feet were firmly planted, the elbow was pushed well forward. Nothing, in fact, was wrong except for the actual position of the bat in space. The ball went past the bat and hit the wicket. Sir Fielding was aware of some derisive cheers which proceeded from a party of supporters of Fancy-under-Edge, who were sitting on the grass near their bus. He could also hear from the pavilion a shrill scream which he knew was uttered by Mrs Helpless. He turned slowly and retraced his steps. As he approached the pavilion, Mrs Helpless rose to her feet. 'How lovely,' she said, 'that you're out. Now you can come and talk to us.' She advanced towards him with outstretched arms.

Sir Fielding broke into a run and his sudden access of speed enabled him to dodge past her. 'Just a minute,' he said, 'while I get my pads off.' He re-entered the pavilion, brushed aside the commiserations of Colonel Bracer who was now ready to go in, and, after removing his pads, climbed out through the small window at the back.

\*    \*    \*

'Marriage,' said Mrs Helpless, 'is such a very lovely thing. I think I really like it best.' She fixed her eyes dreamily upon Sir Fielding, who once more retreated behind his wife's chair.

'Well, this really is nice,' said Lady Average. 'Now we can tell everybody. Teddy will be so pleased. I wish he'd come back. He's been there a long time now and he must be very tired of hitting that ball about. His poor father didn't hit it at all. They call that a "duck" you know, but I don't know why.'

Sir Fielding ignored the comment on his own batting. 'Wait a minute,' he said. 'Teddy's got the bowling. Must see him get his century.'

So fervent was the tone of Sir Fielding's voice that the others remained silent and for a moment or two turned their eyes towards the cricket match. The fieldsmen were spread out along the boundaries as Teddy prepared to receive the first ball of an over from Major Feather. The ball was a long-hop and Teddy hit it high and straight over the bowler's head. Sir Fielding immediately lost sight of the ball. 'Is it a catch?' he inquired urgently, and George reassured him, beginning at the same time to clap. 'It's a six all the way,' he said. Sure enough, though the boundary was a long one, the ball soared over it, hitting the top branches of an oak tree. The fielder on the boundary ran back and waited expectantly below the tree. He caught the ball in his hands as it bounced down from branch to branch. Both players and spectators began to clap in appreciation of the century which Teddy had scored. Teddy himself raised his bat and then began to prepare for the next ball. He, and indeed everyone else, was surprised to hear from the umpire Mr Clear a triumphant shout of 'Out!' The umpire was leaning forward from the waist and one arm was stretched out in a condemnatory gesture towards the batsman.

Teddy remained still in a momentary astonishment. 'Look here,' Major Feather expostulated. 'It was a six, and besides nobody appealed.'

'When I say "out",' said the umpire doggedly, 'then out it is.'

'But that six gave him his century,' said Major Feather.

Mr Clear considered for a moment. He decided to be generous. 'He can have the runs,' he said, 'but out he must go.'

'This isn't cricket,' said Major Feather. He turned to Teddy. 'Jolly sorry about this,' he remarked, and indeed he was in a dilemma. An open quarrel with Mr Clear would seriously affect his supply of meat for the week-end.

Meanwhile, Mr Clear stuck to his point. 'Out is out,' he said.

Teddy did his best to relieve the tension. 'Suppose I was to retire,' he suggested.

Mr Clear considered the proposal. It seemed to him to possess every advantage, satisfying honour on both sides. 'Out, retired,' he pronounced.

'Jolly decent of you, Average,' said Major Feather, greatly

relieved. Teddy smiled and proceeded towards the pavilion, where he was received with an ovation from his own side and from the spectators.

While Inspector Bruch was attempting the almost impossible task of eliciting the truth from Mrs Helpless, and while Miss Parkinson was occupied in her counter-measures, the cricket match had continued and by the early evening had reached an interesting state. Matters had not gone at all as Sir Fielding had expected and his declaration had never been made. Indeed the whole side had added very few runs after the enforced retirement of Teddy. Colonel Bracer, after scoring a dozen runs and appearing well set, had been given out, caught at the wicket. Not even the wicket-keeper himself had appealed for this catch, but the bowler Bragg had not hesitated to do so, justly confident as he was in the support that would be forthcoming from the umpire, Mr Clear. George was the next to go. He had been following his captain's instructions and, in attempting to score fast, had been caught, perfectly fairly, in the deep field. On returning to the pavilion he had been delighted to find that Miss Parkinson had gone and he had sat down with Teddy and Lucinda, amusing them with an account of how he had been able to further their interests.

As the wickets fell the enthusiasm and confidence of Fancy-under-Edge increased. At the time when Teddy had hit the six into the oak tree, their prospects had appeared indeed hopeless, but after the timely intervention of umpire Clear the game had begun to swing in their favour. Of the recognized Average batsmen only Damp and Canon Breather were left. But for Damp this was a day of misfortune. He immediately succeeded, by making a faulty call, in running the Canon out and was so overcome by the consciousness of his error that he allowed himself to be bowled by the very next ball. Briggs was in the police station and unable to bat. Only Boo and Bloom remained, and though the negro batted with some skill, Bloom was valuable only as a bowler, being extremely shortsighted and

seldom capable of observing the flight of balls that were bowled
at him. After being hit several times about the body, he was
mercifully given out leg-before-wicket by Mr Clear, and the
Average innings was at an end. The record of the innings is as
follows:

| | |
|---|---:|
| Darcy, bowled Bragg | 0 |
| Lord, l.b.w., bowled Bragg | 3 |
| Average, E., retired | 100 |
| Average, Sir Fielding, bowled Bragg | 0 |
| Bracer, caught Snapper, bowled Bragg | 12 |
| Breather, G., caught Lumby, bowled Snagge | 4 |
| Breather, Canon, run out | 0 |
| Damp, bowled Snagge | 0 |
| Briggs, absent | 0 |
| Boo, not out | 3 |
| Bloom, l.b.w., bowled Bragg | 0 |
| Extras | 13 |
| | **135** |

Two and a half hours remained for cricket after tea. There
was thus plenty of time for Fancy-under-Edge to pass the
Average score. There was also plenty of incentive, and here not
only ancient rivalry and ambition, but also guilt and anger
played their parts. Remarks had been exchanged during the tea
interval which had embittered feelings on both sides and, as so
often happens in human affairs, the more guilty of the two sides
was the more indignant. Some, indeed, there were among the
eleven of Fancy-under-Edge who had felt shame at the conduct
of their umpire, but this feeling had not been strong enough to
admit of being expressed. Moreover, whatever might be thought
of Mr Clear, he had certainly put victory within their reach. So,
just as great Powers, after evident breaches of faith, plunge all
the more madly forward on their aggressive courses, the players
of Fancy-under Edge were spurred on rather than deterred by

their guilty consciences. And Mr. Clear himself, like Macbeth, having once committed himself to the powers of evil, was in no mood to turn back until final victory had been achieved.

It was with an air of resolution and confidence that the opening batsmen went to the wicket, and their confidence was increased when they observed that Sir Fielding Average was proposing to open the bowling himself, an action which correspondingly depressed the feelings of his own side. Sir Fielding, however, had, on theoretical grounds, reached the conclusion that few except the greatest batsmen would be able to survive his leg-trap, and was himself confident that his theory could not be demonstrated in practice. No evidence for his views, however, could be collected from his first over, since every ball was bowled rather wide of the off stump. The first two balls were hit with extreme violence towards Canon Breather at silly mid-off, and were fielded painfully and courageously. After this, it evidently occurred to the batsman that it would be more profitable to play the ball into the great undefended areas where the clergyman was not. Sixteen runs came easily off the last four balls of Sir Fielding's over.

Bloom, at the other end, was more successful. He bowled fast, and off his first ball the batsman gave a catch in the slips. Unfortunately, however, the catch went to Sir Fielding. The ball hit him hard upon the chest and dropped to the ground. Off the next ball Boo, who, in the absence of Briggs, was keeping wicket, appealed loudly for another catch. The appeal was immediately dismissed by Mr Clear. The next ball knocked the middle stump back. Bloom stood menacingly over the umpire as though challenging him to deny the evidence of his senses. Mr Clear hesitated, but the batsman was already on his way back to the pavilion. The next three balls were played carefully and correctly by Major Feather.

In his second over Sir Fielding bowled more accurately than before, yet still the leg-trap proved totally unavailing. Every ball was pitched on the leg stump, but every ball was short, and the batsman, to Sir Fielding's disgust, adopted exactly the methods which had previously been suggested by Lady Average. He stepped back from his wicket and cut every ball to the off boundary. Sir Fielding had conceded forty runs in two overs. There had been no occupation at all for any of the fielders in the leg trap. To the unorthodox methods of this batsman Sir Fielding had no answer and he reluctantly took himself off, inviting Damp to bowl in his place.

Still, however, the runs came steadily and still every appeal for leg-before-wicket was confidently rejected by Mr Clear. At the end of an hour eighty runs had been scored and only one wicket had fallen. Sir Fielding, though as a rule he was reluctant to share responsibility, now consulted with Colonel Bracer and with his son Teddy as to what tactics should be adopted. Colonel Bracer immediately suggested that Boo should be allowed to bowl and Teddy seconded the suggestion. Sir Fielding nodded his head. 'I might keep wicket myself,' he said. The other two looked dubiously at each other. Both saw the implications of the proposed action. There would be catches missed, there would be byes, but, on the other hand, Sir Fielding would at least be prevented from bowling himself. So, without ever making use of the word 'long-stop' they made it their business to persuade Sir Fielding to reorganize his field in such a way that while he himself kept wicket there were always two fieldsmen stationed almost directly behind him.

The new move was immediately successful. Boo brought to his task not only skill but a literally religious enthusiasm. There had been occasions in the past when, before beginning to bowl, he had knelt devoutly on the grass for his preliminary prayers, but having once found himself the object of ridicule for so doing, he had abandoned this practice, not wishing to bring religion into contempt. Now as he prepared to bowl and tossed the ball from one hand to the other, he pronounced softly to himself the words: 'O Great God, Thy servant Boo now bowls. If it be Thy will, let him take many wickets, or at least one or two. But only if it be Thy will. Strengthen also the feeble hands of Sir Average, so that there be no byes. Amen.'

After these supplications he began to bowl. Off his first ball Major Feather was caught in the slips. With the next ball he bowled Snapper, the wicket-keeper, and now the fielders began to cluster close about the bowler Bragg, who took guard carefully, determined, if possible, to prevent the hat trick. However, instead of meeting the ball with the middle of his bat, he just touched it with the edge and the catch went straight to Sir Fielding behind the wicket. 'How's that!' cried Sir Fielding, but the ball was not in his hands as he pronounced these words. It had hit him smartly on the thumb and been diverted in the direction of fine leg, where George Breather, plunging forward, made a brilliant catch an inch or two from the ground. The players surrounded Boo, clapped him on the back and expressed their congratulations. Boo grinned as he received them, but to himself he murmured: 'Save Thy servant, O Lord, from vainglory, or at least until the match is over.'

Boo's successes renewed the confidence of Average, and roused the emulation of Bloom, who had been bowling well throughout, though under the tremendous handicap of having the umpire Mr Clear at his end. Two wickets fell in his next over. One was clean bowled, the other was pronounced run out, a decision which was perhaps dubious, if looked at from the point of view of the particular case, but, as at any rate the umpire from Average considered, justified from a perspective of the game as a whole. Indeed the Average umpire, Mr Dulling, after having for some time viewed the monstrous decisions of Mr Clear with a high moral indignation, had in the end come to the conclusion that it would be impossible for the right cause to triumph, unless he were to adopt the same methods as his opponent. Moreover he was an innings and a half behind. He therefore had no hesitation in reaching his decision, which was approved by the whole of the Average team, except for Boo whose principles were of the highest.

Though two wickets had fallen in Bloom's over, the score of Fancy-under-Edge was increased by ten, all byes. Sir Fielding, on three occasions, had not only failed to stop the ball himself, but had prevented the two fieldsmen behind him from doing so by diverting its flight above their heads.

In the next half-hour more wickets fell, and still more runs were scored. It was now 120 for nine, but the resistance of the last pair of batsmen was both determined and effective. At one end the bowler Snagge was facing Bloom. Snagge did not lack courage and of his courage he now gave ample proof. Confident that he would never be given out leg-before-wicket by Mr Clear, he stepped in front of every straight ball, shielding his wicket now with legs, now with stomach, now with thigh. Every appeal from bowler or wicket-keeper was dismissed with equal contempt by Mr Clear. And in the case of balls that were off the wicket, Snagge was content to let them pass him without interference. Thus, though he never employed his bat at all, the score rose regularly in byes. Meanwhile at the other end a new-comer to Fancy-under-Edge, the dentist Mr Thrill, was playing a watchful and an accomplished innings. He realized that the combination of Snagge and Mr Clear was virtually unshakable by any bowler and was certain to yield runs, and so he contented himself with playing a mainly defensive game against the bowling of Boo. Occasionally he would score two runs, but never a single. Boo's skill failed to pierce his defences, and Boo's prayers remained unanswered.

Finally a point was reached when the visiting team needed only one run to equal the Average total. Mr Thrill had survived an extremely good over from Boo and it was now the turn of Bloom to bowl to Snagge. Both Snagge and Mr Clear were confident that victory was now in sight. A deep depression was settling on the Average players, since no over from Bloom so far had failed to yield at least two runs in byes. It was Canon Breather who, by precept and practice, transformed the situation, and gave to Average the victory it deserved. While passing Bloom on his way to his position at silly mid-on, the Canon had suggested to the bowler that it would be safer, in present circumstances to bowl much more slowly. It was not a course which Bloom liked to take, since his whole renown rested on his ability to bowl fast; and now, with Mr Clear at one end and Sir Fielding at the other, Bloom was both bewildered and disappointed. The Canon's advice seemed to him to be worth trying and he bowled a very slow and straight ball to Snagge. Snagge, now confident that his ordeal was nearly over, had been bracing himself to meet the shock of something much faster and was so greatly surprised to find his anticipation incorrect, that he forgot to take his bat out of the way. Off the bat the ball curved gently into the air and was caught with ease and certainty by Canon Breather. The players of Average watched the ball's trajectory with delight. It was a catch which might have gone to their captain and, had it done so, they would have felt very different emotions. But their delight was short-lived. No sooner had the Canon caught the ball firmly in his hands than a defiant shout came from Mr Clear, 'No-ball!' This time, however, the wickedness of the umpire was to go unrewarded. Mr Clear was to be frustrated by the Clergyman's fast-moving brain and nimble limbs. Snagge, partly in astonishment at what he had done, partly in a kind of enthusiastic gratitude to Mr Clear, had moved a few paces out of his crease and towards the umpire. Quick as lightning, the Canon threw down his wicket, aiming at the base of the stumps so that there would be no possibility of Sir Fielding's getting in the way. 'Out!' shouted Mr Dulling in a voice even louder than that of Mr Clear, and without bothering precisely to notice whether or not Snagge had returned to his crease. Virtue was rewarded and Average had won the match.

*from* ESCAPADE *1953*

# A Norfolk Visit

## L. P. HARTLEY

I have never voluntarily watched a cricket match since, but I realize that conditions at Brandham were exceptional: the Triminghams had always been interested in the game and Mr Maudsley carried on the tradition; we had a score-board, scoring-cards, white sheets, and a chalk line to mark the boundary. All these correct accessories gave the match the feeling of importance, of mattering intensely, which I required from life; had it been conducted in a slipshod manner I could not have taken the same interest in it. I liked existence to be simplified into terms of winning or losing, and I was a passionate partisan. I felt that the honour of the Hall was at stake, and that we could never lift our heads up if we lost. Most of the spectators, I imagined, were against us, being members of the village, or neighbouring villages; the fact that they applauded a good shot did not give me a sense of unity with them; had we worn rosettes or colours to distinguish us I could hardly have looked the other party in the eye, while I would willingly have clasped the hand of the biggest blackguard on our side.

Above all I was anxious that Lord Trimingham should do well, partly because he was our captain, and the word captain had a halo for me, partly because I liked him and enjoyed the sense of consequence his condescension gave me, and partly because the glory of Brandham Hall – its highest potentialities for a rhapsody of greatness – centred in him.

The first wicket fell for fifteen runs and he went in. 'Trimingham's a pretty bat,' Denys had said on more than one occasion; 'I grant you he's not so strong on the leg side; but he has a forcing stroke past cover point that's worthy of a county player and I very much doubt if even R. E. Foster can rival his late cuts. I very much doubt it.'

I watched him walk to the wicket with the unconscious

elegance of bearing that made such a poignant contrast with his damaged face; the ceremony of taking centre – actually he asked for middle and leg – a novelty in those days – had its awful ritual solemnity. And he did give us a taste of his quality. The beautiful stroke past cover point reached the boundary twice; the late cut, so fine it might have been a snick, skimmed past the wicket, and then came a bumping ball on the leg stump – looking dangerous as it left the bowler's hand – and he was out, having added only eleven to our score.

A round of applause, subdued and sympathetic and more for him than for his play, greeted his return. I joined in the muted clapping and, averting my eyes, muttered 'Bad luck, sir,' as he came by; so what was my surprise to see Marian applauding vigorously, as for the hero of a century; and her eyes were sparkling as she lifted them to his. He answered with a twisted look that served him as a smile. Can she be mocking him? I wondered. Is it another joke? I didn't think so; it was just that, being a woman, she didn't know what cricket was.

Further disasters followed; five wickets down for fifty-six. These Boers in their motley raiment, triumphantly throwing the ball into the air after each kill, how I disliked them! The spectators disposed along the boundary, standing, sitting, lying, or propped against trees, I imagined to be animated by a revolutionary spirit, and revelling in the downfall of their betters. Such was the position when Mr Maudsley went in. He walked stiffly and stopped more than once to fumble with his gloves. I suppose he was fifty but to me he seemed hopelessly old and utterly out of the picture: it was as though Father Time had come down with his scythe to take a turn at the wicket. He left behind a whiff of office hours and the faint trail of gold so alien to the cricket field. Gnome-like he faced the umpire and responded to his directions with quick, jerky movements of his bat. His head flicked round on his thin lizard neck as he took in the position of the field. Seeing this, the fielders rubbed their hands and came in closer. Suddenly I felt sorry for him with the odds so heavily against him, playing a game he was too old for,

trying to look younger than he was. It was as though an element
of farce had come into the game and I waited resignedly for his
wicket to fall.

But I waited in vain. The qualities that had enabled Mr
Maudsley to get on in the world stood by him in the cricket
field – especially the quality of judgement. He knew when to
leave well alone. It cannot be said that he punished the loose
balls – he never hit a boundary – but he scored off them. He had
no style, it seemed to me; he dealt empirically with each ball that
came along. His method was no method but it worked. He had
an uncanny sense of where the fielders were, and generally
managed to slip the ball between them. They were brought
in closer, they were sent out further, they straddled their legs
and adopted attitudes of extreme watchfulness; but to no
purpose.

A bowler whose fastish swingers had claimed two wickets
earlier in the innings now came on. One of his deliveries hit Mr
Maudsley's pads and he appealed, but the appeal was dis-
allowed, and after that his bowling became demoralized and he
was taken off. In the next over a wicket fell and Denys joined his
father. The score was now 103 of which Mr Maudsley had made
28. The ladies, as I could tell from their motionless hats, were
now taking a proper interest in the game: mentally I could
see the searchlight beam of Mrs Maudsley's eyes fixed on the
wicket.

Before he left the pavilion Denys had told us what he meant
to do. 'The great thing is not to let him tire himself,' he said. 'I
shall not let him run a single run more than I can help. I wanted
him to have someone to run for him, but he wouldn't. When a
ball comes to me I shall either hit a boundary or I shall leave it
alone. I shall leave it absolutely alone.'

For a time these tactics were successful. Denys did hit a
boundary – he hit two. He played with a great deal of gesture,
walking about meditatively when his father had the bowling,
and sometimes strolling out to pat the pitch. But his methods
did not combine well with his father's opportunist policy. Mr

Maudsley, always anxious to steal a run and knowing exactly when to, was frequently thwarted by Denys's raised arm, which shot up like a policeman's.

Once or twice when this happened the spectators tittered but Denys appeared to be as unconscious of their amusement as he was of his father's growing irritation, which also was visible to us. At last, when the signal was again raised against him, Mr Maudsley called out, 'Come on!' It was like the crack of a whip; all the authority that Mr Maudsley so carefully concealed in his daily life spoke in those two words. Denys started off like a rabbit but he was too late; he had hardly got half-way down the pitch before he was run out. Crestfallen and red-faced he returned to the pavilion.

There was now no doubt as to who dominated the field. But oddly enough though I did not grudge my host his success I could not quite reconcile it with the spirit of the game. It wasn't cricket; it wasn't cricket that an elderly gnome-like individual with a stringy neck and creaking joints should, by dint of head-work and superior cunning, reverse the proverb that youth will be served. It was an ascendancy of brain over brawn, of which, like a true Englishman, I felt suspicious.

Mr Maudsley did not find anyone to stay with him long, however. The last three wickets fell quickly, but they had raised our score to 142, a very respectable total. Tremendous applause greeted Mr Maudsley as he came back, undefeated, having just made his fifty. He walked alone – the footman, his last companion at the wicket, having joined the fieldsmen, with whom no doubt he felt more at home. We all rose to do him honour; he looked a little pale but much less heated than the village team, who were perspiring freely and mopping their faces. Lord Trimingham took the liberty of patting him on the back; gentle as the pat was, his frail frame shook under it.

During the tea-interval the game was replayed many times, but the hero of the hour seemed content to be left out; indeed it soon became difficult to associate him with his innings as with the financial operations he directed in the City. At five o'clock our team took the field; the village had two hours in which to beat us.

I still have the scoring cards but whereas I can remember our innings in detail, theirs, although the figures are before me, remains a blur, until the middle. Partly, no doubt, because our batsmen were all known to me personally, and theirs, with one exception, were not. Also because it looked such an easy win for us – as the scores, all in single figures, of the first five batsmen testify – that I withdrew some of my attention: one cannot concentrate on a walk-over. The excitements of our innings seemed far away and almost wasted – as if we had put out all our strength to lift a pin. I remember feeling rather sorry for the villagers, as one after another their men went back, looking so much smaller than when they had walked to the wicket. And as the game receded from my mind the landscape filled it. There were two bows: the arch of the trees beyond the cricket field, and the arch of the sky above them; and each repeated the other's curve. This delighted my sense of symmetry; what disturbed it was the spire of the church. The church itself was almost invisible among the trees, which grew over the mound it stood on in the shape of a protractor, an almost perfect semi-circle. But the spire, instead of dividing the protractor into two equal segments, raised its pencil-point to the left of the centre – about eight degrees, I calculated. Why could not the church conform to Nature's plan? There must be a place, I thought, where the spire would be seen as a continuation of the protractor's axis, producing the perpendicular indefinitely into the sky, with two majestic right angles at its base, like flying buttresses, holding it up. Perhaps some of the spectators enjoyed this view. I wished I could go in search of it, while our team were skittling out the village side.

But soon my eye, following the distressful spire into the heavens, rested on the enormous cloud that hung there, and tried to penetrate its depths. A creation of heat, it was like no cloud I had ever seen. It was pure white on top, rounded and thick and lustrous as a snow-drift; below, the white was flushed with pink, and still further below, in the very heart of the cloud, the pink deepened to purple. Was there a menace in this purple tract, a hint of thunder? I did not think so. The cloud seemed absolutely motionless; scan it as I would, I could not detect the smallest alterations in its outline. And yet it was moving – moving towards the sun and getting brighter and brighter as it approached it  A few more degrees and then—

As I was visualizing the lines of the protractor printed on the sky I heard a rattle and a clatter. It was Ted Burgess going out to bat; he was whistling, no doubt to keep his spirits up.

He was carrying his bat under his arm, rather unorthodox. How did I feel about him? Did I want him, for instance, to come out first ball? Did I want to see him hit a six and then come out? I was puzzled, for until now my feelings had been quite clear: I wanted everyone on our side to make runs, and everyone on their side not to.

The first ball narrowly shaved his wicket and then I knew: I did not want him to get out. The knowledge made me feel guilty of disloyalty, but I consoled myself by thinking that it was sporting, and therefore meritorious, to want the enemy to put up a fight; besides, they were so far behind! And in this state of uneasy neutrality I remained for several overs while Ted, who got most of the bowling, made several mis-hits including one skier, which the pantry-boy might have caught had not the sun been in his eyes.

Then he hit one four, and then another; the ball whistled across the boundary, scattering the spectators. They laughed and applauded, though no one felt, I think, that it was a serious contribution to the match. More mis-hits followed and then a really glorious six which sailed over the pavilion and dropped among the trees at the back.

A scatter of small boys darted off to look for it, and while they were hunting the fieldsmen lay down on the grass; only Ted and his partner and the two umpires remained standing, looking like victors on a stricken field. All the impulse seemed to go out of the game: it was a moment of complete relaxation. And even when the finder had triumphantly tossed the ball down into the field, and play began again, it still had a knock-about, light-hearted character. 'Good Old Ted!' someone shouted when he hit his next boundary.

With the score card in front of me I still can't remember at what point I began to wonder whether Ted's displayful innings might not influence the match. I think it was when he had made his fifty that I began to see the red light and my heart started pounding in my chest.

It was a very different half-century from Mr Maudsley's, a triumph of luck, not of cunning, for the will, and even the wish to win seemed absent from it. Dimly I felt that the contrast represented something more than the conflict between Hall and village. It was that, but it was also the struggle between order and lawlessness, between obedience to tradition and defiance of it, between social stability and revolution, between one attitude to life and another. I knew which side I was on; yet the traitor within my gates felt the issue differently, he backed the individual against the side, even my own side, and wanted to see Ted Burgess pull it off. But I could not voice such thoughts to the hosts of Midian prowling round me under the shade of the pavilion veranda. Their looks had cleared marvellously and they were now taking bets about the outcome not without sly looks at me; so spying a vacant seat beside Marian I edged my way down to her and whispered:

'Isn't it exciting?' I felt this was not too much a betrayal of our side.

When she did not answer I repeated the question. She turned to me and nodded, and I saw the reason she didn't answer was because she couldn't trust herself to speak. Her eyes were bright, her cheeks were flushed and her lips trembled. I was a child and lived in the society of children and I knew the signs. At the time I didn't ask myself what they meant, but the sight of a grown-up person so visibly affected greatly increased my emotional response to the game, and I could hardly sit still. for

I always wriggled when excited. The conflict in my feelings
deepened: I could not bear to face the fact, which was becoming
more apparent to me every moment, that I wanted the other side
to win.

Another wicket fell and then another; there were two more to
go and the village needed twenty-one runs to pass our total. The
spectators were absolutely silent as the new batsman walked out.
I heard their captain say 'Let him have the bowling, Charlie,' but
I doubted whether Ted would fall in with this; he had shown no
sign of wishing to 'bag' the bowling. It was the last ball of the
over; the new batsman survived it, and Ted, facing us, also
faced the attack.

Lord Trimingham had two men in the deep field, and long on
was standing somewhat to our right. Ted hit the first ball straight
at us. I thought it was going to be a six, but soon its trajectory
flattened. As it came to earth it seemed to gather speed. The
fieldsman ran and got his hand to it, but it cannoned off and
hurtled threateningly towards us. Mrs Maudsley jumped up
with a little cry; Marian put her hands in front of her face; I held
my breath; there was a moment of confusion and anxious
inquiry before it was discovered that neither of them had been
touched. Both the ladies laughed at their narrow escape and
tried to pass it off. The ball lay at Mrs Maudsley's feet looking
strangely small and harmless. I threw it to long on, who, I now
saw, was one of our gardeners. But he ignored it. His face
twisted with pain he was nursing his left hand in his right and
gingerly rubbing it.

Lord Trimingham and some of the other fielders came
towards him and he went out to meet them; I saw him showing
them his injured hand. They conferred; they seemed to come to
a decision; then the group dispersed, the handful of players
returned to the wicket, and Lord Trimingham and the gardener
returned to the pavilion.

Confusion reigned in my mind: I thought all sorts of things
at the same time: that the match was over, that the gardener
would be maimed for life, that Ted would be sent to prison.

Then I heard Lord Trimingham say: 'We've had a casualty. Pollin has sprained his thumb, and I'm afraid we shall have to call on our twelfth man.' Even then I did not know he meant me.

My knees quaking I walked back with him to the pitch. 'We've got to get him out,' he said. 'We've got to get him out. Let's hope this interruption will have unsettled him. Now, Leo, I'm going to put you at square leg. You won't have much to do because he makes most of his runs in front of the wicket. But sometimes he hooks one, and that's where you can help us.' Something like that: but I scarcely heard, my nervous system was so busy trying to adjust itself to my new role. From spectator to performer, what a change!

Miserably nervous, I followed the movements of the bowler's hand, signalling me to my place. At last I came to rest in a fairy ring, and this absurdly gave me confidence, I felt that it might be a magic circle and would protect me. Two balls were bowled from which no runs were scored. Gradually my nervousness wore off and a sense of elation took possession of me. I felt at one with my surroundings and upheld by the long tradition of cricket. Awareness such as I had never known sharpened my senses; and when Ted drove the next ball for four, and got another four from the last ball in the over, I had to restrain an impulse to join in the enemy's applause. Yet when I saw, out of the tail of my eye, a new figure going up on the score-board, I dare not look at it, for I knew it was the last whole ten we had in hand.

The next over was uneventful but increasingly tense; the new batsman stamped and blocked and managed to smother the straight ones; the lower half of his body was more active that the upper. But he got a single off the last ball and faced the bowling again.

It was not the same bowling, however, that had given Ted Burgess his boundaries in the preceding over. As I crossed the pitch I saw a change was pending. Lord Trimingham had the ball, and was throwing it gently from one hand to the other:

he made some alterations in the field, and for a moment I feared he was going to move me out of my magic circle; but he did not.

He took a long run with a skip in the middle but the ball was not very fast; it seemed to drop rather suddenly. The batsman hit out at it and it soared into the air. He ran. Ted ran, but before they reached their opposite creases it was safe in Lord Trimingham's hands. It was evidence of our captain's popularity that, even at this critical juncture, the catch was generously applauded. The clapping soon subsided, however, as the boy who kept the telegraph moved towards the score-board. The figures came with maddening slowness. But what was this? Total score 9, wickets 1, Last Man 135. Laughter broke out among the spectators. The board boy came back and peered at his handiwork. Then to the accompaniment of more laughter, he slowly changed the figures round.

But funny though it seemed, the mistake didn't really relieve the tension, it added to it by suggesting that even mathematics were subject to nervous upset. And only eight runs – two boundaries – stood between us and defeat.

As the outgoing met the incoming batsmen and exchanged a word with him, at which each man nodded, I tried for the last time to sort my feelings out. But they gathered round me like a mist, whose shape can be seen as it advances but not when it is on you, and in the thick, whirling vapours my mind soon lost its way. Yet I kept my sense of the general drama of the match and it was sharpened by an awareness, which I couldn't explain to myself, of a particular drama between the bowler and the batsman. Tenant and landlord, commoner and peer, village and hall – these were elements in it. But there was something else, something to do with Marian, sitting on the pavilion steps watching us.

It was a prideful and sustaining thought that whereas the spectators could throw themselves about and yell themselves hoarse, we, the players could not, must not, show the slightest sign of emotion. Certainly the bowler, digging his heel into the ground, a trick he had before starting his run, and Ted facing him, his shirt clinging to his back, did not.

Lord Trimingham sent down his deceptively dipping ball but Ted did not wait for it to drop, he ran out and hit it past cover point to the boundary. It was a glorious drive and the elation of it ran through me like an electric current. The spectators yelled and cheered and suddenly the balance of my feelings went right over: it was their victory that I wanted, not ours. I did not think of it in terms of the three runs that were needed; I seemed to hear it coming like a wind.

I could not tell whether the next ball was on the wicket or not, but it was pitched much further up and suddenly I saw Ted's face and body swinging round, and the ball, travelling towards me on a rising straight line like a cable stretched between us. Ted started to run and then stopped and stood watching me, wonder in his eyes and a wild disbelief.

I threw my hand above my head and the ball stuck there, but the impact knocked me over. When I scrambled up, still clutching the ball to me, as though it was a pain that had started in my heart, I heard the sweet sound of applause and saw the field breaking up and Lord Trimingham coming towards me. I can't remember what he said – my emotions were too over-whelming – but I remember that his congratulations were the more precious because they were reserved and understated, they might, in fact, have been addressed to a man; and it was as a man, and not by any means the least of men, that I joined the group who were making their way back to the pavilion. We went together in a ragged cluster, the defeated and the surviving batsmen with us, all enmity laid aside, amid a more than generous measure of applause from the spectators. I could not tell how I felt; in my high mood of elation the usual landmarks by which I judged such things were lost to view. I was still in the air, though the scaffolding of events which had lifted me had crumbled. But I was still aware of one separate element that had not quite fused in the general concourse of passions; the pang of regret, sharp as a sword-thrust, that had accompanied the catch. Far from diminishing my exultation, it had somehow raised it to a higher power, like the drop of bitter in the fount of happiness; but I felt that I should be still happier – that it would add another cubit to my stature – if I told Ted of it. Something warned me that such an avowal would be unorthodox; the personal feelings of cricketers were concealed behind their stiff upper lips. But I was almost literally above myself; I knew that the fate of the match had turned on me, and I felt I could afford to defy convention. Yet how would he take it? What were his feelings? Was he still elated by his innings or was he bitterly disappointed by its untimely close? Did he still regard me as a friend, or as an enemy who had brought about his downfall? I did not greatly care; and seeing that he was walking alone (most of the players had exhausted their stock of conversation) I sidled up to him and said, 'I'm sorry, Ted. I didn't really mean to catch you out.' He stopped and smiled at me. 'Well, that's very hand-some of you,' he said. 'It was a damned good catch, anyway, I never thought you'd hold it. To tell you the truth I'd forgotten all about you being at square leg, and then I looked round and there you were by God. And then I thought, "It'll go right over his head," but you stretched up like a concertina. I'd thought of a dozen ways I might get out, but never thought I'd be caught out by our postman.' 'I didn't mean to,' I repeated, not to be cheated of my apology. At that moment the clapping grew louder and some enthusiasts coupled Ted's name with it. Though we were all heroes, he was evidently the crowd's favourite; and I dropped back so that he might walk in alone. His fellow-batsmen in the pavilion were making a great demon-stration; even the ladies of our party, sitting in front, showed themselves mildly interested as Ted came by. All except one. Marian, I noticed, didn't look up.

As soon as we were back at the Hall I said to Marcus, 'Lend me your scoring-card, old man.'

'Why didn't you keep one, pudding face?' he asked me.

'How could I, you dolt, when I was fielding?'

'Did you field, you measly microbe? Are you quite sure?'

When I had punished him for this, and extracted his score-card from him, I copied on to mine the items that were missing.

'E. Burgess c. sub. b. Ld. Trimingham 81,' I read. 'Why, you might have put my name in, you filthy scoundrel.'

' "C. sub." is correct,' he said. 'Besides, I want to keep this card clean, and it wouldn't be if your name was on it.'

*from* THE GO-BETWEEN *1953*

# Cricket in Fiction

## An Essay by GERALD BRODRIBB

Many centuries ago Homer told how Nausicaa indulged in some most eventful catching practice, and since then there have been many references in literature to games which have been played with a ball. In England, cricket is 'more than a game, it's an institution,' and so it is not surprising that writers of fiction should have concerned themselves with cricket more frequently than with any other game.

Most of these fictional accounts of cricket have been introduced incidentally, but there are a few novels in which the playing of cricket has been a central theme. The earliest of these were two books by that great all-round sportsman, Horace G. Hutchinson, whose *Creatures of Circumstance* and *Peter Steele, the Cricketer* trace the careers of two heroes whose cricketing exploits are more successful than their personal affairs. One of them, indeed, is so distressed by the behaviour of the heroine that he gives up cricket and becomes 'A mere frivolous Member of Parliament.' Another cricketing novel which belongs to the last century is J. C. Snaith's *Willow the King*: Snaith himself once played for Notts, and his accounts of the cricket are convincing. Equally good is *A Mother's Son*, written by B. and C. B. Fry: the hero of this book has many ambitions, and the greatest of them is fulfilled when as an Oxford undergraduate he is chosen to play for England in a vital Test match against Australia. A similar rise to Test cricket is enjoyed by Paul Rignold (Eton and Cambridge) in Sir Home Gordon's *That Test Match*, a novel in which most of the achievements of the hero seem to be based upon true fact. Paul's 'composite' career is entirely successful, and we meet here many well-known personalities of cricket who can be identified without much difficulty.

All the heroes of the novels so far mentioned have been somewhat gilded amateurs; the only novels in which the leading character has been a professional are in contrast rather melancholy. Dudley Carew's *The Son of Grief* lives up to its title, and Bruce Hamilton's *Pro* is equally true to its sub-title, *An English Tragedy*. Though it is not strictly a cricket novel, J. D. Beresford's *The Hampdenshire Wonder* opens with a considerable amount of cricket until its professional hero, 'Ginger' Stott (who once took 10 wickets for 5 runs against Surrey) poisoned his finger, and the amputation of it put a sudden end to a brief but spectacular career.

In the opinion of Sir James Barrie (and others) the best book ever written about cricket is Hugh de Selincourt's *The Cricket Match*, which quite apart from its description of the game, is a magnificent study of village life in Sussex. It is a book of great sensibility, and for this reason it excels all the others so far mentioned, but they all have some merit, and if they have been somewhat briefly alluded to it is because they are for the most part straightforward stories of a career, in which the plot is of greater interest than the manner in which the story is told.

While there are comparatively few cricket novels there are a great many works of fiction which include some account of the game, which is approached in various ways. In some of these novels the purpose is to emphasize the character and prowess of the hero; in some the tale of a desperate contest tends to quicken the whole tempo of the story, while the reader becomes interested in others because he is curious to see how a great novelist dealt with the problems of describing a game. A few of these great ones seem slightly to be lacking in technical knowledge, and there are several instances of 'late cuts to leg' and other such oddities.

In the days when stories with a school setting were written primarily for those at school, there were plenty of good cricket accounts, and the prototype of all school stories, *Tom Brown's Schooldays* tells how Tom captains the side against an M.C.C. eleven in a match played at Rugby after the end of term, Dr Arnold having already gone on holiday, after careful warnings 'to keep all spirituous liquor out of the Close.' A noble and sporting game lasts from 10 a.m. until 8.15, with a suitable interval for the dinner at which there are 'the most topping comic songs.' At a critical point in the game we break in upon a discussion about Aristophanes between Tom and one of the masters, while Arthur sits by and listens until he has to bat in a match in which he is perhaps lucky to appear, for Tom has chosen him not so much 'for his play,' as for the reason 'that it will do him so much good.'

As might well be expected, Talbot Baines Reed's inimitable *Fifth Form at St Dominic's* contains some stirring accounts of cricket, and the story of 'the Sixth versus the Fifth' match is full of high, manly conflict. 'The Fifth had "cheeked" the Sixth and the Sixth had snubbed the Fifth . . . and now the opposing forces are to be ranged face to face' while the Lower School suck brandy-balls and 'mark and applaud every ball and every hit as if Empires depended on them.' After many dramatic incidents (and a fine crop of exclamation marks), the scores are level with the last man in, when a ball is delivered 'to which there is but one way of playing – among the slips.' The batsman plays it there, but the cheers of the Fifth 'suddenly drop,' for a fielder has crept in close and saved the Sixth by one of the neatest low catches ever seen in a Dominican match.

Turning to a more exalted setting, H. A. Vachell's *The Hill* gives us an account of an Eton-Harrow match as seen chiefly through the eyes of the Reverend Septimus Duff, an Harrovian who has come up from a West Country vicarage on a visit to Lord's he has made annually for some thirty years, and who in the interval is invited to lunch by twenty men at least – 'some of them with names known wherever the Union Jack waves.' He is delighted by a great century by the Harrow Captain, who hits two consecutive 'sixers' with the result that 'upon the tops of the coaches countesses, duchesses – ay, princesses – are cheering like Fourth-form boys.' After much exciting play in which there are 'many close squeaks,' Eton are left with 211 to win, and after some wickets have fallen quickly the Eton captain begins to get his eye so well in that the father of his rival captain offers to write a cheque for £10,000 if only Harrow could win. He himself 'had never been a cricketer, but this game gripped him.' With only 40 runs short of victory, the Eton captain is brilliantly caught. 'Pandemonium broke loose. Grey-headed men threw their hats into the air; peers danced; lovely women shrieked; every Harrovian on the ground howled. For Caesar held the ball fast in his lean brown hands.' The excitement continues, and with three to make and one wicket to go, the Reverend Sep's son produces a long-hop. It is 'smitten so hard that no hand, surely, can stop the whirling sphere,' but the Harrow captain is a 'demon'; he snaps it up; he shies and aims – instantaneously; he shatters the wicket with the smiter still out of his ground – and Harrow has won. Similar but less detailed accounts of the Eton and Harrow match occur in Shane Leslie's *The Oppidan*, and in Eric Parker's *Playing Fields*. In the latter book Eton snatch a victory amid 'a shout that ended in a choke and a laugh as the green, sunlit ground suddenly became full of black, hurrying figures.'

Some more good cricket appears in E. F. Benson's *David Blaize*. In a prep-school match the not unpleasantly bumptious David enjoys triumph and disaster by taking eight wickets and then dropping a sitter which costs his side the match. A year or two later he goes in last in a House match final at 'ten to make and the match to win' and helps to carry his House to victory by hitting a somewhat impudent boundary in reply to the advice of his House captain (who is batting the other end) not to take any risks. But the match is won: 'David, old man,' says the House captain, 'isn't it ripping that it's just you and me.'

Another House final is described in Alec Waugh's *The Loom of Youth*, where the hero's school career is brought to a fine close. In the first innings he fails, and when he goes in again 'with nearly everything depending on him,' he is dropped off his first ball, but from then on his success is inevitable. Another boy enjoys 'the supreme moment of his schooldays,' when the hero of Ernest Raymond's *Tell England* bowls out a county player a few minutes before time for the school ('whose ambitions were rather greater than usual') to gain an innings victory over a Team of Masters. The cheering lasted for half an hour until the parties of exultant boys disperse homeward, some of them singing 'Now the day is done.'

There are many excellent accounts of cricket in *Pip* by Ian Hay, and in *Mike*, a public school story, by P. G. Wodehouse, and we hear more of Mike Jackson, who is the youngest of three great cricketing brothers, in *Psmith in the City*. Mike and his friend Psmith have achieved jobs in a London bank, but their banking careers are soon ended when Mike absents himself from his work in order to fill a place in the Middlesex match – and to score a brilliant century. The author shows a profound knowledge of the game, and knows when to curb his fine boisterous humour.

A similarly competent fictional cricketer is the 'amateur cracksman' A. J. Raffles, who professes to play cricket only from the very lowest motives. 'What's the satisfaction,' he asks, 'of taking a man's wickets when you want his spoons?' He finds, however, that his ability to appear for the Gentlemen against the Players 'as perhaps the very finest slow bowler of his decade' affords a glorious protection to a person of such proclivities as his. His creator, E. W. Hornung, wrote many short stories which deal with cricket (mostly in a volume called *Old Offenders and a Few Old Scores*) and his public school novel, *Fathers of Men*, is largely concerned with the exploits of Jan Rutter, 'a natural left-hand bowler,' whose greatest feat is told of in a long and detailed account of an Old Boys match.

Another Old Boys match, this time at a Scots school, affords Bruce Marshall, the author of *Prayer for the Living*, many opportunities of amusing and penetrating observations on the inevitable difficulties of school cricket in war-time. Very different in tone from this book is a long short-story by Henry Drummond called *Baxter's Second Innings*. While convalescing from a hit on the head young Baxter has explained to him the allegorical significance of cricket in which the bowler stands for Temptation and attacks a boy's three stumps (Truth, Honour and Purity) by means of 'Swifts, slows and screws.' This conversation ends in Baxter enjoying a highly successful second innings. This is not the only occasion when a cricket story has been steeped in morality, for there is a very interesting tale called *The Cricket Club*, or *Warned Just in Time – a Story for Mothers' Meetings*, which presents the miseries of a married life in which the cricketer's wife is not sufficiently appreciative of the glories of the game.

Even in these days, when women can enjoy the rigours of playing in Test matches, there have been no accounts of cricket as played by 'young ladies' more interesting than that by Helen Mathers in her novel *Comin' Thro' the Rye*. Although it dates back to some seventy-five years ago the account of the heroine's eventful visit to the wicket is still very fresh, and expresses more convincingly than most cricket books the strange feeling of apprehension felt by a young player before going in to bat.

Even longer ago Miss Mary Mitford wrote the words, 'I doubt if there be any scene in the world more animating or delightful than a cricket-match . . . a real solid old-fashioned match between neighbouring parishes,' and since then village cricket has been praised and written about until at one time it became almost a literary cult. Hugh de Selincourt's short stories of village cricket in *The Game of the Season* increase our lasting affection for Paul Gauvinier and the rest of the Tillingfold team.

Among other serious accounts of village cricket 'The Flower Show Match' from Siegfried Sassoon's *Memoirs of a Fox-Hunting Man* is outstanding, and charmingly recalls the glories of village cricket of forty years ago. It provides a finish desperate enough for any tale as 'young Master George,' wearing his House eleven scarf, snatches the winning run after nine wickets have fallen. In a somewhat similar manner Edmund Blunden described a well-fought village match in *The Face of England*. Here the attention is focussed on a young player 'born with the zest of the game in him,' but who is so afflicted with nervousness that 'even cricket could torment him.' Once set however he plays a fine innings, and later, 'amid inhuman excitement,' bowls out the last man for his team to win by eight runs. Edward Bucknell's novel *Linden Lea* includes a description of a village match in which an old Wykehamist plays his first game for ten years, and spins his side to a close victory. The Squire 'in a faded Forester blazer,' the ground 'with a view of the Hall nestling among ancient trees,' the crowded brake, the comments of Lady Pilsdon, the blacksmith with his celebrated four-pound bat, all go to make up a typically 'pastoral' account of the cricket.

Similar atmosphere is provided in a wistful short story called *The Match* in which Stacy Aumonier (writing in 1916) recalls 'the white-clad figures on the sunlit field' where the grass is now long, and which some of the village players will never see again. Graham White's *Cricket on Saturday* contains several stories in which village cricket is described faithfully without either sentiment or farcical humour.

With the words 'are you a cricketer?' (to which Mr Winkle replies with a discreet 'No') Dickens introduces us to perhaps the most famous of all humorous accounts of cricket matches. It is not a long account because the efforts of Mr Dumkins and Mr Podder 'who blocked the doubtful balls, missed the bad ones, and took the good ones and sent them flying to all parts of field' are so successful that they gained All-Muggleton 'an advantage too great to be recovered,' with the result that at an early period of the game Dingley Dell 'gave in and allowed the superior prowess of their opponents.' The account of the actual play is so short that it seems that Dickens is anxious to join Mr Pickwick and 'partake of a plain dinner at the Blue Lion,' at which Mr Jingle follows up his fantastic story of Sir Thomas Blazo's single-wicket match, with a lively and convivial song.

In more recent years there have been several accounts of village cricket that are undeniably farcical. M. D. Lyon, the Somerset county player, wrote a novel called *A Village Match and After* that has plenty of humour, but the funniest account of all appears in A. G. Macdonell's *England, their England*. After many desperate and fantastic episodes the scores are equal when the blacksmith comes in and hits his first ball straight up in the air. 'Up and up it went and then at the top it seemed to hang motionless in the air, poised like a hawk, fighting as it were a heroic but forlorn battle against the chief invention of Sir Isaac Newton, and then it began its slow descent.' Three uproarious pages describe what happens during this descent, until at last the ball is grabbed off the seat of the wicket-keeper's trousers, and the match is a tie. It is one of those rare pieces of humorous writing which can be read over and over again with increasing enjoyment.

Though not quite so hilarious, there is another amusing account in R. C. Hutchinson's fine novel *The Unforgotten Prisoner*. This tells of how the hero of the book is reluctantly persuaded to play cricket for his parson brother's village team, and how he takes with him a somewhat irresponsible friend, who plays a peculiar but successful innings. The match is a good one, but the hero reflects (with shame) that the thing he enjoyed most was the squire's unfortunate adventure with a cheap deck-chair. No one who reads Chapter VIII of J. C. Masterman's remarkable *Fate Cannot Harm Me* can fail to appreciate the joys of country house cricket. The chief feature of this account is the deserved discomfiture of Colonel Murcher-Pringle, 'whom most of his own side would cheerfully have drowned.' He is the sort of man who tries to explain away a catch he misses by announcing that 'cricket is a funny game.' The author of this book considers this 'an odious remark' that besets all descriptions of cricket matches, but it certainly is a true one if we judge cricket by the account he gives, for the whole match sparkles with wit and fun, without ever becoming ludicrous. In his introduction to the book, J. C. Masterman forestalls any objections to the inclusion of 'a lengthy tale of a cricket match, wholly irrelevant to the main issue,' and this account is probably enhanced by not being tied up too closely with the fortunes of 'the hero.'

Perhaps the strangest of all references to cricket in the country are those which appear in several of the novels of George Meredith. 'Are there gods in the air?' asks the author, as Nick Frim, the village of Beckley's 'renowned out-hitter' is dropped by a 'butter-fingered beast' at 'long-hit-off,' and subsequently batters the Fallowfield bowling until the ladies 'grow hot and weary' with watching his efforts. Whether he reaches his hundred we never knew, because Evan Harrington, who has been watching the play, has his attention diverted by the arrival of the Countess de Soldar, who finds the 'creeket very unintelligible.' Other spectators are engaged in the contest of polite conversation, for 'many good county names may be pointed out,' and the whole game is subordinate to their chit-chat. Meredith also mentions a cricket match in *Diana of the Crossways* where on their way from London some ladies come upon the 'not very comprehensible' sight of cricketers at work under a vertical sun. One of the players, however, is recognized (he has come down from London to assist the local side), and before 'the heat of the noonday sun compelled the ladies to drive on,' he has stayed at the wicket long enough for one of them to come to the conclusion that 'he looks well in flannels.'

It is possible that Meredith would have found the atmosphere of first-class cricket more congenial, and if he had done so he would have been the first novelist to describe 'big' cricket.

Apart from the accounts in some of the so-called cricket novels there are a few incidental descriptions of county cricket. Christopher Hollis's *Death of a Gentleman* and *Fossett's Memory* have some admirable references, and the heroine of Lou King-Hall's *Fly Envious Time* is the wife of a county secretary, and tells us of some of the problems concerned with such a job. Michael Sadleir's *Desolate Splendour* contains a short but deft account of a scene at Lord's during a 'Varsity match. On the whole there are rather more allusions to Test matches, though oddly enough most of them border on satire or fantasy. A. G. Macdonell's *How Like an Angel* refers to 'the usual sirocco of excitement that swirls round' Test cricket, and tells how a 'mystery' fast bowler is chosen to play for England, and is unwise enough to bowl at the leg-stump and put five men on the leg-side. This causes such an uproar among the Borealian supporters that on the request of the Secretary of State for the Dominions, the fast bowler is summarily dismissed, and the match started all over again. At this the gratified Borealians strike up 'Land of Hope and Glory,' and 'smite the slow and medium-paced deliveries of the remaining English bowlers all over the field.' This description by Macdonell is perhaps the only good thing that resulted from the unhappy 'leg-theory' incidents of the 1932-33 tour.

Of all cricket short stories Sir Arthur Conan Doyle's *The Story of Spedegue's Dropper* is one of the most entertaining. It tells how the English Selection Committee come to hear of an unknown schoolmaster who is able to bowl a remarkable ball which is lobbed up to over 50 ft. and then descends sharply in the area of the bails. After a secret 4 a.m. trial they decide to risk playing him in the final decisive Test match against Australia, and amid great astonishment, and after some nervous beginnings, he proves entirely successful and captures 15 wickets. 'How can you play with a straight bat at a ball that falls straight from the clouds?' ask the bewildered Australians, but fortunately no strife arises, and presently both countries join 'in appreciation of the greatest joke in the history of cricket.'

An equally good short story is Lord Dunsany's *How Jembu played for Cambridge* which tells how an African chieftain who is in residence at Cambridge obtains a cricket Blue through his magical powers of consistent scoring which enable him always to reach a score of 50. Unlike Bradman (who had much the same powers) Jembu was not permitted to exceed this ration. On one occasion he does so, with disastrous results. It is a great pity that Conan Doyle, who was a player good enough to play for M.C.C. in several first-class matches, did not write more about cricket. Apart from the Spedegue story and a brief but amusing description of Brigadier Gerard's strange efforts at the game when a prisoner-of-war, there is little else.

The novels of Anthony Trollope have recently been enjoying great popularity and those who read his book *The Fixed Period* will find an amazing Test match fantasy, for there is a full description of a contest between England and Britannula played in the spring of 1980.

In their endless search for new settings the writers of detective fiction have occasionally turned to the field of cricket. Adrian Alington's *The Amazing Test Match Crime* is more properly a fantasy than a detective story, but C. A. Alington's *Mr Evans* contains rather more detection, and Miss Dorothy Sayers' *Murder Must Advertise* shows Lord Peter Wimsey trying to make runs without disclosing his identity, a difficult task for such a brilliant player. *Murder Isn't Cricket*, *Death Before Wicket* and *The Test Match Murder* are three more recent detective stories, and equally ingenious is Nicholas Blake's *A Question of Proof*, in which the concentration of the spectators on a thrilling finish in a prep-school fathers' match enables one of the assistant masters to murder his headmaster without being noticed. Harold Hobson's *The Devil in Woodford Wells* is a fantasy in which a problem connected with a century-old score sheet is solved only by a personal visitation of the devil.

Several very well-known names do not appear in this brief and no doubt incomplete survey of cricket in fiction as their writing does not really come under this heading. E. V. Lucas' cricket writing is mostly in the form of essays; A. A. Milne (apart from the sketches in *The Day's Play*) is better known for his cricket verse; Sir James Barrie has a charming passage in *The Little White Bird* but not much else of cricket in his novels.

The last few years have produced several good cricket novels. William Godfrey's *Malleson at Melbourne* and Maurice Moiseiwitch's *A Sky Blue Life* both have a full-scale Test match background, and in *The Friendly Game* the exploits of the England captain 'Abdul' Malleson are continued in the different, but no less tough, atmosphere of village cricket. Village Green fantasy is maintained in various degrees in episodes from Rex Warner's *Escapade*, Denys Roberts's *The Elwood Wager*, and John Hadfield's *Love on a Branch Line*. John Moore in *The White Sparrow* has a village setting and a young cricketing hero.

The Oval appeared as background for a detective story in John Creasey's *A Six for the Toff*, and Lord's figures in Ernest

Raymond's *To the Wood No More*, where the Wood is St John's Wood.

There has also been a book of short stories – *Century of a Lifetime* by R. T. Johnstone, which follows to some extent the Macdonell tradition. Jeff Glanville has written of the adventures of *The Schoolboy Test Cricketer*, with all the usual trappings; but now that recent years have produced – especially in Pakistan – Test cricketers who are genuine schoolboys the glamour of such an idea seems a bit thin.

Finally, if it seems that some of the novelists have produced rather melodramatic contests, it should be remembered that even in first-class cricket things have happened that are even 'stranger than fiction.' P. G. Van der Byl once made 28 runs off a last over to win a Currie Cup match in 1937-38: what writer of fiction would have dared to invent such a fantastically exciting finish?

*from* ALL ROUND THE WICKET *1951* (*revised*)

# PART II

# Great Players

'There's music in the names I used to know,
And magic when I heard them, long ago.'

*Thomas Moult*
THE NAMES

### LEG HALF-VOLLEY

                           'Beware
Of entrance to a quarrel, but being in
Bear it, that thy opposer may beware of thee.'
                                  *Hamlet*

# W. G. Grace – The Champion

## A. A. THOMSON

*'No monument, no portrait, no book can adequately represent either the vitality of W.G. or his superb skill in the game he loved.'*

Lord Hawke.

In the celebrated oil-portrait that was painted in 1888 by Archibald Stuart Wortley and now hangs in the Long Room at Lord's you see W.G. in characteristic stance. His cheeks are bronzed and his beard dark and bushy. His right foot stands squarely along the popping crease, his left well forward, the toe of his brown boot raised. (Billy Murdoch said he raised his toe to tread on a yorker but, in fact, it was next to impossible to bowl him a yorker because he could automatically convert it into a full toss.) The bat, which looks small in those huge hands, is raised in a high back-lift. The pose is easy, balanced and, most clearly and plainly, poised for attack. ('But, Dr Grace, would you stand as easily if the game were in a tight place?' the artist asked. 'Certainly,' said W.G., 'because, after all, I should only be facing the next ball.')

All his life he was facing the next ball. He was not 'the greatest batsman the world has ever seen' merely because in his career he scored just under 55,000 runs, including a thousand in a season twenty-eight times. Four batsmen – Hobbs, Woolley, Hendren and Mead – have surpassed the first of these feats and Woolley has equalled the second W.G.'s records are immensely impressive by any standard of any time, and by those of his period stupendous, but records do not tell the whole story. Mere figures do not tell his stature among his fellows or explain that he was a giant among giants, an Everest, not above the

205

foothills, but above the Himalayas. Figures do not depict the dramatic hostility of the bowling, or show that during the whole of his career, from 'Fearful' Jackson and 'Tear-'Em' Tarrant to the Demon Spofforth and Ernest Jones, it was hostile to the point of physical violence; they do not tell how evil many of the pitches were, even (and indeed especially) at Lord's and the Oval; and they do not tell you that, unless you had hit the ball, say, into St. John's Wood Road or its territorial equivalent, everything had to be run out.

His supremacy rested on two foundations: the first was his superb physical health from which he drew his quickness of eye, strength of arm and, above all, his unquenchable energy. There is a story from fairly unimpeachable sources that he had only one lung, but medical friends are apt to be disrespectful when the supposition is mentioned. The man who made 282 on a bitter-cold day towards the end of his forty-seventh year and a gay 74 on his fifty-eighth birthday was unlikely to be a lung short. The second basis of his mastery was the inspired early coaching of Uncle Pocock in the orchard at the Chestnuts, coaching which insisted above all things on sound defence and the straight bat. It is not genuinely paradoxical, when the question is reconsidered, that the methods of this hard-hitting, swift-scoring batsman were built on the rock of solid defence. He thought nothing of the two-eyed stance. 'These fellers,' he said, 'don't know how to hold their bats.'

W.G.'s batting had grandeur and not elegance. It was massive and ingenious. W.G. was not a 'beautiful' bat, as were R. A. H. Mitchell in his earliest and L. C. H. Palairet and R. H. Spooner in his later days. He would seldom dazzle the eye with sheer witchery and enchantment, as did Victor Trumper and as, to this day, Denis Compton can sometimes do. He was not a subtle magician like Ranji, some of whose leg-glances came near to sorcery and were as far removed from credibility as the Indian rope-trick. He was not so polished as Hobbs or so elementally roof-wrecking as his county colleague, Jessop. He did not create the game of cricket or invent the elements of batsmanship. There were handsome batsmen before him, such as Silver Billy Beldham of Hambledon and William Ward and Fuller Pilch; there were, as we know well, imperial batsmen after him: Hobbs and Hammond and Bradman and Hutton and Compton and a few, but not many, more. His career was immensely long and at each end of it there were great batsmen. They were, however, considered great only as coming near to himself. For all the years of his playing life, then, he was cricket's overlord.

Ranji said of him – 'he turned the old one-stringed instrument into a many-chorded lyre'. He also said: 'W.G. discovered batting; he turned its many straight channels into one great winding river.' W.G. played all the old strokes with greater force than had been known before and, indeed, as a rueful Kent bowler observed: 'There's only one thing the Doctor has to learn and that is to hit 'em up high.' He also brought in one stroke which he made peculiarly his own: a hard push to leg with a straight bat. This was the stroke of which it was said: 'Oh, yes, he blocks the shooters but he blocks 'em to the boundary.' Of this stroke, too, he is himself reputed to have said (no doubt apocryphally): 'I don't like defensive strokes: you can only get three off 'em.'

'There is something monumental in his stance at the wicket,' said Andrew Lang, 'wholly free from a false refinement, without extraneous elegances. His is a nervous, sinewy, English style, like that of Fielding'.* He could, and did, hit all round the wicket and he could keep this hitting up all day. His superb skill as a batsman can never be dissociated from his energy, stamina, and quick clearness of eye. There were few firework displays but every ball was regarded as something that could be hit. He hit the ball hàrd and he did not relish the thought of failing to score off any ball sent down. 'Leaving the ball alone,' he said, 'never won matches.' He would have scorned the half-hearted modern habit of leaving alone any ball outside the off stump. Indeed, he felt it somehow immoral that a ball should be allowed to pass

* See page 346.

his bat. Old Parson Wickham, who kept wicket in his brown-topped pads in the game when W.G. made his hundredth hundred (and then another hundred-and-eighty more), said that in all that time W.G. let only four balls go by. Some commentators have said it was five and some have said six, but Wickham should be allowed the last word. He was there all the time.

One of the hardships that drove W.G.'s opponents to admiring exasperation was the extreme difficulty of setting a field for him. His power of placing, gained in the hard school of batting against Eighteens and Twenty-Twos, seemed uncanny. As soon as you moved a fieldsman, the ball went whizzing past the spot he had just vacated.

Not merely did W.G. hit almost every ball: he hit it in the middle of the bat. Critics of style have claimed that that was his highest distinction. In 1884 the Australian tourists complained that English bats were wider than they ought to be. Some English players conscientiously measured and even planed the edges of their bats. But W.G. only laughed and said he didn't care how much they shaved off his bat. 'All I want,' he said, 'is the middle.'

It was, of course, part of his character and of his devotion to the game that he hated not making the best of every single innings. What else did you have a bat for? Almost everybody who batted with him grew tired as time wore on, but W.G. never. His imperviousness to fatigue made him seem relentless, for the bowlers grew weary so long before he did. In the golden 'seventies it was said that he 'made all the bowling plain and all the bowlers desperate'. The professional bowlers were so overjoyed to see the back of him that when one of them finally got rid of him he would fling his cap in the air with delight. Once Tom Emmett missed him off a simple caught-and-bowled and was so mortified that he flung his cap on the ground and danced on it. He then kicked the ball to the boundary.

'Kick it again, Tom,' said W.G. 'It's always four to me.'

At the end of each over throughout the day Tom apologized. 'I weren't mad with thee, Doctor. I were mad with my-sen.'

You had only to look at W.G.'s brown, hairy, massive fore-arms to see the power which he could put into a stroke. In his earliest period he never retreated from his maxim of the firmly fixed right leg. He even advocated that the beginner's right foot should be pegged down until he gained ease and confidence in playing back and forward. He disagreed with the notion that the weight should be equally distributed on both legs. 'The weight should be chiefly on the right foot and kept there when you raise your bat to play the ball.' Watching an early Test match, A. G. Steel said of him: 'Other men keep their right foot steady, but W.G. never moves it during the actual stroke, and that is what I have always envied in him most.' He would cut, as E. H. D. Sewell said, 'off the right foot the long-hop which others often cut off the left foot'.

Twenty years later when told that his methods were out of date he stuck to his guns, but maintained that the policy of the firm right leg was not aimed at the correct disposal of the body's weight but to prevent the novice from drawing away his foot, and therefore his body, from a rising ball towards short-leg. (This was what Patsy Hendren afterwards called 'kicking the square-leg umpire'.) 'And,' W.G. added, 'I have always believed in footwork, but pulling away from the wicket and footwork are two different matters. Footwork comes with experience, after a batsman has learnt to take up a proper position.'

There were critics who half-humorously approved of W.G.'s firm-footed stance because, as they maintained, if he had added to his own princely gifts the star-twinkling footwork of a Ranji, it would have been impossible even to hope to get him out. If he had learned and practised the quick-footed back-stroke thirty years before in the orchard at Downend, then, they argued, 'an intervention of Providence would be required to shift him'.

He loved, and chastised, the fast bowlers and their medium-fast colleagues, though he greatly respected George Freeman and Tom Emmett. A fifty against those two on a difficult wicket, he reckoned, was as good as any hundred scored in any condition against anybody else. He respected Spofforth, too, if only because the Demon was not crippled by reverence for him. Morley was a fierce fast bowler, too, but he said of W.G., after being sadly hammered by him on a rough pitch at Trent Bridge, 'He hit me for a couple of sixers off his eyebrows and then I bowled him through his flaming whiskers!' There was a memorable occasion when, on an appalling wicket at Lord's, W.G. blocked four venomous shooters in succession from the same bowler. They would so obviously have bowled any other living batsman that the crowd rose and cheered him as though he had just completed a century. It is also a fact that he hated the bowling that was called 'slinging'. His method of dealing with slingers did not include appealing to the umpire against an unfair delivery, as was his undoubted right. His way was to subject them to retributive chastisement. There was another memorable occasion when W.G. was savagely hit about the body by Crossland, to the vocal anger of the large crowd. Limping haughtily to the boundary, he told the spectators to mind their own business. He then went back to the crease and subjected the bowlers, and especially Crossland, to a positively sadistic century.

With the slow bowlers he was perhaps not quite so happy, but happy enough. Alfred Shaw clean bowled him twenty times, Barlow thirteen, Briggs ten and Peate nine times. Here were fifty-two separate feats spread over many years. But nobody has calculated how many of his 55,000 runs were scored off the slow bowlers. 'I love 'em all,' he once said in an expansive moment. Broadly, this was true and certainly none of them had any serious terrors for him, not even Wilfred Rhodes, who played his first Test in 1899 when W.G. played his last. 'I never saw such a fellow for hiding the ball,' said W.G. 'He kept the ball out of sight such a time and didn't seem to let you have a look at it until it was almost upon you. . . .'

Though his technique was masterly, he did not surround it

with a smoke-screen of pretentious nonsense. I once heard J. M. Barrie tell how he came upon Thomas Hardy, sitting among a crowd of people, all talking at once, about Art. 'He was the only one who knew anything about it and he never said a wor-rd.' W.G.'s attitude to his undoubted art was similar. When asked what was the best way to play a particularly awkward ball, he replied thoughtfully: 'I should say you ought to put the bat against the ba . . all.' And as he said it, his vowel was as broad as his bat. The reply was neither facetious nor pompous. It was both simple and profound, because, however clever the techniques you might invent for dealing with a difficult kind of ball, they would come to naught if you failed to observe the elementary precept of putting the face of the bat squarely against the ball. There is no substitute for first principles.

He was no great believer in an anxious watching of the bowler's hand. He preferred to watch the ball and not to anticipate the break. This, he argued, applied especially to googly bowlers who in his later days had begun to bowl an off-break with a leg-break action. He quoted with strong approval the counsel given on this problem by Arthur Shrewsbury, whom he considered the next best batsman in England to himself. 'If this kind of bowler,' said Shrewsbury, 'pitches a ball outside my off stump, I expect it to break in from the off and I'm ready to play it that way. If it breaks the other way I leave it alone. But if it pitches on my legs or between my legs and the wicket, I expect it to break in from leg; if it does, I play it, if it doesn't, I leave it alone. And what's more,' added Arthur shrewdly, 'I bide my time, because I never saw one of those chaps who didn't bowl one or two bad balls in an over, and I'd get a four off those. . . .'

That was the principle – it was no secret – on which W.G. batted. Everything that could be hit he hit hard and straight. For a kind of sunlit magic he could not be compared with Ranji and Trumper, but for sheer dominance of the scene there was none to compare with him before and only one after: Sir Donald

Bradman. Similarly, one may say of Bradman that his batting was not so lovely a spectacle as that of his contemporary, Stanley McCabe, but of his absolute subjugation of the bowlers on the field of play there is no shadow of doubt. Wilfred Rhodes, who took more wickets in first class cricket than anybody else and had as richly varied an experience in taming batsmen as W.G. had of battering bowlers, had no doubt in his own mind who was the greatest batsman he had ever bowled against. This man who had bowled Trumper, Jessop, Ranji, MacLaren, Fry, Hobbs, Hammond and Woolley told me: 'Why, Bradman, of course. I once saw him come in and put his first ball past the bowler for four. And the second. And the third. Just like that. Without getting his eye in or anything. You should have seen the power of it, and every one a defensive stroke off a good ball. . . .' This was a true description of Bradman's dominance and, by the same token, it could have stood as a description of W.G.'s as well.

Each of these great batsmen towered above his age, with the difference that Bradman's age was shorter and that he retired on health grounds, as Hutton retired later, before his powers had waned. There was a striking difference in the physical presence of the two men, the difference between the heavy hunter and the racehorse, the bulldozer and the Bentley. Grace's height and reach were commanding, even before he began to put on weight, and his limbs were long and sinewy; Bradman was neat, not obviously muscular, and almost a little man, achieving the opposite effects of looking both dapper and dynamic.

Both practised with almost fanatical concentration when young. Grace was master on bad wickets and on good. The wickets of his stupendous triumphs in the 'seventies were, by modern standards of groundsmanship, almost uniformly bad; indeed, they were literally lethal, as in the fatal match at Lord's in 1870 that killed poor Summers. Bradman shone less often on bad wickets, but I have always felt that the reason for this was no reflection on his competence. Bad wickets were, in his view, outside the realms of serious cricket. He believed that a great batsman should no more be asked to perform on ruined wickets than that, say, Walter Lindrum should have been called on to play on 'a cloth untrue with a twisted cue and elliptical billiard balls'. W.G., not to put too fine a point upon it, was not so fussy. Philosophically or perforce, he put up with whichever wickets he could get.

W.G. had astonishingly keen eyesight at the age of fifty-eight, so that in the years between twenty and thirty his vision must have been more than remarkable. Watching Bradman, you would have said that his eye was equally matchless. You would have been wrong: his eyesight was normal rather than super-normal. His jet-propelled speed in moving to the pitch of the ball came not from eyesight but from his footwork, to which not even Ranji's was superior. This is another reason for believing that Bradman was contemptuous of, rather than inadequately equipped for, play on a bad wicket. A cricketer who combined Grace's eyesight and forearms with Bradman's footwork would have been even further outside the limits of human achievement (and credibility) than either of these great men in fact was. Both were massively effective in execution, not in any dull or mechanical way, but in the sense that their batting was potent far beyond that of any of their contemporaries and almost invulnerable.

I was once in company where the venerable question was in its perennial process of being tossed about: how much had cricket methods changed since the time of W.G. and how would the Old Man get on today? The opinion was rather freely expressed that, with the advance of bowling techniques and the increased concentration on a tight leg field, he would have been hard put to it to survive. My own view, offered without disrespect to anyone, was that the Titan would not, so to speak, be tamed by a Titmus. He might pull his beard over the first ball or two and have a good old-fashioned look at the bowling for the first over or two, but all the time he would 'put the bat to the ball'. Then, having taken its measure, he would settle down, as he had done any summer day in forty years, to play the new bowling comfortably.

The question came round to a very old cricketer who had played against W.G. in his London County days and, as a boy, had watched him in the eighteen-nineties. His tone was courteous and almost compassionate.

'Why,' he said, 'he'd murder 'em.'

You will remember that W.G. began his career as a round-arm bowler of medium pace with an action as high as the laws would allow at the time. Gradually he adopted the slower, guilelessly guileful delivery, well remembered today by elderly Gentlemen who saw it when they were boys. His success in his first Gentlemen v. Players game was with the ball rather than with the bat and nobody doubted his worth as an all-rounder. It may have been a pardonable exaggeration when Bob Thoms, whom we might call the Frank Chester of his day, asserted that if W.G. had not been the best batsman of all time, he would have been the best bowler. There are many candidates for that hypothetical honour. It depends on your period and your allegiance: David Harris, Alfred Mynn, Alfred Shaw, F. R. Spofforth, Sydney Barnes, E. A. Macdonald, Harold Larwood, 'Tiger' O'Reilly. . . . For myself, I should plump for Wilfred Rhodes, whose figure of more than four thousand wickets over a period of more than thirty years is fantastic and almost unanswerable.

But while W.G. could hardly be considered among the greatest half-dozen bowlers, he was well worthy to march in their company. He was a great – the greatest – natural batsman. His contemporaries agree that he was a 'made' bowler; that is, by resource and perpetual practice, he made himself into something far more than a creditable performer. One thing is certain: if he were not a 'great' bowler, he was an almost maddeningly successful one. You cannot take nearly three thousand wickets in first class cricket without being a formidable attacker. These wickets were taken in a career during the greater part of which first class matches were far less frequent than in a modern season. Counties were few and in the other 'big' matches the opposition was formidable. Yet he took 2,864 wickets in first class games. How many he took in games that were less, some only a little less, than first class, only God and Mr Neville Weston know.

It is an added wonder that many of his most stupendous bowling feats were performed immediately after he completed some big innings, lasting four or five hours. And without doubt he was the most ineluctably persistent of bowlers. 'Just one more over.' 'I'll have him directly.' Or, as when his captain suggested a change: 'All right, then, I'll go on at the other end.' These were phrases cherished and remembered by those who had been with him on the field. His bowling figures were remarkable and good judges surmise that, had he been content to bowl a little less, they would have been more remarkable still.

A. G. Steel left a pretty picture of the Old Man in action: an enormous ogre of a man rushing to the wicket with both elbows out, great black beard blowing on each side of him, red and yellow cap on top of a dark, swarthy face. . . . Thus confronted, the batsman expected something more deadly than a gently lobbed-up ball that actually arrived; he could hardly believe that this milk-pudding sort of bowling was really the great man's. Consequently he became flustered and lost his wicket. W.G.'s bowling looked difficult when it was easiest and easy when it was genuinely tricky. There is evidence, too, that he had a firm command of length. Nearly every bowler of W.G.'s era, in contrast to some in our own, kept a reasonably consistent length; otherwise he would not have found a place in a county side at all. W.G.'s length was unexceptionable and though no wizard as a contriver of break, he could turn the ball sufficiently to bother an inexperienced batsman, particularly when, as has been noted, he was looking for non-existent terrors in an innocent delivery. To a newcomer he would murmur blandly: 'I'll get you out, boy; I always get young 'uns out.' And he usually did, but if you looked downcast, he would say: 'Come along to the nets in the morning, and I'll show you how to play that ball.' W.G. at all times used his height and used his head. It was his heart that prompted him to suggest the nets in the morning.

He got many of his wickets from catches at long-leg, for even an experienced batsman found it difficult to resist having a swing at a slow ball on the leg side, apparently sent down for the purpose of offering a bonus in the shape of an easy and satisfying six. This hit did not as a rule quite go for six. Instead, it came down after a period practically in the stratosphere, descending into the safe hands of cousin Gilbert or of brother Fred, the most predatory and prehensile of long-legs. W.G. was once heard to say: 'You saw old Mary Ann (Ephraim Lockwood) look round to see how the field is placed? I'll make him put one right into Fred's mouth.' And, as by some act of hypnosis, that is exactly what he did. Everything happened as if the ball had been on the end of a long piece of string. But although he took many wickets in this way and loved to tempt the demented to destruction, he did not like it to be thought that this was the sole weapon in his armoury and he would not have been pleased to hear that E. V. Lucas called this his 'bread-and-butter ball'. There was far more than bread-and-butter on W.G.'s plate. In the famous match against Notts in 1877 he took seventeen wickets for about five runs each: the last seven of these fell to him in seventeen balls for no runs at all, three of them in one over. It is no compliment to the batting side to call it bread and butter. It was, in more modern phrase, a piece of cake.

W.G. believed in trying every form of cunning attack. He even believed that, in the last resort, a bad ball would sometimes steal a wicket, particularly from a good batsman who treated it with contemptuous carelessness. In the Gentlemen v. Players game at Lord's in 1896 he had been audaciously hit about by Frank Sugg. Imperturbably placing every fielder except himself and the wicketkeeper out in the deep, he saw Sugg caught at long-on in the next over. He sometimes even bowled the googly, as M. Jourdain spoke prose, without knowing it. The lumbering sway of his body as the ball left his hand with a slight leg-break could, if the wind was blowing across the wicket, achieve an off-break with a leg-break action.

He seemed to sum up every batsman's weakness and he would play on it as a dentist plays on a hollow tooth with his drill. Most of all he took an impish delight in bamboozling you out.

When he was young, W.G. was a notable outfield, though, in fact, in his first Gentlemen v. Players match, he fielded brilliantly at cover-point; in later years he was a sturdily courageous point, but his most spectacular fielding was done in none of these positions. At his most brilliant he regularly took catches – hard and low or hard and high – off his own bowling somewhere between cover and silly mid-off.

In 1866, in his eighteenth year, W.G. was reckoned outstanding in the long-field, and especially at long-leg, the position in which young Fred was to achieve even more sensational renown. W.G.'s throw-in on the run was one of the sights of the period. The ball seemed to be bowled rather than thrown. It had, according to the records, a peculiar spin that often baffled the wicketkeeper. Sympathies go out almost automatically to the wicketkeeper, for W.G.'s throw-in at this time when he was at his fastest as a runner and hurdler, must have been a formidable affair. His record for throwing the cricket ball was 122 yards, set up at Eastbourne. At the athletic sports held at the Oval in 1868 when the team of Australian aboriginals were paying their solitary visit to England, he threw the cricket ball 116, 117 and 118 yards in successive throws and, although these came nowhere near the absolute record of 140 yards 2 feet, achieved by R. Percival sixteen years later, it was an impressive feat, especially as, when he had finished, he threw the ball back a hundred yards in sheer exuberance.

W.G. gave up fielding in the deep fairly early in his career because of a damaged shoulder and took up a position near the wicket. He disliked fielding at slip but, as we have observed, he never minded keeping wicket. (There is a record, late in his life, of his keeping wicket in a club match at Eltham, joyously whipping off the bails as the batsman missed the insidious lobs bowled by his youngest son, C.B.) He was never as hostile and thrusting a fieldsman at point as E.M., who was an almost sinful performer in this position, but he was a point to be feared. It was not true, as E.M.'s admirers alleged, that W.G. was 'not within streets of E.M.'; he was practically in the next street.

Even when older and bulkier, he never lost a certain degree of agility. When the ball collided with either of his huge hands, there was a sound like a smack on a board, and the board was extremely hard. The ball went into those hands, as C. T. Studd said, like a pea into a top hat. On his American trip a startled critic wrote: 'It would seem as if the ball were fascinated by Mr Grace's basilisk eye, for it seems to jump into his hand.' When on his first trip to Australia, he and his friends were afflicted in the small back-blocks town of Stawell by a plague of Egyptian dimensions. Smiting a fly-covered table with one mighty hand, he slew seventy-six. It was the hand of fate and the hand of a master-fieldsman.

But the form of fielding he enjoyed most was a gallop towards silly mid-off directly he had delivered the ball. He always had his mid-off straight behind him to cover the empty space. There was something mesmeric about this action which was not wholly dependent on the subtlety of the delivery. Without any good reason within the laws of physics, the ball would get itself cocked up, as if under some malign influence, in his direction. Some of the catches he made off balls of this kind were easy, some were brilliant, but almost all of them were willed and dictated by a personality stronger than the batsman's. In the Old Trafford Test match of 1888 he took four of these catches, none of which, in the ordinary conceptions of fielding, might have been regarded as catches at all.

Once, in a country game, a ball sent down by W.G. was skied high and hard above square-leg. Yelling to square-leg to get out of the way, W.G. came pounding forward like a charging buffalo. As, with one hand stretched out in front of him, he seized an astonishing catch at full gallop, the bewildered batsman was heard to mutter: 'That chap won't be satisfied till he's keeping wicket to his own bowling.'

In his first class career W.G. took 871 catches. It is usual in such comparisons to leave out wicketkeepers, and if this is done, the only fieldsman with a greater number of catches to his credit than W.G. is the long-armed Frank Woolley.

W.G.'s unconquerable might as a batsman, his craftiness as a bowler and his agility as a fieldsman, need no emphasis. These qualities in combination comprise the most striking phenomenon that has ever appeared on the cricket field. Added to this concentrated wealth of talent was the natural confidence that he possessed and with which he inspired the rest of his side. If W.G. was with you, the game was not lost until the last ball had been bowled. Conversely, if he was against you, the game was never won till the last moment. He revelled in a crisis but did not approach it, 'grim and pallid'. His determination was strong; it was also cheerful. Being human, he occasionally failed with either bat or ball, but failure instantly became a thing that had to be redeemed and redeemed handsomely. Think of those two first-innings ducks for which the misguided James Shaw dismissed him. The retribution exacted in the second innings of each of those two games was overwhelming. You literally never knew when you had him. His consistency over the years was unique.

When someone ventured the opinion that W. L. Murdoch was as good as W.G., Alec Bannerman scornfully replied: 'Murdoch? Why, W.G. has forgotten more than Billy ever learnt.'

As for Murdoch himself, hero of the first Test match played on English soil, he had no illusions about the comparison, and his own tribute was sincere in the Murdoch manner.

'What do I think of W.G.? Why, I have never seen his like and never shall. I tell you my opinion, which is that W.G. should never be put underground. When he dies his body ought to be embalmed and permanently exhibited in the British Museum as "the colossal cricketer of all time".'

*from* THE GREAT CRICKETER *1957*

# W. G. Grace

## CLIFFORD BAX

Most cricketers regard the eighteen-nineties as the Golden Age of the game, though something depends on the date of the enthusiast's birth. If Keats, who tried his hand at batting, had lived to be elderly, he would probably have refused to admit that there was ever a finer player than Alfred Mynn; whose death inspired one of the most charming lines in cricket verse –

'Lightly lie the turf upon thee, kind and manly Alfred Mynn'.*
Any contemporary of Grace would have been irritated to hear
that Lohmann was a better bowler and Ranjitsinhji a better
batsman. We know how Francis Thompson sighed for 'my
Hornby and my Barlow long ago',† though nothing but
Lancastrian loyalty can explain why anybody should sigh for
Barlow. And other 'supreme masters' have captured the admira-
tion of later onlookers – as for instance MacLaren, Jessop, Fry,
Tom Richardson, Hayward, John Tyldesley, Hobbs, Sydney
Barnes and Bradman.

Certainly the 'nineties produced many brilliant rivals to
W.G. – too many for citation; and at first it really seemed that
his mastery might be declining. He had become so heavy that,
as with the Duke of Bracciano, there was difficulty in finding a
strong enough horse to carry him a-hunting. Moreover, he was
now in his forties, while E.M. had advanced to the age of fifty.
This may explain why Gloucestershire, first or second in the
Championship table in 1870, 1873, 1876, 1877, 1878 and 1880,
thereafter sank low, often finishing last. Notts and Surrey
easily displaced them, and then came the triumphant and
unended magnificence of Yorkshire. Or was there a contributory
cause of Gloucestershire's eclipse? At the Oval, while we were
watching their players in the field, C. B. Fry remarked, 'There!
You see? It's always like that with these West Countrymen;
they bowl superbly for an hour or so, and then they begin to
think about apples.' The 'nineties merit their glory because in
those days there were still innumerable 'Gentlemen' who could
play cricket throughout the summer. Certain county teams,
particularly those in the West, frequently fielded sides that
contained eight or nine 'Esquired', and country-house cricket
still flourished, though it may have been at its most delightful
in the 'eighties. We should reflect that amateurs rarely 'played
for their averages', whereas W.G. himself says that the Nottinghamshire players, most of whom were professionals, did for
some years notoriously think of that final table of Batting

* See page 448.                              † See page 459.

Averages which, appearing in September, looks like an immense funeral procession lamenting the dead summer. We are told that three days is not now long enough for the completion of a Test Match and that the trouble comes from the doping of the wickets; but it may be the enterprising spirit of the amateur batsmen which made three days quite long enough for a Test Match victory in the Golden Age.

In his middle forties the Doctor could not expect to bowl and bat as he had when he was fifteen years leaner and suppler. He still did more than well, but in the early 'nineties other and younger players naturally did even better. And then! In the year of his forty-seventh birthday the 'Old Man' astounded the whole sporting world. Indeed his achievements in 1895 continue even now to amaze all cricket lovers. What he achieved is therefore pretty well known, but it must be rehearsed once more. In the month of May he scored over a thousand runs, a feat never previously accomplished; he was second in the First-Class Batting Records with an average of 51; he completed his century of centuries with a score of 288; and in one game when he made 257 and 73 not out, this veteran was on the field of play from the first ball of the match until the last – for three days, in a word. Little wonder if another National Subscription was instituted by the *Daily Telegraph* with its 'Shilling Testimonial', by the *Sportsman* and by the M.C.C. The 'good old man' received more than nine thousand pounds.

It is now that *Punch* takes his part in the cheering. 'Mr Grace's favourite dish? Batter Pudding.' 'Dr Grace, C.B. (Companion of the Bat).' 'Classic title: the Centurion.' 'Dr Grace to be Cricket-Field-Marshal.' In June, adapting an old popular song ('The Two Obadiahs'), *Punch*, with a reference to young W.G.'s glasses, wrote:

> Says the young W.G. to the old W.G.
>  'How I wish that I could time and place like you!
> I should like to hear them clap me but my giglamps
>    handicap me;
>  Still I'll do my little best to pile a few!'

It was also in June that *The Times* referred roundly to 'Dr W. G. Grace whose name has been everywhere of late – except where it might well have been – on the Birthday Honours List.' Here was a bold opinion which *Punch* eagerly supported:

> True, 'Thunderer', true. He stands the test
> Unmatched, unchallengeable Best
> At our best game! Requite him!
> For thirty years to hold first place
> Please a stout, sport-loving race;
> By Jove, Sir William Gilbert Grace
> Sounds splendid. *Punch* says 'Knight him'.

Even considering that Queen Victoria was still on the throne (who may never have heard of any cricketer) and that 1895 was less democratic than 1948, it is surprising that a suggestion advanced by two much-respected papers should have been ignored.

At the end of this season, in September, *Punch* remains faithful to the great player, as we see in this verse, one of several:

> Oft have I seen that cricketer or this
> Bat, bowl or field or catch (or even miss)
> And oft, astounded by some piece of play,
> Have marked with letters red the auspicious day;
>
> Yet ne'er before three heroes have I seen
> More apt and splendid on the well-rolled green;
> Men of one skill, though varying in race—
> MacLaren, Ranjitsinhji, Grand old Grace.

He could not quite sustain such an amazing standard of skill when playing among men who were half his age – and against the largest assembly of first-rate bowlers (I surmise) in the chronicles of the game; but for the remaining years of the century he still figured near the top of the Annual Batting Averages, and was obviously still a useful slow bowler who could tease fifty little victims to their doom.

It was, I should guess, at the end of the imposing nineteenth century or in the early years of our less agreeable era that Grace had his revenge upon Old Murdoch, as indeed I promised to relate. The friendly reader will recall that, as a stripling, Grace played against Twenty-two of Corsham (Wiltshire). For more than twenty years, beginning in 1911, I took a team of holiday cricketers to try our luck against Eleven of Corsham; and one year among our opponents was a Mr Tanner, who, if I remember rightly, was a little lame. We liked him at once, and we liked him the more when, bleeding copiously from his nose which a leaping ball had struck, he refused to retire hurt. We liked him still more when, at the end of a happy game (for even he seemed to think it so) Mr Tanner said to me, 'A good match, and a hot day. Would you and your lads care to drive to my farm, have a drink and take a dip in the river – it flows to one side of my garden, under willows?' Of course we accepted, got into our fleet of cars and followed Mr Tanner.

A fine August evening in the West Country, with a keen but friendly cricket-match aglow in your thoughts, is, we may assume, a very fair foretaste of Paradise. John Drinkwater once musingly said in Charles Fry's box at Lord's, 'To sit here watching a Test Match equates with my requirements in Heaven'; but to be a little leg-weary after actually contending in a match with your favourite enemy, and to visit an old farm that possessed a water-wheel which is mentioned in Domesday Book, to be kindly greeted by a not surprised Mrs Tanner, to sip her whisky-and-soda – well, that is to gain a foreknowledge of Nirvana. A writer who is not widely read may sometimes be lucky. I wrote of our present experience long ago, in 1936, but I can confidently reproduce my account of that evening, nor will I bother the reader with quotation marks.

We had packed our bags, and we made the journey to fifteenth-century Lacock, a village that I had known and admired for more than twenty years. We arrived at Mr Tanner's farmhouse. All around us were meadows for which, I do assure you, the only true adjective is 'lush'; and what with the slanting gold of the sun, the rich emerald of the grass, the tall slumbering aureate trees and the length of willow-shadowed water, that scene was perhaps the most gently beautiful, the most heart-easing and most English that I ever absorbed. It was hard to remember that in a world which was here so idyllic (Pan might have been peeping at us from under the willows) there could be swindlings, wars and political manœuvres. Within a few minutes two of my players had stripped and were swimming under the low-branched trees.

Meanwhile I – no swimmer, unhappily – had followed our host into his home and here, he told me, his father and his grandfather had lived out their years. . . . Just inside the front door stood a heap of large, round white stones. Most of them were cricket-ball size, but the one on top, the prize piece, was as large as a football. These mysterious relics mystified me. Tanner, who had known them from infancy, said, 'Well, in years gone by, people fed their horses on bran, and in the bran there were imperceptible scraps of metal. The scraps coagulated and, given fifteen or twenty years, became solid blocks. Lift that one,' he suggested; and we thought with compassion of the slave-horse who had trudged about with such a cruel weight in its belly.

Presently, when the bathers had rejoined us, we noticed among several glass cases one which provided a stuffed immortality for a large and particularly lugubrious fish. 'That,' said our host, 'was caught by W.G.' This was like suddenly finding Agamemnon's autograph, and we soon learned that the mighty man had often stayed at the farm. 'When I was a boy,' said Mr Tanner, 'I knew him quite well. Once he took me into the garden where we had put up a cricket net, and he began by bowling to me for a long while, and then he called out, 'Come along, laddie, you shall bowl to me now.' After some time he managed to let me hit his off-stump, and he'd done it so cleverly that I didn't suspect for many years that he missed the ball in order that I should have one triumph to remember always. Of course, like most men of his period he was selfish, and he could be something of a bully, but he certainly had his kindly moments toward a small boy in this house.' 'There was also,' resumed our friends, 'an amusing occasion when Grace was staying here while W. L. Murdoch was to play in a county match. W.G. wagered that on the first day of the match he would catch more fish than the number of runs which Murdoch would make, and the Australian accepted the odds. So as to make sure of winning, W.G. began fishing in the river there at four in the morning, and he actually caught a hundred, mostly roach, and by supper-time he packed up his tackle, pretty well contented. But what do you think? Murdoch had scored a hundred and three.'

The two old cronies must have twinkled as Grace handed over his golden sovereigns.

*from* CRICKETING LIVES – W. G. GRACE *1952*

# Ranji, Fry and Jessop — The Golden Age of Batting

## H. S. ALTHAM

It may, I hope, be of some little interest to attempt some general estimate of English cricket as it was in the opening years of this century, and to appreciate, if we can, in what ways it differed from the game as we know it today. In the first place, then, the County Championship had by this time extended itself to something very like its present dimensions, and complaints were already to be heard that our bowlers were being bowled to death. More wearing, however, than the actual amount of work they were called upon to do, were the conditions under which they had to do it. This was the era of the perfect wicket. The preparation of the pitch by such artificial aids as marl and liquid manure had now been reduced to a fine art, and whereas when the Champion first began to roll off his centuries there were not more than five grounds in England where run-getting was positively easy in fine weather, there were now more than double that number on which, given fine weather throughout, two evenly matched county sides might fairly be backed to fail to arrive at a decision in three days. Certainly the proportion of drawn games was very high, and, as MacLaren pointed out in an interesting article contributed to *Wisden* for 1905, it was the last four or five hours of play, with no prospect of a result, that tended to kill our bowlers and handicapped them so heavily as compared with the Australians with their much smaller first-class programme and the stimulus of a certain finish in all their games.

But at least some of the explanation lay in the personal balance between bowlers and batsmen. It was not that our bowling in the opening years of the century was weak – far from it. A batsman who played regularly in county cricket for the decade 1895–1905 would, I believe, have been far more severely tested than anyone could be today. On difficult wickets, Briggs, Blythe, Wilfred Rhodes, and Sam Hargreave of Warwickshire, to say nothing of Dennett and Cranfield, were certainly a more formidable combination than any left-handers he would now have to face. The off-theory was being to some extent abandoned, and a crop of right-hand leg-break bowlers was arising to confront him with new problems. Of these Charles Townsend was the prototype, Braund the best, and C. M. Wells and Vine both very good. George Hirst had in 1901 suddenly discovered that he could swerve, and, from being an ordinarily good fast bowler, became a positive portent in the cricket world. As one batsman plaintively remarked, 'I don't really see how one can be expected to play a ball which, when it leaves the bowler's arm, appears to be coming straight, but when it reaches the wicket is like a very good throw-in from cover-point!' He was a terror to even the best of the opening batsmen; if they escaped being clean bowled, there were the serried ranks of his leg-traps to negotiate – a new proposition, but not 'leg theory' and still less 'body line'. The right-handed swerve, too, was beginning to appear, on the model of M. A. Noble, and no one today can bowl it better than did Ted Arnold of Worcestershire.

But by far the greatest contrast between then and now is surely presented by the fast bowlers. If we are not today quite so badly off for real speed as we were when cricket was resumed after the war, yet neither in quantity nor quality can we compare in this respect with the situation that our batsmen of the last generation had to face. In those days practically every county side possessed a bowler of real pace – pace, that is to say, great enough to make him definitely unpleasant to anything like a faint heart. It is safe to say that the great majority of these fast bowlers would, at his best, be today something of a phenomenon, and a strong candidate for a place in our England Eleven; yet a quarter of a century ago they were bowling up and down the country. They were all in the day's work, and our batsmen were wholly undismayed.

To judge from an article contributed by D. L. A. Jephson to the 1901 *Wisden*, the fielding of the period left a good deal to be desired. Possibly the stalemate of the perfect wicket and the vast number of drawn matches was conducive to a spirit of lethargy on the part of some elevens. Nevertheless there were a great number of fine fieldsmen playing, and particularly fine slips and deep-fields, the two areas in which we are weakest today. Now, it is certain that on good wickets the former play much the largest part of all fieldsmen in capturing the wickets of the best batsmen. The placing of the field at the beginning of the century was still more orthodox and less elastic than such as we are accustomed to today. On-side play had not yet developed to any very great extent, and the scoring strokes chiefly to be guarded against were still the straight-drive, and the cut. The Australians had not yet, under the inspiration of Noble, shown us how to adjust the field to any particular batsman, on the system of the inner and the outer ring, which they subsequently worked out with such cramping efficiency. Still, there were great captains in the land, and men like A. C. MacLaren, Hawke, MacGregor, A. O. Jones, Ranjitsinhji, Sam Woods, and Harry Foster were very much alive to any situation, and very far from likely to make the batsman's task any easier than it had necessarily to be.

Neither excellence of pitches, nor weakness of attack, can supply an adequate explanation of what, to my thinking, is the outstanding feature of English cricket at this time – the superiority of bat over ball. The truest explanation is, I believe, the simplest, that our batting was at least as good as, if not better than, at any period before or since. The latter end of most county sides were not so difficult to get rid of as they are now, when the genuine non-striker seems almost to be disappearing from our ranks, but the first half-dozen or so on most sides included two or three men of really outstanding ability. The general level of defence on turning pitches may not have reached the present level, but as against this we must set the fact that there were far more aggressive batsmen playing – men

who would use their feet and would never surrender the
initiative to the bowler without a struggle, whose 'half-hour'
was as good as many of our modern players' afternoons. Above
all on fast wickets would the contrast be apparent. The great
majority of the leading batsmen had no use for the short back-
lift, the double shuffle with the feet, the push for one, or the
tickle for two. They were masters of the drive; the cut was not
yet *démodé*, and the now common spectacle of the medium-
paced bowler with no man on the boundary would have been
laughed at and hit out of court.

If the general level of batsmanship was high at the beginning
of the century, the relative level of amateur to professional
batsmen was higher still. In the season of 1923 there were only
seven amateurs in the first twenty-five places in the averages; in
1900 there were eighteen amateurs in the first twenty, while
two years later, of the thirty-four men who averaged 30 or over
for the year, only ten were professionals.

Collectively, then, amateur batting outstripped professional;
selectively, the amateurs' lead was equally marked. One instance
must suffice. Of the side that went into the field for the first
Test Match of 1902 – considered by many the best we have ever
produced – the men chosen for their batting alone were, with
the exception of Johnny Tyldesley, all amateurs – MacLaren,
Jackson, Jessop, Fry, and Ranjitsinhji.

The first two, wonderful players as they were, never bulked
quite so big in the imagination of contemporary England as did
the last trio, and, inasmuch as first-class cricket depends for
public support to a great extent upon the personalities and
methods of its greatest exponents, these three wonderful
batsmen perhaps did more for the popularity of the game than
any cricketers since the Champion himself. Wherever they went,
crowds flocked to see them. With Gilbert Jessop it was a
glorious gamble; with the Prince and Charles Fry on the same
side, the spectators must have felt that their entrance money was
on the nearest approach to a certainty that the game was ever
likely to afford. As a matter of fact, in their greatest seasons

together, 1899, 1900, and 1901, they practically never failed; if one was dismissed for a single figure, the other would generally come along with a century, often with two. But as a rule they both got runs, and hour after hour the bowlers would pound away on the then utterly pitiless Hove wicket, sheer artistry at one end, supreme self-mastery and physical perfection at the other; and day after day, on every variety of wicket, and against every type of bowling, the telegraph would proclaim the greatest pair of batsmen that ever played together on the same county side.

K. S. Ranjitsinhji, as he was then universally known, came to England in his twentieth year, having played the game as a boy in India, with a fixed determination to master the art of batting. It is a popular fallacy that he was a heaven-born genius who had no need for apprenticeship at all; as a matter of fact, no cricketer has ever practised more arduously. He would engage the best professional bowlers for a month or more in the spring, and bat against them for hours every day, to learn the defence which his Indian experience had not given him. Of course, he was blest with supreme natural gifts, and an alert and receptive mind, physique that was at once strong, supple, and perfectly co-ordinated, and, as a result, a lightning quickness of conception and execution that no man, not even Victor Trumper, has ever quite equalled. But it was by unremitting application that he trained himself to make the utmost of these innate advantages. He was underrated as a batsman at Cambridge, though his slip-fielding was something of a wonder; and, though he did win his 'blue' in '93, it was not until two years later, when fully qualified for Sussex, that he leapt in a single month into fame. At his very first appearance for his county – against the M.C.C. at Lord's – he scored 77 not out and 150, and from that start he never once looked back. In the following season, 1895, he broke W.G.'s record aggregate with 2,780 runs for an average of 57; but his greatest years were 1899 and 1900, in both of which he passed the 3,000, in the latter averaging 87 for forty innings, and scoring over 200 five times.

Of these great scores, the most remarkable was an innings against Middlesex at Hove. It was the last day of the match; the wicket was considerably affected by a heavy thunderstorm, and he was opposed by Albert Trott, Hearne, and Rawlin. Overnight, Fry and Killick had scored well, but on the Saturday the rest of the side found run-getting terribly difficult: Vine scored 17, no one else got into double figures, and the Prince got 202! One more story illustrating his supreme ascendancy. In the next season Sussex had had a dreadful gruelling in the field at Taunton, and at the end of the second day it was agreed that they should get their own back on the morrow, and that their captain should make 300. The latter complacently agreed; he failed to keep his promise by 15 runs, but he was still not out!

In method, Ranji was a law unto himself. His extraordinary quickness of eye and mind allowed him to do things utterly impracticable for others. He would play back to the fastest bowlers on the fastest wicket, and never had to hurry his stroke; his cutting was marvellous; his leg-side play has never been approached, and he broke the hearts of the best bowlers by the way he deflected their fastest breakbacks to the boundary. It was not a glance, as we now understand the term: the ball was met with the full face of the bat, and at the psychological moment those wrists of steel pivoted, and the ball sped away to leg. But it is less commonly realized that he was always a wonderful driver, and, indeed, in his later years discarded defence more and more for attack, and often played the innings of a pure hitter, only that it was backed throughout by his marvellously resourceful back-play.

It is an open secret, which he himself would be the first to admit, that it was his association with the Indian Prince that raised Charles Fry from a good into a great player. Gifted with keen powers of observation, an acute and highly analytical mind, unlimited resolution and patience, he was supremely calculated to profit by the example of genius, and it is by no means mere coincidence that back-play and driving were the predominating features of his batting. It was not that Fry could not play the off-strokes; in the wet season of 1903 his driving past mid-off and extra cover was one of the finest things about his play, whilst in the final Test Match against the 1905 Australian side he further confounded the critics by his brilliant cutting in an innings of 144. But, on the whole, he concentrated on the straight drive and on every variety of on-side stroke, finding that type of game the safest and at the same time most profitable, and it was just this ability to know what he could do best, to concentrate on that, and to do it supremely well, that made him for years the greatest run-getting machine that modern cricket has known. His marvellous physique made him impervious to fatigue, his self-control never slackened. More markedly than any of his contemporaries he adopted a distinct secondary position at the wicket, and as he stood there, upright and perfectly balanced, with the bat lifted back over the middle stump, he presented to the unfortunate bowler a most dominating and discouraging figure.

Statistically, his record is stupendous, though he played by no means as regularly as some others; let him get 30, and he was as likely as not to get 200. His defence was as consummate as his driving was terrible; he mastered the best bowlers almost as readily as he took toll from the worst. Five times he exceeded 2,000 runs in the season, and once, in 1901, 3,000. This was his greatest year, in which he scored six consecutive hundreds. Five times in his career he scored 100 in each innings of a match, and on three other occasions he only missed doing so by one run.

It is one of the tragedies of English cricket that, with his many other interests and activities, he could never manage to visit Australia. Had he gone there, and once become acclimatized to the conditions, there is no saying what he might not have done.

Had C. L. Townsend been able to play regularly for his county in the years when he had become an England batsman, it is possible that he and Gilbert Jessop together would have played almost as big a role in Gloucestershire cricket as did Ranji and Fry for Sussex. As things were, Jessop had to shoulder the greater part of the burden alone. Inevitably, from the nature of his method, he was a match-winner rather than a consistent match-saver, and the county, with their weak bowling, could not avoid defeat often enough to be a serious rival throughout a season to the strongest sides. As a hitter, Jessop stands absolutely alone; others, such as C. I. Thornton and Bonnor, may have driven the ball farther and higher, but no cricketer that has ever lived hit it so often, so fast, and with such a bewildering variety of strokes. His very stance, like a panther's crouch, bespoke aggression. The secret of his hitting lay in his speed, of eye, of foot, and of hand. He combined in a unique degree strength and flexibility of shoulder, arm, and wrist. Length had no meaning for him; it was the length ball he hit best, and he hit it where the whim or the placing of the field suggested. One moment he would drive it along the ground or lift it, straight or with pull, over the deep-field's head; the next he would drop on his right knee and sweep the off-ball round to square-leg, or lie back and cut it like a flash past third man. It was impossible to keep him quiet, impossible to set the field for him. When he was in form, the best bowlers were as helpless against him as the worst; he hit them just when and where he pleased. Nowadays we call a batsman a quick scorer if he makes 40 runs in an hour; the 'Croucher's' average rate in any of his best innings was approximately double! In his little brochure on Gloucester County Cricket Mr Ashley-Cooper has summarized his greatest feats. They make almost unbelievable reading. Four times he scored 100 in both innings of a county match, and on each occasion at the rate of about 100 an hour; against the West Indian team of 1900 he made 157 runs between 3.30 p.m. and 4.30 p.m.; and in the same year he made over 100 at Lord's in just over an hour. His longest innings, 286 against Sussex at Brighton in 1903, took him less than three hours; but perhaps his most astonishing feat of sustained fast scoring was his 191 in ninety minutes against the Players of the South, at Hastings, in 1907.

His century which won the Oval Test Match of 1902 was, of course, one of the most famous innings of all history; but almost equally notable was his 93 at Lord's against the famous quartet of South African googly bowlers in 1907. In that innings he received only sixty-three balls! The Australians were outspoken in their opinion that no representative side was complete without him. One other point in connection with his batting deserves to be noticed. His capacity for quick scoring was so incalculable that he must have saved many a match before the last innings was ever begun. His opponents simply did not dare venture a normal declaration, knowing as they did that an hour or less of Jessop might confound their best calculations. As a fieldsman at extra cover he has never been equalled. His return – and it was often so masked as to deceive the runners – was so fast that he could afford to stand much deeper than the average good field, and so cut off the four as well as save the single. As a fast bowler he was good enough to be selected, even if erroneously, to play that role for England.

I have dwelt at some length on these three great cricketers because I conceive them to have exercised an unequalled influence upon their generation. Gilbert Jessop was the living embodiment of that sensationalism which will always make the most direct and compelling appeal to the man who pays his shilling and wants his money's worth. The two great Sussex batsmen, by their mastery of back-play and the on-side game, orientated the field afresh, and, by their influence on bowlers and example to batsmen, laid down the lines which, for good or evil, their successors have followed in the development of 'modern cricket.'

*from* A HISTORY OF CRICKET *1926*

# C. B. Fry

## DENZIL BATCHELOR

Magnifico on Olympus.

It is half-past ten: time for the caravan to start from Brown's Hotel. The Bentley is at the door; Mr Brooks, the chauffeur, is wise-cracking out of the side of his guttapercha mouth. Aboard are writing pads and binoculars and travelling rugs, a copy of Herodotus, a box of Henry Clay cigars, and reserve hampers of hock and chicken sandwiches in case there has been a strike of caterers in North-West London. A monocle glitters. A silver crest passes, high and haughty, above the cities of the plain. C. B. Fry is off to Lord's.

When the car is held up by the queue milling round the W.G. gates, a greeting comes through the open window. It is uttered by a thin grey Colonel with the neatly folded look Soames Forsyte wore before he grew up to be imperious and hectoring like Errol Flynn. 'Excuse me, sire, but aren't you C. B. Fry?' It is probably the only time in his life the Colonel has ever spoken to a complete stranger. He does not blush, but he grows a richer grey with sheer embarrassment.

Charles Fry holds up a benevolent forefinger. 'I know exactly what you're going to tell me. You saw me bat in 1909 at Southampton. I made two.'

These shock tactics rattle the Colonel, who has expected nothing more than a little harmless long-distance trench warfare. 'As a matter of fact it *was* Southampton in 1909. But you only made one.'

By rights that should round off the campaign, but it doesn't. The Colonel is taken aboard and transported to Charles's box. Here he sits, day after day. At twelve he is given the cocktail a visitor from Mars has introduced into the box; a straightforward tumbler filled with equal measures of gin and whisky which as soon as it has been christened a Bamboo-shoot is somehow accepted by the company as innocent to the point of being non-alcoholic. He eats lobsters for lunch with that fine Traminer '26, and has strawberries for tea and hears Charles Fry declaim (but not translate) Herodotus, and meets, perhaps, E. V. Lucas, Dr Dalton, Sir Pelham Warner, Clifford and Arnold Bax, Peggy Ashcroft, James Agate and a lady dressed in bridal white from veil to shoe-buckle to celebrate her divorce which becomes absolute during the lunch interval.

Moreover, sometime in the afternoon, another lady whom the host calls My Madam, pays a call. In youth Mrs Fry was an honorary whip with the Duke of Beaufort's Hounds, and the model for a G. F. Watts' painting: an unusual double. When Charles was a selector of England teams she gave him the benefit of her valued advice. Sometimes she had not actually seen the players in action, but she appeared to have an instinct about their very names which reacted no less sensitively than a dowser's twig. She does not show up for lunch, preferring to eat her sandwiches in the stand, but one feels that when she arrives the cricketers had better pull themselves together. If they don't, some telepathically conveyed barbed paragraph will spring up in the genial flow of Charles's report for the *Evening Standard*.

For while the small talk sparkles, glittering and undangerous as indoor fireworks, and everyone with a nodding acquaintance comes to call, Charles in tussore coat, wide grey felt hat and monocle, continues his effortless production of paragraphs for the column called 'C. B. Fry Says'. He writes in staccato style, bringing the picture of the gracious battlefield at Lord's sharply before the reader's eye. He seeks to dramatize the scene, or to offer it to the reader as a film script, not forgetting that, until he tells them, most of his readers have no idea whether or not Paynter is a giant with a cavalry moustache, or that O'Reilly's right arm coils up like a cobra as the snake-charmer calls the tune. He says that he is writing for nursemaids in Wimbledon: for in those days there are nursemaids in Wimbledon. To make quite sure that these ladies are being properly catered for, he occasionally appeals for the veto or imprimatur of the Colonel, sitting in helpless hypnosis at the back of the box. And so the day wears on.

Late in the afternoon it is remembered that an old Wadham friend, now a Colonial Bishop, is believed to be in the President's box. Mr Brooks is sent off to fetch him for a Bamboo-shoot or a cup of China tea. You see the two of them ambling along past the little mound below the Press Box, where Neville Cardus is generally to be found. Mr Brooks is in full spate. 'Of course you understand, sir, I don't only drive the Commander, I also do a turn now and then on the Halls. "Public Enemy Number One" – that's the way I'm billed, see. Well, the other night, on I come, dressed up like a Boy Scoutmaster, but still wearing my dog-collar, see. Now this is the point, if you get me, and mark you this story's clean, dead clean, and yet you know you've got to laugh, quite as much as the yarns you really do laugh at when there's only you and the missus. Well, in I come, see, innocent as a babe that's only a twinkle in his father's eye. But what I *don't* know, see, is that this isn't no jamboree at all, it's the Annual General Meeting of Birth Control for Central Africa, see and the lady in the chair says. . . .'

The Bishop waves away the weak tea and opts for the Bamboo-shoot.

That is Charles Fry's box in the great days of old. It will never be the same again. The war wafted Mr Brooks into industry, and for all I know the Bentley was melted down into a tank, and Charles is no longer a mere Commander, but a Captain, R.N.V.R., and James Agate is dead, having dined with me a night or two before the end, and told me that his final regret was that God would not allow him to last long enough to see the Third World War in which mankind would destroy itself – at the sight of which God would laugh himself to death.

And Madam is dead too. I went down to her memorial service, and Charles wrung me by the hand and said, to hide his emotion, 'Look, I'll show you an infallible way to play a googly.' He had picked up a cricket bat and was demonstrating imperiously,

when the chapel bell rang. 'Never mind. We'll finish afterwards.'
At which moment, I was reminded of the bereaved friend:
'Dear Otis, You lucky bum. You had forty years with that
delightful woman. How I envy you. Yours sincerely. . . .'

Yes, it was all a long time ago, when the grey Colonel, with
his features neatly folded like the features of Soames Forsyte,
sat at the back of the box during the four days of a Test Match
without anyone discovering his name. You see, if not the
Colonel, someone exactly like his unidentified self was always
there, in Charles's box at every big game. If not the grey
Colonel, a pink clergyman who had strayed out of the very
heart of *The Private Secretary*. If not the clergyman, a very old
gentleman indeed, who had just returned from Africa, whither
he had buried himself in '79, who asked innocently half-way
through the third day whether his host had ever taken an active
part in cricket himself.

There were years, of course, when there were no boxes to be
had. On one midsummer day during one of these, I had a rather
bored lady in tow when I ran into Charles. He thought of a way
of mellowing this gelid Diana, who only uncurled a nostril
when he unbosomed himself of the view that polo was the best
of all possible games because the ponies did the work while the
men got the applause. He sent a page (I do not know whether
M.C.C. has pages on its strength – but he sent a page) to the
Langham at which he had dined on the previous night to fetch
a bottle of Liebfraumilch of a vintage which he considered might
be worthy of the occasion. The boy (who undoubtedly went both
ways on a 53 'bus) was given strict instructions to drive back in
a taxi which never exceeded fifteen miles an hour, even if it
travelled all the way in second gear. The lady drank the great
wine with an air of condescension. She said she had always
liked Alsatian wines and could not understand why all her
friends affected to despise them.

Then there were the jovial nights, when stumps were drawn
and it could be forgotten that Billy Brown, with no strokes at
all to which MacLaren could have given august approval, had

made a utility double century that would stand in the record book for ever, and be forgotten before the next Test Match. The nights were the signal for white tie and tails, and dancing from ten o'clock till three in the morning. For Charles might (and did) say that polo was probably a better game than cricket, and that Rugby was a better game than soccer, but the one opinion he stood fast on was that the beginning and the end of all the games he respected was dancing. The Greeks knew the secret. A game was not worth the trouble it put you to, unless it was first and last a physical fine art. Cricket was a dance with a bat in your hand, or with the encumbrance of a ball. What was exquisite and memorable was the lyric movement of the artist in action. What was incidental was the score that resulted from his having a bat in his hands, or the analysis that came about from his handling of the ball.

In the dance itself there were no such ignoble impedimenta. The art was pure, not applied. On with the white tie and tails, and let the evening be given over to abandonment to the graces of movement! To surrender oneself to this delight was the surest cure for self-consciousness, which Charles Fry saw as a national failing. Watch the young Englishman enter the ball-room. His hand goes inevitably to his Adam's apple to straighten his tie. When he learns *not* to do that he is at least on the way to the rhythmic control of his body which is the fundamental necessity for success in every game.

Make no mistake about it, Charles Fry has pondered the reason for his pre-eminence as an all-round sportsman. At the end of all his ruminations on the subject, he has no doubt whatsoever that if a man will consent to become an expert dancer first, all these accomplishments shall be added unto him. And almost as a matter of course.

*from* CRICKETING LIVES – C. B. FRY *1951*

# G. L. Jessop

## A COUNTRY VICAR

Jessop's performance in his first match v. Oxford was decidedly modest. In the first innings his score could not have been smaller; in the second innings he was stumped after making 19. In bowling he captured five wickets at a cost of 173 runs. People said he lacked patience – that he began to hit too soon – that he ought, first, to have 'played himself in'. People always make these assertions when the great hitter fails. And there is, I admit, some wisdom in getting the pace of the ground. But had Jessop, throughout his career, listened to the advocates for caution he would not have been his true, glorious, incomparable self. Half his value to the side for which he played would have gone. He was always an individualist. He played his own game – for him. He was not a model example for callow youth; few of any age would dare to try and imitate him. He was unique. He had the eye of a hawk, the strength of an ox, and the courage of a man who knows his own powers and his own mind. The faster the bowling the more he liked it and the harder he hit.

Jessop showed Oxford his capabilities in 1897. The Light Blues won the toss and were all out for 156. N. F. Druce (41) and J. H. Stogdon (20) were the highest scorers. Jessop was bowled by J. C. Hartley for 4; but there were other good batsmen who did little or nothing. C. J. Burnup made 0, F. Mitchell 6, H. H. Marriott 13, C. E. M. Wilson 19, E. H. Bray 6. It was a disappointing show. F. H. E. Cunliffe bowled uncommonly well, and Hartley seemed difficult to play, but it was a poor performance on a wicket which was fast and true. We all thought Oxford would secure a long lead. Jessop was the main cause of their failing to do so. He bowled at a great pace, and the Cambridge fielding was brilliant. At the end of the first day the Dark Blues had scored 130 for 8 wickets.

On the second morning Hartley and Cunliffe battled bravely,

and the Oxford total reached 162 – 6 runs ahead. An even game so far! But Cambridge again began badly. Mitchell fell with the score at 11, whilst Burnup and Marriott were obviously in difficulties. However, they struggled on, gradually mastered the bowling, and added 103 invaluable runs before Marriott was caught for an admirable 50. Druce failed, and it was once more anybody's game. Then Jessop came in. In less than twenty minutes – with thirteen scoring strokes – he knocked up 42 runs out of 51. It was a marvellous display – his driving was astonishing – and the ease and rapidity with which he scored had an undoubted moral effect on the later batsmen. The total reached 336. So Oxford had to make 331 to win. They never looked like getting them, and were all out for 151.

A week later, on a badly worn pitch, for Gentlemen v. Players at Lord's, Jessop punished the best professional bowling in England to the tune of 67 runs, out of 88, in thirty-five minutes. The batsman at the other end was Francis Ford – hardly a stone-waller, but, in comparison with Jessop, he looked like one that day!

A fortnight afterwards, at Harrogate, playing for Gloucestershire, Jessop took 101 out of 118, in forty-five minutes, off the Yorkshire bowlers!

He was the idol of the crowd. They loved him – as well they might! We all loved him!

'It's Jessop next!'

Those words used to cause a strange shiver of expectation and delight. I always felt it myself – a cold sensation running down the spine – and the ring of spectators swayed with it as corn waves in a sudden breeze on a summer day. One could watch the tremor encircle the whole field of play; it was like an electric shock. And when the figure of the hero emerged from the pavilion the public roared a welcome.

I can visualize the scene, at Lord's, on the occasion of a big match – Oxford v. Cambridge, or Gentlemen v. Players, or, perhaps, England v. Australia. The great throng of people – tense with excitement – their faces all turned to the pavilion.

'Here he comes!' Then the applause began.

A Light Blue cap moving swiftly above the members' silk hats – whatever the match I believe I always saw Jessop in a Cambridge cap; it became very faded as the years went by. A broad, sturdy form descending the steps – his immense chest and shoulders made him look shorter than he was – advancing rapidly towards the wicket. He walked with an air of the most intense determination – as though he said: 'Let's get this business over! What in the world are the people shouting for? So silly!'

The fieldsmen moving back. The opposing captain waving men to the boundary – wishing, no doubt, the ground was bigger.

Guard taken. A quick glance round the field. Then absolute immobility. And a dead silence.

He stooped very low over his bat – so low that the cricket scribes called him 'The Croucher'. But it was the crouch of the panther – ready to spring – waiting for the precise moment to make his attack.

It came. The bat flashed through the air.

Sometimes – very seldom – the bails flew. Far more often it was the ball! When he failed it seemed a national calamity to the disappointed multitude. There were one or two occasions when it was actually as serious as that.

I want to make one fact quite plain – in case anyone who does not remember Jessop, or remembers him imperfectly, should read these lines.

He was a mighty hitter. Not a blind slogger, however, who smites wildly at everything and, more by good luck than good management, now and then strikes the ball. He was dashing, daring to a degree, seemingly reckless. But, behind it all, there was the cool, calculating brain of the super-batsman. Jessop always knew exactly what he was doing. He was as reasoned in his methods as 'W.G.' himself. His eye was perfect. And eye, brain, and hand were usually in entire sympathy. Hence his triumphs.

He made strokes which no ordinary man would even attempt.

Tom Wily – that master of perfect length – might say to himself, 'Aha, young feller, I'll larn yer! A hitter, are yer? Well, have a go at this!' And he, with three men out in the deep, would toss one up. Jessop would promptly hit it, over the fieldsmen's heads, out of the ground. That was Tom's bait and Jessop's method of accepting it!

The bowler, perhaps a little nettled, might then bowl one a trifle shorter – a good deal faster – dead on the middle stump. Jessop, lying back, would cut it, to the boundary, through the slips.

Tom might try to feed that stroke. A good-length ball, with plenty of spin, well outside the off-stump. Jessop, with a sweeping horizontal bat, would as likely as not pull it round to square-leg.

It was all very disconcerting – often most disheartening – for the bowlers. Jessop was ever ready to accept every challenge, but in his own way – which was not the obvious. Length had no meaning and no terrors to him. By his quickness he would convert Tom's – or Bill's, or Jack's, or anybody else's – best ball into a half-volley or a long-hop, as suited his purpose. In this respect he resembled Ranji.

Of course, he failed at times. He had 'bad patches' like everybody else. ' 'Tis not in mortals to command success', but Jessop always deserved it; he was so gallant – so dauntless – so greathearted.

In recent years I have often sighed 'Oh! for a Jessop!' I said it to myself in 1921, when J. M. Gregory and E. A. MacDonald were frightening England's batsmen. I say it aloud when I see half-volleys patted gently back to the bowler, and balls wide of the off-stump allowed to pass untouched. Which means I say it pretty often!

For Jessop was not just a fearless batsman with a wonderful eye and a stout heart. He was a great all-round cricketer. So long as he remained sound he was a fine fast bowler; and, if he had never made a run, he would have been worth his place in most sides for his fielding alone. I have seen some admirable cover-points – Johnny Briggs, S. E. Gregory (the Australian), and Jack Hobbs have been three of the best – but G.L.J. was, at least, as good as any of them. We can count up the total number of runs he made, but we can never calculate the number of runs he saved! I verily believe that – per innings – it would well exceed his batting average.

My first epithet, I think, most aptly describes him – a 'Phenomenon'. That he was. There have been fieldsmen as great and bowlers who far excelled him, but I doubt if there was ever a hitter so likely to rise to the big occasion – who could, and did, more often turn the course of an apparently lost match and carry his side triumphantly to victory.

'Here was a Caesar! When comes such another?'

*from* CRICKET MEMORIES *1930*

## *Parr, Spofforth and Trumper*

### F. S. ASHLEY-COOPER

Early in the season of 1926 there occurred two events which served to reveal the very prominent parts played in the game by George Parr and F. R. Spofforth, for the centenary of the former's birth fell on May 22nd, and the latter died at his home in Surrey a few days later.

Although over fifty years have passed since Parr took part in his last match of any public note, his name is still familiar to everyone who takes any interest in the game, as for years he was acknowledged without a superior as a batsman. In Nottinghamshire cricket annals especially he occupies a most prominent position but, besides assisting the county regularly for about a quarter of a century, he also took part in all the greatest matches of his time. He led Notts, the Players and England, and took teams to America in 1859, and to Australia and New Zealand in

1863-4, both of which returned undefeated. He was thoroughly acquainted with every fibre of the game, and was always a chivalrous opponent. Respecting the last-mentioned point, E. M. Grace furnished an interesting and illuminating instance. Just after 'The Coroner' had pulled a ball from John Jackson for four in a match at Lord's, Parr, whilst the ball was being recovered, went up to him from point and said softly: 'You had better look out, sir, for old Jack is almost sure to send the next ball straight at your body.' 'E.M.' when relating the incident, used to add: 'Knowing what to expect, I hit his next delivery for another four!' Think what one will, it was a kindly act on Parr's part to warn a young cricketer at the expense of his best bowler. Both Daft and Alfred Shaw declared that the old 'Lion of the North' was the best captain under whom they ever played, which was praise indeed coming from two such excellent judges.

George Parr's fame, however, rests on his batting. He could hit well all round the wicket, but it was as a leg-hitter that he was unrivalled. He himself declared, and doubtless believed, that he never made such a stroke off a ball on the wicket; but there can be no doubt that at times he did. In those days it was considered 'not cricket' to send a straight ball to leg, and some-times when Parr made one of his favourite strokes he would in consequence, be greeted with shouts of protest from the fielding side, and even from the spectators! Of his contemporaries, no bowler held more emphatic views on that point than Diver, of Cambridge. Once, whilst the ball was being retrieved from such a hit, he strode down the wicket and asked the striker in angry tones: 'Do you know where that ball pitched?' The batsman, misunderstanding the drift of the remark (or pretending to do so) replied: 'In the hedge, I think.'

The certainty with which Parr made his famous leg-hits was quite remarkable. It was useless to try to set the field to stop them, for he could steer the ball through almost any number of men – when he did not hit it over their heads. Generally he did not seem to hit the ball with very great force, but it travelled

hard and fast as a rule – the result of perfect timing. Such strokes
on his part were often more like mowing than genuine hitting,
but were beautiful to see.

Parr stood at the wicket with his left knee bent and his back
arched, and, when preparing to receive the ball, held his bat
slanting so much that his hands were often battered and bruised
in consequence. This was especially the case when he played his
historic innings of 130 against Surrey at the Oval in 1859 – the
greatest personal triumph he ever enjoyed. When he was out
on that occasion, the spectators swarmed over the ground,
cheering as they ran, and formed a narrow passage from the
wicket to the pavilion down which Parr hobbled with his
peculiar limp, and with his bat in one hand and his straw hat in
the other. Upon arriving at the pavilion, he was at once
presented with a sum of money which had been collected, in a
coconut shell, for him among the spectators. The batsman
always declared that it was the proudest day of his life.

George Parr was a kind-hearted man of a retiring disposition,
though some people who did not know him well mistook his
shyness for surliness. He had his foibles, of course – most people
have – and if, when conducting the affairs of the All-England
Eleven he at times spoke strongly, it must be remembered that
there were probably good causes. He was, however, a man who
would never willingly have caused a moment's pain or irritation
to anyone. Once, at Stoke, a gentleman who subsequently
became President of the M.C.C. went up to him and said: 'I hope,
Parr, you will remember me being at Harrow whilst you were
coaching there.' George at once replied: 'Of course, sir; of
course. Those were happy days, weren't they?' A few minutes
later, however, Parr inquired of a friend: 'Who was that?' and,
when told, said: 'I did not know him from a crow; but he will go
home much happier thinking I did.'

He was a man of much quiet humour, and many stories are
told respecting his quaint observations. Thus, he used to say
to young cricketers: 'When you play in a match, be sure not to
forget to pay a little attention to the umpire. First of all inquire

after his health, then say what a good player his father was and, finally present him with a brace of birds or rabbits. This will give you confidence, and you will probably do well.'

Parr was an excellent shot, and in shooting, as in cricket, was a true sportsman. He never took a shot that he thought belonged to a neighbour, and he would often turn to the next gun and shout, 'Your shot, sir!' He preferred to miss than to wound, for nothing caused him more pain than the cry of a maimed animal. Perhaps one personal reminiscence on this point may be allowed. During a shoot at Shelford Manor a hare was wounded, and endeavoured to run on its hind legs whilst crying like a child. It was more than Parr could stand, and hastily passing over his gun to his cartridge carrier, he put his hands over his ears and called out to the keeper: 'For heaven's sake, loose that dog!' When the hare was killed, he added: 'Poor as I am, I would not have wounded anything like that for a five-pound note.'

Those whose pleasure and privilege it was to know George Parr – he died in June 1891 – will always recall him with something very like affection. Dick Daft referred to him as 'a man under whose banner I am proud to have fought, for a more honest and straightforward cricketer never took hold of a bat.'

### F. R. SPOFFORTH

It would be an easy matter to write many pages about 'The Demon' for he occupied a place in cricket history which is unique. It was as much to his undoubted genius as to any other cause that Australia proved her right to meet England on even terms, and it is not too much to say that he reached the place among bowlers that 'W.G.' did amongst batsmen. Although he had played, and with success, in good-class cricket before he ever came to England, his great days may be said to date from 1878, when he was seen in this country for the first time. That was for the pioneer Australian team which, under the captaincy of D. W. Gregory, arrived unheralded and almost unnoticed. Defeat by an innings and 14 runs at the opening match caused no comment – it was much what had been expected by those who had troubled to think at all about the matter; but, exactly a week later, at Lord's they disposed of a strong M.C.C. side for 33 and 19, and won, in a single day, by nine wickets, thirty-one men actually being dismissed for 105 runs in four and a half hours. Boyle took nine wickets for 17 runs; Spofforth, who did the hat trick, ten for 20; and, although the former had slightly the better average, it was 'The Demon' who made the greater impression. It was a wonderful success on the part of the visitors, one which electrified the whole cricketing world, and one which caused May 27, 1878 to mark the commencement of a new epoch in the history of the game. Until then Englishmen had quietly assumed that they were without rivals in a game they had made peculiarly their own, and their awakening was both rude and emphatic.

It was in such dramatic fashion that Spofforth gained recognition, and wherever he played that season crowds flocked to see him perform. He was then twenty-five years of age, and so presumably at about his best, and, that being so, it was unfortunate that the side – it was the same with that of two years later – played so few eleven-a-side matches. For the teams of 1878 and 1880, Spofforth's figures, even allowing for the many games in which he took part against odds, were altogether remarkable. For the former side he obtained 746 wickets at a cost of 6·08 runs each, and for the latter 763 for 5·49 apiece. These figures include his doings in the Colonies and (in 1878) in America.

'The Demon' himself has told how he developed his skill and attained such a state of excellence as caused him to be dreaded by the strongest opponents, whatever the conditions. As a small boy at Eglington College, Glebe Point, Sydney, he bowled fast underhand, and, when he saw the success with which George Tarrant, of Cambridge, met, he determined to be as fast a bowler as possible. In that resolve he persevered for some years, until, in fact, he saw Southerton and Alfred Shaw perform, when he decided, if possible, to combine the methods of all three men. It was a great undertaking, but Spofforth was ambitious, and, besides, was never a man to be daunted by any seeming difficulties. He was a tall, wiry man, 6 feet 3 inches in height, with a high delivery, good length, a deceptive break and a deadly yorker. Add to all this that he had wonderful command over the ball, and could vary his pace without any apparent change of action – he could be exceedingly fast – and it will readily be understood why many batsmen funked him. He was always most energetic, and he was the man before all others that one would have wished to have on one's side in an up-hill game. When endeavouring to pull off a match by his bowling he would brace every nerve to accomplish the task, and in such circumstances one required an iron nerve to face him with any confidence, for even in his run up to the wicket he was intimidating. In that respect one cannot help recalling the most prominent part he played in Australia's memorable seven-runs victory at the Oval in 1882 – England's first reverse in a Test on her own soil. Several of our greatest players were so unnerved that their teeth chattered whilst waiting their turn to go in. Spofforth never did anything greater, considering the importance of the occasion, than he did in that match, for he took seven wickets in each innings – fourteen altogether for 90 runs. Some good judges were inclined to rank C. T. B. Turner as his equal, but the general opinion seems to be that 'The Demon' stood in a class apart. Both W.G. and George Giffen, whose authority is entitled to all respect, held the latter view.

Apart altogether from his outstanding ability as a bowler, Spofforth was quite a useful man to have on one's side. He was a long-headed individual, and his advice on matters of policy was always valued. Like so many of his companions in some of the early Australian teams, he could throw the ball a great distance – he has been credited with 120 yards; he was, too, a safe catch and a plucky, hard-hitting bat. His best innings in a match of note was played in a Test in Melbourne in 1884-5, when, going in number eleven, he made the highest score for his side, and obtained 50 of the 64 runs which the last wicket added in fifty-five minutes.

It is much to be regretted that Spofforth never wrote his reminiscences, for he was a capital raconteur, and such a volume, dealing, as it would have done, with cricket for a period covering sixty years, would have been most interesting and valuable. The articles he penned were characteristic of the man – thoughtful and making clear in few words what he wished to impart. He was a man of considerable personal charm and with a decided sense of humour, and his death was felt very keenly by many.

## V. T. TRUMPER

Just as Spofforth ranks as the greatest bowler yet produced by Australia, so must Victor Trumper be regarded as the Commonwealth's most pronounced genius so far as batting is concerned.

Trumper's batting was *sui generis*, and, although he could play an orthodox game as successfully as anyone, it was his ability to make big scores when customary methods were unavailing that placed him above his fellows. His timing has never been excelled, and in the art of placing the ball he was unsurpassed. He always seemed to divine far quicker than most men the best way in which a ball should be played, and then brain, wrist and bat acted in perfect unison. At times he would apparently change his mind at the last moment – he was always very quick on his feet – but, even then, the resulting hit was, more often than not, pre-eminently a master-stroke. So many were his devices, in fact, and so pronounced his versatility that, when at his best, even the greatest bowlers seemed to be at his mercy. At times it was useless for a captain to attempt to place the field for him, for his repertoire of strokes was remarkable and, as stated, his ability to place the ball was exceeded by none. His wonderful pulling was so successful because it was due to a combination of great confidence in himself and a marvellous eye.

In his prime he would often get a yorker to the square-leg boundary, and it was by no means unusual to see him cut a ball off the middle stump for four. Some of his biggest hits, which sent the ball over the ring, were made without any apparent effort – the result of perfect timing and judgment. His swing was as graceful as that of Mr F. G. J. Ford, and at times the length of his hits rivalled those of many of the greatest hitters among his contemporaries. It is no exaggeration to say that he was great under all conditions of weather and wicket and against all kinds of bowling.

When he visited England for the first time, as fourteenth man, with the Australian team of 1899, he did very well, scoring 135 not out in the Test match at Lord's and 300 not out v. Sussex at Hove; but during the tour of three years later he was even more successful. Then he obtained eleven hundreds – two in one match against Essex – and an aggregate of 2,570. Not once did he fail to score, and only Shrewsbury, who had far fewer innings and seven not-outs to help him, was higher in the averages. It was a very wet year, but apparently the conditions under which he played made little difference to him, for he scored well and readily throughout the tour. The exhibitions he gave were alone sufficient to make the season of 1902 memorable. Not since W.G. was in his prime had any batsman met with such brilliant success. Well might 'Felix' (Mr Tom Horan) say that 'then it was that the welkin rang with the tumult of sustained applause in recognition of his glorious play', for glorious his cricket certainly was, and Englishmen would not have been human had they failed to mark their deep appreciation. For him the season was one long triumphal progress, and those who were fortunate enough to witness his amazing brilliance will never be able to forget the unrivalled skill and resource he displayed. On sticky wickets he hit with freedom and scored well, often whilst his companions were puddling about the crease, unable to make headway and seemingly content if they could keep up their wickets.

That he should have failed to repeat such wonderful doings on his subsequent visits to England was not surprising: in his greatest year he attained heights which may never be reached by any other player, and in that season alone he did sufficient to achieve cricket immortality. He was always to be feared on Australian wickets, but followers of the game in England were privileged to see him at his zenith. Much of his old brilliance, however, was apparently again in evidence in 1910–11, during the visit of the South Africans to Australia, but then he was not afforded so much scope for displaying his genius as on the ever-changing paced wickets of England almost a decade earlier, and, of course, he played far fewer innings. Mr Guy Eden in his 'Bush Ballads and Other Verses' included a tribute to him of which the following is a specimen verse:

> Oh! he's just a dandy batsman, he's a rajah, he's a toff,
> Widout any fancy feelin' for the 'on' or for the 'off'.
> He just takes his bat, and thin wid one apologetic cough,
> Sets to work to play the divil wid the bowlin'.

Trumper, who was always particularly neat in his attire, was the *beau ideal* of a cricketer, alike in build, temperament and skill. He possessed a charming personality, which caused him to be the most loved, as he was certainly the most gifted, of all Australian batsmen, and it must have been due largely to the fact that he was the most good-natured and popular of men that his testimonial match – New South Wales v. Rest of Australia at Sydney in 1912–13 – produced almost £3,000. Notwithstanding his confidence in his own ability, he was the most modest of men in the hour of triumph – not with a studied modesty (which is often the most objectionable form of egotism), but with a natural reserve, amounting almost to shyness, which won all hearts.

*from* CRICKET HIGHWAYS AND BYWAYS *1927*

# The Great Bowling of S. F. Barnes

## JACK FINGLETON

Write the name of S. F. Barnes, of Staffordshire, England, and set against it this bowling analysis: 11 overs, 7 maidens, 6 runs, 5 wickets. There you have the finest piece of bowling ever seen in Test cricket, for it was performed on a true pitch at Melbourne and the wickets were those of Bardsley, Kelleway, Hill, Armstrong and Minnett.

There was a mix-up over the 1901 English side to Australia. The M.C.C. could not get a satisfactory side together and passed the job over to Archie MacLaren with their blessing. Yorkshire made the task no easier by withholding Hirst and Rhodes, and MacLaren, as a brave and knowledgeable man should often do, backed his own judgment – he did so by plucking Barnes out of the Lancashire League. Barnes had played a few games for Warwickshire as a fast bowler, but he was a spinner when MacLaren spotted and selected him.

Barnes had played only two Tests in Australia when he was being acclaimed as the finest hard-wicket bowler England had sent abroad. A few years later M. A. Noble singled him out as the world's finest bowler, and to this day Sir Pelham Warner plumps for him as the greatest bowler he has ever seen.

Barnes's first Test wicket was that of Victor Trumper; he caught and bowled him for two in Sydney. Also, he clean-bowled Clem Hill in the same innings. Barnes took 5–65 in that innings (he got only 1–74 in the second), but in the next Test, at Melbourne, his name was being spoken everywhere because he took 6–42 and 7–121 (he got Trumper and Hill in both innings). Melbourne was to be his best Test ground.

Misfortune hit him hard in the next Test at Adelaide. He suffered a knee injury, withdrew from the match, and didn't play in another Test until the July one at Sheffield in 1902. He took there 6–49 in the first innings and 1–50; yet, unaccountably, he wasn't chosen in the immortal next Test at Old Trafford, which Australia won by three runs. Barnes didn't play against Australia again in England until 1909, and he missed another trip to Australia.

It is interesting that Noble should have placed Barnes on a pedestal for, in fact, Barnes learnt a lot about swing bowling from Noble. Barnes began, as most bowlers do, as a fast bowler, but he soon learned that there was more to the business than sheer speed. He experimented with finger-spin both off and leg, and it was as a medium-paced spinner that he was singled out for the Australian tour by MacLaren. Barnes possessed a very shrewd and deductive cricket brain. He closely watched the other leading bowlers of that day and quickly applied some of their technique to his own bowling.

Monty Noble, in particular, captivated him. Here was an off-spinner of the old and original school (very similar to the latter-day Jim Laker) who possessed all the variations of the art. Noble would gain tricks of flight by delivering the ball at various heights – gaining this by dipping or straightening his right leg at the moment of release – and he had an outcurve as distinct from the ordinary off-break. If a breeze came in from fine-leg, Noble was in his element as he curved, floated, and dropped the ball with side-spin and over-spin. He brought to the cricket field much of the technique of the baseball pitcher.

I don't know whether modern Test bowlers have a union in which they swop the tricks of the trade – I think not – but Syd Barnes found that Noble lived up to his name, for the great Australian all-rounder and captain gave him many tips on bowling.

Barnes not only wanted off-breaks and leg-breaks from the pitch. He wanted movement in the air as well, and in England he studied the great English left-hander, George Hirst. The normal swing of a right-hand bowler to a right-hand batsman with the new ball is from leg to off. Similarly, a left-hand bowler will swing in from off to leg – as Hirst did.

Barnes practised with his leg-break allied to a certain body action at the moment of delivery and, hey presto! he found movement in the air similar to Hirst's natural swing.

But observe these important differences in the technique of Barnes and let me illustrate them by referring to Maurice Tate, one of the greatest of all bowlers. Tate was a glorious mover of the new ball, mostly from the leg and with tremendous whip off the pitch. His swing (as distinct from swerve, which comes from spin) was gained by holding the ball in the normal fashion with the line of stitches facing the batsman. This swing comes late in the ball's flight, and the ball, off the pitch, continues on the direction of the swing – that is, towards the slips. A nightmare of a ball, too!

When Barnes swung in the air from the leg, by spin, the ball turned back from the off. When he swung in from the off, with his leg-break action, the ball gripped the pitch with its spin and turned from the leg. In the case of Hirst – and Alec Bedser, with his in-swing, being a right-hander – the ball, on hitting the pitch, continues out towards the leg-slips. Thus Barnes's swerves broke from the pitch in directions different from the normal swings.

'At the time I was able to bowl these,' Barnes recently told me by letter, 'I thought I was at a disadvantage in having to spin the ball when I could see bowlers doing the same by simply placing the ball in their hand and letting go; but I soon learned that the advantage was with me because by spinning the ball, if the wicket would take spin, the ball would come back against the swing .... I may say I did not bowl a ball but that I had to spin, and that is, to my way of thinking, the reason for what success I attained.'

In Barnes's first Test innings against Australia, Charlie Macartney was at the bowler's end when Barnes clean-bowled Trumper. 'The ball was fast on the leg stump,' said Macartney, 'but just before it pitched it swung suddenly to the off. Then it pitched, broke back, and took Vic's leg-stump. It was the sort of ball a man might see if he was dreaming or drunk.'

Those who have played against Barnes – unfortunately, there are now not many left – have told me that he was accurate and kept a perfect length. He had variations of pace and flight and could regulate the spot at which his swing became effective. He could also regulate the amount of break. Moreover, he used the width of the crease, first over the stumps, then from halfway, and then from the edge.

'But I never bowled all out at the stumps,' he maintained. 'I liked to study the batsman and then bowl at his strokes. I intended him to make a stroke and then I tried to beat it. I tried to make the batsman move. It is amazing how often a batsman will make a mistake if you induce him to use his feet.'

I asked him about that December morning of 1911. 'Naturally, I was very pleased,' he said, 'but I did not consider it the high-light of my career, for I knew that it was possible to bowl well with little or no result. On the other hand, one could bowl not nearly so well and reap quite a harvest of wickets – you know as well as I do that there is a very small margin between success and failure.'

And then, after a pause: 'Still, I think I did bowl well that day.'

Of course he did. I looked up the files.

They had bands at Test matches in those days – they did in Sydney right up to 1931 when the Springbok captain, Jock Cameron, asked the band not to play as he could not concentrate while the music was in the air.

The band in Melbourne was playing comic-opera tunes as the Englishmen were led out by Johnny Douglas. The early morning was dull and close and around eleven o'clock there were a few drops of rain. The weather looked like developing into a thunderstorm. But Clem Hill, winning the toss, feared neither the light nor the moisture-laden atmosphere – lending swing to a new ball – nor even the pitch. 'Bad luck, Johnny,' he said to Douglas, 'we'll bat.'

There was a slight mist as the umpires walked out. Bardsley had been put through a pretty rigorous physical test and had been pronounced fit, although, after a battering from Foster in Sydney, he was well strapped up as he walked out with Kelleway to open the innings.

Kelleway was very wary in playing the first over from Foster. Then Barnes prepared to bowl to Bardsley. Barnes, in collaboration with Douglas, took a long time to settle his field. He was most pernickety in this matter.

At last he was satisfied and over came the first ball. It was on a good length and Bardsley shaped at it very cautiously. He missed, and it hit him on the leg and went into his stumps – an in-swinger that would have had the Australian l.b.w. had it not bowled him.

Another left-hander, Hill, was next, and he took a single from the first ball, a fact to be noted because it was a long time before another run was scored from Barnes.

Hill faced up to Barnes again for his next over, and a torrid one it was. There was an immediate and loud appeal for l.b.w. but it was rejected, and Hill, defending desperately, saw the over through.

Kelleway faced Barnes for his next over. He missed completely an in-swinger on his leg stump that straightened up and he was out l.b.w. Australia: 2 for 5.

In came Armstrong and he saw Hill in all manner of trouble. Barnes gave him one that was an off-break to him, and followed with an in-swinger. Then came one a little wider, going away which Hill allowed to pass. The final ball of the over pitched on Hill's leg stump and hit the top of the off-stump. Australia: 3 for 8.

As captain, Hill had put Trumper lower on the list so that he could bat with the sheen gone from the ball. But Trumper came now with the ball still almost new. Meanwhile, spectators were busy recalling an earlier tour by Warner's team when Australia batted in Sydney on a perfect pitch under a thundery sky, and Hill, Trumper and Duff were out for 12, leaving Noble and Armstrong to stop the collapse. This time, as Trumper walked out in the tense atmosphere, a great cheer went up. Trumper would succeed where the others had failed!

Armstrong drove Foster for three and then faced Barnes. Immediate exit! He snicked his first ball and Smith caught him behind.

Four Australian wickets were gone for eight, and of that very modest figure only a single run had been scored from Barnes. He had taken four wickets for one run! Test cricket had not seen the like of this before.

Ransford, on his home ground, now joined Trumper, and the latter brought a relieved cheer, like a clap of thunder, as he brilliantly back-cut Foster. The ball went like a streak, incidentally hitting Douglas on the shins, and the batsmen ran two. Rain began to fall now and the players came off after 45 minutes of play.

They were back again 15 minutes later. Barnes bowled a maiden to Ransford, feverishly defensive. Then in the next over, from Foster, Trumper made two delicious late cuts to the rails. It looked like another maiden over from Barnes to Ransford, but the left-hander got Barnes away to leg for a single off the last ball. It had been an hour since the previous and only run had been taken from Barnes.

Barnes didn't seem himself in his next over. He bowled a full toss that went high over Ransford's head for four byes. At the end of the over he spoke to Douglas. Barnes had been ill during the preceding week and there was a doubt whether he would play. He told Douglas that he couldn't see the other end. Everything seemed to be going round and round.

So, to the great relief of the Melbourne crowd – and also of the batsmen at the wickets – Barnes left the field. He didn't return until after lunch.

The Australian players, on their way from the dressing-room to lunch in another pavilion, had to run the gauntlet of many an anxious inquiry from the spectators. What was wrong? Was something amiss with the wicket? To all inquiries the humbled Australians gave the one reply, 'Barnes!'

Foster knocked Trumper's stumps back after lunch, and then Barnes took the ball again. Australia: 5 for 33.

Minnett, a notable performer in the preceding Test at Sydney, came next and promptly snicked Barnes to third slip. He was dropped. But after scoring two, he skied Barnes to cover, where Jack Hobbs was waiting. Six down for 38, and Barnes had the remarkable bowling figures cited in the first paragraph of this chapter – 11 overs, 7 maidens, 6 runs, 5 wickets.

Barnes got no more wickets in that innings. He finished with 5-44 off 23 overs. Actually, he should have had another wicket when Hordern spooned one up in front, a catch that could have been taken by any one of five men but for the fact that each one left it to the other fellow. He might, too, have had the last man, Whitty. All the players, including Whitty, himself, thought he had been clean bowled. Indeed, the usual procession to the pavilion had begun when Umpire Crockett, who was at square leg, held that the ball had come back from the keeper's pads and called out 'No, no!' The other umpire then gave Whitty not out, and 35 more runs were added to the score.

Ransford was Australia's best batsman; he played coolly and intelligently for 43. Hordern, after his let-off, got 49 not out, Carter a cheeky 29, and Whitty and Cotter 14 each.

The day provided many other incidents. With the score 8–125 Barnes came on to relieve Hearne. Very carefully, Barnes motioned his fieldsmen this way and that, upon which a portion of the crowd in the Outer began to hoot him for not 'getting on with it.'

Barnes resented the hooting. He threw down the ball and stood with his arms folded. While a few still hooted, members and others cheered. 'It was', wrote a Sydney critic, 'a most unwarranted display against a man who had bowled magnificently. It evidenced, too, a most partisan spirit. It was confined to a hostile section in the shilling stand, and such unfair treatment undoubtedly interfered with Barnes's bowling. In his next over there was a similar outbreak by the hoodlums, but the occupants of the members' reserve cheered him and the noisy element was quickly quelled by the counter-demonstration.'

'During the tea interval,' the Sydney critic added, 'the demonstration against Barnes was universally condemned, and it was suggested that the Victorian authorities should at once follow the example of the New South Wales Association and announce that they would prosecute offenders for unruly or riotous behaviour. After the interval, when Barnes bowled again, the crowd was perfectly quiet, a couple of policemen being in the middle of the noisy section. But it was the worst demonstration of partisanship seen on the ground.'

Spectators cheered Barnes all the way to the pavilion when the innings ended. It was said of Barnes then that he was too reserved, too stern, to be popular with his fellows, but I imagine that he, like the latter-day O'Reilly, looked upon all batsmen as his natural enemies. Not for him frivolities on the field or the happy exchange of pleasantries. He meant business from the first ball, and never more than on that Melbourne morning of December 30, 1911.

It was perhaps the most historic morning in Test history. England won finally by eight wickets, Hearne and Hobbs getting centuries and F. R. Foster 6-91 in the second innings. Some said the Foster-Barnes partnership was the greatest bowling one ever.

Now, in his eighties, Barnes is courteous, gentle and gracious. He is as straight in figure as on that Melbourne morning, a splendid specimen of physical fitness, and his mind is alert and discerning. He pays tribute to the modern bowler, if not many modern bowling methods, and I like very much this expression of opinion, one which the world of officialdom must listen to some day: 'The l.b.w. rule, as it is now, has done much harm to cricket. It has shut out the lovely off-side strokes. There is too much defensive bowling outside the leg stump to leg fields and too much playing by the batsmen off the back foot. If you are going to get wickets, you must attack the batsman. If you are going to get runs, you must attack the bowler. That is the game of cricket. One must attack the other, and every bowler should welcome it when a batsman shows a desire to step into him.

It is then, if he uses his head, that a bowler has most chance. But that l.b.w. rule – no! It has done too much harm already.'

*from* MASTERS OF CRICKET *1956*

# *Victor Trumper*

## JACK FINGLETON

On June 28, 1915, Victor Trumper* died at Sydney in his thirty-eighth year. His funeral caused the streets of the city to be blocked and he was carried to his grave by eleven Australian cricketers. In London, in the midst of World War I and all its momentous happenings, the event was featured on newspaper posters, as, for example, 'Death of a Great Cricketer'.

Men said then – and some in both Australia and England still say it – 'There will never be another like Vic Trumper.'

I never saw Trumper bat; I was only a few years old when he died. But so often have I listened to stories of him, so often have I seen a new light come into the eyes of people at the mention of his name, so much have I read of him, that I am prepared to believe that nobody, before or since, ever achieved the standards of batsmanship set by Trumper.

Many players, it is true, made more runs; but runs can never be accepted as the true indication of a player's greatness. A fighting innings of thirty or so under difficult conditions is lost in cold statistics, yet its merits may far outweigh many staid (and unnecessary) centuries that are recorded for all time.

Trumper went to bat one day against Victoria in Sydney on a wet pitch. The first ball from Jack Saunders ( a terror on such pitches) beat him completely. Saunders' eyes lit up. His fellow-Victorians grinned in anticipation. Trumper smiled broadly.

* See also 'Opposing my Hero', page 355.

'Why, Jack,' he called down the pitch, 'what a thing to do to an old friend. Well, it's either you or me for it.'

And then, by dazzling footwork and miraculous stroke-play, Trumper hit a century in 60 minutes.

At the beginning of 1904, in Melbourne, Trumper faced up to Rhodes and Hirst on a wet pitch. These Yorkshiremen were two of the greatest left-handed bowlers of all time and a wet Melbourne pitch was known as the worst in the world, with balls from a good length lifting quickly around the chin.

Trumper was first in and last out, for 74, in a total of 122. Hopkins made 18 and Duff 10. Noble, Syd Gregory, Trumble and Armstrong made 9 between them!

That innings caused Charles Fry, in one of his unpredictable moments, to rise suddenly from a reverie during a dinner in London and say: 'Gentlemen, charge your glasses. I give you the toast of the world's greatest batsman. Drink to Victor Trumper, first man in, last man out, on a bad pitch and against Hirst and Rhodes.'

Fry knew the full value of such an innings on such a pitch and against two skilled left-handers. His short and unexpected speech brought down the house.

No less interesting is the fact that Mrs Fry (who may or may not have had some knowledge of cricket) shared her famous husband's admiration of Trumper. My information on this point comes from the Sydney Bulletin of the period. It appears that Mrs Fry declared in a London periodical that Vic Trumper was an artist and that some day someone would paint his portrait and have it hung in a National Gallery. 'He will be,' the lady said, 'dressed in white, with his splendid neck bared to the wind, standing on short green grass against a blue sky; he will be waiting for the ball, the orchestra to strike up.'

My formative days in cricket were spent in the Sydney suburb of Waverley. We adjoined Paddington, the club of Trumper and Noble, but we yielded to no Sydney club in the proud possession of internationals and other first-class players. Carter, all the twentieth-century Gregorys, Kippax, Hendry, Collins, and many other proficient players figured with Waverley and established the high standards of the district. One of the great sources of the club's strength was that cricket, and talk of it, flowed through the life of the district. All the internationals I have mentioned showed themselves on the local oval at practice during the week and played there in the club games on Saturday afternoons.

Saturday evenings and Sunday mornings were given over to post-mortems.

These critics – some lovely characters among them – knew their cricket. When they had disposed of the present they drifted, fondly, to the hallowed ground of the past, and always, I found, the day's reminiscences ended on Victor Trumper.

As I walked home I used to wonder how one cricketer could so capture the imagination above all others; and the imagination, moreover, of men so steeped in the game that they were the severest of critics. Yet even years after Trumper's death they spoke wistfully of him and would brook no interlopers. Nor criticism. Trumper was unique in that nobody ever criticized him as a cricketer or as a man. In England, in Australia, in South Africa, listening to men who knew and played against him, I never at any time heard a derogatory word said against Trumper. That could not be said of any other cricketer of any generation.

A mark of a great man is the power of making lasting impressions upon people he meets. Winston Churchill once wrote of F. E. Smith, the first Earl of Birkenhead: 'Some men when they die after busy, toilsome, successful lives leave a great stock of scrip and securities, of acres or factories or the goodwill of large undertakings. F.E. banked his treasure in the hearts of his friends, and they will cherish his memory until their time is come.'

That could also have been written of Trumper. He left no stock or securities. He was a singularly unsuccessful business man. He ran a sporting goods firm in the city of Sydney but he was too generous with his gifts to accumulate money. Once, on the morning of a Test, he was working in his shop and allowed time to elude him. He hurried into his coat, took down a new bat from the rack, caught a taxi to the Sydney Cricket Ground – and made 185 not out!

It has been said that this was the most brilliant and versatile innings ever played by the Master. The match was the famous one in which R. E. Foster, the Englishman, hit a brilliant 287 in his first Test and Clem Hill was concerned in the most tumultuous run-out in the history of Test cricket.

An admirer of Trumper came into his shop after the match and asked whether he could buy a bat Trumper had used.

Yes, he was told. There was the bat used in the recent Test. The admirer's eyes sparkled. How much would it be?

'Well,' said the impractical Victor, 'it was a 45s. bat but it is now second-hand. You can have it for a pound.'

What a difference, this, from a modern I know who swapped a bat with which he had made a record for one of the most fabulous cars seen on a roadway (but that is another story that doesn't belong here).

Another tale of Trumper – there are dozens – was told me by Vernon Ransford, his comrade in many Australian Elevens.

The Australians were dressing at Melbourne for a Test, against Sherwell's South Africans, when there came a knock at the door. Was Mr Trumper available?

Trumper went to the door and found a young man, a complete stranger, holding a bat. He was anxious to begin in the bat-making business. This was one of his bats and he wondered whether Mr Trumper would use it in the Test.

This usage of material is one of the niceties of 'amateur' sport. A successful player is retained to use the material of a certain sports outfitter. Not only, by his play, is he expected to bring glory and advertisement to the firm's goods, but he must also be well practised in presenting the name on his equipment whenever his photograph is being taken. Thus, when you see a triumphant winner of Wimbledon in a photograph, you have a fair chance of seeing also the name of the racquet used as the hero pushes it to the front. Strictly speaking, of course, amateurs are not allowed to associate their names with sporting goods – and knowing editors now sometimes help them to observe the proprieties by blacking-out the name in the printed photograph!

That angle on sport was not developed in Trumper's day. He would have had in his bag several bats that suited him in weight and balance but, nevertheless, he didn't hesitate about accepting the young applicant's gruesome-looking bat. It weighed almost 3 lb. 6 oz. and it staggered his team-mates.

'Surely,' one of them said, 'you won't use that blunderbuss, Vic?'

'He's only a young chap and he's starting out in business,' replied Trumper. 'If I can get a few runs with this it might help him.'

He made 87 (probably wearying of lifting it!), inscribed it on the back with a hearty recommendation, and gave it back to the delighted young man.

Hanson Carter, the great wicket-keeper, was my first club captain. 'You must never,' he once sternly told me, 'compare Hobbs, Bradman or anybody else with Trumper. If you want to try and classify the great batsmen in the game, put Victor Trumper way up there – on his own – and then you can begin to talk about the rest.'

So, too, with Charlie Macartney, upon whose shoulders the mantle of Trumper was supposed to have descended. He revelled in talking of the things Trumper did. So did Ransford. I sat with him in his office a few years ago when he was secretary of the Melbourne Cricket Ground and he went into rhapsodies regarding the dismally wet season in England in 1902 when Trumper made 2,570 runs.

'If Vic had been greedy, it could have been 4,000,' said Ransford. 'His highest score, despite all the centuries he scored, was only 128. He could, obviously, have turned many of those centuries into double ones had he wished. But he was too generous. He looked around for some deserving character, a youngster maybe, or some player down on his luck, and unostentatiously gave him his wicket. That was Vic.'

*Wisden's* wrote of Trumper and that tour: 'Trumper stood alone. He put everybody else into the shade. No one, not even Ranjitsinhji has been at once so brilliant and so consistent since Dr W. G. Grace was at his best.'

The English bosie bowler, Bosanquet, clean bowled Trumper with the first bosie he sent down to him. 'Plum' Warner describes it:

It was in Sydney in 1903. Trumper and Duff had gone in first and in 35 minutes had scored 72 runs by batting, every stroke of which I remember vividly to this day. Bosanquet went on to bowl and his first ball pitched a good length just outside the off-stump. Trumper thought it was a leg-break and proceeded to cut it late, as he hoped, for four, but it came back and down went his off-stump. Subsequently, he used to 'murder' Bosanquet but it is worth recording that the first 'googly' ever bowled in Australia bowled out the man who, in spite of all the fine deeds of Don Bradman, many Australians regard as the finest batsman their country has ever produced.

It is very doubtful if there has ever been a greater batsman and his wonderful deeds would have been even greater but for indifferent health, which, in the end, cut short his life.

No one ever played so naturally, and he was as modest as he was magnificent. To this day in Australia, he is regarded as the highest ideal of batsmanship. He was, I think, the most fascinating batsman I have seen. He had grace, ease, style and power and a quickness of foot both in jumping out and in getting back to a ball that can surely never be surpassed.

He had every known stroke and one or two of his own. When set on a good wicket it seemed impossible to place a field for him. He was somewhat slightly built, but his sense of timing was so perfect that he hit the ball with tremendous power. Most bowlers are agreed that he was the most difficult batsman to keep quiet. I have heard a great bowler remark, 'I could, in the ordinary way, keep most people from

scoring quickly, but I always felt rather helpless against
Trumper, for he was so quick, and he had so many strokes.'
His brilliant batting stirred cricketing England. His unrivalled
skill and resource will never be forgotten. No cricketer was
ever more popular, and he deserved it, for he preserved the
modesty of true greatness and was the *beau-ideal* of a cricketer.

On one occasion, after batting brilliantly at Kennington
Oval, Trumper, 'ducked' an official dinner at night. The fact
was, simply, that he didn't want to be talking 'shop' among
cricketers and receiving plaudits. He was duly fined for missing
an official engagement!

The South Africans had a quick introduction to Trumper.
An Australian team called at the Union on the way home from
England, where Trumper had had a most successful tour.
There were opinions that Trumper wouldn't find the matting
pitches of South Africa too easy and money changed hands to
say that, in the few matches played there, Trumper wouldn't
make a century. He hit a double-century in his very first game
on the mat!

The South Africans in Australia in 1910–11 were mesmerized
by his skill. This was the team with all the bosie bowlers, but
Trumper cut, hooked and drove at will. He had a fascinating
stroke against a fast yorker. He lifted his back foot, jabbed down
on the ball with his bat at an angle and it streaked away to the
square-leg boundary. Somewhat naturally, they called it the
dog-stroke.

He teased Percy Sherwell, the Springbok captain. When a
fieldsman was shifted, Trumper deliberately hit the next ball
where that man had been. He was a consummate master at
placement. Later, somebody commiserated with Sherwell at
having his captaincy, his bowlers and his fieldsmen torn to
tatters while Trumper made 214; whereupon the Springbok
said, 'Ah, don't talk about it. We have seen batting today'

Neville Cardus, the Trumper of cricket writing, once wrote,
'The art of Trumper is like the art in a bird's flight, an art that

knows not how wonderful it is. Batting was for him a superb dissipation, a spontaneous spreading of fine feathers.'

How unfortunate it is that Trumper slightly preceded the movie-camera age!

Posterity has the chance of seeing all the moderns in action, as it has of hearing all the great singing voices. Mr Menzies, our Prime Minister, has a thrilling film of Don Bradman – there are a number of copies of the same film in existence – and to see Bradman on the screen is to realize again, instantly, his great stature as a batsman. The speed of his footwork, the flay of his bat, the manner in which he 'smelt' the ball, so over the ball was his head – all this has been caught and kept for the years to come and, in the evidence of the film, there can be no possible disputation over Bradman's status in the game.

With Trumper it is different. All we have, so far as I know, are the several photographic 'stills' of him at the beginning of an off-drive and at the finish and, also, of his stance at the crease. But these do portray his art. The two of him laying the off-drive are technically perfect in every detail – his feet, his shoulders, his head, his back swing, his follow-through with the proper transfer of weight and then, finally, the full, flowing arc of the bat. His stance is perfection.

Those who saw and knew Trumper used to say that Macartney, Jackson and Kippax were reminiscent of him; but that even when they were at their greatest they served only to rekindle memories of the Great Man. He was, obviously, supreme on the field; and a man of kind and generous nature, of consideration for his fellow-man, off the field. He embodied, to those who knew him, all that was good and noble in cricket and life.

'Where would you like your field placed?' 'Plum' Warner, as captain, once asked George Hirst. And Hirst replied, 'It doesn't much matter, sir, where we put 'em. Victor will still do as 'e likes.'

The evidence, then, would seem to be conclusive. Many of Trumper's greatest innings were played in the full face of adversity, the true test of worth. He rose to heights on wet wickets where others tumbled to earth. Although some half a dozen or so players down the years could be regarded as really great, Trumper, as Carter said, merits a niche of his own. He brought to the game an artistry, a talent, and an inherent modesty not manifested by any other cricketer. In short, he possessed all the graces.

*from* MASTERS OF CRICKET *1956*

# George Gunn

## NEVILLE CARDUS

George Gunn played for Nottinghamshire from 1902 until 1932, in which late summer, in his fifty-third year, he scored 200 runs in five innings and probably would have continued playing until old age really set in; but he was knocked unconscious, more or less, by a fast full-toss from Alfred Gover at Trent Bridge, an accident from which he never, as a cricketer, recovered. The irony of this mishap is that George Gunn toyed with fast bowling as no other cricketer. He would walk slowly but quite purposely yards down the pitch, even to the pace of E. A. McDonald, prince of fast bowlers.

McDonald never lost his temper, but once at Old Trafford, on a fiery dry pitch, George sauntered out to flick flying balls deliberately over the slips. He nearly achieved a six high over the head of third man, a fanciful, almost indolent stroke, performed with George on his toes. This was too much for McDonald, who had his dignity to look after, so before receiving back the ball to send flying his next one, he called down the wicket: 'George, get back to your crease or I'll knock your head off,' whereat Gunn replied, to the fastest bowler of his time, 'Ted, you couldn't knock the skin off a rice pudding!'

A genius, of course, if genius means a technique so masterful that a man can express himself through it, and give scope for every mood and inclination. 'I always bats according,' said George, when I asked him (to draw him) to explain his method and first principles. According to what? – his own sweet will! Sometime in the remote pre-war 1914 years, at Trent Bridge, Yorkshire won the toss and amassed 471. Nottinghamshire had nothing to play for but a draw, so George Gunn defended for six hours, declining to make a run more than 132 in all that long time. The Yorkshire attack, consisting of Hirst, Booth, Rhodes, Drake, Haigh and Kilner (an England attack!) waxed sarcastic about George's dilatoriness and asked him, between innings, 'Ast t'a lost all thi stroakes?' And George answered, quietly and slowly, 'Oh, you'd like to see some strokes, would you, some swashbuckle, like? Well, I'll see what I can do about it next innings.'

Next innings, when Nottinghamshire were batting out time, Gunn scored, in an hour and a half, 109 out of 129 for four before the end came. Nobody else reached double figures; the score card, preserved in silk at Trent Bridge to this day, read:

| | |
|---|---|
| G. Gunn not out | 109 |
| G. M. Lee b Haigh | 4 |
| J. Hardstaff run out | 3 |
| J. Gunn run out | 8 |
| E. Alletson c Booth b Rhodes | 0 |
| Extras | 5 |
| Total (for 4) | 129 |

As he said, he batted 'according'. Again, at Trent Bridge, in August 1928, less than a year from his fiftieth birthday, he astonished a crowd and the Kent XI out of their senses on an afternoon of golden sunshine. A grand match suddenly collapsed after lunch on the third day, so Nottinghamshire were left with ample time to score 158 for victory. The runs were made in an hour and thirty-five minutes, Gunn being exactly 100 not out. Years afterwards I asked why he had been in such a hurry on a gorgeous summer afternoon when nobody wanted to go home. 'It was like this,' he explained in his slow, pleasant way, 'when Dodge Whysall and myself went out to get the runs, I asked him, "Dodge, how many do we want?", and he said, "158". So I said, "Very well, Dodge, we'll go fifty-fifty". And then a member on the pavilion side spoke to me and said something that annoyed me – I can't tell you what it was, but it put my back up, I can promise you.' 'Yes,' I said, 'but what had that to do with the fact that you hurried and spoiled the afternoon and sent everybody home too early?' 'Well,' replied George, 'As I'm telling you, that member put me into a temper – so I goes out and takes it out of the Kent bowling!'

In his career George Gunn scored 35,190 runs, average 35·90, with 62 centuries. But what has the science of statistics to tell us of George Gunn? Nothing at all. He changed batsmanship into a means of private (and public) art and entertainment. Sometimes the crowd were rather at a loss to follow his vagaries. He might decide to drive and cut brilliantly, he might – in the same innings – decide to toy with the bowlers, cat with mice. One day Arthur Carr, having lost the toss on a good wicket against Yorkshire, with his attack severely crippled by injury, came to Gunn in the dressing-room before Notts batted and said: 'I want you, George, to stay in until tea and keep one end going. We must get 400 at least.' But George pointed out to Carr that he, George, was getting on in years. 'My legs won't stand it,' he argued. But Carr persisted. And George once more argued, then said, 'Make it a pound an hour, Mr Carr, and I'll stay there till half-past four.' And Carr, with a growl, agreed. George batted five hours that day for 40, then went to Carr and claimed time and a half for overtime!

He belongs to the great company of batsmen not blessed by too many inches. A slight and agreeable suggestion of bandiness made him look a little less tall than actually he was – and thrive he did though perceptibly bandy. At the wicket he presented a compact appearance, splendidly proportioned in build, and absolutely relaxed. His style was hard to describe, but at the bottom it was classic, combining the straight back-play, pads well in front, of Arthur Shrewsbury, and the upright forward action, especially the cover-drive, of his famous uncle, William. But mingled with these classic elements was his own modernity, his unorthodox improvisations, his glances and his late cut from the stumps, his sudden cross-bat last-minute pulls, which stupefied all bowlers.

Tradition and the latest surrealism! Often an innings by George Gunn made me think of Louis Armstrong playing in the Philharmonic Orchestra, while a symphony by Mozart was being performed. His cover-drives, as I say, were as handsome as could be, as strong and effortless as any ever seen. On the defensive he would use a bat of exemplary straightness. Then, without warning, he would transform the diagrammatic textbooks into a sort of contemporary collection of elliptical sketches, with half the usual lines left out. In a Test match at Sydney he cocked up his left leg and flicked a good-length off-break under it for four. He happened to be in Australia for his health in 1907, when the England team was there. To fill a place left vacant by illness, he was asked to play in the first Test at Sydney. He obliged and scored 119 and 74, following up these innings with 15, 0, 65, 11, 13, 43, 122 not out, and 0.

He was chosen as one of the England team in Australia in 1911–12 and in the five Tests he contributed scores of 4, 62, 10, 43, 29, 45, 75, 52 and 61. The outstanding fact is that he was invited only *once* in his career to play for England in England – at Lord's in 1909, when he got out for 1 and 0. Even in 1921 when McDonald and Gregory's forked lightning and thunderbolts sent the Selection Committee into panic, so that for five Tests no fewer than 30 of our players were called on, Gunn was neglected. Yet in 1919, at Trent Bridge, he had enjoyed himself to the extent of 131 against the Australian Imperial Forces XI, which included Gregory at his fastest. George liked to tell of the band that played music while he was stroking his way to a century in his first Test match at Sydney, in December 1907. 'I like music,' he said, 'but trumpet was out of tune, and they were playing Gilbert and Sullivan, and I was humming "Regular Royal Queen" to myself, and tryin', at same time, to watch out for Warwick Armstrong's top-spinner; and trumpet kept worrying me all the time. . . .'

He was worrying about the trumpet while scoring a century against Cotter (fast as a whirlwind), Saunders, Hazlitt, Armstrong, Macartney and M. A. Noble! No wonder 'Sammy' Carter, the Australian wicket-keeper said: 'George, you seem to be more concerned with that b— band than with our music.' George played the piano quite well; he once surprised me by sitting down in the Bentinck Hotel at Nottingham, which he managed at the time, and performing a Chopin waltz. He assured me he had never taken piano lessons. 'I play by ear,' he said. And, I imagine, he batted by ear. A short while before his death he discussed cricket of today with me. 'Batsmen make two big mistakes,' he maintained, 'they always have made same two mistakes. They take too much notice of the wicket, pattin' it and looking at it. Then they make a worse mistake – they take too much notice of the bowling.'

In the summer of 1928 George told me that he would reach his fiftieth birthday on 13 June 1929, and said he would make a century 'for me' if I would come to the match. 'I can't promise a year ahead,' I replied, 'who will Notts be playing that day?' 'I don't know,' said George, 'but I'll make a hundred for you to write about.' As it happened, Lancashire had an engagement on 12 June 1929 that I dared not neglect, so I couldn't attend George Gunn's match which celebrated his fiftieth birthday. It was played at Worcester, and though rain cut down cricket to fifty minutes the first day, on the next, George's birthday, the 13th, he attained the promised century – 164 – whether I could be there to see it or not.

A week later, at his own Trent Bridge, it was arranged to honour the birthday by a presentation on the field of play. Glorious sunshine blessed the scene. Obviously, a poor score by George would have meant a disappointing anti-climax. So he stayed at the wicket two hours for 59, then allowed somebody to run him out. He never was seen to hurry. One of his daily philosophical maxims was: 'Never hurry – either on the field or off it.' He was happy in a grand Nottingham lass for a wife, one of the best. She told me of one Monday when she went to waken him and give him his morning cup of tea. 'Then I went downstairs and got breakfast ready and busied about. George seemed a long time coming down, so I called to him. No answer, not a sound. So I went up to the bedroom again, and there he was, fast asleep. I woke him and said, "George, come and get up at once – it's nearly ten o'clock, and it's a lovely morning. You'll be late getting to the ground." And he said: "There's no hurry lass, skipper won't declare for another hour or so." ' 'But,' Mrs Gunn reminded him, 'you were not out on Saturday night.' On Saturday night George had been not out 72, and had forgotten!

What a man! What is the use of adding up his runs and finding his 'average'? The figures can tell nothing of character as free as this, or of skill as masterly. At Cheltenham, in 1926, when comparatively young at the age of forty-seven, he batted throughout Nottinghamshire's first innings, in first and undefeated for 67, out of a total of 155 against Charles Parker at his nastiest. He played with a composure and leisure that rather disturbed Parker's equanimity and vocabulary. So George explained it all to him. 'You see, Charlie,' he said, 'I just plays with tide.' If the ball span in he played it to the on; if it span away, he persuaded it to the off behind point or through the slips. He walked out of his ground so much, here, there, and everywhere, one day against Yorkshire, that George Macaulay pulled himself up in his run to the wicket. 'For God's sake, George,' he called out, 'stay thi still. Ah dunno know which is bluddy off-side or leg side.'

O, rare George Gunn, Scion in an historic house, nephew of the eminently Victorian William; and brother to John, himself one of Trent Bridge's characters and today not forgotten for his all-round prowess. But we'll never see another George. He was himself, morning, noon and night, and inimitable. His death in 1958 took from us an artist, a philosopher, and a man of great courage.

*from* CRICKET HEROES *1959*

# J. B. Hobbs –
## England's Greatest Batsman

### JACK FINGLETON

| Melbourne | 1911–12 | 126 not out |
|-----------|---------|-------------|
| Adelaide  | 1911–12 | 187 |
| Melbourne | 1911–12 | 178 |
| Lords     | 1912    | 107 |
| Melbourne | 1920–21 | 122 |
| Adelaide  | 1920–21 | 123 |
| Melbourne | 1924–25 | 154 |
| Adelaide  | 1924–25 | 119 |
| Sydney    | 1924–25 | 115 |
| Lords     | 1926    | 119 |
| The Oval  | 1926    | 100 |
| Melbourne | 1928–29 | 142 |

That is the Test story, in centuries, of John Berry Hobbs – now Sir Jack – against Australia. Twelve centuries, more than those of any other Englishman, against the Great Enemy!

Those centuries, of course, tell only part of the story of the man who, as Australian Test players agree, was the best batsman ever produced by England. You don't judge a cricketer by centuries alone. Quite often such a score is not nearly as valuable to a side as a 40 or 50 made in difficult circumstances – that is, when the strain is on with every pressing minute a test of temperament and resource. And Jack Hobbs was at his very best when the fight was toughest. One other important point: from his first Test match in Melbourne, on January 1, 1908, to his last at his home Oval in Kennington, Surrey, in 1930, Jack Hobbs always opened the innings. He got no easy runs, after the sting was taken out of the bowling. He did his own de-stinging.

Furthermore, that long list of centuries could well have been half as long again. In his first Test innings Hobbs almost made a century. He had scored 83 in three hours of correct batsmanship when Cotter clean-bowled him. He later scored 72 in the same series in Sydney. He made a brilliant 62 not out – scoring twice as fast as the redoubtable C. B. Fry – to push England home to a ten wickets win against Australia in a low-scoring game on a horrible pitch at Birmingham in 1909. In 1926 he scored 88 at Leeds, 74 in the next Test at Old Trafford, 74 at Adelaide in 1929, 65 in his last Test innings in Australia at Melbourne, and 78 and 74 at Nottingham in 1930.

It is readily seen, therefore, that Hobbs, given just a little luck, could have added another half dozen or more centuries to his list against Australia.

He played in 41 Tests against Australia and had 71 innings for 3,636 runs at an average of 54·23. He played in 18 Tests against South Africa with 29 innings for 1,562 runs at an average of 60·07. He had only two Tests against the West Indies, for 212 runs at an average of 106.

In all Test cricket, then, with his average not buttressed by games against India, Pakistan and New Zealand, he made 5,410 runs at an average of 56·94. His record number of first-class centuries is 197. He made 61,221 first-class runs at an average of 50·63. Although figures indicate the greatness of Hobbs they don't convey the grandeur of his batting, his faultless technique, and the manner in which he captivated those who could recognize and analyse style. Australians who played against him over the years believe cricket never produced a more correct batsman than Hobbs.

From 1907 to 1930 Hobbs batted against this imposing list of Australian bowlers: Saunders, Noble, Armstrong, Macartney, Cotter, Laver, Whitty, Hordern, Minnett, Kelleway, Gregory, McDonald, Mailey, Arthur Richardson, Grimmett, Ironmonger, Oxenham, Blackie, Wall, Hornibrook, McCabe, Fairfax, and a'Beckett.

They were, too, players who had shrewd captains such as Noble, Clem Hill, Sid Gregory, Armstrong, Collins, Ryder and Woodfull to set fields to the best purpose.

Hobbs took them all in his century-making stride. He played Test cricket until he was 48; he played for Surrey until he was 52.

During tours of England, I used to think fondly of Hobbs, Tom Hayward and Ranjitsinhji as I walked on various mornings across Parker's Piece to the Cambridge ground. It was on the Piece that Hobbs and Hayward first played cricket and it was there, too, that the Indian prince first began to reveal his genius to England.

The Piece must have had much to do with the correct moulding of Hobbs's technique. Provided a young batsman has inherent ability there is no better place to build a solid defence than on a turf that scoots, jumps and imparts abnormal break to the ball. Given too much of it a batsman could form bad habits, such as drawing away from the ball, but the correct amount at a formative time leads to a sharpening of the eyesight, quick footwork and deft wielding of the bat. Such an experience leads the youngster to notable deeds when he finds himself on better, truer pitches.

Hobbs has acknowledged his debt to Tom Hayward in his early days – Hayward introduced him to Surrey – but it is well to note Hobbs's claim that he never had an hour's coaching in his life. He was a self-made cricketer – observing, thinking and executing for himself.

He didn't copy Hayward's stance at the wickets, although there was a similarity. Hobbs improved on Hayward's stance, which was decidedly two-eyed, with the left foot pointing almost straight up the pitch, the two shoulders round and the face practically full on to the bowler. Hobbs, like Denis Compton, had his face, and thus his right shoulder, a little fuller to the bowler than most top-ranking batsmen and herein, as with Compton, could have been the secret of his remarkable prowess in playing on-side strokes. I think that was the case, although, and in this consideration I include Compton again, Hobbs could not have played the cover-drive and the square-drive – both forward – had his body not been admirably positioned to allow of the correct back-swing. Such strokes are immediately denied the 'two-eyed' stancer because he can't swing back through his body.

Hobbs was one of the twelve children of a groundsman at Jesus College, Cambridge. His own first job was as groundsman at Bedford school, where he also did some net-bowling against the schoolboys. His life was thus inseparable from cricket but he had an early set-back when he was recommended to the Essex County Club and found not good enough! Essex turned him down.

Then he tried with Surrey, was immediately accepted and in his second match scored a glorious 155 against Essex. Every run must have given him a special pleasure and, knowing that their club had spurned him, the Essex players must have had some galling thoughts at the end of that game – and forever afterwards through Hobbs's great career.

Fittingly enough, for he was years afterwards to displace the Great Man as a scorer of centuries, Hobbs played his first game for Surrey against the Gentlemen of England, captained by Dr W. G. Grace. The game of cricket was to know no greater stealer of a run than Hobbs and, facing up to Grace, he should have got off the mark with a quick single.

Hobbs, very nervous against Grace, played several balls and then played one a few yards up the pitch. He quickly sensed there was a run to be 'stolen' but just as he began his run the quavery voice of the Doctor came down the pitch; 'Thank you, youngster, just tap it back here and save my poor old legs!'

And Hobbs, suitably impressed by the Old Man, who was a terror to the game's newcomers, tapped the ball back to him. He made 18 in the first innings and 88 in the second.

Hobbs played for Surrey against Darling's great Australian side of 1905. He batted beautifully against Cotter, then at his fastest, and had reached 94 when a thrilling throw-in by Clem Hill from the Kennington Oval boundary hit the stumps and ran him out. It was a compliment Hobbs often returned to the Australians. Perhaps the greatest cover-point ever – quick in anticipation, swift to the ball and unerring in his under-the-shoulder return – he had 15 run-outs on his second tour of Australia in 1912.

No cover-point can ever be considered great unless he has deft, tinkling footwork. As the ball speeds towards him, cover-point must be on the way in to meet it, for a split second thus gained could bring the run-out and, moreover, he should so position his movements in to the ball and throw it to the desired end with one action. A champion cover-point must possess an additional sense. He must sense what the batsmen are doing, for his own eyes never leave the ball. He must, too, be a 'fox', yielding a single here and there to snare the batsman into a feeling of safety and, when his chance comes, cover-point must be able to hit the stumps from side-on nine times out of ten. Jack Hobbs had the lot – all the tricks.

Hobbs's Test career against Australia was preceded by disappointment. A. O. Jones brought the English side to Australia in 1907 with Hobbs making his first trip. Jones became ill on the eve of the First Test in Sydney and Hobbs seemed certain to get the position. But the selectors did an odd thing, although it was to prove most successful. George Gunn, of Nottinghamshire, had travelled with the team on a health trip and he was asked to play, instead of Hobbs.

Hobbs was not only bitterly disappointed; he thought he had been badly treated, even though Gunn proved the hero of the game, scoring 119 and 74 in a masterly manner in his first Test. Anyway, Hobbs almost equalled the century feat with 83 in the following Test in Melbourne. Gunn headed the Test averages of the tour, 462 at an average of 51·33, and Hobbs was second with 302 runs at 43·14. Together, Gunn and Hobbs put on 134 in the final Test in Sydney. It was a partnership, according to those who saw it, which hasn't been excelled, for classical batsmanship, by any other two Englishmen in Australia.

Hobbs went home to make a 'duck' in his first Test innings against the Australians in England. The Birmingham pitch then was helpful to bowlers. Blythe and Hirst ran through

Australia for the meagre total of 74. Hobbs opened for England but Macartney, with the new ball, had him quickly for a 'duck'. But in the second innings Hobbs made a brilliant 62 not out, top score for the match – and England won by ten wickets. His stroke play was classical, so much so that Englishmen described it as the best since Vic Trumper's performances of 1902.

That was a time of outstanding batting strength in English cricket. There were so many men of brilliance knocking at the Test door that those inside could barely afford to fail. Yet, with his own place by no means assured, Hobbs was responsible at Leeds for what Australians thought was a remarkable gesture.

The captain, M. A. Noble told the story thus:

'Hobbs forced a ball off his back foot between short-leg and mid-on. In doing so he knocked off one of the bails. Believing that it was done in the act of making the stroke we appealed for hit wicket, but the umpire gave him not out on the ground that he had completed the stroke before his foot touched the stump.

'Two or three balls later Hobbs made a weak attempt to play a straight one and was bowled. My impression was then – and still is – that Hobbs believed himself legally to be out and deliberately allowed himself to be bowled. It is a most difficult thing to allow yourself to be bowled without betraying the fact to the bowler or someone fielding near the wicket. It was a match of small scores and the loss then of a player of Hobbs's ability probably had a determining influence upon our success in that game.'

Another Australian captain who spoke in warm terms of Hobbs's outstanding sportsmanship was H. L. Collins. Hobbs gave himself out once at Kennington Oval against the Australians after the umpire had said not out. Few Test cricketers down the years have done that. Most accept an umpire's blunder when it is their way on the principle that they are sometimes given out when they are not and, indeed, some of the moderns stay when an obvious catch has been made in the hope, unworthy as it is, that the umpire will make a mistake!

As I have said, Hobbs's greatness as a batsman lay not only

in the fact that he got many runs with incredible consistency but also in the manner in which he made them. He was perfect in the execution of every stroke. His footwork was a model for all players and his style was irreproachable. He was always attractive to watch – a neat, compact figure, faultlessly attired in flannels – whether he was moving along at a fast rate or was on the defensive.

I asked him once which innings he considered the best he had played in Australia.

'Well,' he replied, 'it's a long time since I retired from first-class cricket, twenty-three years, and it was five years earlier that I last played in Australia. Memory grows dim. Quite naturally, I suppose, on being asked which was my best innings I try to recall which was the best of the nine Test centuries I scored in your country. There was that one in 1912 when I made 178 and along with Wilfred Rhodes put on 323 for the first wicket. England won the rubber by winning that match.

"Then there was the 122 in the second Test at Melbourne in 1921, made for the most part on a rain-damaged wicket: but we lost that match. Both of those innings gave me a lot of pleasure because I felt that I had played pretty well – if I may, with modesty, say so.'

I put it to him that an achievement that will never be forgotten in Australia was the 49 he made in England's second innings of the third Test in Melbourne of the 1928–29 tour.

'Yes,' he agreed, 'perhaps it would be wise to select that innings as England won the match against all the odds. You would be surprised at the number of Aussies who mention that match when they call to see me in Fleet Street. Just the same as folk here speak about the fifth Test at the Oval in 1926 – another "sticky".' (Hobbs made a brilliant 100 on this later occasion, England winning back the Ashes.)

He continued: 'I well remember waiting in Melbourne for the wicket to dry so that we could continue the match. Australia still had two wickets to fall. I can recall very well how our friends came to the pavilion to commiserate with us, saying what a pity it was the rain came. We thought so too. We considered we didn't have a chance of getting the runs. That old campaigner Hughie Trumble, then secretary of the Melbourne Cricket Club, told us in all seriousness that 70 would be a good score in our second innings. Well, as you know, we chased 332 and eventually won by three wickets. Our success caused quite a stir at home. I remember that a London newspaper cabled out £100 each to Herbert Sutcliffe and myself.'

It was the opening partnership of 105 between Hobbs and Sutcliffe that enabled England to win that match. Not only was it rich in runs but it defied the Australian attack on one of the worst wickets known in Melbourne. Considering the difficulties, that opening partnership would possibly rank as the most outstanding one in Test history.

The wicket was bad all day, going through different phases. Thirty points of rain had fallen and the English innings began in gentle sunshine, increasing in intensity and drying the pitch in patches so that there were spots off which the ball kicked disconcertingly. It was at its most dangerous period from lunch to the tea interval.

The Australians had no fast bowler in this match, the opening bowlers, Hendry and a'Beckett, being no more than medium-pace, but there was an abundance of varied spin in Oxenham (medium off-breaks), Grimmett (leg-breaks) and Blackie (slow to slow-medium off-breaks).

On such a pitch against such spinners, the English task should have been an impossible one but, right from the beginning, the two great opening batsmen dominated the pitch and the Australians.

For over after over, Blackie bowled around the wicket with a packed leg-side field, but by superb dead-bat play and adept pad-play, together with the most astute judgment in not playing at the ball when it wasn't necessary, Hobbs and Sutcliffe went on for one hour, then two hours and finally came to tea with the score 0–78 – Hobbs 36 and Sutcliffe 32. The whole members' stand rose to them in acclamation.

In effect, the leg-theory tactics of the Australians played into the hands of two such proficient batsmen. Ryder, fast-medium, often hit the body but never seemed likely to hit the stumps. Both batsmen were black and blue on the body – Hobbs was once hit on the head by Ryder – but they never flinched, even though the sharply rising balls yielded many byes off Oldfield's body. Indeed, one ball from Oxenham rose so sharply off a length that it cleared Oldfield's head (the keeper was standing up to the stumps) for two byes. Three successive balls from Oxenham particularly revealed the conditions – one rose high and went from Oldfield's gloves to the first slip, the next hit Sutcliffe on the shoulder and the next went for a bye off Oldfield's shoulder.

While Hendry was bowling, Richardson, Blackie, Ryder, Bradman and a'Beckett formed a complete circle of under ten yards diameter around the batsman from silly-point to forward short-leg.

The two Englishmen on that day demoralized the Australian bowling, the fielding and the captaincy of Ryder. They gave their usual superb lesson of running between the wickets. One never let the other down. This was exemplified time after time in their calling and acceptance, many of the runs, of a seemingly dangerous nature at the beginning, being completed at a walk. Once, Hobbs walked out of his crease several yards before Blackie bowled and placed him to the on for two.

The century came in 133 minutes. Just before this the old field-marshal, Hobbs, using the stratagem of signalling for a bat, sent a message to Chapman in the pavilion to change his batting order, sending Jardine in next before Hammond.

It was a shrewd piece of advice. Hobbs went l.b.w. to Blackie at 49, but at stumps England were 1–171 – Sutcliffe 83 and Jardine 18. There were 13 byes in that total. Commenting on this in England, Strudwick said: 'A wet wicket in Melbourne is about the worst of its kind, especially for the wicket-keeper. The ball does all sorts of funny things.'

In short, the old firm of Hobbs and Sutcliffe, making their

eighth opening stand of a century against the Australians out-generalled and out-played Ryder and his men. The next day, with three wickets falling for 14 after the match was all but won, England took the honours by three wickets. Sutcliffe played perhaps his greatest innings, 6½ hours for 135 – but undoubtedly it was that opening stand that won the match.

Hobbs found his first great opening partner for England in Wilfred Rhodes and it was fitting that another Yorkshireman, Sutcliffe, should have been his second. Hobbs and Rhodes made a record 221 for the first wicket against South Africa in Cape Town in 1910: and in Melbourne in 1912 they put on 323 against Australia. This still stands as a record for Tests.

Hobbs was at his best in Melbourne, as his records show. In 1926, after Australia had hit up a record first innings tally of 600, one London newspaper announced on its placard: 'Australia 600: Come on Hobbs!' With Sutcliffe, Hobbs batted all the next day, the opening being worth 283. The same newspaper said on its placard next day: 'Thank you Hobbs!'

'Figures,' an admirer once wrote of Hobbs, 'can convey no idea of the Master, of his full-blooded hooking when he was young, of his driving on light, swift feet, of his peerless square-cut, of his leaning leg-glance, of the natural growth of his talents to a quite regal control and superiority.'

There was all that success, too, as I have stressed, when the fight was hardest, when the pitch was cranky. Somebody once aptly observed that it was Hobbs who took the description 'unplayable' out of the category of pitches.

Douglas Jardine, who saw many great batsmen at close quarters, was once asked to name the greatest. He didn't hesitate. 'Hobbs,' said Jardine, 'is number one every time. He was so good on bad pitches.' The interviewer interposed another name. Jardine looked out the window – and refused to answer.

*from* MASTERS OF CRICKET *1956*

# H. Sutcliffe

## R. C. ROBERTSON-GLASGOW

Herbert Sutcliffe is the serenest batsman I have known. Whatever may have passed under that calm brow – anger, joy, disagreement, surprise, relief, triumph – no outward sign was betrayed on the field of play. He was understood, over two thousand years in advance, by the Greek philosophers. They called this character megalo-psychic. It is the sort of man who would rather miss a train than run for it, and so be seen in disorder and heard breathing heavily.

He sets himself the highest available standard of batting and deportment. His physical discipline equals his mental; shown in the cool, clear eye and the muscularity of frame. If he is bowled, he appears to regard the event less as a human miscalculation than some temporary, and reprehensible, lapse of natural laws. There has been a blunder, to which he is unwillingly privy and liable. The effects of this blunder will be entered, with other blunders in a score-book, and the world may read of it in due time. He does not regret that it has occurred, for he is never sorry for himself; but he is sorry that Nature should have forgotten herself. To the later comers to the ground he would so to speak, announce: 'Mr Sutcliffe regrets he's unable to bat today, being, ludicrously enough, already out.' Yet he is not proud. He leaves pride to little cricketers. There is nothing little in Sutcliffe. He is great. Great in idea and great in effect.

In the matter of round numbers he has scored over 50,000 runs in twenty-one years at an average of 52. In Test matches against Australia his average stands at nearly 67 for 2,741 runs – easily the highest average among English batsmen. On his first appearance against Australia, at Sydney, he played an innings of 115. He took part with Holmes (P.) in the world's record first-wicket stand of 555 for Yorkshire at Leyton in 1932. These are but a few of the feats in a career of resounding triumph.

When I first saw him in 1919, he was a debonair and powerful stylist. He didn't look Yorkshire; even less a Yorkshire Number One. He looked, rather, as if he had remembered and caught something of an earlier and not indigenous grace of manner. Pudsey was his home, but his style was not Pudsey. He had easy offside strokes and a disdainful hook. I would not say that with the years he lost this manner, but it was increasingly seldom seen in its fullness. Two visits within five years to help Hobbs for England against Australia must mark any batsman of Sutcliffe's will and intelligence. It became hard to discern which predominated, the pleasure of batting or the trick of staying in.

As you bowled opening overs to the later Sutcliffe you noticed the entire development of every defensive art: the depressingly straight bat, the astute use of pads (as with Hobbs), the sharp detection of which outswinger could be left; above all, the consistently safe playing down of a rising or turning ball on leg stump, or thighs. This last art you will, I think, find only in the best players; Makepeace, Holmes (P.), Hutton, D. R. Jardine, Sandham and Hobbs as a matter of course, spring to the mind's eye. Professionals generally acquire it more readily than amateurs, whose early coaching often tends to a neglect of the on-side strokes.

Sutcliffe added a defensive stroke of his own; not exactly pretty, nor easily imitable. It was often played to a rising ball on about the line of the off stump. The bat started straight, on a restricted forward stroke; then with a swivel or overturn of the wrists he caused the ball to lie 'dead' a few yards down the pitch, or where a silly-point would have stood if such a liberty had been taken; as if Sutcliffe had thought: 'Ball, you irk me. There. Be strangled, and lie quiet.'

He has always been capable of scoring at a great speed, especially from fast bowling. His hook is imperious. Some remark that this stroke has often been his downfall. They forget the many hundreds of runs that it has brought him, from balls which make lesser batsmen dodge and murmur of danger. I hope we shall soon see his like again.

*from* CRICKET PRINTS *1943*

# Maurice Tate

## JOHN ARLOTT

In the eleven months between the beginning of May 1924 and the end of March 1925, Maurice Tate, in his thirtieth year, placed himself among the really great bowlers of the modern, or overarm, age of bowling – F. R. Spofforth, Lohmann, C. T. B. Turner, S. F. Barnes, Maurice Tate and Bill O'Reilly. There have been other outstanding bowlers but, for attack, for ability to defeat the best batsmen on unhelpful wickets, for bowling the virtually unplayable ball, these men must stand alone. Even in such company, Tate has one unique quality, in that he lacked that support without which – it is an axiom of cricket – no bowler can achieve consistently great results. Each of the others had a partner little less mighty than himself – it was Spofforth and Boyle or Spofforth and Garrett, Turner and Ferris, Lohmann and Peel or Lohmann and Briggs, Barnes and Foster, O'Reilly and Grimmett – but Maurice Tate had no one of comparable stature to share with him the task of bowling out England's opponents. He achieved his great place in cricket history without real support, for the partnership of Tate and Gilligan which had promised to be so immense, was unhappily broken for ever as an effective weapon. Cecil Parkin, who had the gifts to be little lower than his Sussex contemporary, did not remain in the Test cricket world – for reasons not connected with his playing ability; what a great pair those two might have been. Thus, in two ways, Maurice Tate was unique among the great bowlers. When a master bowler lacks support, his opponents can regard him as a problem separate from the remainder of his team's outcricket. That is to say, a single defensive batsman can be deputed to 'farm' the outstanding bowler while his less safe fellows play themselves in and score runs against the lesser bowling: meanwhile the spearhead is slowly blunted by purely defensive batting directed to the end

of tiring him out. Because escape from Spofforth meant facing
Garrett, because at the opposite end to Sidney Barnes was
Frank Foster, in each case a foil only a little less great than the
principal, those great bowlers *had* to be played as an alternative
to stalemate at both ends and a rate of scoring which could not
hope to win a match. Tate, however, for many years, gave many
wickets to his fellow-bowlers by driving the batsmen to them
in a state of partly-relaxed relief while, against him, resistance
was the normal course of strategic batting.

Above all, Maurice Tate was unique in that he made the ball
leave the ground faster, in relation to its speed through the air,
than any other pace bowler in the history of the game. Great
batsmen have said that he could be of medium pace through the
air and positively fast off the pitch. Certainly, at the start of an
innings, it was impossible to play back to him; the batsman who
tried to do so would find his stumps leaping before his bat was
fully down. Thus more than one young cricketer playing
against Sussex has been sent out with strict instructions from
his senior pro not to do anything but play forward to Maurice
Tate until he has scored at least twenty.

1923 had been a great season for Tate, but in 1924 he was the
greatest problem batsmen had faced since Sidney Barnes. It was
excitement to go to Brighton to watch him. At any moment he
might whisk away the entire batting of a county in a burst of
inspired bowling. For years, to win the toss at Brighton had
been to take a day-long lease on the friendliest stretch of turf
ever tamed by sun and groundsman for the delight and pros-
perity of batsmen. Now it was different; captains won the toss
there and took first innings half-reluctantly.

When the sea-fret was on the wicket and Tate was playing,
the Sussex team went out to field almost with joy. He would
take the end which enabled him to bowl into the wind and
measure out his run – seven full paces and a four-feet jump – and
there he made his mark. 'Tich' Cornford – wicket-keeper of
Sussex after the sad death of George Street – would crouch at
the wicket, standing close, his head no higher than the bails,

for Tate believed he could not bowl so well with the wicket-keeper standing back. Then you saw the most perfect bowling action that theory or practice can conceive. Two short walking steps, falling into six accelerating running strides and – midway between the fifth and sixth – the body rocked easily back. The left arm was thrown up, the ball held in the back-slung right hand so that, at one point of the swing, the left hand pointed high forward and there was a pure straight line from the fingers of the left hand diagonally across the body to the right hand. But this was momentary, and comes back only in the analysing memory, for the eye and mind at this time were consumed by the immense unchecking power of the bowler's movement. Then, with the final leap, came the full rhythmic swing of those heavy shoulders: he delivered at the highest point of his vertical swing and followed through with his hand seeming to press heavily into the air. The left foot, square, plunged into the ground just off the line of the stumps, so that, in any appreciable spell, he would dig a pit just where the batsman stood and which might have to be filled-in several times in the course of a single match. And, ask any man who ever fielded at cover-point for Sussex in Tate's day and he will tell you how, even there, he could feel the ground shake as that left foot pounded it in his follow-through. Tate's arm swept on after the delivery in a huge circle right round past his legs and, as he pulled away to the off-side of the wicket, he had completed the finest bowling action of our time. The approach, delivery and follow-through, fathered, concentrated and directed every fraction of their combined energy into the pace of the ball.

After he had bowled a few overs on a wet day, you would see his run clearly marked in sharp, complete footprints, showing black against the green, for he put his feet down in *exactly* the same place each time he ran up to bowl. And he always delivered from the same point of the crease – close against the stumps – he did not 'use the crease' – which telegraphs to the batsman the type of ball the pace bowler is about to bowl. There is no suggestion of strain or pressing in his action and, in his entire career, Maurice Tate never once bowled a no-ball! At Brighton, on one occasion, he threw up a slow 'floater' which a violent wind carried away – and that was his only wide. That delivery apart, every ball he ever bowled was finely controlled and, simultaneously, impelled with immense ferocity.

Bowling into the wind on a heavy seaside morning, he would make the ball dart and move in the air as if bewitched. The in-swing and the out-swing were there as a matter of course but, as every man who batted against him at his best will testify, the ball would sometimes seem to begin to swerve and then straighten again before it struck the ground. Once it pitched, the bounce was full of fire and, because Tate was a 'long-fingered' bowler, on a green-topped wicket the ball would some-times strike back in the direction opposite to the swing. That is to say, an out-swinger would become, in effect, an off-break off the pitch, or an in-swinger a leg-break. Sometimes this happened to his 'cutter' because of the tendency of the cut break to swerve; but it could also happen to deliveries which were not 'cutters'. Tate, of course, like any other swing bowler, could only produce the swing *deliberately*, the subsequent tricks of the swung ball off the 'green 'un' happened, according, we may assume, to the angle of seam to ground on pitching, but not within the command of the bowler. When he bowled thus on a green wicket, no batsman in the world was too good to be his victim; the ball pitched and left an ominous black mark on the damp turf where it landed; that was the danger sign. Batsmen, when they saw Tate's mark on the pitch at Hove, resolved to play forward, hold their bats very straight and hope. The ball would whip into Tich Cornford's gloves with a villainous smack and the little man would hollow his belly and was lifted to, or off, his toes as the ball carried his heavy-gloved hands back into him.

There was no 'new' l.b.w. rule in those days to prevent the batsman from covering up with his pads to the ball which nipped in late off the pitch. More than one batsman with a great record against the finest bowlers would shuffle across the wicket to Maurice Tate, keeping his bat away from the ball which,

sinfully late, would swing away at fierce pace towards the slips –
where Ted Bowley, Bert Wensley, Duleep, Tommy Cook, John
Langridge, over the years, were great fieldsmen to the bowling
of Maurice Tate. But when that out-swinging ball struck back
off the pitch, the pads would be there, it would thunder against
them in its denied course to the wicket and there could not even
be an appeal. A fraction shorter and it would race across the
face of the pad and rise high to hit the batsman's thigh and
produce an excruciating agony so that even those batsmen who
did not rub themselves because 'it encourages the bowler',
broke their rule when this ball of Tate's crashed home on the
unprotected muscle.

Because we have not his like among us today, it is difficult to
convey the power of Maurice Tate's bowling for those nine
years from 1923 to 1932. Certainly no batsmen in the world
could expect with any real confidence to weather Tate's first
hour of bowling in the morning. Of those who did survive, and
their number is small, none ever 'middled' every ball at which
he played. And, with it all, Tate, by the judgment not only of
his team-mates but also of his opponents, was the unluckiest
of all great bowlers. He was also bowling at the wicket or around
the edge of the off stump and he probably beat the bat more often
than any other bowler of his time. Again and again the ball would
miss the wicket when Cornford had turned his head away to
avoid being struck by a flying bail: it would miss by the nar-
rowest margin so that the bails seemed to shake in their grooves
at its close passage. Then Maurice Tate would turn his follow-
through into a gesture of suffering to the Gods at the narrowness
of the batsman's escape. The next ball would be bowled to
adjust the misfortune of the preceding ball and so, on and on
through the hottest day, his ferocity burned beyond the power
of sweat to quench it. His stamina was such that he bowled
unwaveringly through the longest spells. Sometimes, coming
back to the Sussex side after two days of bowling in a Test
Match, he would, after ten or so overs, ask for one of the slips
to be moved to short-leg – for the first sign of Tate tiring was the

lapse of power of his out-swing. But, even when he was tired or the pitch denied him help, he still expected a wicket with every ball, still put the ferocity of five bowlers into stock-bowling and again and again turned defence into attack.

Often he was bowling too well: batsmen just good enough to get an edge to his out-swinger were hit in the middle of the bat by the ball as it struck back: when he was bowling at his best with the new ball, only the greatest were good enough even to edge him in the early stages of their innings. Most dangerous of all was his out-swinger, which moved in at the line of the middle-and-off stumps and then, in the last yard, moved away towards the slips. No pitch was quite so dead but he could startle the batsman into the hasty stroke, no position so hopeless but he could muster enthusiasm and magnificent bowling to meet it.

In the year 1924, he took more than a third of the wickets which fell while he was in the field for a fifth of the runs scored. There was not a great batsman in the country that year who did not fall to him, not a single county against which he played without having one of his great spells.

Sussex started the season with a run of six 'out' matches before they played in Sussex. After a rain-ruined match at Trent Bridge in which not even a first innings decision could be reached, Tate settled down to his historic season. A match record of nine for 51 against Cambridge University at Fenners, five for 35 against Hampshire, ten for 74 in the match against Gloucester, and six for 50 in the only Warwick innings at Birmingham, led up to six for 24 against Worcester, seven for 45 and four for 50 *and* the top batting score against Essex at Ilford. Thus, when the side came to its first match at Brighton, Tate had taken 48 of the 100 wickets which had fallen to Sussex – almost half the wickets, for a quarter of the runs scored against them: his bowling average was less than eight and more than a third of the overs he had bowled had been maidens.

Immediately afterwards, in the course of a heroic week in London, he took six for 22 against Surrey on a good wicket at

The Oval – including the legendary opening pair of Hobbs and Sandham for 4 runs. At Lord's in the Whitsun Bank holiday match against Middlesex, he took seven for 36 in the Middlesex first innings of 104, two for 13 in the second and his 51, top score of his side, was the match-winning innings.

He was eagerly selected to play in the first Test against South Africa at Birmingham, when Taylor, captaining South Africa, won the toss and put England in to bat. That first English innings did not end until the second day, at 438 all out. The last three wickets added 40 runs that morning on an easy wicket and, immediately afterwards, when the wicket was rolled, Tate and Gilligan began the bowling for England.

Gilligan bowled the first over to Herby Taylor, greatest of South African batsmen, who opened the innings with R. H. Catterall. Taylor scored a single and then Gilligan bowled Catterall; Susskind came in at number three and scored a three to take him to the other end to face Maurice Tate's first over in a Test Match. The first ball was a late in-swinger, Susskind came quickly down on it but not quickly enough; it hit his bat before his timing expected it and flew off to Roy Kilner – a catch at short leg – and Tate had taken a wicket with his first ball in a Test.

At the end of the over he went to field at short leg and, cupping his hands confidentially, even portentously, about his mouth, turned to Bill Reeves the square-leg umpire. Bill, ever interested in everything, inclined a listening ear to the young man who had just begun his Test career so impressively but, as Tate was about to speak, Gilligan came up to bowl and he turned to his fielding again. Between each ball this happened, with Tate unable to find time to communicate his news to Bill Reeves. With the last ball of the over, Maurice, without moving from his position, turned to Bill Reeves, and, with a glance to see that no one else was listening, said, hand confidentially shielding his mouth, "Ot, ain't it?' Bill, stunned beyond reply, walked darkly in to the wicket, but, after the initial disappointment of his thoroughly roused expectations, Bill Reeves cherished and repeated the conversation, thus perpetuating the first recorded 'Tateism'.

In three-quarters of an hour, Tate and Gilligan bowled out South Africa for 30 – 11 of them extras – the lowest total ever made in a Test in England. Tate took four wickets – three of the first five batsmen – he cleaned bowled the redoubtable Herby Taylor, the best batsman in the side, and dismissed Susskind and Blackenberg, numbers 3 and 6 – Number 5 – Commaille – was not out 1! The figures of the two Sussex bowlers, who bowled unchanged, were –

|  | Overs | Maidens | Runs | Wickets |
|---|---|---|---|---|
| A. E. R. Gilligan | 6·3 | 4 | 7 | 6 |
| M. W. Tate | 6 | 1 | 12 | 4 |

Following on, the South Africans batted hard to avoid the innings defeat, but did not succeed. Gilligan again took the greater number of wickets – five for 83 – but Tate, who bowled as many as 54 overs, again got Taylor's wicket, that of Catterall, the top-scorer, and the dour Commaille, in his four for 103. *Wisden* said, 'Arthur Gilligan . . . took in all eleven wickets, for 90 runs. Tate, to whom fortune was unkind in the last innings, had a record for the match of eight wickets for 115 runs. The other England bowlers did not look at all difficult.' Those 'other England bowlers' were Parkin, Kilner, Fender and Woolley!

Immediately from the Test to a wonderful Tate spell of eight for 18 against Worcester – and he and Gilligan had taken 76 wickets in a fortnight. As a pair, they were utterly superior to every batting side they met until the match with Yorkshire at Sheffield. There Tate had four wickets – Percy Holmes, Oldroyd, Rhodes and Wilson – for 66 runs in 37 overs in the first innings and followed his bowling with a century which was more than half his side's total – 102 not out in a score of 192. In the second Yorkshire innings, however, Sutcliffe and Holmes got on top after some very narrow escapes and last-minute pad-play against Tate's opening overs. This defeat was the beginning of a Sussex slide from a strong position, for, of their next five match-dates, Tate and Gilligan played two Tests and the two Gentlemen and Players matches at Lord's and The Oval. The second Test was another innings win for England with five wickets to Gilligan and four to Tate. The entire spell, four representative matches and the game against Kent, brought Tate 29 good wickets and lost him his bowling partner. In the Gentlemen and Players match at The Oval, a ball from Arthur Pearson, the Worcester player, rose off a good length and struck Arthur Gilligan over the heart. Tate, who was fielding at slip, was the first to reach him and, loosening his shirt, saw the huge bruise over his heart; Gilligan was revived, and insisted on playing on: he was out almost immediately and the Gentlemen followed on. They had lost seven wickets for 207 and seemed in utter defeat when Arthur Gilligan came in for his second innings and, characteristically, hit 112 in an hour and a half. This innings, which changed an entire game, between some of the finest players in the land, added to the bruising over his heart, has been held responsible for the trouble which, within a few days, was virtually to end Arthur Gilligan's career as a fast bowler. He played much after, scored many good runs, fielded well and took valuable wickets at medium pace, but his effective days as an England fast bowler in the mighty combination of Gilligan and Tate were over. He, as captain of Sussex, was to realize its effect all too bitterly, and Tate, though he bowled as well as ever, was not again to know such support and became, for county and country, an isolated attacker, the only real menace to opposing batsmen.

Those who saw Tate and Gilligan at their greatest will never greatly respect the in-swinger. Each of them bowled the out-swinger as his deadliest ball: each could pitch straight enough to compel a stroke *and* make the ball rear, finding and leaving the bat's edge and diving into slips. It is tempting, if profitless, to speculate what might have happened if Arthur Gilligan had never received his injury, even if he had rested immediately afterwards, or even if he had not scored that epic century on the 4th of July 1924. Sussex might well have won the County Championship at least once, possibly twice: England might have won the Ashes in Australia in the season of 1924–25. Above all, Maurice Tate might never have had to be 'bowled into the ground' as the saying is. The master batsmen would not have comforted and protected their younger colleagues with 'All right, I'll look after Chub Tate, you stay out of harm's way' if Arthur Gilligan had been at the other end. Never again that season did Sussex look so dangerous as in the early months, except in a solitary August match when Arthur Gilligan took the risk of bowling himself full out again, and he and Tate twice ran through the Leicestershire side, for 113 and 45, to give Sussex an innings win. With this weakening of its bowling, the county's immense weakness in batting could no longer be concealed: for a week in June Sussex were at the top of the Championship table, but they finished the season tenth. Tate was effectively top of the bowling averages (N. J. Holloway who came out above him took only seven wickets). Despite his absences at representative matches he bowled twice as many overs as any other bowler in the side, took over a third of the wickets credited to Sussex bowlers for less than a quarter of the runs scored off them, and almost a third of his overs were maidens. In addition to these labours, he was also top of the Sussex batting averages! He was the only member of the side to score a thousand runs, made the highest score of the season for the county, scored two of the three Sussex centuries and averaged a little over thirty runs an innings with very little support.

In all cricket for the season, he again took two hundred wickets (205) and scored a thousand runs (1,419). His wickets cost only 13·74 apiece and well over a quarter of his fourteen hundred overs were maidens.

It was a foregone conclusion that he would be picked as a member of the M.C.C. side to challenge for the Ashes during the Australian season of 1924–25 and, indeed, his name was one of the first group among Hobbs, Sutcliffe, Hearne and Hendren, with Arthur Gilligan as captain. There were those in England as well as in Australia who doubted if a bowler of his type could succeed on Australian wickets but, on his record, he had to be selected.

*from* CRICKETING LIVES – TATE *1951*

# W. R. Hammond

## R. C. ROBERTSON-GLASGOW

W. R. Hammond is the sort of cricketer that any schoolboy might wish to be. Schoolboys are very good judges of most things and people. They think and look straight on, un-apprenticed to prejudice.

It might be interesting, and it would be unprofitable, to argue Hammond's place as a batsman in the ranks of all the great, or to compare his ability with that of famous contemporaries. It has been tried, and it ends in futility. To me he is, quite simply, the great cricketer who began playing in the last twenty years, and that, too, by a long distance. In the word 'cricketer' I count not only batting, bowling and fielding. In these combined arts there is not one, not Bradman, not Constantine, who could stand a full and unbiased comparison with Hammond as he showed himself in the decade from 1925 to 1935; when he would make a hundred or two against Australia, then bowl down their first three wickets, then make with ease a slip-catch which others would not merely miss but would not even have rated as a miss. But I count also those things which cannot be translated into words, far less into print, but belong to the brain and the heart. I mean the effect on a match of his presence alone; the influence on a bowler's feelings of the sight of Hammond taking guard at about 11.50 a.m., when lunch seemed far and the boundary near.

Such abstractions belong as surely to a batsman's greatness as do his technical ability and his power to make the numbers rattle on the board. It is something to have seen Hammond walk out to the Australians from the pavilion at Lord's; a ship in full sail. There is a pride in possessing such a player. There was an anxiety for his success, not only from party reasons but because his failure would be an affront to sense, a slap in the face to Nature. Surely he would do it today. And none that saw it will forget his batting on a June Saturday in 1938. He gave one chance in an innings of 240, and that split a fieldsman's finger.

As a batsman he has it all; and with double the strength of most players; strength scientifically applied. In his prime his hitting, mostly straight and through the covers, was of a combined power and grace that I have never seen in any other man. I can't think that human agency could do more to a ball. To field to him at cover-point was a sort of ordeal by fire. You would take a ball, perhaps, with as much give as possible and in the middle of the hands, then wring them. I have heard the criticism that he is not a good hooker. I never noticed the deficiency when I bowled him a straight long-hop. It is nearer the truth to say that his method and strength enabled him to play straight, or nearly straight, many short balls which other batsmen find easier to hook.

I have seen him in trouble to leg-break bowling, but not often. Far oftener I have seen a leg-breaker preparing footwork for a dodge from violent death. I have known him lose his wicket through what looked like a sudden failure of concentration, generally to fast bowling. And I believe that from the first, when he was a free and sometimes abandoned hitter, he had to learn and hardly acquire concentration. It was not born in him. For his method, when he is allowed to play as he wishes, and his conversation, both show that he regards fun as the first reason for cricket. He got as far as acquiring the iron temperament of Test Matches for the necessary period. But he never wholly enjoyed that mood, and it never sat comfortably on him. You should see him in a Festival.

As you would expect in such a player, he has generosity and humour, especially in his judgments of other cricketers, given quietly and with a twinkling eye. I chanced to meet him soon after close of play, when he'd been cut over the eye by a rising ball in the Old Trafford Test against West Indies in 1933. 'Well,' he said, 'we began it, you know; and now you can see just a bit of what it was like. Just the luck of the game.'

Hammond is not only a great cricketer.

*from* CRICKET PRINTS *1943*

# D. G. Bradman

## NEVILLE CARDUS

Bradman, who played his last innings in England in 1948, is already becoming legendary in a way, after the manner of legends, that deprives him of human appeal as a cricketer. The notion is getting about which suggests he was a mechanical batsman, slave to his own heartless technique, an adding-machine crushing out of the game all hazard and glorious uncertainty. It is a notion true only in so far as it does honour to a mastery of skill not excelled by anybody in the conditions in which he played. It is indirectly untrue because it doesn't stress Bradman's consistent brilliance and range of strokes. It is entirely false in so far as it conveys that Bradman at the wicket was ever dull, without imagination and the personal touch. He was, if we may abuse language, a *deus ex machina*.

A hundred years after the birth of W. G. Grace the curtain fell on Bradman's career in Test matches when Hollies of Warwickshire bowled him for nothing at Kennington Oval. Twenty years earlier he had gone to the wicket for the first time in a Test match in Australia at Brisbane, a terrible match for Australia too; for J. M. Gregory broke down in it physically and, so melodrama delightfully assures us, gulped to the dressing-room: 'Boys, I'm finished. I'll never bowl again.' Nor did he. In this match England, leading by 399, went in again and in five hours and a half compiled 342 for eight wickets, then, mercifully if not gallantly, declared – to trap Australia on a vicious pitch and finish them off for 66 all out. An appropriately austere baptism for the boy from Bowral. He scored 18, l.b.w. to Tate and, c. Chapman, b. White. 1. Then he was discarded from the Australian XI for the second match of the rubber, or rather he had to be content to act as twelfth man and carry the drinks to the field. When the third Test match was played at Melbourne, Ponsford could not be chosen on account of an injury, so Bradman received a recall. He jumped at the opportunity, and scored 79 and 112.

He never looked back after that, proceeding to stagger every cricketer's credulity. He changed batsmanship into an exact science, but a science with a difference; he dwarfed precedent and known values. He came fresh to England in 1930, his age twenty-one, and began at Worcester with 236. Day after day he cut and drove and hooked bowlers right and left, never raising the ball from the ground. I followed him up and down the land for two or three weeks in May, then another engagement called me to London. One afternoon as I was walking along Whitehall I saw a newspaper placard: 'Bradman Fails', and in the stop-press I read, 'Bradman, b. Ryan, 58'. At Nottingham in the first Test of the summer, he scored 131, and while he was making it I asked the one and only Sidney Barnes what he thought of him. 'Well,' he said, 'I won't say I couldn't have got him out at my best, but I would have needed to be at my very best.'

It was Ranjitsinhji who gave to batsmanship a new and revolutionary direction. 'Play back or drive' – it is a delusion that Ranji couldn't drive. The old lunge at the pitch of the ball became, or should have become, more or less obsolete. The Aristotle to Ranji's Alexander as he conquered new worlds was, of course, C. B. Fry. 'The fallacy of reach,' wrote Fry, 'is fatal in true cricket. None but a giant, by advancing the left foot and pushing down the wicket, can reach within feet of the pitch of a good-length fast ball. Why, the very thing the bowler wants one to do, what he works to make one do, is to feel forward at the pitch of his bowling.' At his high noon Bradman was seldom to be seen drawn out of his crease or elongated an inch. His footwork took his body closer to and more above the ball than any batsman before him.

But it was not by advancing technique that he began a new chapter. Jack Hobbs had already organized every discovered principle and device of batsmanship into a synthesis beyond which to this day no further advance seems possible. There has never been a more complete batsman than Hobbs. Bradman's

contribution was eternal vigilance and a new economy. Every
ball was for him a problem in itself, to be solved with no
concern about its place in a context and no reference to what
had happened to preceding balls. I asked him once what was his
secret. 'Concentration. Every ball is for me the first ball, whether
my score is o or 200.' And then he took my breath away by
adding: 'And I never visualize the possibility of *anybody* getting
me out.' (The italics were his.) In 1947 at Melbourne, Yardley
clean-bowled him on a good wicket when he was thoroughly
established, his score 79; it was a straight ball too. As he turned
round and saw the disturbed stump he said to Evans, the wicket-
keeper: 'I must be losing my concentration.' He altered the
currency. In 1930 his first sequence of scores was 236, 185, 78, 9,
48 not out, 66, 4, 44, 252, 32, 191. J. S. Ryder, himself an
Australian, was asked by a friend round about this period:
'What sort of a batsman is this Bradman?' Ryder, not given to
abstract thinking or definition, answered: 'Well. he just belts
the hell out of every ball he can reach.'

Not since W. G. Grace has a cricketer appealed to a public
as large and world-spread as Bradman's. He filled grounds
everywhere and held in thrall people with whom cricket is not
a passion. He beggared description and achievement. He made
the then world's record individual score – 452 not out; he scored
a century before lunch for Australia against England and 300
in the same day. He equalled the miracle of C. B. Fry – six
centuries in six consecutive innings. He scored on an average a
century in every third of his innings. But, as I say, he combined
mass-production with the performance of swift and often
thrilling strokes, murderous of intent and execution. He was
never the conventional stylist; he was dynamic rather than
polished. There was always the Bowral boy peeping out from
under the armoured machine. The critics who have said he
didn't enjoy himself at cricket have missed the pathos and
irony of his case, like the poor lad who in a night finds himself
rich beyond all dreams. Bradman could never accept his good
fortune as a natural thing to squander or take for granted. It is

astonishing, in fact, that he seldom, if ever, seemed to bat with the care and tempo of thriftiness. No bowler was able to keep him quiet at his best; all were put to the sword, massacred without the turning of a hair. After he had pulverized Larwood, Geary, Tate and Richard Tyldesley at Leeds in 1930 for his 304 in a day, he came from the field at half-past six as cool and neat as though fresh from the bathroom; forty boundaries and not a spot of perspiration.

Perhaps his most remarkable innings in a Test match occurred at Lord's during the same summer of 1930, which was his 'wonderful year'. I doubt if he subsequently equalled, for verve and complete mastery, his batsmanship of 1930. In the Lord's Test, Ponsford and Woodfull scored 162 for the first wicket, then Bradman in two hours and forty minutes before half-past six scourged the England attack for 155 not out. The power and the ease, the fluent, rapid, vehement, cold-blooded slaughter were beyond sober discussion. I recollect that J. C. White was brought into action at once – to keep Bradman quiet – J. C. White the untouchable, or at least the scarcely drive-able. To his first ball Bradman leaped yards out of his crease and drove it to the long-on rails, near the clock at the nursery end; the stroke was just one flash of prancing white and yellow, with a crack that echoed round the ground and sent the pigeons flying. He cut and hooked G. O. Allen that evening until it seemed that soon his bat must be red hot and catch fire.

He always knew what was within his power and would, without boastfulness, face a heavy responsibility as though it had presented itself merely to be set aside. At Leeds in 1934 Bowes ran amok at the first day's end and dismissed Brown, Woodfull and Oldfield for 39, after England had collapsed on an easy wicket against a truly great attack by Grimmett and O'Reilly. That night I saw Bradman in his hotel at Harrogate; he withdrew from a dinner engagement, went to bed early with the explanation: 'Thanks, but I must make 200 tomorrow, at least'.

He caused a revolution in bowling; for of course the methods of Jardine with Larwood the spearhead – fast bowling on the leg-side rising head high, and a packed leg-side cordon of fieldsmen – were designed to reduce if possible Bradman's batting average by half. The plan was successful, no doubt; but no other batsman of our or any other period could have coped as Bradman did with this formidable expedient – against Larwood faster than at any other time in his life. In spite of Larwood and the Jardinian theory, Bradman's innings were 0, 103 not out, 8, 66, 76, 24, 48, and 71.

In 1905 when Armstrong bowled slow 'leg theory' at Nottingham, also to a crowded field on the leg-side, J. T. Tyldesley drew away to the on-side and, having made the pitch of the ball fall on the off-side, cracked through the covers. Against the fastest bowling seen in Australia for decades – or nearly seen – Bradman employed the same plan. Astounding and audacious! Desperate maybe; but what else could have been done in the circumstances? Bradman's measures against the fast leg-side attack were severely censured by several of his playing contemporaries. Their main argument was that his improvisations suggested no long tenure at the crease and were therefore likely to disturb the confidence of less gifted colleagues sitting in the pavilion, pads on, if not securely buckled, waiting and watching, while the moth darted in and out of the flame. But there was no rational means of 'digging-in', or of planning a long, deliberately executed innings against Larwood and the leg-field. The situation called for nerve and originality. In all his career Bradman did little that was more wonderful and so highly charged with his own force of character than his dazzling improvisations, his neck-or-nothing brilliance, in the face of the ruthless challenge of Jardine thrown down in 1932–1933.

We needn't call him the greatest batsman of all time, though he was the most prolific. But when W. G. Grace scored 2,739 runs in 1871, with an average of 78, the next batsman on the list was Richard Daft, whose average was not half as high. Bradman might lead the list with thousands of runs, average 90; but somebody would be on his heels, averaging 70, and somebody else averaging 60, and so on, down the rungs of the ladder.

Grace in 1871 was twice as good, to say the least, as the next best; he played in another dimension, so to say. And we must remember the pitches he had to tackle, dangerous as the bowling.

It is argued, too, that Bradman seldom mastered a 'sticky' wicket. Certain it is that at Lord's in 1934 he shaped against Verity as a tyro, striking horribly at the spin until he sent the ball straight up like a water-spout, and Ames came forward from behind the stumps and waited for the catch while Bradman stood aside and stroked his forehead with a sweep of the back of his right hand, a picture of humiliation. He held obtuse ideas about 'sticky' wickets, arguing that they reduced science to nonsense, the best batsman to the levels of the crudest. 'You might as well,' he said to me, 'expect an Inman to play on a torn table.' But nobody expects to find a torn table in the highest circle of billiards; a 'sticky' pitch is part of the natural order of things in cricket, and a great batsman should set himself to answer the challenge when it comes along.

Still, when we contemplate the cavalcade of Bradman's Test match innings from 1927 to 1948, we are forced to confess that if a cricketer with less than a masterful 'sticky-wicket' technique was able to go on and on, from one prodigious performance to another, why then, 'sticky' wickets would seem of no consequence whatever and seldom to occur. Besides, Bradman by the very quickness of his eye and feet, was born to conquer any turning ball; if he often appeared not to 'try' on a 'sticky' pitch it was surely because of his curious mental approach to such conditions. And if he did fail on 'sticky' pitches – well, then, this was a proof that there really is a natural law of compensation. His Test match record is 80 innings, 6,996 runs, average 99·94.

Never, as I say, did he play an innings of dull negation. Always was he ready to pick up the gauntlet if it was boldly thrown before him. Whenever Bradman fell back on defence it was because the opposition had set a protective field and bowled for safety, without intent to attack. In his heyday no known species of bowler could keep him quiet or stay his course, and despite the pace of his scoring he hardly ever lifted the ball unbeautifully. Sometimes before he had scored at all, he would get a single in a rather undignified way, a mishit from the bottom of the blade; and he would run like a hungry hen – the Bowral boy again, not born for riches but a self-made millionaire!

He kindled ravaging fires of batsmanship, but scarcely ever burned his own fingers lighting them. It has been said of him that he couldn't bear admitting he was ever out: that is, technically beaten. But to use such an assumption as evidence in him of conceit is humourless and very English, as though Heifetz were accused of conceit if he expressed bewilderment if for a split second he played his violin other than impeccably.

Bradman 'murdered' all sorts of bowling, not only loose or mediocre stuff but the best. In a match between South Australia and South Africa at Adelaide, S. J. Pegler bowled his leg-spin and 'googlies' over after over, and Bradman belaboured him mercilessly. At the tea interval one of the South African players came to Pegler and said: 'What's the matter today, Sid; can't you turn 'em to the little devil?' And Pegler replied: 'I have never bowled better in my life.' Every bowler did his utmost to bring down Bradman, if only momentarily, from his eminence. Nobody ever 'gave' him an easy one to get off the mark or to complete a double – or triple century. That is why Bradman was himself reluctant to make a batsman an object for his charity. I firmly believe that throughout his career most bowlers would have supported any legal means whereby, before a match, Bradman could have been bought off, or compounded with, by the gift of 100 runs on condition that he did not bat. But day by day he was himself under an obligation to bat; crowds came from far and near to see him, and departed in disappointed droves when he got out. If he announced his inability to play through sheer physical and mental staleness, some English county club was likely to drift nearer than usual to bankruptcy. When Bradman is accused of not knowing the English secret of cricket, the jolly approach in the school cap, the fact is conveniently forgotten that the master was made slave to circumstances not of his choosing. It is doubtful if any cricketer of our time has responded with more than Bradman's conscientiousness to all demanded and expected of him. If he didn't throw his wicket away after reaching a century might he not have been thinking of those of us, myself included, who were content to watch him all day? In any case, how many batsmen have we known, since Jack Hobbs, who do throw their wickets away? Unfortunately they do not. If Bradman stayed in all day he was not only placing his team in a position which in a few hours would be pretty safe from defeat; he was winning the match all the time, holding the crowd in thrall all the time, old and young, connoisseur and layman. Of how many English batsmen can as much as this be said, how often even of Compton or Hutton? There is probably, as I write these lines, only one English cricketer of whom it can be said that he never bores or disappoints his admirers – he either plays true to his spirit or gets out. I refer, of course, to Gimblett. I can recollect only two or three occasions on which Bradman batted with the mute on and sternly held his strokes in check. He was then past his meridian. At Trent Bridge in 1938 he was not out on the closing morning. Australia was faced with more than the possibility of defeat. The wicket was dusty too. That morning, before we went to the ground, I saw him in the hotel writing a letter to his wife in Adelaide. He called me over to him and very frankly and simply told me the gist of his message. He was very serious as he read: 'A pretty gruelling day's work is before us but I'm going to see it through, and I don't think we'll lose.' He scored 144 and was not out after five or six hours' martyrdom. At Melbourne in 1937, after the terrible 'sticky' pitch which broke the heart of G. O. Allen and all of us, the wicket rolled out comfortably on the Monday, but Australia had lost five wickets for 90 or so runs when Bradman joined Fingleton. For an hour he hardly lifted his bat. I happened at the time to be reporting for an evening paper, so I was obliged to send messages away piecemeal in a sort of running commentary. I had just written a paragraph to the effect that Bradman after all could be kept quiet in a Test match, when applause in the crowd announced that he had reached fifty – in seventy-five minutes. He had got them in ones and twos by thoroughly safe placing, with an entirely protective bat.

He played hard but not meanly. He was all for the rigour of the game. He respected an opponent and declined to patronize him. There is a point of view from which something 'soft', if not hypocritical, can be seen in the English show of condescension in games. The style should be romantic; execution should not run away from challenge. But the temper, the will to play without flabbiness of smile, should in great cricket never be relaxed. Bradman seldom patronized and insulted keen antagonism or ran away from it. And he rightly was ruthless in the presence of the Laodicean. Occasionally his ruthlessness had a grim humour. During G. O. Allen's tour of Australia in 1936–1937, Worthington of Derbyshire couldn't find his form until the fifth Test match at Melbourne; then, having gone in first and after scoring a brilliant 44, he trod on his wicket while making a superb pull to the fence. That evening I said to Bradman I thought poor Worthington had been shabbily treated by fortune. 'There he was, thoroughly happy, looking like a hundred; and he gets out that way.' Bradman was sympathetic; but after consideration he said: 'Still, you know, a batsman ought not to tread on his wicket, ought he?'

It is forgotten as we wonder for ever at the runs he amassed that when he was young he had no superior as an outfielder, none more thrilling in chase and pick-up and deadly return. He could run a man out from strokes which it seemed might be 'walked' with time to spare. He threw Hobbs's wicket down at Leeds in 1930 with a rapidity and dash which snatched the breath away. His catching was equally agile; I have seen him run after a ghost of a chance on the off-side and hold a spinning mishit while his body was swivelling round like a top released from the whip. And he was a shrewd far-seeing captain who commanded from everybody an emotion less common in ordinary human nature than affection: he commanded respect. He didn't easily make friends, and appeared not to go out of his way to retain those who were proud to call him a friend. He was, they say, a bad mixer; but many of us come under this designation if we decline to go half-way to meet all sorts of birds of passage and prefer our own company. His unpopularity was partly the price he had to pay for his mastery and power: his achievement transcended normal humanity's scope and normal humanity's magnanimity. He easily aroused the most common failing of our kind – jealousy. I found him difficult as a man but not – as Doctor Johnson might say – impossible. His integrity to his conception of the game was not to be questioned. Much of his austerity sprang from that almost moral economy which is the self-made man's guiding principle. When he first came to England in 1930, a socially uninstructed youth, he asked me to make him a list of books which I thought might help him to develop his mind and enlarge his conversation. I wrote out for him a number of titles, none of them easy reading and covering a wide field of politics and letters. A year or two later he had got through them all – and he had assimilated much.

The greatest batsmen of them all? We are bound to answer the question, because generations yet young insist on asking. We elders can see with the mind's eye a man with a great beard, stroking it contemplatively, looking down from Olympus on the years from 1928 to 1948. 'He was a good 'un, not the least of my progeny. Eh yes – he put the bat to the ball all right. And he knew how to deal with umpires. What? – one of my first choices for a World XI? . . . eh, yes . . . but all the same, give me Arthur.'

So the game goes on, its genius fruitful and multiplying. Bradman is already a legend, and the imagination boggles at the thought of the like of him again.

*from* CRICKET ALL THE YEAR *1952*

# A Compton Innings

## E. W. SWANTON

It is a dangerous thing when the crowd sets up an idol who tends
to be of more moment than the game itself, as the great career of
Sir Donald Bradman illustrates. To any who think on these
lines I would say that the only thing that might ever spoil
Compton as a cricketer is the effort of trying to live up to the
dizzy standards his admirers have set for him; and that perhaps
the best safeguard I can offer against this is an attempt to give
an impression of the man himself, as he is on the cricket field.

When Compton first came into the Middlesex eleven at the
age of eighteen he was quickly appreciated in his true colours
by all who see a little more in cricket than the players taking
exercise in the sunshine, and a series of numbers flicking round
on the score-board.

Here, it was plain to observe, was a natural player of games,
who combined the eye of a hawk with an instinctive gift of
balance. To be analytical for a moment, it is an unusual measure
of harmony between the eye and the brain controlling the movement of the body that produces the perfection of timing which
differentiates the masters from other very excellent players.
This formula applies equally to the exponents of all games
played with a moving ball. In cricket one has seen it exemplified
by such artists with the bat as Hobbs and Woolley and K. S.
Duleepsinhji. To put the thing slightly differently, the secret of
the skill of the Hobbs and the Comptons is surely the exceptionally swift and sure transference in their brain of the
knowledge of what to do with the ball, that they see so quickly,
to the limbs which are brought into the making of the stroke.
There is no conscious process but an instinctive reflex action.
Similarly instinctive is the acknowledgement of this virtue by
the spectator. You might say that balance and timing add up to
rhythm, and that it is rhythm which the unsophisticated spectator

is appreciating when an especially delicious stroke evokes murmurs of 'Lovely, sir, lovely!'

There are many cries of 'Lovely!' when Compton is at the wicket, and there are plenty of those amiably sadistic chuckles which acknowledge the outwitting of the poor, honest bowlers and fielders. He is one of those lucky people whose genius the crowd is always quick to recognize. He can hardly help entertaining them. Batsmanship comes as naturally to him as golf came to Bobby Jones and to Miss Joyce Wethered, as she was; or football to Stanley Matthews and to Cliff Jones.

Let us take a look at Compton as he begins an innings. You will notice the breadth of shoulder which, with all else in proportion, suggests the strength of his frame. There have been great batsmen who were anything but powerful, and brute force must be subservient to the more delicate items of machinery. But there is no denying that good muscles are a great help, as the famous golfer somewhat brutally reminded his anaemic pupil who asked him what he should do to increase his length. 'What should you do?' barked the old warrior, 'I'll tell you what you should do. Hit it a damn sight harder!'

Compton then, without being unduly tall, is well made and powerful and I would say that the particular characteristic that has most strongly affected his style of batting is his remarkable strength of forearm. People seeing him for the first time sometimes find him a little ungainly. That is a thing one tends not to notice when one has spent many hours watching him play. But it is not hard to see what is meant. It is as though when the construction of this creditable machine was completed no one thought to go round and give the nuts and bolts a final turn. Some of the joints are a shade on the loose side.

Having noticed this peculiarity or not on his way to the wicket, and remarked the serene, confident smile which he usually wears as he walks down the pavilion steps, we can settle down to watch his method. What is the first thing the expert would observe? I think it is probably the fact that from the moment the bowler reaches the stumps until the stroke is completed Compton's movements are deliberate, almost leisurely. That is an unfailing sign of quality, meaning that the batsman has both focused the ball very early in its flight and followed it until it has come almost on to the bat. Thus he has been able to give himself ample time to decide on the stroke and also to execute it. Lesser mortals, who achieve only a briefer focus of the ball, often in their haste choose the wrong stroke, and when they choose the right one dangerous faults are apt to interfere with their hurried making of it.

It will be unusual if we have to wait long before he begins tuning up his strokes. Going clock-wise round the field, there is first the leg-glance in all its varieties, and so keen is the eye that he rarely fails to make contact with even the finest flick he attempts. Then comes the leg-sweep that he is so fond of, made with right knee bent, an almost horizontal bat and a quick turn of the wrists. If, by the way, this is not a situation of any particular moment or gravity Compton might choose the wrong ball for this stroke and pay the penalty. It is one that allows a very small margin of error, and it is not to be recommended strongly to ordinary mortals. It would be a very expensive bait for a bowler to go on pitching a fraction wide of the leg stump hoping for a mistake, for on a true pitch Compton generally times and controls his sweep to perfection; but it represents one of the very few possible chinks in his armour. Personally I never like to see him playing the stroke if the ball is coming slowly off the turf, or if the bowlers have cut up the pitch with their follow-through.

The hook (that is the leg-side hit off the back foot) is another and more orthodox favourite, and woe betide the bowler, fast or slow, who drops them short! The on-drive he plays too, and plays well, with a characteristic touch of wrist in the finish of the stroke, though the pet sweep absorbs some balls that the average batsman would hit wide of mid-on. Next comes a narrow segment of territory that Compton chooses rather to neglect. Perhaps because he is so very strong from elbow to wrist he rarely swings straight-armed from the shoulders, and thus, in contrast to Edrich, for instance, he uses the drive between mid-on and mid-off much less frequently than the other strokes in the book. The captain who allows the same field-setting to serve for these two betrays weak powers of observation.

Anyone who has discovered to his cost on the golf course what impressive distances Compton cracks a golf ball with a short sharp forearm punch probably comprehends why he normally prefers to hit a cricket ball in the same way rather than through a wide arc from the shoulders. I am reminded, however, of a diverting moment at Lord's which indicates his ability to drive if he wishes, and also perhaps sheds a light on his attitude towards the game.

One afternoon Compton came in from batting at the tea interval, and was enduring with his usual indulgence the shafts of genially abusive humour which are a long tradition of the Middlesex dressing-room. Someone, probably Walter Robins, said: 'It's a funny thing a strong chap like you can't drive the ball straight. We never see you hit it over the bowler's head.' Compton said: 'Yes, it is funny; look out for the third ball after tea.' A few minutes afterwards the third ball bowled came whistling straight and true into the Members' seats in front of the pavilion, and, as the umpire was signalling 'six' Compton waved his bat cheerfully to his companions. A slight incident perhaps, but significant of his outlook: least of anyone is he in danger of forgetting that cricket is a game to be enjoyed.

Proceeding still clockwise round the field we come next to the favourite Compton country. It ranges really from mid-off right round to second slip, but the angles in most frequent use are those to either side of cover-point. And I write advisedly 'to either side' because of Compton's remarkable knack of beating the fielder there by disguising the direction of the stroke. One of his captains describes him as the best teaser of cover-point he has ever seen. His off-side strokes off the forward foot are not orthodox because normally he does not bring that foot right across on to the line of flight. He prefers to give himself more room, to bring his wrists into the stroke, and, in consequence, to aim the bat squarer than he strictly should. In theory this is a dangerous departure from the text-book, and it is a sure indication of Compton's unusual gifts of eye and timing that he makes the stroke look safe – almost obvious.

The ball is hit off the back foot as severely as might be expected from his physique, all the way round the off-side, except that when it comes to the square cut he still is apt to prefer to use the wrist and play forward. The later cuts, including the one very late and therefore very fine, complete an armoury which is more varied than that of anyone playing today.

There is only one flaw in Compton as a batsman, only one art, almost, that he does not command: he is still not a good runner between wickets. Here his judgment and his confidence are apt to stray, and on the worst days there is apt to be a deal of calling, counter-calling, scufflings back and forth and general disorder. There are run-outs, too, and though these dire calamities do not befall very often, the sum of safe runs lost mounts high. As a malady, of course, it is infectious in the case of all but the soundest runners, and Compton perhaps is unfortunate in that few among his contemporaries, either in the Middlesex or the England teams, fall into that category. If he is in with Yardley or Barnett or Mann there is less to fear, and not too many singles will be neglected. Unfortunately there are too many days when Compton and Bill Edrich seem to find it impossible to run smoothly, and each in turn sends the other back when the run could have been taken at a gentle canter. Against weak bowling sides this does not so very greatly matter; the better the bowling the more necessary it is to keep the fielding machine under steady pressure. It was a fair estimate that at Lord's against South Africa in 1947 this Middlesex pair lost a dozen runs an hour at the very least, and since they spent five and a half hours together they could be said to have been more than sixty runs short of the true value effect of good running on a fielding side over the period of a long partnership.

A word about him as a fielder and bowler. It is almost tedious to have to record so many virtues, but the cold truth is he can field extraordinarily well anywhere. When he was just starting it was found that, although he was a very quick mover, and had an exceptionally quick eye for the slips, his mind was apt to stray far away, and then accidents sometimes happened. On the other hand, without looking exactly fast, he covered the ground pretty quickly and, as he had a strong left-arm throw, he made a thoroughly good fielder in the country. I tended myself to think that, if it fitted into the general plan of the side, a compromise was best – the old-fashioned combination of slip at one end and deep field the other. Thus it be hoped his concentration would stand the strain! In South Africa last winter, he was usually very close, at short leg, silly mid-off, or the gully, and with practice he became outstandingly quick and safe in all these positions.

*from* DENIS COMPTON: A SKETCH *1948*

"ONE OF THE MODERN TIME."

# K. R. Miller – Touch of a Hero

## RAY ROBINSON

Long before Keith Miller gets near the wicket you can tell that something extraordinary is going to happen. The erect set of his capless head on his square shoulders, the loose swing of his long legs, the half-smile on his handsome face and his general ease of manner all signify that no ordinary cricketer approaches.

Then there is the crowd's greeting. In weight and duration the applause may be no more, often less, than Bradman was accustomed to receive as tribute to the weight of his run-getting, the duration of his innings, the skill of his batting and the dramatic crescendo of his scoring. The ear detects different qualities in the applause for Miller. It contains so much pleasurable expectation, as if the hands are clapping, in some kind of morse of their own: 'This will be good.' But the keynote is a shriller sound – the whistling of the boys. Especially at Sydney or Melbourne it swells to a joyous volume not heard since Jack Gregory came out to play in the years after World War I. It is a sign that here is the youngsters' hero. The place these two strapping adventurers of cricket won in the hearts of the keenest watchers present is not to be earned by enough runs to pack a warehouse, or an average like a skyscraper, or enough wickets to fill a quarry. It is a place involuntarily given them by those who have enjoyed seeing them bat and bowl and catch more excitingly than anybody else, unless it has been Constantine in his inspired moments.

To young eyes, quickest to perceive the things that make cricket, Miller is as an Olympian god among mortals. He brings boys' dreams to life. He is the cricketer they would all like to be, the one who can hit more gloriously and bowl faster than anybody on earth. When Neville Cardus called him a young eagle among crows and daws Miller was not a champion playing out of his class; sharing the field with him were the elect of the world's two greatest cricketing countries, Bradman, Hammond and bearers of other famous names, Compton and other men of personality.

Masculine as Tarzan, he plays lustily. Style suffuses his cricket with glowing power, personality charges it with daring and knocks bowling and conventions sky-high.

Since World War II Miller has made his mark on pavilion roofs across half the earth. He was not clear of his teens when the war began; before long it hid from view a youth from Melbourne High School who at 18 had scored 181 against Tasmania in his first innings in first-class cricket and, just twenty, overcame the difficulties of Grimmett's bowling in making 108 against South Australia in his fourth match in the Sheffield Shield competition. As a flying-officer of twenty-five he gave up piloting Mosquitoes in 1945 to become the mainstay of the Australian Services' batting. As such, he seldom lifted the ball in the Victory Tests, but towards the end of the season he began coping with coping-stones and other upstair targets around English cricket fields. In his 185 for the Dominions he drove England's bowlers to seven spots among the buildings enclosing Lord's ground. *The Times*' own R. B. Vincent, discriminating and droll, began to wonder whether Lord's was a big enough ground for such terrific hitting. The first and farthest six crashed into the top-tier seats between the towers of the pavilion. Next morning one with less carry struck the southern tower, above the broadcasters' eyrie. They were among the highest blows Lord's pavilion had felt this century though they left intact the all-time record by an earlier exile from Victoria, Albert Trott, who in 1899 drove a ball over the hallowed edifice. Miller lifted his overnight total by 124 before lunch on the last day of the match. Only such an innings as his 185 could have won the game. A week later he opened his 40-inch chest at Manchester and hit eight sixes in a hundred against an English XI.

The cannonading and his carefree demeanour were too much for some people, with conventional concepts of high-class batsmanship, to swallow; when he succeeded with things no other would attempt they discounted him as something of a slogger enjoying a lucky break. Though his deeds helped the uneven Services XI to square the rubber of Victory Tests against the strength of England, and he scored most runs at the highest average, they could not accept him as a member of batting's aristocracy, one of the world's best half-dozen, who at his top could out-bat even Hammond and Hutton in the dawn of post-war cricket. Among those who saw him in true light were G. O. Allen, former fast-bowling captain of England, and those tall, wise and witty observers, R. C. Robertson-Glasgow and C. B. Fry. Allen said: 'It almost makes me happy to think I shan't have to face up to this in the future.' Robertson-Glasgow wrote: 'From the moment Miller takes guard he plays each ball just that much below its supposed merits that scratches a bowler's pride. . . . It is dignity with the brakes off.' Over the B.B.C., Fry said: 'In our eyes Miller is Australia's star turn. We know we have been watching a batsman, already great, who is likely, later on, to challenge the feats of Australia's champions of the past. Apart from his technical excellence, Keith Miller has something of the dash and generous abandon that were part of Victor Trumper's charm.' The Services' captain, Hassett, put it: 'In our team Miller stands out. He hasn't Hutton's solidity yet, but as a stroke player he is second to none in the world today.'

Except in the moment when effort is needed Miller is enviably relaxed. Waiting, padded up, to go in for his first Test innings against England (usually a time of chain-smoking and other signs of tension), non-smoker Miller dozed off until applause woke him. In heraldry, his escutcheon would show a jolly miller and the motto 'I couldn't care less', if that free-and-easy sentiment could be expressed in Latin. In the field he looks up to identify every aircraft that flies over the ground. When a wicket falls he is the first to sprawl on his back, with an arm shielding his eyes. He relishes jokes with fellow-fieldsmen, and as he walks away he finishes conversations with a hand-language of his own, as if brushing bushes aside or patting toddlers on the head. He pulls out his handkerchief, holds it by two corners and lets it flutter like a flag before mopping his face or tailing it around his neck.

Even at tense moments in Test matches he is as ready for a bit of fun as for a good ball or a sharp catch. When a bowler goes through an experimental run-up and delivery without the ball he promptly hooks an imaginary long-hop to the fence. The crowds share his enjoyment of cricket and he enjoys their presence. In a Test at Lord's he was in line to be third victim of a hat-trick; as the next ball struck his leg the crowd excitedly shouted: 'How's that?' Miller shook his head sorrowfully to the mass appealers, as if it grieved him to disappoint them. Onlookers are amused by his mimicry of the umpire signalling a wide against him, his drop-kicking the ball to the wicketkeeper after a running catch, his boyish exuberance in the scrambling horseplay for souvenir stumps at the end. No stage villain looks more melodramatic than Miller the bowler, staring at an umpire who refuses one of his whirling appeals. Once he toppled over backwards and appealed sitting on the pitch. When a bowler stops Miller's hard drive and menaces to throw him out, the tall batsman does not scamper back to the crease but holds up a stern hand, forbidding all tomfoolery.

Superb technique has enabled Miller to look for runs where others look for trouble. He blends with Melbourne forthrightness the allurements of style typical of Sydney, with a dash of Kent and Gloucestershire to bring out the full flavour. Watch him stride into the field, toes straight ahead but eyes looking about, following the fieldsmen's throwing to become accustomed to quick focusing in the outdoor light. At the wicket he takes in the position of the backing-away fielders as he spins his bat upright with his left hand and stops it revolving with his right. Taking 'two legs' block, he marks the spot between middle and leg stumps by drawing a V back from the crease with two geometric strokes of his right toe. He adjusts his shirt-neck and smooths his long brown hair back with his left hand as he settles in his stance, the most easy and natural stance of all. In this he combines everything to produce dominating reach. His legs are straight but not taut, his body leans just enough for him to hold the bat comfortably. Comfortably and commandingly, because Miller's hands clasp the handle high – as unwelcome a sight as bowlers and fieldsmen can see. Whitington called him 'the man with the long hair and the long handle'. The bottom of the bat is on the line, almost between his toes. His feet, the whole length of them, seem to cling closer to the earth than other men's, as if made specially to fit a cricket pitch and give balance and purchase. Six inches apart, they rest on either side of the crease, parallel with it, and share his $13\frac{1}{2}$ stone equally. Awaiting the bowler, he stands motionless – not even a tap of the bat; it is the stillness of death for any balls except the best.

Between long lashes, his blue eyes watch the ball as searchingly as any stonewaller's, but with different intent. His wrists lift the bat back just outside the off stump on a direct course – no wavings to delay getting it straight down in a hurry if the ball skids through quickly. Every movement of his footwork is designed to bring his head and shoulders over the ball. In back-play his right foot plumbs the depth between the creases, his front elbow goes up, and bat and forearm form almost a vertical line as blade and ball meet. What in other batsmen are defensive blocks become positive strokes when Miller plays them; fieldsmen have to get down smartly to stop them. No other right-hand batsman in my memory has consistently hit the ball so firmly in this way. And he cuts late with precision and artistry not possessed by other tall, driving batsmen.

Miller's forward play is unrivalled in splendour. He is the grandest player of cricket's grandest stroke, the drive. Left shoulder and elbow lead his body in unison with the thrust of his left foot towards the ball. As a thermometer responds to the sun's warmth, the height of his backswing varies in accordance with his estimate of the ball's quality. If he judges it to be coming within range of his matchless drive his swing is as full as a six-footer can keep in control throughout its menacing arc; his hands extend back to neck-height and cocked wrists point the bat skyward. At the moment of impact straight arms transmit the energy of true-lined shoulders to whipping wrists. Usually the ball is close to his front pad before the bat smashes through and onwards in the direction the shot has taken. To put the kernel of his style in one sentence he wields the straightest bat with the greatest power. When Miller springs a stride or two forward both feet grip the pitch for the drive as firmly as when he advances only the front leg, and the purchase they obtain forces his knees inward.

Distinctively his own is a rhythmic lunge with leg and bat seemingly moving together towards the ball, and his body bowing into the stroke as if giving it a benediction. This is more noticeable because nothing like it has been seen in an Australian since the back foot began to rule Test batting in the 1930s, and even before that no stylist made quite the same motion. To me, Miller's lunge is the truest gauge of his form. When playing well, he delivers it as positively as a boxer's classic straight left, whether he drives at boundary-finding strength or extends himself to the limit to kill a testing ball in its tracks. If he is out of touch, good bowlers draw him into it too often; the lunge becomes overborne as he stretches to a ball he should have jumped to or perhaps gone back on. Instead of being a firm anchor, his back leg drags across the crease as a shuffling extra line of defence. Sometimes balance fails him and he props himself up with his right hand or sprawls, full length, on both hands, like a physical culturist doing the body-press.

In this manly athlete's straight-bat strokes force is harnessed to a line as classic as a Corinthian column, but it bursts into full view, unrestrained, when he lets go for a hit to leg. His left side leads so strongly into the blow that the follow-through screws his clean-cut frame into spiral shape; he looks as if a willy-willy* has spun his body around, as if he would revolve if it were not for his staying right foot, twisted over on its outside by the blockhole. No other batsman puts such plunging power into

* A spiralling cyclonic wind, so named by West Australian aborigines.

a pull or similar swinging leg-hit. After adding its part to the speed of the bat his right arm sometimes gets left behind; the hand slips off, like a wheel from a racing car careering around a bend. When this happened as he hit the accurate Toshack's left-arm bowling for three sixes in one over it looked as if he swept the ball over the leg fence of the Melbourne ground with one hand. Watching the ball cannoning about the vast concrete stand, Ponsford (who fielded against Woolley, Constantine, Chapman and all the other famous hitters between the World Wars) said Miller's strokes were the most powerful he had ever seen.

His bowling has been chock full of life and personality, and full of shocks for batsmen – some of them nasty shocks. He gathers momentum in a much shorter run than other fast bowlers, shorter than Wright takes for a slow-medium googly. Nine loose-jointed strides are usually enough, sometimes fewer. He is the only Test-class bowler with such a flexible approach, and the only one I have seen drop the ball as he ran, scoop it up and deliver it without a trace of the interruption. Once he bowled in odd boots, one size nine and a borrowed ten, because the stress of fast bowling had broken his own. After his short run Miller generates pace with such a convulsive body effort that it is a wonder his back and sides have not troubled him more often. His delivery is high-handed (in more senses than one), especially for his in-dipper. Not satisfied with late swerve either way, break-backs and a wide range of pace-changes, he rings in a leg-break or a round-armer now and again. Batsmen find it hard to understand Miller's bowling. Some of it is well over their heads.

We came to expect one like that whenever he was hit for four. That indignity stung the same combative streak in him as a bowler that a crisis did as a batsman (I preferred to see him hit the roof when he was batting). Tossing back his mane like a mettlesome colt with dilated nostrils, he would stride back. giving a hurrying clap to the fieldsman and thrusting out his hand to command a quick return, in eagerness to get at the bats-

man again. Rushing up, he would fling down a bumper that
made the batsman duck penitently; or occasionally it would be
an exaggerated full-toss instead. For the most frequent bouncer
in post-war cricket he seldom hit a batsman – the ball usually
bounded too high – but such moments transformed him from
hero to villain, and he has been hooted at Nottingham, Madras,
Perth, Adelaide, Brisbane and other points east and west. How
much of his apparent anger was simulated only those close at
hand could tell. As he ran up Miller did not always look at the
batsman, and once started to bowl without noticing that the
umpire's arm barred his path because the striker was not ready.
When he almost collided with it he changed in a flash from his
bowling action to shake the umpire's outstretched hand. His
personality abolishes the boundary and brings the crowd into the
game with him.

Cardus writes of him: 'His strokes are lordly and pedigreed,
his attitude to cricket is almost as obsolete as chivalry.'

It has been truly said that the real artist either makes music as
he wants to or he makes no music. Miller's qualities are stimulating; his faults are of the kind lesser men can avoid with ease.

*from* FROM THE BOUNDARY *1953*

# PART III

# Men and Moments

'But for an hour to watch them play
Those heroes dead and gone
And pit our batsmen of today
With those of Hambledon.'

*Alfred Cochrane*

ENGLAND, PAST AND PRESENT

## THE DRAW

'Then lend the eye a terrible aspect.'
*Henry V*

# The Cricketers of My Time

## JOHN NYREN

The game of Cricket is thoroughly British. Its derivation is probably from the Saxon 'cpyce, a stick'. Strutt, however, in his *Sports and Pastimes*, states that he can find no record of the game, under its present appellation, 'beyond the commencement of the last century, where it occurs in one of the songs published by D'Urfey.'* The first four lines of 'Of a noble race was Shenkin' ran thus:

> '¹Her was the prettiest fellow
> At foot-ball or at cricket,
> At hunting chase, or nimble race,
> How featly her could prick it.'

The same historian of our games doubts not that cricket derived its orgin from the ancient game of club-ball, the patronymics of which being compounded of Welch and Danish (clwppa and bol), do not warrant his conclusion, the Saxon being an elder occupant of our island. The circumstance, however, of there being no illustration extant – no missal, illuminated with a group engaged in this king of athletic games, as is the case with its plebeian brother, the club-ball; also, from its constitution, being of a more civil and complicated character, – we may rationally infer that it is the offspring of a more polite, at all events, of a maturer age than its fellow.

The game of club-ball appears to have been no other than the present well-known bat-and-ball, which, with similar laws and customs prescribed in the playing at it, was, doubtless, anterior

* *Pills to Purge Melancholy*, 4th edit., 1719, vol. 11, p. 172.

to trap-ball. The trap, indeed, carries with it an air of refinement in the 'march of mechanism'.

They who are acquainted with some of the remote and unfrequented villages of England, where the primitive manners, customs, and games of our ancestors survive in the perfection of rude and unadulterated simplicity, must have remarked the lads playing at a game which is the same in its outline and principal features as the consummate piece of perfection that at this day is the glory of Lord's, and the pride of English athletae – I mean the one in which a single stick is appointed for a wicket, ditto for a bat, and the same repeated, of about three inches in length, for a ball. If this be not the original of the game of cricket, it is a plebeian imitation of it.

My purpose, however, is not to search into the antiquities of cricketing, but to record my recollections of some of the most eminent professors of my favourite pastime who have figured on the public arena since the year 1776, when I might be about twelve years of age. From that period till within a few seasons past, I have constantly been 'at the receipt of custom' when any rousing match has been toward; and being now a veteran, and laid up in ordinary, I may be allowed the vanity of the quotation,

'Quorum magna pars fui'*

I was born at Hambledon, in Hampshire – the Attica of the scientific art I am celebrating. No eleven in England could compare with the Hambledon, which met on the first Tuesday in May on Broad-Halfpenny. So renowned a set were the men of Hambledon, that the whole country would flock to see one of their trial matches. 'Great men,' indeed, 'have been among us – better none'; and in the course of my recollections I shall have occasion to instance so many within the knowledge of persons

---

* I learned a little Latin when I was a boy of a worthy old Jesuit, but I was a better hand at the fiddle; and many a time have I taught the gipsies a tune during their annual visits to our village, thereby purchasing the security of our poultry-yard. When the hand of the destroyer was stretched forth over the neighbouring roosts, our little Goshen was always passed by.

now living, as will, I doubt not, warrant me in giving the palm
to my native place.

The two principal bowlers in my early days were Thomas
Brett and Richard Nyren, of Hambledon; the *corps de reserve*, or
change-bowlers, were Barber and Hogsflesh. Brett was, beyond
all comparison, the fastest as well as straightest bowler that was
ever known; he was neither a thrower nor a jerker, but a
legitimate downright *bowler*, delivering his ball fairly, high and
very quickly, quite as strongly as the jerkers, and with the force
of a point-blank shot. He was a well-grown, dark-looking man,
remarkably strong, and with rather a short arm. As a batter, he
was comparatively an inferior player – a slashing hitter, but he
had little guard of his wicket, and his judgment of the game was
held in no great estimation. Brett, whose occupation was that
of a farmer, bore the universal character of a strictly honourable man in all his transactions, whether in business or in
amusement.

Richard Nyren was left-handed. He had a high delivery,
always to the length, and his balls were provokingly deceitful.
He was the chosen General of all the matches, ordering and
directing the whole. In such esteem did the brotherhood hold
his experience and judgment, that he was uniformly consulted
on all questions of law or precedent; and I never knew an
exception to be taken against his opinion, or his decision to be
reversed. I never saw a finer specimen of the thorough-bred old
English yeoman than Richard Nyren. He was a good face-to-
face, unflinching, uncompromising, independent man. He placed
a full and just value upon the station he held in society, and he
maintained it without insolence or assumption. He could differ
with a superior, without trenching upon his dignity, or losing his
own. I have known him maintain an opinion with great firmness
against the Duke of Dorset and Sir Horace Mann; and when, in
consequence of his being proved to be in the right, the latter
has afterwards crossed the ground and shaken him heartily by
the hand. Nyren had immense advantage over Brett; for,
independently of his general knowledge of the game, he was

practically a better cricketer, being a safe batsman and an excellent hitter. Although a very stout man (standing about five feet nine) he was uncommonly active. He owed all the skill and judgment he possessed to an old uncle, Richard Newland, of Slindon, in Sussex, under whom he was brought up – a man so famous in his time, that when a song was written in honour of the Sussex cricketers, Richard Newland was especially and honourably signalized. No one man ever dared to play him. When Richard Nyren left Hambledon the club broke up, and never resumed from that day. The head and right arm were gone.

Barber and Hogsflesh were both good hands; they had a high delivery, and a generally good length; not very strong, however, at least for those days in playing, when the bowling was all fast. These four were our tip-top men, and I think such another stud was not to be matched in the whole kingdom, either before or since. They were choice fellows, staunch and thorough-going. No thought of treachery ever seemed to have entered their heads. The modern politics of trickery and 'crossing' were (so far as my own experience and judgment of their actions extended) as yet 'a sealed book' to the Hambledonians; what they did, they did for love of honour and victory; and when one (who shall be nameless) sold the birthright of his good name for a mess of pottage, he paid dearly for his bargain. It cost him the trouble of being a knave – (no trifle); the esteem of his old friends, and, what was worst of all, the respect of him who could have been his *best* friend – himself.

Upon coming to the old batters of our club, the name of John Small,* the elder, shines among them in all the lustre of a star in the first magnitude. His merits have already been recorded in a separate publication, which every zealous brother of the pastime has probably read. I need, therefore, only subscribe my testimony to his uncommon talent, shortly summing up his chief excellencies. He was the best short runner of his day, and indeed I believe him to have been the first who turned the short

* See also page 420.

hits to account. His decision was as prompt as his eye was accurate in calculating a short run. Add to the value of his accomplishment as a batter, he was an admirable fieldsman, always playing middle wicket; and so correct was his judgment of the game, that old Nyren would appeal to him when a point of law was being debated. Small was a remarkably well-made and well-knit man, of honest expression, and as active as a hare.

He was a good fiddler, and taught himself the double bass. The Duke of Dorset having been informed of his musical talent, sent him as a present a handsome violin, and paid the carriage. Small, like a true and simple-hearted Englishman, returned the compliment, by sending his Grace two bats and balls, also *paying the carriage*. We may be sure that on both hands the presents were choice of their kind. Upon one occasion he turned his Orphean accomplishment to good account. Having to cross two or three fields on his way to a musical party, a vicious bull made at him; when our hero, with the characteristic coolness and presence of mind of a good cricketer, began playing upon his bass, to the admiration and perfect satisfaction of the mischievous beast.

About this time, 1778, I became a sort of farmer's pony to my native club of Hambledon, and I never had cause to repent the work I was put to; I gained by it that various knowledge of the game, which I leave in the hands of those who knew me in my 'high and palmy state' to speak to and appreciate. This trifling preliminary being settled, the name and figure of Tom Sueter first comes across me – a Hambledon man, and of the club. What a handful of steel-hearted soldiers are in an important pass, such was Tom in keeping the wicket. Nothing went by him; and for coolness, and nerve in this trying and responsible post, I never saw his equal. As a proof of his quickness and skill, I have numberless times seen him stump a man out with Brett's tremendous bowling. Add to this valuable accomplishment, he was one of the manliest and most graceful of hitters. Few would cut a ball harder at the point of the bat, and he was, moreover, an excellent short runner. He had an eye like an eagle – rapid and comprehensive. He was the first who departed from the custom of the old players before him, who deemed it a heresy to leave the crease for the ball; he would get in at it, and hit it straight off and straight on; and, egad! it went as if it had been fired. As by the rules of our club, at the trial-matches no man was allowed to get more than thirty runs, he generally gained his number earlier than any of them. I have seldom seen a handsomer man than Tom Sueter, who measured about five feet ten. As if, too, Dame Nature wished to shew at his birth a specimen of her prodigality, she gave him so amiable disposition, that he was the pet of all the neighbourhood; so honourable a heart, that his word was never questioned by the gentlemen who associated with him; and a voice, which for sweetness, power and purity of tone (a tenor) would, with proper cultivation, have made him a handsome fortune. With what rapture have I hung upon his notes when he has given us a hunting song in the club room after the day's practice was over.

George Lear of Hambledon, who always answered to the title among us of 'Little George', was our best long-stop. So firm and steady was he, that I have known him stand through a whole match against Brett's bowling, and not lose more than two runs. The ball seemed to go into him and he was as sure of it as if he had been a sandbank. His activity was so great and, besides, he had so good a judgment in running to cover the ball, that he would stop many that were hit in the slip and this, be it remembered, from the swiftest bowling ever known. The portion of ground that man would cover was quite extraordinary. He was a good batsman, and a tolerably sure guard of his wicket; he averaged from fifteen to twenty runs, but I never remembered his having a long innings. What he did not bring to the stock by his bat, however, he amply made up with his perfect fielding. Lear was a short man, of a fair complexion, well looking, and of a pleasing aspect. He had a sweet counter-tenor voice. Many a treat have I had in hearing him and Sueter join in a glee at the 'Bat and Ball' on Broad-Halfpenny:

'I have been there, and still would go;
'Twas like a little Heaven below!'

Edward Arburrow, a native of Hambledon, was one of our best long fields. He always went by the name of Curry; why, I cannot remember, neither is it of the utmost importance to enquire. He was well calculated for the post he always occupied, being a sure and strong thrower, and able to cover a great space of the field. He was a steady and safe batter, averaging the same number of runs as Lear. We reckoned him a tolerably good change for bowling. Arburrow was a strong and well-made man, standing about five feet nine; he had a plain, honest-looking face, and was beloved by all his acquaintance.

Buck, whose real name was Peter Steward, is the next Hambledon man that occurs to my recollection. He, too, played long field, and was a steady man at his post; his batting, too, reached the same pitch of excellence; he could cut the balls very hard at the point of the bat – nothing like Sueter, however – very few could have equalled *him*. Buck was a dark-looking man, a shoemaker by trade, in height about five feet eight, rather slimly built, and very active. He had an ambition to be thought a humourist. The following anecdote may serve both as a specimen of his talent, and of the unfastidious taste of the men of Hambledon. When a match was to be played at a distance, the whole eleven, with the umpire and scorer, were conveyed in one caravan, built for their accommodation. Upon one occasion, the vehicle having been overturned, the whole cargo unshipped, Buck remained at his post, and refused to come out, desiring that they would right the vessel with him in it; for that 'one good turn deserved another'. This repartee was admired for a week.

The following old-fashioned song, and which was very popular fifty years ago, may bring back pleasant recollections to those of my countrymen who remember the Hambledon Club in the year 1778:

### CRICKET

By the Rev. Mr Cotton of Winchester

Assist, all ye Muses, and join to rehearse
An old English Sport, never praised yet in verse;
Tis Cricket I sing, of illustrious fame,
No nation e'er boasted so noble a game.
  Derry down, etc.

Great Pindar has bragg'd of his heroes of old –
Some were swift in the race, some in battles were bold;
The brows of the victor with olives were crown'd:
Hark! they shout, and Olympia returns the glad sound!
  Derry down, etc.

What boasting of Castor and Pollux's brother –
The one famed for riding, for boxing the other:
Compared with our heroes, they'll not shine at all –
What were Castor and Pollux to Nyren and Small?
  Derry down, etc.

Here's guarding and catching, and throwing and tossing,
And bowling and striking, and running and crossing;
Each mate must excel in some principal part –
The Pentathlum of Greece could not show so much art.
  Derry down, etc.

The parties are met, and array'd all in white –
Famed Elis ne'er boasted so pleasing a sight;
Each nymph looks askew at her favourite swain,
And views him, half stript, both with pleasure and pain,
  Derry down, etc.

The wickets are pitched now, and measured the ground;
Then they form a large ring, and stand gazing around –
Since Ajax fought Hector, in sight of all Troy,
No contest was seen with such fear and such joy.
  Derry down, etc.

Ye bowlers, take heed, to my precepts attend;
On you the whole fate of the game must depend;
Spare your vigour at first, now exert all your strength,
But measure each step and be sure pitch a length.
    Derry down, etc.

Ye fieldsmen, look sharp, lest your pains ye beguile;
Move close like an army, in rank and in file;
When the ball is returned, back it sure, for I trow,
Whole states have been ruined by one overthrow.
    Derry down, etc.

Ye strikers, observe when the foe shall draw nigh;
Mark the bowler, advancing with vigilant eye;
Your skill all depends upon distance and sight,
Stand firm to your scratch, let your bat be upright.
    Derry down, etc.

And now the game's o'er, IO victory! rings,
Echo doubles her chorus, and Fame spreads her wings;
Let's now hail our champions all steady and true,
Such as Homer ne'er sung of, nor Pindar e'er knew.
    Derry down, etc.

Buck, Curry and Hogsflesh, and Barber and Brett,
Whose swiftness in bowling was ne'er equalled yet;
I had almost forgot, they deserve a large bumper;
Little George, the long stop, and Tom Sueter, the stumper.
    Derry down, etc.

Then why should we fear either Sackville or Mann,
Or repine at the loss both of Boynton and Lann? –
With such troops as those we'll be lords of the game,
Spite of Minshull and Miller, and Lumpy and Frame.
    Derry down, etc.

Then fill up your glass, he's the best that drinks most.
Here's the Hambledon Club! – who refuses the toast?
Let's join in the praise of the bat and the wicket,
And sing in full chorus the patrons of cricket.
    Derry down, etc.

And when the game's o'er, and our fate shall draw nigh,
(For the heroes of cricket, like others, must die,)
Our bats we'll resign, neither troubled nor vex'd,
And give up our wickets to those that come next.
    Derry down, etc.

The tenth knight of our round table (of which old Richard
Nyren was the King Arthur) was a man we always called 'The
Little Farmer'; his name was Lambert. He was a bowler – right-
handed, and he had the most extraordinary delivery ever I saw.
The ball was delivered quite low, and with a twist; not like that
of the generality of right-handed bowlers, but just the reverse
way: that is, if bowling to a right-handed hitter, his ball would
twist from the off stump into the leg. He was the first I remember
who introduced this deceitful and teasing style of delivering the
ball. When all England played the Hambledon Club, the Little
Farmer was appointed one of our bowlers; and, egad! this new
trick of his so bothered the Kent and Surrey men, that they
tumbled out one after another, as if they had been picked off by
a rifle corps. For a long time they could not tell what to make of
that cursed twist of his.

This, however, was the only virtue he possessed, as a cricketer.
He was no batter, and had no judgment of the game. The
perfection he had attained in this one department, and his otherwise general deficiency, are at once accounted for by the circumstance, that when he was tending his father's sheep, he
would set up a hurdle or two, and bowl away for hours together.
Our General, Old Nyren, after a great deal of trouble (for the
Farmer's comprehension did not equal the speed of lightning),
got him to pitch the ball a little to the off-side of the wicket, when

it would twist full in upon the stumps. Before he had got into this knack, he was once bowling against the Duke of Dorset and, delivering his ball straight to the wicket, it curled in, and missed the Duke's leg-stump by a hair's breadth. The plain-spoken little bumpkin, in his eagerness and delight, and forgetting the style in which we were always accustomed to impress our aristocratical playmates with our acknowledgment of their rank and station, bawled out – 'Ah! it was *tedious* near you, Sir!' The familiarity of his tone, and the genuine Hampshire dialect in which it was spoken, set the whole ground laughing. I have never seen but one *bowler* who delivered his balls in the same way as our Little Farmer; with the jerkers the practice is not uncommon. He was a very civil and inoffensive young fellow, and remained in the club perhaps two or three seasons.

With Tom Taylor the old eleven was completed. There were, of course, several changes of other players, but these were the established picked set – the *élite*. Tom was an admirable field – certainly one of the very finest I ever saw. His station was between the point of the bat and the middle wicket, to save the two runs; but Tom had a lucky knack of gathering in to the wicket, for Tom had a licence from our old General; so that, if the ball was hit to him, he had so quick a way of meeting it, and with such a rapid return (for no sooner was it in his hand, than with the quickness of thought it was returned to the top of the wicket) that I have seen many put out by this manœuvre in a single run, and when the hit might be safely calculated upon for a prosperous one. He had an excellent general knowledge of the game; but of fielding, in particular, he was perfect both in judgment and practice. Tom was also a brilliant hitter, but his great fault lay in not sufficiently guarding his wicket; he was too fond of cutting, at the point of the bat, balls that were delivered straight; although, therefore, he would frequently get many runs, yet, from this habit, he was commonly the cause of his being out. I have known Lord Frederick Beauclerc (certainly the finest batter of his day) throw away the chance of a capital innings by the same incaution – that of cutting at *straight* balls, and he has been bowled out in consequence. Taylor was a short, well-made man, strong, and as watchful and active as a cat; but in no other instance will the comparison hold good, for he was without guile, and was an attached friend.

*from* THE YOUNG CRICKETER'S TUTOR *1830*

## A Chapter of Accidents

### JAMES PYCROFT

William Beldham saw as much of cricket as any other man in England, from the year 1780 to about 1820. Mr E. H. Budd and Caldecourt are the best of chroniclers from the days of Beldham down to George Parr. Yet neither of these worthies could remember any injury at cricket which would at all compare with those 'moving accidents of flood and field' which have thinned the ranks of Nimrod, Hawker, or Isaac Walton. A fatal accident in any legitimate game of cricket is almost unknown. Mr A. Haygarth, however, kindly informed me that the father of George III died from the effects of a blow from a cricket ball. His authority is Wraxall's Memoirs:

'Frederick, Prince of Wales, son of George II, expired suddenly in 1751, at Leicester House, in the arms of Desnoyers, the celebrated dancing master. His end was caused by an internal abscess that had long been forming in consequence of a blow which he received in the side from a cricket ball while he was engaged in playing at that game on the lawn at Cliefden House in Buckinghamshire, where he then principally resided. Death did not take place, however, till several months after the accident, when a collection of matter burst and instantly suffocated him.'

A solicitor at Romsey, about 1825, was, says an eye-witness, struck so hard in the abdomen that he died in a week of mortification. There is a rumour of a boy at school, about twenty-five years since, and another boy about thirty-five years ago, being severally killed by a blow on the head with a cricket ball. A dirty boy also, of Salisbury town, in 1826, having contracted a bad habit of pocketing the balls of the pupils of Dr Ratcliffe, was hit rather hard on the head with a brass-tipped stump, and by a strange coincidence, died, as the jury found, of 'excess of passion' a few hours after.

The most likely source of serious injury, is when a hitter returns the ball with all his force, straight back to the bowler. Caldecourt and the Rev. C. Wordsworth, severally and separately, remarked in my hearing that they had shuddered at cricket once, each in the same position, and each from the same hitter! Each had a ball hit back to him by that powerful hitter Mr H. Kingscote, which whizzed, in defiance of hand or eye, most dangerously by. A similar hit, already described, by Hammond, who took a ball at the pitch, just missed Lord F. Beauclerk's head, and spoiled his nerve for bowling ever after. But, what if these several balls had really hit? Who knows whether the respective skulls might not have stood the shock, as in a case which I witnessed in Oxford in 1835; when one Richard Blucher, a Cowley bowler, was hit on the head by a clean half-volley, from the bat of Henry Daubeny – than whom few Wykehamists *used* (fuit!) to hit with better eye or stronger arm. Still 'Richard was himself again' the very next day; for, we saw him with his head tied up, bowling at shillings as industriously as ever. Some skulls stand a great deal. Witness the sprigs of Shillelah at Donnibrook fair; still most indubiously tender is the face, as also – which *horresco referens*; and here let me tell wicket-keepers and long-stops especially, that a cricket jacket made long and full, with pockets to hold a handkerchief sufficiently in front, is a precaution not to be despised; though 'the race of inventive men' have also devised a cross-bar india-rubber guard, aptly described in Ulysses' thread to Thersites, in the Iliad.

The most alarming accident I ever saw occurred in one of the many matches played by the Lansdowne Club against Mr E. G. Budd's Eleven, at Purton, in 1835. Two of the Lansdowne players were running between wickets; and good Mr Pratt – *immani corpore* – was standing mid way, and hiding each from the other. Both were rushing the same side of him, and as one held his bat most dangerously extended, the point of it met his partner under the chin, forced back his head as if his neck were broken and dashed him senseless to the ground. Never shall I forget the shudder and the chill of every heart, till poor Price – for he it

was – being lifted up, gradually evinced returning consciousness; and, at length, when all was explained, he smiled, amidst his bewilderment, with his usual good nature, on his unlucky friend. A surgeon, who witnessed the collision, feared he was dead, and said afterwards, that with less powerful muscles (for he had a neck like a bull-dog) he never could have stood the shock. Price told me next day that he felt as if a little more and he never should have raised his head again.

And what Wykehamist of 1820–30 does not remember R— Price? or what Fellow of New College down to 1847, when

'*Multis ille bonis flebilis occidit,*'

has not enjoyed his merriment in the Common Room or his play on Bullingdon and Dowley Marsh? His were the safest hands and most effective fielding ever seen. To attempt the one run from a cover hit when Price was there, or to give the sight of one stump to shy at, was a wicket lost. When his friend, F. B. Wright, or any one he could trust, was at the wicket, well backed up, the ball, by the fine old Wykehamist action, was up and in with such speed and precision as I have hardly seen equalled and never exceeded. When he came to Lord's, in 1825, with that Wykehamist Eleven which Mr Ward so long remembered with delight, their play was at first unknown, and the bets on their opponents; but when once Price was seen practising at a single stump, his Eleven became the favourites immediately; for he was one of the straightest of all fast bowlers; and I have heard experienced batsmen say, 'We don't care for his underhand bowling, only it is so straight we could take no liberties, and the first we missed was Out.' I never envied any man his sight and nerve like Price – the coolest practitioner you ever saw; he always looked bright, though others blue; and you had only to glance at his sharp grey eyes, and you could at once account for the fact, that one stump to shy at, a rook for a single bullet, or the ripple of a trout in a bushy stream, was so much fun for R. Price.

Some of the most painful accidents have been of the same kind – from collision; therefore I never blame a man who, as the ball soars high in the air, and the captain of his side does not (as he ought if he can) call out 'Johnson has it!' stops short, for fear of three spikes in his instep, or the buttons of his neighbour's jacket forcibly conflicting with his own. Still these are not distinctively the dangers of Cricket; men may run their heads together in the street.

The principal injuries sustained are in the fingers; though, I did once know a gentleman playing in spectacles, who saw two balls in the air, and catching at the shadow, very nearly had the substance in his face. The old players, in the days of underhand bowling, played without gloves; and Bennet assured me he had seen Tom Walker, before advancing civilisation made man tender, rub his bleeding fingers in the dust. The old players could show finger-joints of most ungenteel dimensions; and no wonder, for a finger has been broken even through tubular india-rubber. Still, with a good pair of cricket gloves, no man need think much about his fingers; albeit flesh will blacken, joints will grow too large for the accustomed ring, and finger-nails will come off. A spinning ball is the most mischievous; and when there is spin and pace too (as with a ball from Mr Fellowes, which you could hear humming like a top) the danger is too great for mere amusement; for when, as in the Players' Match of 1849, Hillyer plays a bowler a foot away from his stumps, and Pilch cannot face him – which is true when Mr Fellowes bowls on any but the smoothest ground – why then, we will not say that any thing which that hardest of hitters and thorough cricketer does, is not cricket, but certainly it is any-thing but *play*.

Some of the worst injuries of the hands occur rather in fielding than in batting. A fine player of the Kent Eleven, some six years ago, so far injured his thumb that one of the joints was removed, and he has rarely played since. Another of the best gentlemen players broke one of the bones of his hand in putting down a wicket; but, strangest of all, I saw one of the Christchurch Eleven at Oxford, in 1835, in fielding at Cover, split up his hand an inch in length between his second and third fingers; still, all was well in a few weeks.

Add to all these chances of war, the many balls which are flying at the same time at Lord's and at the Universities and other much frequented grounds, on a practising day. At Oxford I once could see, any day in summer, on Cowley Marsh, two rows of six wickets each facing some other, with a space of about sixty yards between each row, and ten yards between each wicket. Then, you have twelve bowlers, *aos à dos*, and as many hitters – making twelve balls and twenty-four men, all in danger's way at once, besides by-standers. The most any one of these bowlers can do is to look out for the balls of his own set; whether hit or not by a ball from behind, is very much a matter of chance. A ball from the opposite row once touched my hair! The wonder is, that twelve balls should be flying in a small space nearly every day, yet no man hit in the face – a fact the more remarkable because there was usually free hitting with loose bowling. Pierce Egan records that, in 1830, in the Hyde Park Ground, Sheffield, nine double-wicket games were playing at once – *two hundred players* within six acres of grass! One day, at Lord's, just before the match bell rang after dinner, I saw one of the hardest hitters in the M.C.C. actually trying how hard he could drive the ball among the various clusters of sixpenny amateurs, every man thinking it fun, and no one dangerous. An elderly gentleman cannot stand a bruise so well – matter forms or bone exfoliates. But then an elderly gentleman – bearing an inverse ratio in all things to him who calls him 'governor' – is the most careful thing in nature; and, as to young blood, it circulates too fast to be overtaken by half the ills that flesh is heir to.

A well-known Wykehamist player of R. Price's standing, was playing as wicket-keeper, and seeing the batsman going to hit off, ran almost to the place of a near Point; the hit, a tremendously hard one, glanced off from his forehead – he called out 'Catch it', and it was caught by the bowler! He was not hurt – not even marked by the ball.

*from* THE CRICKET FIELD *1851*

# Introduction to
# *Richard Daft's 'Kings of Cricket'*

## ANDREW LANG

Mr Daft has requested me to write an introduction to the volume of his *Kings of Cricket*. It is an old saying that 'Good wine needs no bush', and I scarcely see how the remarks of one who is a living disproof of a maxim of Mr Daft's can help the cause of the game. 'Anyone ought to make himself into a fair player by perseverance', observed this authority. Alas! a long and bitter experience has taught me that there was one exception, at least, to a rule which observation convinces me is far from general. A cricketer is born, not made. A good eye and stout muscles are necessary: and though Mr Daft thinks highly of the intellectual element in cricket, it remains true that 'muscles make the man, not mind, nor that confounded intellect'.

As to intellect, it is not so very hard to invent 'head balls'. After weeks of reflection, I once invented a 'head-ball' myself. First, you send your man a ball tossed rather high, but really pitched rather short. The batsman detects this, or if he does not and goes in to drive it, so much the better. If he does detect it, you follow it up by a ball really pitched up, but of the same height in curve as the former. The batsman plays back again, thinking it is the same ball, and usually makes a mistake. Such studies in the subjectivity of the batsman are easily elaborated in the closet, but when it comes to practice he usually hits across the hop of the first ball and drives the second over the pavilion. In consequence of these failures to make the means attain the end, I have never taken part in really first-class cricket – not beyond playing once for my college eleven. But one beauty of cricket is that, if you cannot play at it, you can at least look on and talk very learnedly, and find fault with the captain, showing how you would order matters if you were consulted. This is the recreation of middle age, and is permitted to an incapacity for actual performance which the audience never heard of or have had time to forget.

About Mr Daft's own play it is not possible, were it desirable, for me to offer criticism, as I never saw him save on one occasion. I had gone to Nottingham to view Gloucestershire play Notts, as two Clifton boys, friends of mine, were playing for the western county. One of them was bowling, and it is not ungracious to say that he was far from being a colossus. As Mr Daft came in, one of the crowd observed: 'I would like to see the little 'un bowl Daft!' which surely was a chivalrous expression of an Englishman's preference for the weaker side. However, the prayer was scattered to the winds. The ball, too, visited the boundaries of the Trent Bridge ground, and Notts made over five hundred.

Though one did not see very much first-class cricket before 1874, the memories of what one has seen and read about abide among our most pleasant reminiscences. Cricket is among the few institutions in England which Time has not spoiled, nay, has rather improved. The wickets are better, immeasurably better than of old. The bowling is better, the fielding is as good as ever; probably the wicket-keeping is improved, and the general temper of players and spectators leaves nothing to be desired. A fine day at the Oval makes us all akin, and a pleasant sight it is to see the vast assembly, every man with his eyes riveted on the wicket, every man able to appreciate the most delicate strokes in the game, and anxious to applaud friend or adversary. An English cricketing crowd is as fair and as generous as any assembly of mortals may be. When the Australians defeat us, though we do not like it, we applaud them till these bronzed Colonists almost blush. It is not so in all countries, nor in all countries is there the ready acceptance of the umpire's verdict, without which cricket degenerates into a wrangle.

Mr Daft is not inclined to believe that the veterans of a middle-aged man's youth were inferior to the heroes of our later day. With Dr W. G. Grace, indeed, no man competes or has competed. The hardness and the subtlety of his hitting and placing of the ball, his reach and certainty at such a field as point, and the sagacious perseverance which he displays as a bowler, combine to make him unique – 'W.G.'– a name to resound for ages.

There is something monumental in his stance at the wicket, wholly free from a false refinement, without extraneous elegancies. His is a nervous, sinewy, English style, like that of Fielding. Better graced cricketers we may have seen, such as Mr Edward Lyttleton, Mr Charles Studd, Mr A. G. Steel, all of them, in their day, models of classical dexterity and refinement. But it is always, or almost always, Dr W. G. Grace's day: his play is unhasting, unresting like the action of some great natural law. With him, then, nobody can compare; and we who have seen may report to the age unbred that ere they were born the flower of cricket had blossomed. Nevertheless, methinks that even before Fuller Pilch and Clarke, there had been very great cricketers, who, could they return in their prime, after a few weeks' practice might match our best.

Aylward, of Hampshire, must have been a truly sterling batsman. Lambert may also be reckoned among the immortals, and it is highly probable that David Harris, on those wickets which he knew how to prepare, would puzzle even men like Shrewsbury.

In those days the bowler laid out his wicket to suit himself. None of us now living can equal the old underhand bowling, which, in some mysterious way, was delivered high, from under the armpit, got up very fast and erect from the pitch, and was capable of many changes of curve and pitch. Brown, of Brighton, and others, appear to have bowled under-hand as fast, or faster, than Tarrant, or Jackson, or Mr Cecil Boyle.

This seems quite probable. Perhaps the swiftest bowling I ever saw was the underhand of a fast round-hand bowler, now in Canada, and at no time known to fame. He is a clergyman of the Scottish church, the 'Jointer', so styled of yore. 'He says he's a meenister, he says he's a beginner; I think he's a leear,' observed the caddie, when asked, at golf, who this gentleman might be. Hail, Jointer, across the wide seas and the many years, I salute thee. *Bayete!* as the Zulu says.

Now, allowing for odd wickets, and for the peculiarities of very fast underhand with a high delivery, it seems likely, that, on an old Hampshire wicket, Nyren's team might have tackled as good as eleven as we moderns could send to meet them. In the fields of asphodel (which, of course, would need returfing), some such game may be played by heroes dead and gone.

But in this world one can never thus measure strength any more than we can judge of old actors, and compare Molière to Garrick, and Garrick to Monsieur Poquelin. The cricketer, unlike the actor, leaves something permanent – his scores; but we cannot discover the true equation, as the different conditions cannot be estimated. Thus in golf, a round of 94, on St Andrews Links, in 1761, with feather balls, and unkempt putting greens, and whins all over the links, is surely, at least as good as Hugh Kirkcaldy's round of 73 today, now that the iron age has come in, and the baffy spoon exists only as venerable relic. Men's thews and skill have ever been much on a level.

It is the conditions that alter, and all old cricketers will believe in the old heroes of the past. To do so is pleasant, pious, and provides a creed not to be shaken by criticism. We who remember Carpenter and Hayward, Caffyn and H. H. Stephenson, are not to be divorced from these idols. They wore 'billycock' hats (the true word is 'bully-cock') and oddly-coloured shirts, and blue belts with snake clasps, and collars and neckties, as their great-grandfathers had worn jockey caps and knee-breeches, and their fathers tall hats. But these were unessential details.

The style in bowling of that age – Caffyn's age – with a level arm, was peculiarly graceful. The command of the ball was less than at present. Peate's delivery was level, or nearly level; yet his dexterity was unsurpassed. The most favourable admirers can hardly call Mr Spofforth's style a model of grace. It has withal a something truculent and overbearing. Yet, on the modern wickets, bowling needs every fair advantage that it can obtain, and throwing has gone distinctly out of favour. I remember an excellent cricketer and most successful bowler, concerning whom I chanced to remark to a friend that I thought him quite fair. 'I think him a capital man to have on our side', was the furthest to which my companion's lenity of judgment would stretch. Probably no bowler throws consciously, but it was certainly high time that umpires should bring some fast bowlers to the test of an objective standard.

When round-hand bowling came in, the veteran Nyren declared that all was over with the game; that it would become a mere struggle of physical force. But, for this once, pessimism was mistaken, and prophecy was unfulfilled. Still there was the grace of a day that is dead in the old level deliveries, while some slinging bowlers, of whom Mr Powys, I think, was the last, could be extremely dangerous, if occasionally erratic. The regrets of him who praises times past are natural, but are tempered.

As for the present day, we are all tired – Mr Daft is tired – of the Fabian policy which leaves balls to the off alone, in a scientific cowardice. Once Mr Ernest Steel, then by no means a big boy, playing for Marlborough, at Lord's, taught a Rugby boy the unwisdom of this course. He bowled two balls to the off which were left alone; the third looked like them, but broke viciously, was let alone, and down went the off stump. This was not in first-class cricket, but it was a pleasant thing to see and remember. Many such pleasant memories recur to an old spectator.

There was Ulyett's catch, at Lord's, when the gigantic Mr Bonnor drove a ball to the off, invisible for its speed, and the public looked to see where the ring would divide. But the ball was in Ulyett's hands. There was Mr A. J. Webbe's catch of Mr Edward Lyttleton, who had hit a ball, low and swift as a half-topped golf ball, to the ropes. Running along the ropes, Mr. Webbe caught it, low down, at full speed, a beautiful exhibition of graceful activity. Pindar would have commemorated it in an ode, and Dioscorides in a gem. Mr G. F. Grace's catch, under the pavilion at the Oval, I had not the fortune to witness, but Mr Gale has described it in impassioned prose.

Then there was Mr Steel's bowling, in his youthful prime, a sad sight for Oxford eyes, when the ball seemed alive and unplayable.

Mr Berkeley's bowling at Lord's, in 1891, at the end of the second Cambridge innings, was also a thing to dream upon, when for a moment it seemed as if the glories of Mr Cobden were to be repeated; but Mr Woods was there! As to Mr V. T. Hill's innings, in 1892, I cannot speak of it in prose.

Mr Daft has not dwelt much on University cricket, the most powerfully exciting to the spectator whose heart is in the right place (not unfrequently 'in his mouth') when we wait for a catch to come to hand.

The memories of old players in these affairs – Mr Mitchell, Mr Ottaway, Mr Yardley, Mr Steel, Mr Kemp (who won matches by sheer pluck and force of character), are fragrant and immortal. There is no talk, none so witty and brilliant, that is so good as cricket talk, when memory sharpens memory, and the dead live again – the regretted, the unforgotten – and the old happy days of burned out Junes revive. We shall not see them again. We lament that lost lightness of heart, 'for no man under the sun lives twice, outliving his day', and the day of the cricketer is brief. It is not every one who can go on playing, 'once you come to forty years', like Mr Daft and Dr W. G. Grace; the eye loses its quickness. An old man at point must be a very courageous old man; the hand loses its cunning, the ball from the veteran fingers has no work nor spin, and the idea of throwing in 'from the country' is painfully distasteful. Dr E. M. Grace, of course, is not old; he reckons not by years. Fortunately, golf exists as a solace of old age, and trout can always be angled for; and to lose a trout is only loss, not 'infinite dishonour', like missing a catch.

Cricket is a very humanizing game. It appeals to the emotions of local patriotism and pride. It is eminently unselfish; the love of it never leaves us, and binds all the brethren together, whatever their politics and rank may be. There is nothing like it in the sports of mankind. Everyone, however young, can try himself at it, though excellence be for the few, or perhaps not entirely for the few. At Nottingham, during the practice hour, how many wonderfully good bowlers you see, throwing off their coats and playing without even cricket shoes. How much good cricket there is in the world!

If a brief and desultory sermon may end with a collection, as is customary, I would fain ask cricketers to remember the London Playing Fields Committee, and send their mites to provide the grounds for those eager young players who draw their wickets with chalk on the wall, or bowl at a piled heap of jackets. Their hearts are in the right place, if their wickets are not, and we can help to get them better grounds. Many good cricketers are on the Committee of the Playing Fields. I believe a cheque to Mr Theodore Hall, Oxford and Cambridge Club, Pall Mall, will go to the right place also. So pay up, that young town-bred boys may play up, ye merry men of England.

Cricket ought to be to English boys what Habeas Corpus is to Englishmen, as Mr Hughes says in *Tom Brown*.

At no ruinous expense, the village cricket might also be kept alive and improved; for cricket is a liberal education in itself, and demands temper and justice and perseverance. There is more teaching in the playground than in schoolrooms, and a lesson better worth learning very often. For there can be no good or enjoyable cricket without enthusiasm – without sentiment, one may almost say: a quality that enriches life and refines it; gives it, what life more and more is apt to lose, zest.

Though he who writes was ever a cricketing failure, he must acknowledge that no art has added so much to his pleasures as this English one, and that he has had happier hours at Lord's, or even on a rough country wicket, than at the Louvre or in the Uffizi. If this be true of one, it is probably true of the many whose pleasures are scant, and can seldom come from what is called culture.

Cricket is simply the most catholic and diffused, the most innocent, kindly, and manly of popular pleasures, while it has been the delight of statesmen and the relaxation of learning. There was an old Covenanting minister of the straitest sect, who had so high an opinion of curling that he said if he were to die in the afternoon, he could imagine no better way than curling of passing the morning. Surely we may say as much for cricket. Heaven (as the bishop said of the strawberry) might doubtless have devised a better diversion, but as certainly no better has been invented than that which grew up on the village greens of England.

*from* KINGS OF CRICKET *1893*

# The Famous United XI

## RICHARD DAFT

The rival of the All England Eleven, the United Eleven, was composed of principal players of the South of England with a few from the North, notably Carpenter and one of my own country-men James Grundy. No cricketer was better known in those days than Old Jemmy. He was one of the best medium pace round-arm bowlers then about, having great command over the ball, but had not much break and consequently on a good wicket was not difficult; but if the pitch broke up a little and he found a 'spot', he was then very dangerous. This happened on one occasion when Notts and Yorkshire played on Trent Bridge. The victory appeared to be as good as won by the latter, who had few runs to get and plenty of wickets in hand. Grundy, however, got on a worn place, and kept pegging away at it with such persistency that the Yorkshiremen's wickets fell one after the other in a most remarkable manner, and the home county achieved a brilliant victory.

I never in my life, I think, saw so much excitement as was evinced by the spectators on this occasion. When the match was won the uproar was indescribable. Old Charles Brown, seeing as he thought inevitable defeat for his county, had gone home and to bed hours before, and many of the spectators, surrounding his house on their way from the ground, made Charlie get up and put his head out of the window to hear the result of the match, which he no sooner understood than he declared he would dress himself and come out and make a night of it, which I have no doubt he did.

Grundy always wore a black velvet cap, which, when bowling, he generally took off and thrust in his belt. His delivery was wonderfully easy, and he could bowl for almost any length of time without fatigue. He was a remarkably neat, bright-looking man, always as keen as possible when in the field. He had a great weakness for fat mutton chops and would devour it all eagerly. He once at Lord's bowled to George Parr and myself twenty-one overs without our scoring a run.

Tom Lockyer I have already mentioned.

A very good man the United Eleven possessed in John Lillywhite, of whose batting George Parr had at one time a very high opinion. His defence and hitting were both excellent.

Tom Hearne was another most useful all-round man. He made lots of runs and took plenty of wickets. He was more successful with the old-fashoned 'draw' than any batsman I can remember. In a match at Islington a curious incident occurred. A pigeon came flying across the ground high in the air, at which Hearne threw the ball, hit the bird, which dropped dead at his feet. The pigeon Tom afterwards had stuffed.

I never saw anything of this kind done on a cricket ground before or since. But I saw a dog killed only a few years ago when some friends and myself were practising cricket on an asphalt tennis-court which I have at my house. The dog was a fox terrier belonging to one of my friends. It happened to run across the pitch just after the ball had left the bowler's hand, when the ball, striking the dog full on the head, killed it instantly.

Young Walker, a son of the old groundsman at Trent Bridge, was the bowler.

Of William Caffyn's play I cannot speak too highly. It is a pity such players as he should ever grow old. A superior man in every way was Caffyn. He always dressed well, and had a smart and neat appearance at all times. I have often heard related a trick which that great practical joker, Sam Parr, once played him during a tour they were on. Caffyn always took with him when travelling a hat-box, in which was a splendid tall silk hat that he wore on Sundays.

Well, during this tour Sam Parr happened to find a dead mouse, which, having flattened out as well as he could, he deposited under the lining of Caffyn's hat. This was early in the week, and the weather being very hot the head vermin soon began to be very offensive. Caffyn, who kept the hat in his bedroom at the hotel where he was staying, soon perceived this, and declared something was wrong with the drains; but when Sunday came, and the hat was required, of course the mystery was solved. He at once suspected who had played him the trick, and was so exasperated that Sam thought it advisable to keep out of his way for some time after.

Old Tom Box was the victim of a still more cruel joke of Sam's about this time, when the All England Eleven were playing away somewhere. Sam, seeing a barber's shop, went in to be shaved, and told the proprietor he had come to see the great cricket match; and that he was in charge of a gentleman who was not quite right in his mind, and that, as the weather was warm, he intended bringing him to have his hair cut very short on the following morning. 'It will be so much better for him this hot weather,' Sam said, 'though he has a great objection to having much taken off; but you never mind what he says, and dash away with the scissors, and be sure and keep him away from a looking-glass till it is over.' All this the barber promised to carry out.

Now, if there was one thing Old Box was prouder of than another, it was his hair, which he wore rather long (the short crops of the present day were then unknown) and he was always extremely particular about the way he had it cut. It was not difficult for Sam to persuade him to go and have it trimmed on this occasion; and away the pair went, and the 'mad gentleman' was soon under the hands of the barber. Sam diverted Old Tom's attention by keeping up a conversation while the scissors were being plied freely.

'Be sure and don't take too much off,' Tom kept saying.

'All right, sir,' replied the hairdresser; 'pray be calm, and leave it to me.'

And such good use did the latter make of his time that Tom soon had his head shorn as close as a convict's. Sam had quietly disappeared before the performance came to an end.

The barber at length finished his task, for there was literally nothing left for him to do, and Tom rose up and walked to a mirror to look at himself. He had no sooner done so that he cursed the unfortunate barber till he was black in the face; and the latter, now perceiving for the first time the absence of the keeper of the supposed lunatic, fled for his life. Sam had meanwhile made his way back to the hotel, where were the rest of the eleven at breakfast. He told them of the whole performance; and presently, when poor Box arrived minus his hair, he was received with roars of laughter.

'Well,' said Tom, after a considerable flow of strong language, 'I intended going home at the weekend, but I'll be hanged if I'll do so till my hair grows again, if I stop away six months!'

John Wisden was for years one of the best all-round men in England, being a splendid fast bowler with a beautiful length, a grand little batsman, and an excellent fellow withal. Wisden was known as the 'pendulum' player, from the way in which he swung his bat backwards and forwards.

As I remarked before, the match, All England Eleven v. United Eleven, was always one of the best of the season. This match was not confined to Lord's, but sometimes took place at the Oval and elsewhere. Once, when it was played at Manchester, I made 111 for All England Eleven. For really enjoyable games, both for players and spectators alike, there never have been, in my opinion, and never again will be, any to equal those played between the All England Eleven and United Eleven in their best days.

*from* KINGS OF CRICKET *1893*

## Opposing my Hero

### ARTHUR MAILEY

More unemployment – and still I carried a cricket ball as I trudged the streets.

I had drifted into a lower grade of cricket, though it was still of a fairly good standard, and I was told by some of my team-mates that I was capable of bowling a very dangerous ball. It didn't come up as often as it should, but it might lead to something. However, I would be well advised to lessen the spin and concentrate on length.

I was flattered that my fellow-cricketers should think that even a few of the balls I delivered had devil in them. All the same, there was a rebellious imp sitting on my shoulder that whispered: 'Take no notice, cobber. They're crazy. Millions can bowl a good length but few can really spin the ball. Keep the spin and practise, practise, practise.'

Then came a commission for a house-painting job. It was a house near Botany Bay and it belonged to my brother-in-law. Wages? A bat that had been given to my brother-in-law by a distant relative who had taken part in the 1904 English tour. But what a relative! It was Victor Trumper* himself – the fantastic, legendary Trumper, my particular hero. A hundred pounds could not have given me more pleasure.

Fancy getting a bat which my hero had actually used in a Test

* See also pages 251 and 262.

at Lord's; a flattish bat with a springy handle and a blade curved like the bowl of a spoon. This was another link closer to the great batsman and I was more than ever determined to improve my bowling.

The 'wrong 'un', that legacy from the great Bosanquet, like Bateman's 'one-note man' seemed to be getting me somewhere, for after several seasons in Sydney lower-grade teams I found myself in first grade, a class of cricket in which inter-state and Test players participate.

At the same time, and having done my house-painting, I got another regular job. I became an A Class labourer on the Water and Sewerage Board.

Things were certainly coming my way; I had never worn a collar and tie to work before. My mother had always hoped that I would get a 'white collar' job like Mr Rumble some day – and here it was.

It is difficult to realize that a relatively minor event in one's life can still remain the most important through the years. I was chosen to play for Redfern against Paddington – and Paddington was Victor Trumper's club.

This was unbelievable, fantastic. It could never happen – something was sure to go wrong. A war – an earthquake – Trumper might fall sick. A million things could crop up in the two or three days before the match.

I sat on my bed and looked at Trumper's picture still pinned on the canvas wall. It seemed to be breathing with the movement of the draught between the skirting. I glanced at his bat standing in a corner of the room, then back at the gently moving picture. I just couldn't believe that this, to me, ethereal and godlike figure could step off the wall, pick up the bat and say quietly, 'Two legs, please, umpire', in my presence.

My family, usually undemonstrative and self-possessed, found it difficult to maintain that reserve which, strange as it may seem, was characteristic of my father's Northern Irish heritage.

'H'm,' said Father, 'Playing against Trumper on Saturday. By jove, you'll cop Old Harry if you're put on to bowl at him.'

'Why should he?' protested Mother. 'You never know what you can do till you try.'

I had nothing to say. I was little concerned with what should happen to me in the match. What worried me was that something would happen to Trumper which would prevent his playing.

Although at this time I had never seen Trumper play, on occasions I trudged from Waterloo across the Sandhills to the Sydney cricket ground and waited at the gate to watch the players coming out. Once I had climbed on a tram and actually sat opposite my hero for three stops. I would have gone further but having no money I did not want to take the chance of being kicked in the pants by the conductor. Even so I had been taken half a mile out of my way.

In my wildest dreams I never thought I would ever speak to Trumper let along play against him. I am fairly phlegmatic by nature but between the period of my selection and the match I must have behaved like a half-wit.

Right up to my first Test match I always washed and pressed my own flannels, but before this match I pressed them not once but several times. On the Saturday I was up with the sparrows and looking anxiously at the sky. It was a lovely morning but it still might rain. Come to that, lots of things could happen in ten hours – there was still a chance that Vic could be taken ill or knocked down by a tram or twist his ankle or break his arm. . . .

My thoughts were interrupted by a vigorous thumping on the back gate. I looked out of the washhouse-bathroom-woodshed-workshop window and saw that it was the milkman who was kicking up the row.

'Hey!' he roared – '– yer didn't leave the can out. I can't wait around here all day. A man should pour it in the garbage tin – that'd make yer wake up a bit!'

On that morning I wouldn't have cared whether he poured the milk in the garbage tin or all over me. I didn't belong to this world. I was playing against the great Victor Trumper. Let the milk take care of itself.

I kept looking at the clock. It might be slow – or it might have stopped! I'd better whip down to the Zetland Hotel and check up. Anyhow, I mightn't bowl at Trumper after all. He might get out before I come on. Or I mightn't get a bowl at all – after all, I can't put myself on. Wonder what Trumper's doing this very minute . . . bet he's not ironing his flannels. Sends them to the laundry, I suppose. He's probably got two sets of flannels, anyway. Perhaps he's at breakfast, perhaps he's eating bacon and eggs. Wonder if he knows I'm playing against him? Don't suppose he's ever heard of me. Wouldn't worry him anyhow, I shouldn't think. Gosh, what a long morning! Think I'll dig the garden. No, I won't – I want to keep fresh. Think I'll lie down for a bit . . . better not, I might fall off to sleep and be late.

The morning did not pass in this way. Time just stopped. I couldn't bring myself to doing anything in particular and yet I couldn't settle to the thought of not doing anything. I was bowling to Trumper and I was not bowling to Trumper. I was early and I was late. In fact, I think I was slightly out of my mind.

I didn't get to the ground so very early after all, mainly because it would have been impossible for me to wait around so near the scene of Trumper's appearance – and yet for it to rain or news to come that something had prevented Vic from playing.

'Is he here?' I asked Harry Goddard, our captain, the moment I did arrive at the ground.

'Is who here?' he countered.

My answer was probably a scornful and disgusted look. I remember that it occurred to me to say, 'Julius Caesar, of course' but that I stopped myself being cheeky because this was one occasion when I couldn't afford to be.

Paddington won the toss and took first knock.

When Trumper walked out to bat, Harry Goddard said to me: 'I'd better keep you away from Vic. If he starts on you he'll probably knock you out of grade cricket.'

I was inclined to agree with him yet at the same time I didn't fear punishment from the master batsman. All I wanted to do was just to bowl at him. I suppose in their time other ambitious youngsters have wanted to play on the same stage with Henry Irving, or sing with Caruso or Melba, to fight with Napoleon or sail the seas with Columbus. It wasn't conquest I desired. I simply wanted to meet my hero on common ground.

Vic, beautifully clad in creamy, loose-fitting but well-tailored flannels, left the pavilion with his bat tucked under his left arm and in the act of donning his gloves. Although slightly pigeon-toed in the left foot he had a springy athletic walk and a tendency to shrug his shoulders every few minutes, a habit I understand he developed through trying to loosen his shirt off his shoulders when it became soaked with sweat during his innings.

Arriving at the wicket, he bent his bat handle almost to a right angle, walked up the pitch, prodded about six yards of it, returned to the batting crease and asked the umpire for 'two legs', took a quick glance in the direction of fine leg, shrugged his shoulders again and took up his stance.

I was called to bowl sooner than I had expected. I suspect now that Harry Goddard changed his mind and decided to put me out of my misery early in the piece.

Did I ever bowl that first ball? I don't remember. My head was in a whirl, I really think I fainted and the secret of the mythical first ball has been kept over all these years to save me embarrassment. If the ball *was* sent down it must have been hit for six, or at least four, because I was awakened from my trance by the thunderous booming Yabba who roared: 'O for a strong arm and a walking stick!'

I do remember the next ball. It was, I imagined, a perfect leg-break. When it left my hand it was singing sweetly like a humming top. The trajectory couldn't have been more graceful if designed by a professor of ballistics. The tremendous leg-spin caused the ball to swing and curve from the off and move in line with the middle and leg stump. Had I bowled this particular ball at any other batsman I would have turned my back early in its flight and listened for the death rattle. However, consistent with my idolization of the champion, I watched his every movement.

He stood poised like a panther ready to spring. Down came

his left foot to within a foot of the ball. The bat, swung from well over his shoulders, met the ball just as it fizzed off the pitch, and the next sound I heard was a rapping on the off-side fence.

It was the most beautiful shot I have ever seen.

The immortal Yabba made some attempt to say something but his voice faded away to the soft gurgle one hears at the end of a kookaburra's song. The only person on the ground who didn't watch the course of the ball was Victor Trumper. The moment he played it he turned his back, smacked down a few tufts of grass and prodded his way back to the batting crease. He knew where the ball was going.

What were my reactions?

Well, I never expected that ball or any other ball I could produce to get Trumper's wicket. But that being the best ball a bowler of my type could spin into being, I thought that at least Vic might have been forced to play a defensive shot, particularly as I was almost a stranger too and it might have been to his advantage to use discretion rather than valour.

After I had bowled one or two other reasonably good balls without success I found fresh hope in the thought that Trumper had found Bosanquet, creator of the 'wrong 'un' or 'bosie' (which I think a better name), rather puzzling. This left me with one shot in my locker, but if I didn't use it quickly I would be taken out of the firing line. I decided, therefore, to try this most undisciplined and cantankerous creation of the great B. J. Bosanquet – not, as many may think, as a compliment to the inventor but as the gallant farewell, so to speak, of a warrior who refused to surrender until all his ammunition was spent.

Again fortune was on my side in that I bowled the ball I had often dreamed of bowling. As with the leg-break, it had sufficient spin to curve in the air and break considerably after making contact with the pitch. If anything it might have had a little more top-spin, which would cause it to drop rather suddenly. The sensitivity of a spinning ball against a breeze is governed by the amount of spin imparted, and if a ball bowled at a certain pace drops on a certain spot, one bowled with identical pace but with more top-spin should drop eighteen inches or two feet shorter.

For this reason I thought the difference in the trajectory and ultimate landing of the ball might provide a measure of uncertainty in Trumper's mind. Whilst the ball was in flight this reasoning appeared to be vindicated by Trumper's initial movement. As at the beginning of my over he sprang in to attack but did not realize that the ball, being an off-break, was floating away from him and dropping a little quicker. Instead of his left foot being close to the ball it was a foot out of line.

In a split second Vic grasped this and tried to make up the deficiency with a wider swing of the bat It was then I could see a passage-way to the stumps with our 'keeper, Con Hayes, ready to claim his victim. Vic's bat came through like a flash but the ball passed between his bat and legs, missed the leg stump by a fraction, and the bails were whipped off with the great batsman at least two yards out of his ground.

Vic had made no attempt to scramble back. He knew the ball had beaten him and was prepared to pay the penalty, and although he had little chance of regaining his crease on this occasion I think he would have acted similarly if his back foot had been only an inch from safety.

As he walked past me he smiled, patted the back of his bat and said, 'It was too good for me.'

There was no triumph in me as I watched the receding figure. I felt like a boy who had killed a dove.

*from* 10 FOR 66 AND ALL THAT *1958*

# Eton v. Harrow at Lord's

## DUDLEY CAREW

She was not really old, not, I thought looking at her with covert carefulness, not over sixty-four. The whole day she had sat there on one of the lines of benches drawn up in front of the coaches by the tavern, watching the cricket with unswerving and, as I thought, unintelligent attention. Her black dress, elaborately pleated, spoke of another age, and the white feather in her hat, a full voluminous feather, gave her, for all her ampleness, a faint but startling resemblance to the women that Gainsborough delighted to paint. Her hands were amazingly patient; all day they had lain folded on her lap, and my eyes, constantly straying from the cricket back to them, delighted in the nervous slimness of the fingers, the archness and delicacy of the wrists. They were made the more attractive by the contrast they afforded to the rest of her. She was, as I have said, ample, and, were one to take her in at a free unsubtle glance, one would add another adjective, florid. But that, while describing perhaps the full contours of her face and her rich complexion, would leave unaccounted for the hands and the exquisitely shaped feet that her long skirt half hid, half revealed. She broke through adjectives, rather she beckoned to so many contradictory and bewildering ones that one was forced to reject them all. She spread herself through your consciousness, massively, satisfyingly. All day long she sat, speechless, her face lifted at a curious unnatural angle, her hands unmoving.

There had been little in the cricket to make me forget her. With the glass high and the wicket plumb, there was little probability from the very beginning that the match would have a definite result, and one was becoming a little tired of the succession of drawn matches.

Eton had won the toss, and their innings had progressed unevenly but not very interestingly until the total of 312 had been reached. P. V. Cazalet, whom one was particularly anxious to see make runs, failed, and H. E. H. Hope, the captain as well as the best bat on the side, was out, just when he seemed to be getting a good sight of the ball. M. H. de Zoete proved that he could hit a cricket ball as worthily as his father can drive a golf ball, and, so long as he was in, the cricket had vitality about it, but, for the most part, the men were more busy with memories and boys with relations and friends than with the actual game that was going on.

The Eton and Harrow match keeps up its ritual wonderfully well. Year after year coaches gather round the tavern, the popping of champagne corks is heard, salmon mayonnaise is handed round. Top hats glitter in the sun and gaitered legs perambulate backwards and forwards by the pavilion. The ground itself seems to become jolly and benevolent, like an old gentleman who puts his age and dignity by and exerts himself at a children's party. The party at luncheon and between the innings somehow carries one back to the days when Dan Leno held the Empire in adoring silence and women stood on chairs to catch a sight of Lily Langtry.

Immaculate old men, leaning on sticks as they walk, seem to have come out of Meredith's world and one can imagine their talk run as Victor Radnor's, that magnificent City merchant, did. 'City dead flat. A monotonous key, but it's about the same as fetching a breath after a run; only, true, it lasts too long – not healthy! I was down in the country early this morning looking over the house with Taplow, my architect, and he speaks fairly well of the contractors.' In the City they do not impress one as having the breadth and culture and dignity of Meredith's men, egoists though they were. They cannot rise superior to the background of office and Stock Exchange growing year by year cheaper and shoddier. But Lord's, on the day of the Eton and Harrow match, touches their souls with a magic of its own and they wear their traditions with grace and confidence. The past suddenly becomes close to them; they realize and acknowledge their obligation.

And the women. Does one ignore the passing fashion of clothes, and old songs come clamorously back:

> The Church Parade, the Church Parade.
> The Church Parade is in full swing,
> It's a thing to see and wonder at
> With all the wealth displayed,
> With the millinery art,
> And the costume smart,
> At the Church Parade.

Wealth carried stature in those days, and the goods one bought with it were more worth the having.

My thoughts fluttering over the crowd, lazing indolently over the cricket, came back again to the woman by my side. Surely she would go now that the Eton innings was over, she could not wait all day in that passive attitude of watchfulness. The bell rang and the kaleidoscopic crowd slowly sorted itself out. Hope led the light blue caps from the pavilion, and, a moment later, A. M. Crawley and C. Clover-Brown trotted down the steps.

The woman, for the first time that day I veritably believe, stirred, and with a sudden trembling impulse – trembling because, spreading so on my own consciousness, she affected me strangely – I handed her my score card.

One hand, slim and exquisitely carved, fluttered delicately in denial. 'Crawley and Clover-Brown, we should see some good cricket now. Crawley is the best bat on either side.'

I do not know whether it was her voice or her actual words that startled me most. She spoke as though, leaning out from a crystal tower, she cast her words as white petals on to clear, dark water below. Her every syllable seemed to hang in the air, round and vibrant, and yet so quietly did she speak that I do not believe the young man sitting on the other side of her was aware she had opened her mouth. And her remark that Crawley was the best bat on either side. He was, he was, but how should she know, and how should she know, without looking at the card, who the batsmen were? Unmannerly I gaped at her.

'The covers will have a lot of work to do while he is in,' she went on gently; 'he has the Harrow drive to perfection – a beautiful pair of wrists.'

I stammered, 'Yes! he has. If he hadn't got out early in the second innings last year Harrow would have won.'

In grave agreement she bowed her head, the feather incongruously waving, 'Ford lost that match. Stupid boy playing carefully when there was no need, stupid boy.'

Quickly I asked her, 'Do you then come every year?'

She turned her large vacant eyes on me. 'Oh! no, only since the war and the one year before it,' she said gently and with a faintly surprised air as though she had been asked to explain an obvious thing. She would say nothing more. Indeed she turned away from me, as though she had wasted only too much precious time in talking to me as it was, and, until stumps were drawn, she sat motionless and absorbed.

The covers, as she had prophesied, were kept busy. Directly he came in Crawley set about making runs. He is one of those batsmen who never allow the bowler to dictate to them, and his foot-work enables him to make most balls suit his particular style of play. His off-driving was hard and confident, and, at the close, he had made 83 runs, a vast proportion of the runs made by his side. The other Harrow batsmen had not, indeed, been at all successful, and R. C. C. Whittaker, a slow left-hander who has a seasoned professional's ability for keeping a length over long spells of work, took three wickets. The game balanced evenly enough, but once Crawley was out I doubted whether Harrow were a strong enough batting side to pass the Eton score.

The next day, arriving at the ground a little late, I made my way to the seat I had occupied the day before. As I had somewhat expected, the woman was there, motionless, inscrutable, looking indeed as though she had sat all through the night. This time it was she who spoke first. 'Crawley is out, there is no chance of a Harrow win now.' Her actual voice was more perfect than the ghost of it my memory and imagination had created together in the night. C. K. H. Hill-Wood, a fast medium bowler, who bowls off the wrong leg and comes quickly off the pitch, had got Crawley out and he went on to worry N. M. Ford and G. L. Raphael. Neither played at all confidently, and one felt that both of them were acutely aware that the quick fall of another wicket might mean that Harrow would have to fight hard to save the match.

Ford is a disappointing batsman. With all his height, his racquets player's wrists and his family tradition he should be a magnificent forcing player, but his style is cramped and his foot-work ungainly. In half an hour only 13 runs were added, and soon afterwards Ford, trying to pull a full pitch from G. N. Capel-Cure, gave D. Lomax an easy catch at the wicket. Eight runs later Raphael was out to a simple catch in the slips, and the position was perilous for Harrow. K. R. M. Carlisle and C. M. Andreae faced the crisis gallantly and with determination. Carlisle drove beautifully past extra cover and Andreae, with plenty of experience of Lord's to give him confidence, got many runs by forcing the ball round his legs. The pair of them brought the two hundred up together and the match was now one for the first innings lead, for the moral, if not for the actual victory. Both Carlisle and Andreae scored a number of boundaries, Carlisle's to the off, Andreae's to leg, and by luncheon, with 272 runs on the board, Harrow had the match, so far as the first innings was concerned, in their hands.

Afterwards Andreae quickly got his fifty and immediately afterwards was stumped. When one member of a partnership which has put on a lot of runs goes, the other, seven times out of ten, it seems, goes too. What strange law operates here I cannot say but if one watches cricket uninterruptedly over a long space one learns to call the fact that when one goes the other goes by a stronger name than coincidence. It is almost as though there was some queer fatalism about it, that the remaining batsmen were at the mercy of a power stronger than himself and his skill. At any rate one run later Carlisle was caught in the slips off Whittaker, and, with eight Harrow wickets down for 286, the position was once again desperately open.

What a match it would have been were this Harrow's second innings and not their first, but, even as it was, excitement hung electrically in the air, and the shouts of 'E-ton' 'Harrow', which are supposed to be becoming fainter every year, took on the robust note of an earlier age.

There was, as a matter of fact, no breathless climax after all. G. E. M. Pennefather and D. A. M. Rome hit about fiercely as though they were not worrying themselves about such paltry considerations as first innings leads, but were concentrating on the task of putting Harrow far enough ahead to give their bowlers a chance of getting Eton out before stumps were drawn and winning the match by an innings. Eton had all but collapsed last year; this year they would collapse altogether. Quickly the Eton total was passed and the pair went on hitting until the total reached 363 when Pennefather was bowled by a good length ball from M. S. C. Ward. J. Robinson, as diminutive as one imagines E. M. Dowson looked when he first played for Harrow, came in and played copybook cricket while another nineteen runs were added.

When Rome was caught in the deep field Harrow had secured a first innings lead of 64 runs and, with three hours left for play, there was time for all kinds of interesting developments. Everyone remembered the sensational opening to the Eton second innings the year before when L. R. Percival and Lord Hyde were both out before the end of the second over, and for Harrow supporters there was the exhilarating, fluttering hope that history would repeat itself. It was not to be, however. From the very first ball Hope and Cazalet played nonchalantly assured cricket. The word 'collapse' obviously never occurred to them; they were just enjoying some gentle batting practice before stumps were drawn. As over succeeded over, the sense of urgency relaxed, dwindled, vanished. Where there had been silence before talk now broke vivaciously out.

I turned to the woman beside me.

'Another draw, I wish Harrow could win, it would do them a lot of good.'

Slowly, reluctantly, she turned her eyes from the cricket and in her exquisite voice there was a faint note of rebuke. 'There are years to come,' she said slowly. 'Years and years, years and years.'

It seemed as though as she spoke she saw in her words a vision of those years to come which upheld and elated her.

Feebly I murmured, 'You like cricket, then?' She turned towards me and her vacant, slightly protruding eyes searched my face as though to discover an expression, a feature known to her. 'He said that,' she murmured at last, 'that Harrow would win, he was always so optimistic, so full of plans. The things he was going to do! He loved cricket so. He thought he might even play for Harrow if he stayed long enough. He always said they would win, though. In 1914 he said, "We shall win next year, mother." There was no match in 1915, you see, so he was wrong, he was wrong.'

She looked again towards the cricket, her eyes dwelling on the players with mild and gentle satisfaction.

Horrified, I stammered, 'I am so sorry, so terribly sorry.' I did not think she had heard, but after a moment or so her face, seeming grotesquely large now, bent near mine. 'You are not old enough, young man, to know how easy it is to forget, not half old enough.' She paused, and then with a weary air as of one explaining something familiar and understood she went on, 'When you are old it is difficult to remember, to remember clearly. Memory lives not in the brain but in places, young man. You must go out and find memory if you want her, she waits but does not come.'

She stopped gazing at me, and took in, in a slow and comprehensive glance, the pavilion, the coaches, the stands, the score board as though to illustrate to me how, in this ground at any rate, memory waited for her faithfully and enduringly.

'There is no point in waiting now,' I said. 'Cazalet will get his hundred, I should think. I shan't stop to see him.' I hesitated. 'You will wait to the end?'

Her voice, resonant, deep and beautiful, echoed my words. 'Till the end.'

I walked away from her, but before passing out of sight, I turned back to look at her. She sat still, a massive and incongruous figure, watching with a glowing intensity the last few overs of a dying game. 'Memory waits,' she had said, and I know that I shall never enter Lord's again without finding her ghost there, tragically and pitifully evoking the memories of her dead son.

*from* ENGLAND OVER *1927*

# Hutton, Hobbs and the Classical Style
## NEVILLE CARDUS

The characteristics of the classical style in cricket, or in anything else, are precision of technique, conservation of energy, and power liberated proportionately so that the outlines of execution are clear and balanced. Hutton is the best example to be seen at the present time of the classical style of batsmanship. He is a model for the emulation of the young. We cannot say as much of, for instance, Worrell, who is the greatest stroke-player of the moment; it would be perilous if a novice tried to educate himself by faithfully observing the play of Worrell. A sudden snick through the slips by Worrell might cause us to lift an eyebrow, but we wouldn't think that something had gone wrong with the element in which Worrell naturally revels; for it is understood that Worrell and all cricketers of his kind live on the rim of their technical scope. A snick by a Jack Hobbs is a sort of disturbance of a cosmic orderliness. It is more than a disturbance; it is a solecism in fact, as though a great writer of prose were to fall into an untidy period, or actually commit bad grammar. The classical style admits of no venturings into the unknown, of no strayings from first principles. A dissonance is part and parcel of romantic excess and effort; all right in Strauss, impossible in

Mozart, where not a star of a semi-quaver may fall. The exponent of the classical style observes, and is content to observe, the limitations imposed by law, restraint, taste. He finds his liberty within the confines of equipoise.

I suppose that the three or four exemplars of the truly classic style of batsmanship have been W. G. Grace, Arthur Shrewsbury, Hayward and Hobbs; I can't include Maclaren; for something of a disturbing rhetoric now and then entered into his generally noble and correct diction. Trumper was, of course, all styles, as C. B. Fry has said, from the lyrical to the dramatic. Maclaren once paid, in a conversation with me, the most generous tribute ever uttered by one great player to another. 'I was supposed to be something of a picture gallery myself,' said he. 'People talked of the "Grand Manner" of Maclaren. But compared with Victor I was as a cab-horse to a Derby winner. . . .'

In our own day, Hutton comes as near as anybody to the classical style, though there are moments when the definition of it, as expounded above, needs to be loosened to accommodate him. Dignity, and a certain lordliness, are the robes and very presence of classicism. Frankly, Hutton many times is obliged to wear the dress or 'overhauls' of utility; moreover, his resort to the passive 'dead bat', though shrewd and tactical, scarcely suggests grandeur or the sovereign attitude. The truth is that the classical style of batsmanship was the consequence of a classical style of bowling – bowling which also observed precision, clarity of outline, length, length, length! It is as difficult to adapt classical calm and dignity of poise to modern in-swingers and 'googlies' as it would be to translate Milton into Gertrude Stein, or Haydn into Tin-pan Alley.

But Hutton, in the present far from classical epoch, follows the line of Hobbs, and if all that we know today of batsmanship as a science were somehow taken from our consciousness, the grammar and alphabet could be deduced from the cricket of Hutton, and codified again; he is all the text-books in an omnibus edition. Compared with him Bradman, who has been accused of bloodless mechanical efficiency, was as a volcanic eruption threatening to destroy Pompeii.

We need to be careful of what we mean if we call Hutton a stylist, which, we have agreed, he is. Style is commonly but mistakenly supposed to be indicated by a flourish added to masterful skill, a spreading of peacock's feathers. (The peacock is efficiently enough created and marvellously beautiful without that.) Style with Hutton is not a vanity, not something deliberately cultivated. It is a bloom and finish, which have come unselfconsciously from organized technique rendered by experience instinctive in its rhythmical and attuned movements. His drives to the off-side have a strength that is generated effortlessly from the physical dynamo, through nerve and muscle, so that we might almost persuade ourselves that the current of his energy, his life-force, is running electrically down the bat's handle into the blade, without a single short-circuit or fusing, thence into the ball, endowing it, as it speeds over the grass, with the momentum of no dead material object compact of leather, but of animate life.

His 'follow through' in his drives is full and unfettered. But the style is the man: there is no squandering in a Hutton innings. Bradman, to refer again to the cricketer known as an 'adding-machine' was a spendthrift compared to Hutton, who is economical always, counting every penny, every single, of his opulent income of runs. We shall understand, when we come to consider the way of life that produced him, his habitat, why with Hutton, the style is indeed the man himself.

Some of us are obliged to work hard for our places in the sun; others have greatness thrust upon them. A fortunate few walk along divinely appointed ways, the gift of prophecy marking their courses. Hutton was scarcely out of the cradle of the Yorkshire nursery nets when Sutcliffe foretold the master to come, not rolling the eye of fanaticism but simply in the manner of a shrewd surveyor of 'futures'. But Sutcliffe knew all the time that the apprenticeship of Hutton had been served in that world of vicissitude and distrust which are the most important factors

forming the North of England character under the pressure of
an outlook which thinks it's as well to 'take nowt on trust' – not
even a fine morning. In his first trial for the Yorkshire Second
XI, May 1933, he was dismissed for nothing against Cheshire.
Four years after, when he was first invited to play for England,
he also made nothing, bowled Cowie. Next innings he was
'slightly more successful' – 'c. Vivian, b. Cowie 1'. Though he
was only eighteen years old when he scored a hundred for
Yorkshire in July 1934 – the youngest Yorkshire cricketer to
achieve such distinction – illness as well as the run of the luck
of the game hindered his progress, dogged him with apparent
malice. When he reappeared on the first-class scene again it was
just in time to take part in that dreadful holocaust at Hudders-
field, when Essex bowled Yorkshire out for 31 and 99. Hutton's
portion was two noughts. In his very first match for Yorkshire
at Fenners in 1934 J. G. W. Davies ran him out brilliant'y – for
nought. Until yesteryear, in fact, the Fates tried him. The
accident to his left forearm, incurred while training in a
Commando course, nearly put an end to his career as a cricketer
altogether.

He has emerged from a hard school. It has never been with
Hutton a case of roses all the way; he had to dig his cricket out
of his bones; a bat and the Yorkshire and England colours
didn't fall into his mouth like silver cutlery. According to the
different threads or warp of our nature and being, a different
texture is an inevitable consequence. There is no softness in
Hutton's psychological or, therefore, in his technical make-up.
And there are broadly two ways of getting things done in our
limited world. We walk either by faith or by reason. There are,
in other words, the born inexplicable geniuses and those we
can account for in terms of the skill they have inherited. They
are in a way the by-products of skill and experience accumulated
and still pregnant in their formative years; their contribution
is to develop the inheritance to a further, though rationally
definable stage of excellence. But we know where they come
from and how. Hutton is one of the greatest of these. But a

Compton, or, better for our illustration, a Trumper seems to spring into being with all his gifts innate and in full bloom from the beginning. He improved in certainty of touch with experience, but as soon as he emerges from the chrysalis there is magic in his power, something that 'defies augury'; he is a law unto himself, therefore dangerous as a guide or example to others who are encased in mortal fallibility. But I am wandering from a contemplation of classicism and Hutton.

The unique or ineluctable genius isn't, of course, necessarily the great master. No cricketer has possessed, or rather been more possessed by genius, than Ranji; for his mastery was the most comprehensive known yet in all the evolution of the game. Hobbs summed-up in himself all that had gone before him in established doctrine of batsmanship. He was encyclopaedic; we could deduce from his cricket not only grammar but history. We could infer from any Hobbs innings the various forces that had produced and perfected his compendious technique over years which witnessed changes which were revolutionary as never before, ranging from the fast bowlers of the post-Grace period, in which Hobbs was nurtured, to the advent of the modern refinements and licences – swerve and 'googly' and all the rest. When Hobbs began his career the attack he faced day by day was much the same in essentials as the one familiar enough to W.G. But very soon Hobbs was confronted by bowling of the new order of disrule, which W.G. couldn't understand; and Hobbs was not only the first to show how the 'googly' should be detected and exposed and how swerve should be played in the middle of the blade; he taught others and led the way. Hobbs was the bridge over which classical cricket marched to the more complex epoch of the present. Hutton is the only cricketer living at the moment who remotely resembles Hobbs by possession of what I shall call here a thoroughly schooled or canonical method. He doesn't commit crudities. The 'wrong' stroke at times – yes, because of an error of judgment. But never an *uninstructed* stroke.

He is a quiet thoughtful Yorkshireman, with widely-spaced

blue eyes that miss nothing. And his batting is quiet and thoughtful; even in his occasional punishing moods, when his strokes are animating as well as ennobling the field, he doesn't get noisy or rampagious. His stance at the wicket is a blend of easeful muscular organization and keen watchfulness. The left shoulder points rather more to the direction of mid-on than would satisfy Tom Hayward; but here again is evidence that Hutton is a creature or rather a creation of his environment; that is to say, he is obliged to solve problems of spin and swerve not persistently put to Hayward day by day. With Hayward and his school, the left leg was the reconnoitring force, the cat's whisker, the pioneer that moved in advance to 'sight' the enemy. With Hutton it is the right leg that is the pivot, the springboard. But often he allowed it to change into an anchor which holds him back when he should be moving out on the full and changing tide of the game. He is perfect at using the 'dead' bat – rendering it passive, a blanket or a buffer, against which spin or sudden rise from the pitch come into contact as though with an anaesthetic. He plays so close to the ball, so much over it that he has acquired a sort of student's slope of the shoulders; at the sight of a fizzing off-break he is arched like a cat. Even when he drives through the covers, his head and eyes incline downwards, and the swing of the bat doesn't go past the front leg until the ball is struck. He can check the action of any stroke extremely late, and so much does he seem to see a delivery all the way that we are perplexed that so frequently he is clean-bowled by a length well up to him. From the back foot he can hit straight for four; and all his hits leave an impressive suggestion of power not entirely expended.

We shall remember, after we have relegated his 364 against Australia at Kennington Oval in 1938 to the museum of records in sport rather than to the things that belong to cricket, his innings at Sydney in the second Test match during the 1946–1947 rubber; only 37 but so dazzling in clean diamond-cut strokes that old men present babbled of Victor Trumper. He has even while playing for Yorkshire more than once caused some raising of the eyebrows. At Nottingham in 1948 he not only played, but played well, Miller, Johnston and Johnson as though for his own private and personal enjoyment. But usually he subdues his hand to what it works in – Yorkshire cricket. I have heard people say that he is not above 'playing for himself'. Well, seeing that he is Yorkshire to the bone's marrow, we should find ourselves metaphysically involved if we tried to argue that he is ever not playing for Yorkshire.

There is romance even in Yorkshire cricket, though they keep quiet about it. Romance has in fact visited the life and career of Hutton. In July 1930, the vast field of Headingley was a scene of moist, hot congestion with, apparently, only one cool, clean, well-brushed individual present, name of Bradman, who during the five hours' traffic of the crease, made at will 300 runs, and a few more, before half-past six. He returned to the pavilion as though fresh from a band-box; the rest of us, players, umpires, crowd and scorers, especially the scorers, were exhausted; dirty, dusty and afflicted by a sense of the vanity of life. In all the heat and burden of this day at Leeds, more than twenty years ago, a boy of fourteen years was concealed amongst the boiling multitude; and so many of these thousands seethed and jostled that one of them, especially an infant in the eyes of the law, couldn't possibly (you might have sworn) have made the slightest difference to what we were all looking at, or to the irony of subsequent history. The solemn fact is that as Bradman compiled the 334 which was then the record individual score in a Test match, the boy hidden in the multitude was none other than the cricketer chosen already by the gods to break this record, if not Bradman's heart, eight years afterwards.

*from* CRICKET ALL THE YEAR *1952*

# Men and Moments

## EDMUND BLUNDEN

I will yield to the temptation to say a word still on men famous in the cricket world of my time. Perhaps brevity of allusion best befits an onlooker. Of Harold Larwood, whose cricket life bewildered, even embroiled the multitudes in Britain and Australia, I chiefly recall something too slight to have been recorded in the press. I was going into the Oval ground, and as I went I was raising my head to spy over the hats of the front rows of spectators; and I saw the most terrifying fast ball wing down that I had seen. It did nothing; it was a full toss. But the authorship even to my eye was unique. I had seen, if I saw nothing more by that hand, the best fast bowler of the day.

Don Bradman has made so much cricket history of the marvellous sort that one scarcely ventures to speak of him; but in a Test on the ground just referred to, he brought off a shot which no doubt was to him just one of a thousand like it. A fast ball was bounced at him, head high; he had not come to the crease more than five minutes before, but he swung his body and bat as if stung to anger, and the ball went flying almost straight behind him like a cannon-ball into the crowd. A. P. F. Chapman was fielding deep on the off side, to Tate's bowling, at Lord's.

Bradman's score was 254, the sunshine was such as conspires with batsmen and not bowlers, and he meant to go well beyond that 254. He drove one of Tate's accurate-length balls as before, but the hit was a little off the ground; Chapman was sensitive to this from the start, and with a long right arm, he collected the hit at a few inches from the floor and Don Bradman was out. I could not have dreamed of this, nor could most of us, but it was done. Chapman mopped his forehead. At Manchester, when the Australian innings was hardening inexorably, Woodfull's partner played the ball well down past Hammond in the slips – a safe run. Hammond moved, gathered, turned and flung and Woodfull, spying danger and making a vast attempt to get home, was out. Nobody in that learned cricket crowd seemed less bewildered than I or very possibly than the batsman. Hammond appears to have cancelled the duration of time. These are but commas written on a spectator's brain. Greatness can be identified, like the touch of a painter, in a detail. Prescience is worth seeing in a sceptical world.

Of Hobbs the well-graced I particularly retain a very simple impression, but it has outlived all the others; it was his ability to make the lightning delivery appear to be in no hurry at all, so far as he and his bat were concerned. There was no fast bowling to that immense clarity. E. Macdonald, in one match, came to this conclusion, and acted on it. It was a pity, for Macdonald bowling fast was good to look upon. Of Hendren, whose powerful refusal to take any situation for lost we shall not all forget, I hold one memory in special, and yet it does not touch his great days, any more than Mr John Betjeman's rhyming his name (not at all irreverently) with 'rhododendron'. It was his adieu to the cricket in which he had from east to west been so general a favourite. He played his little innings of nimble neat shots, just had time for one of his old mighty bangs to the railings, was then bowled with not the slightest doubt in the world, turned at once to go with a shake of the bat at the shattered stumps – and having paced away gaily twenty or thirty yards stopped, looked back rather sadly, waved them all a good-bye. The humorist this once had not the leading part in an action on the green by Hendren.

C. F. Walters never made a century in a Test Match against Australia. A score of 82 at Lord's had in its progress shown every sign of becoming one. It was the most flowing, well-tuned, elegant innings that I saw in those formidable games; the happy discernment and advancing originality of the artist were smiling through it all. And yet it is the end of that composition which haunts me. The batsman played a ball that popped on the leg side a little off the ground, and that little air was enough for A'Beckett (I think it was he) to make a conjurer's catch. Walters, standing at his block, saw this as one witnessing event in detachment, and in the most thoughtful manner he played his stroke again before he left the wicket; the experience presumably would lead to still finer control and selection next time, and the question of a century would be solved accordingly. But it would not be the essential question.

And these notings must cease, and I am alarmed a little that I have been letting them take their course so far. One of the crowd, and not of the most regular or sharp-eyed either, how should I be entitled to any impressions at all on these leaders of the subtlest game in the world, or to conjectures on their motives, their distinguishing qualities? Yet according to the tradition of judges and umpires, I may trust to the benefit of the doubt, and all the more because these little memoranda represent at all events a tried devotion. Not wholly altered from what I was in boyhood, I still find in the master cricketers and the intense and never forecastable competitions between them an apparition of the heroic. Better thus, than in the ancient style. A classical scholar of my acquaintance, who has been if he is not now among the names that count in his field of studies throughout Europe, often tells me that he has ceased to find much pleasure in the poems of Homer; he cannot now endure the cataloguing of heroic carnage in those hexameters. 'And the beauty of the matter was, that the world was no sooner conquered by one hero than it wanted conquering again by another.' This beauty at least continues as an ever prospective force in our cricket, but the world which is conquered there is that of care and dull reality and the strain and dry urgency of the cities; or it is the region of Technique, a god who lends some redeeming virtue to every mortal occupation, and made the child-like De Quincey write a paper on Murder. Cricket will serve us as chivalry, though its armour is limited and simple, and only Hendren ever sped forth into its lists with the addition of a helmet, seemingly supplied from his own comic workshops.

That innovation was not intended otherwise than as a protest against innovation; and though cricket undergoes its changes the affections rest upon its continuity. Then should we resent the inclination of man to possess some central point, some home and haven, to which he may come back at last and not feel estranged?

So we'll go no more a-roving
So late into the night. . . .

Even Byron, in *Don Juan*, is thought to have been uttering a curve of experiences, circling back at last so far as he could see into the England where he too had played cricket. It was not his recreation. But it was part of the appeal which was hovering over him at the age of thirty-six; part of the country life which after all he depicted from the distance to which changefulness had taken him in colours as fresh and in tracery as precise as if he had been walking among his old lawns and lily-ponds and Gothic arches. Byron at Lord's would have been a disconcerting presence to some of the other patrons, but not to the spirit of the place.

Yes, cricket changes – the great matches I should say more than our local attempts. In my father's boyhood, the county player was not the dedicated being that he now is, but the same man to whom, in the evening after he had been serving up his donkey-drops on the big ground, you took your shoes to be cobbled. Though I had no such domestic contacts with these performers I am reminded of a sunny day when I resolved to enter a shop and purchase, with the end of my resources, a clever and inexpensive book called *Who's Who in Cricket*. A mild little man with sandy hair came from among the racks of bats and pads, laid the item in my hands and told me I was doing the right thing. He took the book back for a moment, and through his glasses examined an entry or two, and I thought that it was almost reluctantly he went off to help another and surely more affluent customer. Afterwards I perceived that I had been waited upon by Bobby Abel, whose top score for Surrey on the neighbouring ground was something like 357 – and that is still reckoned a bag of runs, from China to Peru.

The old days, the days that were sunlit, before mine, lacked a formal boundary. A big hit frequently forced the fieldsman to hurl himself among the legs of the spectators, some of whom were quadrupeds. But then the batsmen had to run out their runs. We know the hit for four, to the railings or the ropes or such a definite circumference, and the saving of effort which it makes on both sides. Games on sound wickets naturally go on longer, and an art of economic boundary hits has grown up. I believe too that to hit a six formerly, you had to strike the ball quite out of the ground; these degenerate days require no more than it should soar over the ropes, which run well within the total space. Pampered moderns! But is there much in the effects? One of the last games before the War, bits of which I saw at Oxford over the heads of a swarm of newly hatched priests – the Churches have ever regarded cricket-watching as a venial sin if it is any – was marked by a disorderly deed on the part of Perks, a bowler of merit. He does not usually bat for long. This tall young man arriving at the end of the innings made one or two awkward passes at the bowling and then he connected; and up went the ball, to scare a pigeon somewhere on the roof of the pavilion. The bowler put more pace on the next, but Perks saw it all the way, and it went aerially a bit farther. When it came back, and that took time, our representative tried his yorker on the leg stump, but that seemed merely to solace and allure the batsman, and the ball not only went out of the ground, but almost out of the Parks and out of business. These three sixes might have satisfied the examiners in 1880; or our dear old connoisseur of cricket, cities, literature, anecdote, personality, and indeed all this floating world, E. V. Lucas. I have seldom been more apprehensive for a celebrated man than when at the after-stage of a dinner given by a club in town he was called upon for what he had the utmost misery in supplying – a speech. In a solemn style he got himself to the back of his chair, nervously extracted a bit of paper from his pocket, and slowly recited four lines of verse from it. Despite the sinking tones in which he read, the last words proved to be of an 'uplift' nature:

And a sixer climbs the sky.

To continue, the Press has done much to make the game in its major form more of a total warfare than it used to be. I confess I rather like the excitement and the eloquence. The evening paper during a Test Match is apt to provide us with three several accounts of the play. They fill most of the issue. And not content with that, there are some who listen to the radio descriptions! Well, I may be condemned to some penalty in the underworld for my infirmity, but I cannot help considering all these; I sometimes dwell on the variants in the narratives as fondly as an editor of Shakespeare, deciding whether Hamlet said that he wishes his too solid, his sullied, his sallied, or souled flesh would melt. If only time would run forward merrily, and set this body again in Rupert's little car – that rural vehicle, pulled along not by petrol alone but by an abstractional nannygoat – among the woods of the Thames valley, while with loud beating hearts we listened to the latest facts of the duel between Edrich or Compton and Nupen or Mitchell! But it may not be beyond hope. As for the newspapers, there will be no crashing Letter to the Editor from me when old Time reverting to holiday mood exchanged the issue of essays on the bomb-psychology of the Italian or German public, or the tiff between the agricultural optimists and the Government department, or the superior vitamination of sawdust steaks over the butcher's variety, for one ridiculous plump gazette containing C. B. Fry, P. G. H. Fender, Bruce Harris, Anon and Stop Press on the current fixture at Adelaide. But, all the same, as Charles Lamb observed, 'No one ever put down a newspaper without a feeling of disappointment'.

And does cricket change? Add to all the above all you will of modified rules, of improved equipment, of the horrid ingenuity of groundsmen, of the universal circulation of the best principles as understood by the readers of the averages; add the quickening of our nervous demands; and still cricket is not so vastly other than when I first wonderingly accompanied my father to its healthy feast. On with the dance! Dance it is, and I fancy in naming it so I may be in the school of C. B. Fry himself, whom I cannot forget as he once led the way in the full radiance of the poetry of forward play and unified motion. It is one of the most stately of all dances, and a seventeenth-century poet might have proved it to be not less related to Nature's great round than the ancient Grecian theatre, or Gratiana 'beating the happy pavement'. Among those whom I have caught sight of, quietly revering it, regard for his shyness keeps me from naming the most perfect student, the most poetic seer of the Grecian form whom this century has anywhere produced. To him, if one may interpret his watching face, those white-clad figures in shining constellation about the axis of the two wickets are as the effigies on the friezes, or vases, of his lifelong remodelling. Lovers of the poetry of Keats must not dismiss me as unworthy of further association with them if I say of the cricket of my time that its groups and postures and borders are not unimaginable as pictures on another Grecian Urn such as he contemplated; or else I will attempt to convince them when the passing cloud of war leaves our greensward as golden as it used to be – sometimes.

> A leaf-fringed legend haunts about its shape
> Of deities or mortals or of both.

The cloud of war is passing. May comes in and the hedges are white-clad; the cows sit munching and staring at the first matches still coming to life by the white walls of the villages; this year at last there seems a dispersed feeling that the game may be played and talked over without ghostliness. It was a Yorkshire corporal who told me with a voice of conviction, while he tapped a malevolent wicket almost affectionately as though it created a dream of home, that Sutcliffe will be playing again in the days to come. Hutton too – but that was not in doubt. Sutcliffe is now a cricketer of unknown antiquity – let no one worry me with dates – who has never been a beat behind the newest geniuses, and whose proceeding on his handsome way after his second world war will quite cancel that interruption in an agreeable culture. I see him in the days to come holding the game together; the light will travel from his serene presence on one ground to all of them. This invincible man now represents his partner Hobbs as well – at least, when once again he seats himself on his bat after sweetly delaying to complete his fifty, the imagination will also perceive Hobbs at the other end reflectively twirling his bat or sounding the marl with it, as once upon a time. The inquirer into myths and what underlies them may tell us how such complete understanding is created as ruled the hour when these two ran their sharp runs. It is expressible in the terms of Shakepeare's enigma of the Phoenix and the Turtle:

> Single nature's double name
> Neither two nor one was called.

It might be worth considering whether the official score should not record these adunations of cricketers as single effects, under some shared name (on the analogy of the two poetesses who wrote in identity as Michael Field). Gregory and Macdonald, Hirst and Rhodes, Makepeace and Hallows, Fry and Vine, Larwood and Voce – are these couples not much more, or at least more potent and executive, than the addition of the individuals exerting their powers independently? What was Gilbert, what was Sullivan after that unholy little quarrel over the carpet in the office? which, like the ancient cataclysm said to have severed Dover from Calais, left these inseparables

> Standing apart, the scars remaining:
> A dreary sea now flows between.

Sutcliffe, great and good, like Queen Victoria in the song, will revive in the grey-headed and instil in the young all that his gallant companions have given to the fields of summer – he will perhaps give the boys the autographs of those whose glories shine entwined among his own. But then, there may be in the reconstituted game an edict against autograph ambushes, or rather commandos. It is time to re-educate youth. On the green, the cricketers are above mortality—

> The leaders are fairest
> But all are divine:

and are they to be waylaid with stubs of pencil and little books where bibulous Uncle Josh has drawn his seaside joke and clever Cousin Doreen has illustrated the advice 'Don't be wet' with a pink duck hoisting an umbrella? No: but when Mr C. I. J. Smith recites his selection from 'The Lay of the Last Minstrel' or Mr ('Tich') Cornford lectures on 'Ruskin's Brighton Period' then let them be treated as authors and duly reduced to auto-graph-yielding substrata.

The author who will take for his province The Cricket Spectator has, I believe, yet to appear. Balzac sought his subjects on the wrong side of the channel. The onlooker at the great matches is not always so comprehensible as one might have supposed. I must mention one gentleman who, on a change of bowling which relieved Kent's wizard and gave Todd the ball, loudly informed all in range that Freeman was at length going on, and as for A. P. Freeman he explained with generous pleasure that 'We call him Bill, you know, his real name's not Bill, it's Ernest, but down here we call him Bill'. This private information tangled the audience up and no comment could be offered, but we wondered why this informative man had come to a county match. Especially as he spent the rest of the time, when not spreading his strange tidings, digging into a sort of carpet bag for food. 'Used to play for the Professor's team, ha, that was before *your* time – Professor W. A. G. Grace's side – him and Gilligan – the Rev. Theophilus Gilligan', – a swig of tea and a doughnut.

Alas and alas, too many of us in the crowd on all occasions are not so unlike this warm-hearted but inexact personage. I blush a little as I extract him from the past, for he is recognizable; with very little question he is me. Sitting by him, I make my comments and criticisms on every ball bowled, every stroke played, every tactical move; but to speak truth it is all seen in a glass darkly. We love to sun ourselves in fancy 'out in the middle' but it looks and it is different out there. The fable extends its application beyond cricket, and I need not dwell on its meaning where, for example, 'the conduct of the allies' is being discussed with vehemence over the customary foam. But some of us have been rash enough to write biographies of eminent men who died before we were born, and whose voices we never once heard. Heavens, how did we venture that far? And human nature being what it is we may again. They will forgive us in any Elysian Fields there may be, or they may have been quietly

ignoring all that haps beneath the moon.

But I am uncomfortably suspicious that when we were writing out our plausible and (so we heard) our readable version of their difficult conditions, their intellectual or domestic experiences, feelings in grief or conquest, we were really saying, 'We call him Bill, you know, his real name's not Shakespeare but down here they like to call him Actor Bill – used to do a bit of pelmanism on the stage, previous to the old Britannia being sold', – and the play goes on.

*from* CRICKET COUNTRY *1943*

# Ashes Regained (1953)

## A. A. THOMSON

Nobody can conceive the misery I underwent during the summer of 1953 before the Ashes were safe. During the Lord's Test I gave up cricket; not merely playing cricket, but watching, listening to, arguing about and agonizing over cricket. The time was 6.30 p.m. on Monday, 29th June, 1953. I had just seen England go in to start the task of making 343 in the fourth innings on a worn pitch. The hideously incredible score was 20 for three and the victims were Hutton, the Old Master, Graveney, the Young Master, and Kenyon, the only man who had scored a century for a county against the Australians that season. I could bear no more. Why should I be lacerated by raging, tearing emotion? Even Hamlet, Lear and our other leading sufferers were never asked to sup on horror to that extent. I had devoted far too much of my life to this utterly irrational game. I would chuck the whole thing and take to Strindberg for amusement.

Why, after all that, I should find myself next morning in St John's Wood Road is a question for a psychiatrist, and I would not believe a word a psychiatrist said, anyhow. It may have been the criminal returning to the scene of the crime. It may have been an exceptionally morbid streak in my nature. At any rate, I found myself in my usual place in front of the Tavern and there, beside me, was Albert Osmotherly. Albert is one of the too many Yorkshiremen who infest Lord's. He glared at me:

'Thought you were never coming back?'

'I thought *you* weren't.'

He shrugged his shoulders, frowned across at the Father Time scoreboard – 20-3-2 and delivered judgment.

'They'll never get them,' he said.

This was an understatement of the position. All the morning

386

papers had said, in varying tones of pomposity, recrimination and disdain, that England would never get them. It was, they said, the fault of the weather, the captain, the selectors, the Minister of Education and the worn patch at the Nursery End.

'What's more,' said Albert, 'they don't deserve to win.'

'Why not, if they could?'

'Hutton,' he asserted accusingly, 'dropped three catches.'

'What of it?' I retorted, stung momentarily out of my coma. 'Nelson was often sea-sick.'

Albert plunged back into gloom.

The umpires came out. The fieldsmen came out. The batsmen, Compton and Watson, came out. It seemed almost strange that a clergyman did not meet them at the pavilion gate.

'I'll give 'em till lunch time,' said Albert as though he were making a wildly generous offer.

From the beginning play was quiet, with all the pensive tranquillity of obsequies at which the hearse has not yet turned up. Suddenly Compton forgot he was at a funeral and hit three fours. When I clapped, Albert looked at me disapprovingly.

'Oh, him,' said Albert. He said this with no personal disrespect but from a firm conviction that southerners were not serious characters. And by a southerner he meant, of course, a man born south of a line drawn between Sheffield and Barnsley.

At twenty to one Compton was out for a polished 33 and Bailey came in.

'Oh, him,' said Albert.

At lunch the score, against all probabilities, was 114 for 4.

'At least,' I said, 'they've lasted till now.'

'You wait,' muttered Albert, as though he had a couple of earthquakes up his sleeve.

I do not know what time hope began to revive, like a numbed gum coming out of a local anaesthetic. Slowly it dawned on me that, come rope, come rack, seven men still lived with bats in their hands. Why should not at least some of them survive? Albert looked shocked when I put this to him.

'You must be daft,' he said.

There was something almost uncanny in the way Watson and Bailey supported my daftness. Watson, fair, trim and cool, took the good balls in the middle of the bat and pulled the short ones, with force and velocity, away to leg. Bailey, with consistent courage, got in the way of the ball, mostly with the bat, sometimes with the pad and sometimes, painfully, with the fingers. But if he observed subconsciously: 'this hurts me more than it hurts you,' it gave the bowlers no comfort. The bowlers toiled and spun, Lindwall with controlled fury, Johnston with force and guile, Miller with windmill whirlings, Benaud with quickish tweakers and Ring with waspish cunning. Yet in vain. Were these the avenging furies that had torn England to tatters the evening before? When Watson and Bailey went in for tea at 183 for four, I would willingly have subscribed to a fund for providing both of them with gold cups and platinum saucers.

'You wait,' said Albert. 'Tea always unsettles them.'

It was over an hour after tea before anything unsettled them. Ball by ball, confidence grew, not in the hearts of Watson and Bailey, who had had supreme confidence all along, but in the spectators, who began to gather flickering hope. And hope naturally bred anxiety. As hope gleamed, terrors revived. The crowd showed a slight tendency to gasp and groan, and to sigh with relief when the ball was safe, untouched, in the wicket-keeper's gloves. I died a thousand deaths and would not have missed one of them.

It was at ten to six, when the heroic pair looked as though they would remain for ever in their heroic attitudes that Watson suddenly became mortal, touched one to the slips and then, as fate so often wills, his partner departed soon after. The match was back in the melting-pot and hearts were in mouths again. Were we fair to Freddy Brown, who, though grand, is grandly fallible? The more he made us nervous with his bold and ponderous hits, the more we cheered him, and Evans too, though he was not quite getting the ball in the middle of the bat as he gets them in the middle of his gloves. Ten past six, quarter past six, twenty past, twenty-five past. . . . I shut my eyes. Brown was out. All round me people were frenziedly counting how many balls there were to come. Johnny Wardle came along. If he had a care in the world, it did not show. One, two, three. Wardle, a born survivor, survived. The umpires took off the bails. Who dies, if England lives? The crowd went mad. Albert flung his hat in the air and leaped to meet it in the first steps of a wild Zulu war-dance.

'I knew they'd do it,' he panted, 'but it doesn't do to speak too soon.'

And if I suffered at Lord's, what of Headingley? Do you remember a film in which Naunton Wayne and the ever-lamented Basil Radford wandered round Europe, worrying in a delightfully ridiculous way about what was happening in the Test Match at Manchester? Like so many misfortunes that occur to other folk, it seemed funny at the time. I waited until the Manchester Test was safely over. (If I didn't have a heart attack when Australia finished at 35 for eight, I shall live to be a hundred.) That should have been good enough. Before the 1953 Leeds Test came along I was determined to stand no nonsense. I was going to visit romantic Austria and moonlit Venice, Bride of the Adriatic. Surely, after Wardle had taken four for 7, a man might be allowed to relax for a fortnight. What a fellow wants is to get away from the atom bomb, the cold war and the imminence of national bankruptcy; in short, all the dull routine of everyday life, and soak his soul in peace and beauty. Though, of course, it was difficult for the soul to be at rest, with Hutton suffering from fibrositis. . . .

I deliberately turned my back on my own country. All went well at first. The sea was calm, the journey across Belgium and Germany was full of interest, and there was pleasure, not to mention instruction in seeing Turin, Milan and the long cause-way that leads to Venice. . . . That first glimpse in the soft evening light of the Grand Canal has an enchantment that age cannot wither. Byron saw it. The Brownings saw it. The passenger in the gondola abreast of mine saw it, leaned forward to wonder at it and, as he did so, accidentally dropped his hat in the water.

He said, unexpectedly and rather loudly, that it was a fair cow, and this peculiar ejaculation rather than any marked accent, stamped him as a citizen of the great Australian Commonwealth. When I retrieved his hat for him, we discovered that we were being paddled to the same hotel. He was an amiable companion and our relations from the beginning were extremely pleasant. I was determined not to be the first to mention the Test Match. He talked to me of mediaeval glass, the magic of San Marco and Ruskin's Stones of Venice. I talked to him about Bondi Beach, Chips Rafferty and the ornithorhyncus or duck-billed water-mole. I hope I appeared witty and nonchalant. It was hard work.

'Never mind,' I said to myself, 'I'll find an English paper tomorrow.'

But I was unlucky. The following day I searched Venice from the Bridge of Sighs to the Lido (pavilion end), without even finding out whether England had lost the toss. (I need not have worried about that. Hutton never won the toss that year.) My Australian friend, whose name was Martin, kept slipping away on the pretext of posting post-cards or buying some Venetian glass to send to his wife, but he always came back without (I suspected) having found what he wanted. Before he left Venice he was beginning to have a haggard look. I had, I think, lost several pounds myself.

We came back from Italy to Austria by coach over the historic Brenner Pass. The majestic Dolomites were wreathed in clouds, and Martin and I were wrapped in silence. It was in the Customs shed at the frontier that I first saw an English newspaper. It was stuffed under the straps of a rucksack worn by a big bony citizen in the crowd in front of me. I had virtually to stand on my head to see it and what I saw played havoc with my blood-pressure.

'Feeling faint?' asked Martin considerately.

'If I can read upside down,' I murmured, 'Hutton has got a duck.'

'Ha-ha – I mean, sorry. You'd better have a stiff peg of slivowitz. That should pull you round.'

For the next four days my agony was less in extent but more concentrated. Hampered though we were by the ignorance of foreigners, we managed to ascertain the score once, or nearly once, a day. We had to fight for every paper just as England was fighting for every run. In Innsbruck I followed a respectable old gentleman the length of the famous Maria-Theresienstrasse under the impression that he was carrying the *Manchester Guardian* only to discover that he was really a German professor, flourishing the *Frankfurter Zeitung*.

(England 167, Australia 161 for three.) At the moment when we obtained the news, from a kindly American who little knew how he was turning the dagger in my wound, that Australia had filched – you couldn't call it scored – 48 for the last wicket, we were standing in front of the great cathedral at Salzburg, listening to Mozart, a man whom, in my less agitated moments, I have always considered as good as Victor Trumper in his own line. We were actually hanging by a bit of wire in the hair-raising cable railway car 5,000 feet above the Hungerburg plateau, likes peas in a matchbox, when we learned, from a sympathetic fellow-pea, that England's fate hung equally in the balance. Hutton was out in the second innings, too, but Edrich and Compton, old campaigners both, were making a fight of it. But we never heard another word that day.

It was on the way home that Fate began to turn the screw. We set off on a long railway journey, through a corner of Germany, back into Austria, and then into Germany again. Leaving the train we boarded a steamer, like a Mississippi show-boat, to sail between castled crags and vine-clad slopes along the poet's 'wide and winding Rhine'. It was while passing the notorious Lorelei rock that I learned that five English batsmen had been lured to their doom and that my beloved country was only about 70 runs on. Why did I ever leave home? I should never have strayed all this way from Headingley, much less from my own wireless set.

After that we were on the long night train. I do not suppose Martin slept well. I know I did not. The train roared through the darkness. It was three o'clock before I dozed off. When I woke we were at Cologne. I stumbled out sleepily on to a darkened platform. By some miracle there was a bookstall right in front of me and, what was more, an English paper. I flung the boy a mark (about one and eightpence) and bundled back into the train. What was this? There was only one event in contemporary English history which interested me, and I could find no mention of it. Our return journey had brought us in front of schedule. This was Thursday's paper. I had missed the result, which would have been published in Wednesday's. In quiet despair I tumbled asleep.

When the train stopped next, it was at Aix-la-Chapelle; now it was Martin's turn to forage for a newspaper. I watched him toddle down the windy platform, a flapping overcoat over his pyjamas. I watched him as he located the paper-trolley.

He laid his hand on the newspaper, but, before he could open it, a frolic wind snatched it from his grasp and whisked it, provokingly, exasperatingly, maddeningly along the tracks. As he dashed after it in frenzied pursuit, our train moved off, quietly but inexorably, towards Ostend. I suppose a draw is a fair result.

And, of course, we did win at the Oval. I never saw Martin again. Such a nice fellow.

*from* CRICKET MY HAPPINESS *1955*

# A Hundred Hundreds

## R. C. ROBERTSON-GLASGOW

Leonard Hutton's hundredth hundred in first-class cricket was in more than one sense well-timed. It came as a rounding-off to his wonderful performances in Australia in 1950–1, and as a numerical reminder of his supremacy in contemporary cricket. He reached it with a drive to the off boundary, cricket's and Hutton's loveliest stroke; and he was batting at the Oval, scene of so many of his triumphs.

So, as thirteenth man, he joined the list of the mighty who have had the skill, the time, and the health to score a hundred a hundred times. A great feat. But, as we look at the list, we should remember also some of the very greatest who are not there: K. S. Ranjitsinhji and Victor Trumper, for two. In the judging of art, quantity is not of the first relevance; and, when we look up at the stars in the sky, it is not of their size that we are thinking.

Indeed, as we glance through this list of thirteen, let there be no nonsense about comparative merit. W. G. Grace and D. G. Bradman come seventh and eighth in the order. Let that be a warning to all arithmeticians. Far better to let the memory play around the differences of style and temperament which brought them all to the same triumph. F. E. Woolley and C. P. Mead; alike only in being left-handed and great; Woolley, playing as if batsmanship were an exhibition of beauty, to be broken off at his, not the bowler's will; Mead, conducting business on a pitch of which he had taken lease for this world and the next.

H. Sutcliffe and E. Hendren; Sutcliffe, the megalo-psychic; denying, by attitude, the existence of good luck, or, almost, of the bowlers themselves; Hendren, democratic, busily and gladly sharing the enjoyment and stresses of batting with spectators, umpires, scorers and dogs. J. B. Hobbs and W. R. Hammond; alike in perfection of athletic balance and in judgment that flashes from brain to limb; different in that Hammond chose to go down the pitch to the spin bowling, whereas Hobbs liked more to play it in his crease.

Tom Hayward; I saw him far past his prime, but still with something magnificently military in his stance and moustache. Andrew Sandham and Ernest Tyldesley; both great; but both batting as it were under slight shadow; Sandham daily, under the shadow of Hobbs; Tyldesley, by retrospect and comparison, under the shadow of the immortal 'J.T.'

Apart from these stands L. E. G. Ames, the only wicketkeeper who has scored a hundred hundreds, and who kept, later than most, the gift of the quick foot and eye.

So to Grace and Bradman. No words can add to or subtract from their fame. And now L. Hutton joins the band. He is a worthy member.

*from* ALL IN THE GAME *1952*

# Long Vacation

## R. C. ROBERTSON-GLASGOW

Success at games demands total freedom from care. I first learnt this truth at school when, soon after taking guard at the crease, I saw among the few spectators the unwelcome face of my schoolmaster, who had put me down for detention that sunny afternoon.

Nor is this truth invalidated by the desperate case of the illustrious England batsman who, they say, compiled his record aggregate of runs one summer almost entirely because he knew that there lay in wait, near the pavilion, the lady who, contrary to his expressed advice, had determined to marry him. He just had to bat on.

Freedom from care. The words are 'tolling me back' to the

start of the Long Vacation at Oxford. Work, such as it was, is over. The mind is disburdened of the hideous complexities of that tortuous Teuton, Immanuel Kant. Let the Roman Empire rip. It is up to the examiners now. By the Porter's Lodge I meet my tutor, who has done his best. He is off to try out the wines of France and the architecture of Italy. Parting makes him polite; and he hopes, hesitating for the phrase, that we shall meet with the requisite measure of success at Lord's. As to us, we go off to Brighton, to try out the bowling of Maurice Tate, to fish from rowing-boats, and to shoot in the underground rifle-range on the pier. We could also enter the Aquarium for 2d.

Meanwhile, some who said they must work, and others who had made no particular arrangements, stayed behind and played Long Vacation cricket. I fancy that they made more of these matches in the Victorian era. My old headmaster at school, on the long Sunday afternoon rambles of the Summer Term, used to tell me of the heroic deeds performed by these Long Vacation cricketers when he was young.

The years had enlarged the stature of his early companions. All of them seemed only by some inexplicable mischance to have escaped the favourable notice of the University captain. They were the Blues of the Never-Land. Against heroes, too, they played. The Hon. Alfred Lyttelton detached himself from his Middlesex commitments to keep wicket against these Long Vacationers. Alfred Shaw, of Nottingham, for all his perfect length, could make no headway against young X of Keble College. W. G. Grace himself, in his giant prime, was clean bowled for 45 by the tearaway Z, and made kindly inquiries about his qualifications for a County. But Z went off to be a parson in the wilds of Cumberland, and the Doctor went back to Gloucestershire and forgot all about him.

What does it matter if it was all a legend? As the years lend enchantment to the days of youth, the runs and the wickets of the imagination are as good as any that illumine the pages of *Wisden*.

*from* ALL IN THE GAME *1952*

# PART IV

# The Poetry of Cricket

'Recorded centuries leave no trace
On memory of that timeless grace.'

*John Arlott*
ON A GREAT BATSMAN

## THE CUT

'If it were done when 'tis done, then 'twere well
It were done quickly.'

*Macbeth*

### THE OLD CRICKETER

He sits alone to watch the men
At cricket on the village green,
And savours calmly, once again,
The life-remembered, quiet scene
That to his ageing sight grows dim,
And then he sees, with clearer eye,
That these men's fathers play with him,
Their fathers' fathers standing by.
He leaps once more, with eager spring,
To catch the brief-glimpsed, flying ball
And quickens to its sudden sting:
The brightness dies: the old eyes fall,
They see, but do not understand,
A pursed, rheumatic, useless hand.

### TO JOHN BERRY HOBBS
### ON HIS SEVENTIETH BIRTHDAY
#### 16 December 1952

There falls across this one December day
The light remembered from those suns of June
That you reflected in the summer play
Of perfect strokes across the afternoon.

No yeoman ever walked his household land
More sure of step or more secure of lease
Than you, accustomed and unhurried, trod
Your great, yet little, manor of the crease.

The game the Wealden rustics handed down
Through growing skill became, in you, a part
Of sense, and ripened to a style that showed
Their country sport matured to balanced art.

There was a wisdom so informed your bat
To understanding of the bowler's trade
That each resource of strength or skill he used
Seemed but the context of the stroke you played.

The Master: records prove the title good:
Yet figures fail you, for they cannot say
How many men whose names you never knew
Are proud to tell their sons they saw you play.

They share the sunlight of your summer day
Of thirty years; and they, with you, recall
How, through those well-wrought centuries,
    your hand
Reshaped the history of bat and ball.

CRICKET AT WORCESTER, 1938

Dozing in deck-chair's gentle curve,
Through half-closed eyes I watched the cricket,
Knowing the sporting press would say
'Perks bowled well on a perfect wicket'.

Fierce mid-day sun upon the ground;
Through heat-haze came the hollow sound
Of wary bat on ball, to pound
The devil from it, quell its bound.

Sunburned fieldsmen, flannelled cream,
Looked, though urgent, scarce alive,
Swooped, like swallows of a dream,
On skimming fly, the hard-hit drive.

Beyond the score-box, through the trees
Gleamed Severn, blue and wide,
Where oarsmen 'feathered' with polished ease
And passed in gentle glide.

The back-cloth, setting off the setting,
Peter's cathedral soared,
Rich of shade and fine of fretting
Like cut and painted board.

To the cathedral, close for shelter,
Huddled houses, bent and slim,
Some tall, some short, all helter-skelter,
Like a sky-line drawn for Grimm.

This the fanciful engraver might
In his creative dream have seen,
Here, framed by summer's glaring light,
Grey stone, majestic over green.

Closer, the bowler's arm swept down,
The ball swung, pitched and darted,
Stump and bail flashed and flew;
The batsman pensively departed.

Like rattle of dry seeds in pods
The warm crowd faintly clapped;
The boys who came to watch their gods,
The tired old men who napped.

The members sat in their strong deck-chairs
And sometimes glanced at the play,
They smoked and talked of stocks and shares,
And the bar stayed open all day.

## ON A GREAT BATSMAN

As the gull conceals in easeful glide
The inborn gift to curb and ride
The gale – merging the sea-wind's force
With lovely movement on a chosen course –
So, in timed swoop, he moves to charm
The ball down-swirling from the bowler's arm
Along some glissade of his own creation,
Beyond the figures' black and white rotation.
    Recorded centuries leave no trace
    On memory of that timeless grace.

## CRICKET AT SWANSEA
### (*Glamorgan in the Field*)

From the top of the hill-top pavilion,
The sea is a cheat to the eye,
Where it secretly seeps into coastline
Or fades in the yellow-grey sky;
But the crease-marks are sharp on the green
As the axe's first taste of the tree,
And keen is the Welshmen's assault
As the freshening fret from the sea.
The ball is a withering weapon,
Fraught with a strong-fingered spin
And the fieldsmen, with fingers prehensile,
Are the arms of attack moving in.
In the field of a new Cymric mission,
With outcricket cruel as a cat
They pounce on the perilous snick
As it breaks from the spin-harried bat.

On this turf, the remembered of rugby –
'The Invincibles' – came by their name,

And now, in the calm of the clubhouse,
Frown down from their old-fashioned frame.
Their might has outlived their moustaches,
For photos fade faster than fame;
And this cricket rekindles the temper
Of their high-trampling, scrummaging game:
As intense as an Eisteddfod anthem
It burns down the day like a flame.

*John Arlott*

## CRICKET DAYS

When life was budding and I new-married, I made my home
in a house that stood
Grey in the green of the Wiltshire meadows – a hoary dwelling
of stone and beam;
And there, when summer had burst the poppy and skies were
brazen, the men I loved –
Letting the world go by – would gather for days of cricket in
field or park.

Days of delight! For delight unmeasured it was to fare
through the morning lanes,
And hour by hour, as the sun went over, to strive for victory,
friend with friend;
Or, jogging home as the twilight settled on ancient village or
farm, to see
The curtained windows, the candles lighted, the supper
spread and the cider drawn.

Beautiful too were the nights that followed when, strolling
forth in a glad fatigue
And lazing long where the starlight glimmered on ghostlike
lilies that fringed the lawn,

We shared our thought or our laughter, forging a love
    between us that years of change
Have left but stronger, alike responsive to this man's learning
    or that man's wit.

I knew, indeed, as the days went by, how none of all that were
    yet to be
Could bring delight that was more unclouded. I did not know
    that with every hour
We stored a joy that would last forever – like Arab merchants
    that fill their gourds
With crystal water from some white city and then set forth
    to the desert sand.

*Clifford Bax*

### THE SONG OF TILLY LALLY

O, I say, you Joe,
Throw us the ball!
I've a good mind to go
And leave you all.
I never saw such a bowler
To bowl the ball in a tansy
And clean it with my hankercher
Without saying a word.

That Bill's a foolish fellow;
He has given me a black eye.
He does not know how to handle a bat
Any more than a dog or a cat;
He has knock'd down the wicket,
And broke the stumps,
And runs without shoes to save his pumps.

*William Blake*

## THE SEASON OPENS

'A Tower we must have, and a clock in the tower,
Looking over the tombs, the tithebarn, the bower;
The inn and the mill, the forge and the hall,
And the Loamy sweet level that loves bat and ball.'

So a grey tower we have, and the centuried trees
Have arisen to share what its belfry-light sees,
The apple-plats richest in spring-song of all,
Kitchen-gardens and the field where they take bat and ball.

The stream with its moments of dance in the sun
Where the willows allow, runs and ever will run
At the cleft of the orchard, along the soft fall
Of the pasture where tourneys become bat and ball.

And now where the confident cuckoo takes flight
Over buttercups kindled in millions last night,
A labourer leans on the stackyard's low wall
With the hens bothering round him, and dreams bat and ball;

Till the meadow is quick with the masters who were,
And he hears his own shouts when he first trotted there;
Long ago; all gone home now; but here they come all!
Surely these are the same, who now bring bat and ball?

## PRIDE OF THE VILLAGE

A new grave meets the hastiest passer's eye,
It's reared so high, it lacks not some white wreath;
Old ones are not so noticed; low they lie
And lower till the equal grass forgets
The bones beneath.

His now, a modest hillock it must be,
The wooden cross scarce tells such as pass by
The painted name; beneath the chestnut tree
Sleep centuries of such glories and regrets.
But I can tell you, boys who that way run
With bat and ball down to the calm smooth leas,
Your village story's somewhere bright with one
To whom all looked with an approving joy
In hours like these.
Cricket to us, like you, was more than play,
It was a worship in the summer sun,
And when Tom Fletcher in the month of May
Went to the field, the feet of many a boy
Scarce pressed the buttercups; then we stood there
Rapt, as he took the bat and lit day's close,
Gliding and glancing, guiding fine or square
The subtlest bowls, and smoothing, as wave-wise
Rough-hurled they rose,
With a sweet sureness; his especial ease
Did what huge sinews could not; to a hair
His grey eye measured, and from the far trees
Old watchers lobbed the ball with merry cries.

And when the whitened creases marked the match,
Though shaking hands and pipes gone out revealed
The hour's impress and burden, and the catch
Or stumps askew meant it was Tom's turn next,
He walked a field
Modest, and small, and seldom failed to raise
Our score and spirits, great delight to watch;
And where old souls broke chuckling forth in praise
Round the ale booth, Tom's cricket was the text.

Summers slipt out of sight; next summer – hush!
The winter came between, and Tom was ill,
And worse, and with the spring's sweet rosy flush,

His face was flushed with perilous rose; he stayed
Indoors, and still
We hoped: but elders said, 'Tom's going home'.
The brake took cricketers by inn and bush,
But Tom not there! What team could leave out Tom?
He took his last short walk, a trembling shade.
And 'short and sweet', he said, for his tombstone
Would be the word; but paint and wood decay,
And since he died the wind of war has blown
His old companions far beyond the green
Where many a day
He made his poems out of bat and ball.
Some few may yet be left who all alone
Can tell you, boys, who run at cricket's call,
What a low hillock by your path may mean.

*Edmund Blunden*

### THE BLACK SHEEP

You saw that man. You wonder why
I passed him with averted eye,
Although he nodded affably?

It was a Test Match – anxious days.
Somehow he had secured a place
With us, with the habitués.

We were all there. I mean by 'we'
The Old Guard of the M.C.C.
And, with us, but not of us, *he*.

He talked and laughed, as if unused
To serious cricket. He confused
Fosters with Fords, and seemed amused.

You know the story of the match;
The brilliant start, the rotten patch,
And, last, the unaccepted catch:

Mid-off; a gift; no spin at all;
Pure nerves. He fumbled with the ball,
Retrieved it – and then let it fall.

Lord Nestor gave a groan; the rest
Sat silent, overwhelmed, oppress'd;
And he, that fellow, made a jest!

That man, who muddled up the Fords,
At such a moment played with words!
In the pavilion!! and at Lord's!!

*G. F. Bradby*


ON WINDMILL DOWN, 1789

... Then ther was Beldham,
William Beldham – Silver Billy us always called 'en,
For his hair was so white as a wheatfield, come October.
Harry Hall, the ginger bread-maker, learnt 'en the game:
Hall were no great player himself, but he made young
    Beldham
Keep his left elbow up and hold his bat plumb-straight
In the line of the ball when he swung. 'Twere a gallant sight
To see Silver Billy smack 'em all over the field,
And never lift one. That lad, he danced on his toes
Like Jack Broughton, the boxer. And run! He could lance
    like a deer,

To pick up the ball full-pelt, so neat as a swallow
Nips gnats in the air! You'd ought to a'see'd'en cut
Off the point of the bat, with a crack like a pistol-shot,

The ball shaving daisies all the way to the boundary,
And shepherds a'lepping like lambs of an April evening'
To save their old shins – not one of 'en could a'stopped it
Howsomever he tried. But I 'low the best of all
Was when him and Lord Frederick Beauclerk was in together:
Lord Frederick had royal blood in'en, so 'twere said,
For his grammer were Nelly Gwynn, King Charles's fancy,
But when Billy and him walked out to the pitch, side by side,
You couldn't tell which were the farmer and which the
    gentleman,
The pair on' em looked that majestic and when they got set
You'ld a'thought they was brothers born, the way they
    gloried
In blasting the bowling between 'em. There wasn't ball,
Long or short, high or low, but Lord Frederick went into it
Wrist and shoulder. But Billy the same. They looked
    Something grander
Than human mortals, them two – so light on their feet
As hobby hawks skimmin a hedge, or pewits a 'runnun'
Afore they do light on the down. I can see them now:
Billy Beldham's silvery head and his lordship's white hat
Thridding to and fro like shuttles: the crowd on their feet
Hollerin' out: 'Go hard . . . go hard! Tich and turn, tich and
    turn!
Try another! One more!' – and the fielders running' like
    hares
On every side of the wicket. Ay, that was music!
Afore now I've a'see'd Silver Billy notch ten runs
Off one snick past slip and an overthrow. Them was the days!

                                        *Francis Brett Young*

### BRIGHTER CRICKET

A dozen overs, every ball a dolly:
   The artful Podger watches them for spin,
Then gently pats each succulent half-volley:
   There's talent money and the points to win.
He's going to get his benefit next summer;
   His average is better than last year.
The Glumshire bowlers go from glum to glummer,
   He'll get his thirty e'er the night is here.
Sing hey for Glumshire, that's the teak to stick it!
   Sing ho for Starkshire, who can stick still more!
Sing hey for all the purple hours of cricket!
   What's that? Hurst Park, Fast Flapper. Nine to four
Who'd mock the game or libel British lads,
While Podger's playing time out with his pads?

*Ivor Brown*

### VILLAGE CRICKET

Flowing together by devious channels
From farm and brickyard, forest and dene,
Thirteen men in glittering flannels
Move to their stations out on the green.

Long-limbed Waggoner, stern, unbudging,
Stands like a rock behind the bails.
Dairyman umpire, gravely judging,
Spares no thought for his milking-pails.

Bricklayer bowls, a perfect length.
Grocery snicks and sneaks a run.
Law, swiping with all his strength,
Is caught by Chemist at mid-on.

Two to the boundary, a four and a six,
Put the spectators in fear of their lives:
Shepherd the slogger is up to his tricks,
Blithely unwary of weans and wives.

Lord of the manor makes thirty-four.
Parson contributes, smooth and trim,
A cautious twelve to the mounting score:
Leg-before wicket disposes of him.

Patient, dramatic, serious, genial,
From over to over the game goes on,
Weaving a pattern of hardy perennial
Civilization under the sun.

*Gerald Bullett*


CRICKET AT HARROW

High, through those elms, with hoary branches crown'd,
Fair Ida's bower adorns the landscape round;
There Science, from her favour'd seat, surveys
The vale where rural Nature claims her praise;
To her awhile resigns her youthful train,
Who move in joy, and dance along the plain;
In scatt'd groups each favour'd haunt pursue:
Repeat old pastimes, and discover new;
Flush'd with his rays, beneath the noontide sun,
In rival bands, between the wickets run,
Drive o'er the sward the ball with active force,
Or chase with nimble feet its rapid course.

Alonzo! best and dearest of my friends. . . .
. . . when confinement's lingering hour was done,
Our sport, our studies, and our souls were one:

Together we impell'd the flying ball;
Together waited in our tutor's hall;
Together join'd in cricket's manly toil.

*Lord Byron*


## THE DESERTED PARKS

*'Solitudinem faciunt: Parcum appelant'*

Amidst thy bowers the tyrant's hand is seen,
The rude pavilions sadden all thy green;
One selfish pastime grasps the whole domain,
And half a faction swallows up the plain;
Adown thy glades, all sacrificed to cricket,
The hollow-sounding bat now guards the wicket;
Sunk are thy mounds in shapeless level all,
Lest aught impede the swiftly rolling ball;
And trembling, shrinking from the fatal blow,
Far, far away thy hapless children go.

    The man of wealth and pride
Takes up a space that many poor supplied;
Space for the game, and all its instruments,
Space for pavilions and for scorers' tents;
The ball, that raps his shins in padding cased,
Has wore the verdure to an arid waste;
His Park, where these exclusive sports are seen,
Indignant spurns the rustic from the green;
While through the plain, consigned to silence all,
In barren splendour flits the russet ball.

*Lewis Carroll*

## SHALL I NEVER STORM OR SWEAR?

Shall I never storm or swear
Just because the umpire's fair?
Or from expletives forbear,
'Cause he gives me out with care?
Be he fairer, more upright
Than Carpenter or Lillywhite,
   If he will not favour me,
    What care I how fair he be?


If 'How's that?' I loudly shout,
Let him promptly answer, 'Out!'
If, perchance, I bowl a Wide,
Let him cough and look aside;
If my toe slip o'er the crease,
Let him sigh, but hold his peace.
   If he cry 'No ball!' to me,
    What care I how fair he be?


When they catch me near the ground
Let him think 'twas on the bound;
When against me they appeal
Let him hesitation feel;
Let me profit by the doubt,
Let him never give me out.
   If 'Leg-before' he judges me,
    What care I how fair he be?

*E. B. V. Christian*

## ENGLAND, PAST AND PRESENT

But for an hour to watch them play,
    Those heroes dead and gone,
And pit our batsmen of today
    With those of Hambledon!
Our Graces, Nyrens, Studds, and Wards
    In weeks of sunny weather,
Somewhere upon Elysian swards,
    To see them matched together!

Could we but see how Small withstands
    The three-foot break of Steel,
If Silver Billy's 'wondrous hands'
    Survive with Briggs or Peel!
If Mann, with all his pluck of yore,
    Can keep the leather rolling,
And, at a crisis, notch a score,
    When Woods and Hearne are bowling!

No doubt the Doctor could bewitch
    His quaint top-hatted foes,
Though, on a deftly-chosen pitch,
    Old Harris bowled his slows;
And Aylward, if the asphodel
    Had made the wicket bumpy,
Would force the game with Attewell,
    And Stoddard collar 'Lumpy'.

When Time of all our flannelled hosts
    Leaves only the renown,
Our cracks, perhaps, may join the ghosts
    That roam on Windmill Down,
Where shadowy crowds will watch the strife,
    And cheer the deeds of wonder
Achieved by giants whom in life
    A century kept asunder.

## THE CATCH

Stupendous scores he never made,
But perished ever with despatch:
No bowling genius he displayed,
But once, in a forgotten match,
   He made a catch.

No doubt a timely stroke of luck
Assisted him to do the trick;
He was at cover, and it stuck:
It travelled fairly low and quick –
   The kind that stick.

His friends the proud achievement classed
As fortune's most eccentric whim,
And ere a week or two had passed
The memory of the catch grew dim
   To all but him.

To all but him, for he relates,
With varying ornament and phrase,
The story to the man who waits
Unwilling in Pavilion ways,
   On rainy days.

The catch has grown in splendour now –
He had a dozen yards to run;
It won the match, as all allow,
And in his eyes there blazed the sun,
   And how it spun.

Life of old memories is compact,
And happy he for whom with speed
Blossoms a gorgeous tree, where fact
Has planted, in his hour of need,
   A mustard seed.

## THE SCORE BOARD AT LORD'S

In chequered black and white above the green
This giant register surveys the scene,
And, moving in its own mysterious way,
Above the plot and passion of the play,
Presents the futile or triumphant deed
With cold celerity for all who read.

No quiver of excitement you may trace
In the blank outlook of that sombre face;
No preference in the crisis of the fight
Of Blue and Blue for either Dark or Light;
No shouts, no thrills, no fevers disarrange
The stately process of that silent change.

What though you be the buttress of the side,
The prop on whom the other ten relied,
And, through some antic of malicious luck
Your looked-for century comes out a duck,
No whit does that austere Colossus care,
Your number's vanished and the next one's there.

Nor will it serve that you denounce as bad
The verdict passed on your obstructing pad,
No sympathy it sends, no soothing balm,
But marks the issue with Olympian calm.
A moment since and you were Number Two,
You're the Last Player now – so much for you.

Well may you ask, my disappointed friend,
Is life like this, relentless to the end,
Taking no thought of anything but fact,
Of how men act, not how they meant to act,
Or will it lend an ear to failure's claim,
When accident defeats a worthy aim?

### THEORY AND PRACTICE
*(On reading Prince Ranjitsinhji's Book)*

To buy it all the people press
With a despairing eagerness
   That borders on the tragic;
All men peruse with sighs and vows,
And towels bound about their brows,
   This work of Eastern magic.

Of hidden things – the vigorous drive,
The lightning cut that hums for five,
   The secret here is told us;
Here we may surely learn to score
With that deft glide to leg for four
   Off balls that would have bowled us.

Look you – the mystery will be clear,
For we may find the pivot here
   Whereon the business hinges;
Till, full of lore, one summer day
We shall adventure forth to play,
   And all be Ranjitsinhjis.

Dear devotees of bat and ball,
Do you in childhood's hours recall
   The conjuror's candid habit,
Of showing to unskilful men
How flower-pots may conceal a hen
   Or silk-hats hide a rabbit?

The trick was ours, if only books
Could make us Maskelynes and Cookes;
   We saw completely through it;
Yet then our task was but begun,
For though we knew how it was done
   The nuisance was to do it.

                  *Alfred Cochrane*

## A REMINISCENCE OF CRICKET

Once in my heyday of cricket,
  Oh day I shall ever recall!
I captured that glorious wicket,
  The greatest, the grandest of all.

Before me he stands like a vision,
  Bearded and burly and brown,
A smile of good-humoured derision
  As he waits for the first to come down.

A statue from Thebes or from Cnossus,
  A Hercules shrouded in white,
Assyrian bull-like Colossus,
  He stands in his might.

With the beard of a Goth or a Vandal,
  His bat hanging ready and free,
His great hairy hands on the handle,
  And his menacing eyes upon me.

And I – I had tricks for the rabbits,
  The feeble of mind or of eye,
I could see all the duffer's bad habits
  And guess where his ruin might lie.

The capture of such might elate one,
  But it seemed like some horrible jest
That I should serve tosh to the great one,
  Who had broken the hearts of the best.

Well, here goes! Good Lord, what a rotter!
  Such a sitter as never was dreamt;
It was clay in the hands of the potter,
  But he tapped it with quiet contempt.

The second was better – a leetle;
  It was low, but was nearly long-hop;
As the housemaid comes down on the beetle
  So down came the bat with a chop.

He was sizing me up with some wonder,
  My broken-kneed action and ways;
I could see the grim menace from under
  The striped peak that shaded his gaze.

The third was a gift or it looked it –
  A foot off the wicket or so;
·His huge figure swooped as he hooked it,
  His great body swung to the blow.

Still when my dreams are night-marish,
  I picture that terrible smite,
It was meant for a neighbouring parish,
  Or any old place out of sight.

But – yes, there's a but to the story –
  The blade swished a trifle too low;
Oh wonder, and vision of glory!
  It was up like a shaft from a bow.

Up, up, like the towering game-bird,
  Up, up, to a speck in the blue,
And then coming down like the same bird,
  Dead straight on the line that it flew.

Good Lord, was it mine! Such a soarer
  Would call for a safe pair of hands;
None safer than Derbyshire Storer,
  And there, face uplifted, he stands.

Wicket-keep Storer, the knowing,
    Wary and steady of nerve,
Watching it falling and growing
    Marking the pace and the curve.

I stood with my two eyes fixed on it,
    Paralysed, helpless, inert;
There was 'plunk' as the gloves shut upon it,
    And he cuddled it up to his shirt.

Out – beyond question or wrangle!
    Homeward he lurched to his lunch!
His bat was tucked up at an angle,
    His great shoulders curved to a hunch.

Walking he rumbled and grumbled,
    Scolding himself and not me;
One glove was off, and he fumbled,
    Twisting the other hand free

Did I give Storer the credit
    The thanks he so splendidly earned?
It was mere empty talk if I said it,
    For Grace was already returned.

*Arthur Conan Doyle*

## JOHN SMALL (1737–1826)

Here lies, bowled out by Death's unerring ball,
A Cricketer renowned, by name John Small,
But though his name was Small, yet great his fame,
For nobly did he play the noble game;
His life was like his innings, long and good,
Full ninety summers he had death withstood.

At length the ninetieth winter came, when (fate
Not leaving him one solitary mate)
This last of Hambledonians, Old John Small,
Gave up his bat and ball, his leather, wax and all.

*Pierce Egan*

## THE CRICKETER'S ARMS

On a field vert, symbolical,
A Bowler, diabolical;
A sky of azure, ball of gules;
Above, the LAWS (not, please!, the Rules).

The sun, or, sheds a golden light
On Batsmen rampant, clothed in white.
Couchant and sejant at the side,
Spectators are transmogrified.

An Umpire, keen of eye and ardent,
Dispensing Justice, stands regardant.
Fieldsmen support a blazoned scroll:

FAIR PLAY DOTH ELEVATE
THE SOUL.

*Gavin Ewart*

## THE CALL OF MAY

'Good sirs, who sit at home to-night
And listen in the fading light
To voices floating on the air
From here, from there, from everywhere:
Imagine now that out of space
Comes the deep spirit voice of Grace –
Old W.G. – whose mighty frame

No more shall lumber through the game -
Old W.G., whose burly beard
No more is seen, no more is feared:
Yet, from my corner in the sky,
When, not unenvious, I descry
Flannels in fashion down below –
When old familiar sounds I know
Float up – the heavy roller's sound
Clanking across the county ground –
The busy whirr no spring forgets
Of cricket balls in cricket nets –
The insect hum of shillings spun
Silver and black, against the sun –
The call of the pavilion bell,
Tolling its matin summons – well,
Even an angel or two is stirred
And when the umpire speaks the word,
The first word of the season – 'Play!' –
It has my blessing every May.
Sweet May! ah, month beyond compare!
For now you taste the firstlings rare:
The first square cut, the first clean drive,
The first sharp-shooter you survive,
The first fine glance, the first fair glide,
The first good victory for your side:
Sweet May! once more I smell your oil
Smoothing my bat; and press your soil
Under my thumb; once more I feel
The good soft give of pine and deal
Beneath the nails that pierce the boards
In dressing rooms from Leeds to Lord's:
Sweet May! you hold a thrill apart,
For now the batsman strains his art
To make the loveliest score of all –
A century to a cuckoo's call.
How many, many Mays have burst

Their buds, and spread their boughs, since first
I learned to watch the ball, to wait
And always hold my bat up straight!
How many Mays, alas! since last
I let the ball at point go past!
No more! no more! above the crowds,
Like a Jehovah in the clouds
I sit, sans bat or ball, and dream
A captain now without a team:
Yet, though I miss, I miss my May,
Happy that other men still play
The game all England flocked to see
When W.G. was W.G.
So then! to business! Now, my lads,
Up with the stumps! on with the pads!
Out with the cap! whose gaudy rings
Will mellow in a few more springs,
And, as the colours fade, proclaim
A real old master of the game.
Come! to the pitch! The field is set.
Caution, remember, till you get
Your eye in. 'Two leg, umpire, please'.
The wicket-keeper bends his knees:
The slips, with swinging arms, lean low,
Hawks for a swoop, three in a row;
Long-off, beside the boundary track,
Stands with his arm behind his back,
Lolling; the bowler now has spaced
His run; he turns, his fingers taste
The seam, caress the stitch; he comes;
Through the bright air the new ball hums
A delicate, cleaving note; you sight
Against the screen its clear red flight,
Tense in the sun; and as it spins,
The prologue ends, the play begins.'

*Herbert Farjeon*

### THE MASTER

Overhead a sky of speedwell,
　　Pampered yards of green below;
Girls to flutter each Brightonian
　　Substitute for Romeo;
Tents with beer for barleycorners
　　Husky at the luncheon hour;
All of these are proof that Cricket's
　　Bursting fiercely into flower.

Hove is where I breathe contented
　　Now that lilac in array
Publishes the white and purple
　　Masterpieces due to May.
Here I puff a cloud and wonder
　　What decrees of darling Fate
Govern heroes soon to tackle
　　Every subterfuge of Tate.

Sinfield neck-and-crop to Langridge,
　　Nothing but a leg-bye scored!
Enters now the dreaded Hammond,
　　Gloucester County's overlord.
Deeper, Cover Point! and deeper,
　　You that guard the boundaries there!
When she comes you won't have even
　　Half a tick of time to spare!

Thud! she's made a fat civilian
　　Scuttle to preserve the bone
Threatened by a bomb of leather
　　Wensley could but leave alone.
Thud! She's squandered twenty schoolboys
　　Rolling in a gentle laugh.
Now the antic figures caper
　　Furious on the Telegraph!

This is almost youth recovered!
  Keen I quiver in my chair,
Even sensing those electric
  Crackles common to the hair.
This is England for the English,
  Now that Hammond, come in May,
Drives his flock of Fours, presenting
  Ringside hearts with holiday!


## THE CHURCH CRICKETANT

I bowled three sanctified souls
  With three consecutive balls!
What do I care if Blondin trod
  Over Niagara falls?
What do I care for the loon in the Pit
  Or the gilded Earl in the Stalls?
I bowled three curates once
  With three consecutive balls!

I caused three Protestant 'ducks'
  With three consecutive balls!
Poets may rave of lily girls
  Dancing in marble halls!
What do I care for a bevy of yachts
  Or a dozen or so of yawls?
I bowled three curates once
  With three consecutive balls!

I bowled three cricketing priests
  With three consecutive balls!
What if a critic pounds a book
  What if an author squalls?

What do I care if sciatica comes,
  Elephantiasis calls?
I bowled three curates once
  With three consecutive balls!

*Norman Gale*


### THE VITAL QUESTION

You may have paid your Income Tax
  And bought the wife a hat;
Adjusted each domestic bill;
Reduced anxiety to nil.
Quite likely, too, you've made your will;
  But – have you oiled your bat?

Perchance on questions ponderous
  In conference you've sat;
Mayhap you've met a potentate
And settled grave affairs of State
That call for tact and cannot wait;
  But – have you oiled your bat?

Your conscience may be crystal-clear
  On togs and things like that;
You may be waiting – unafraid –
To turn out, spotlessly arrayed,
Complete with blazer (newly-made);
  But – HAVE YOU OILED
              YOUR BAT?

## 'SHINE'

When the sport-lover reads of our cricketer's deeds,
He needs hardly the instinct detective
To deduce from it all that without the new ball
No fast bowler today is effective:
That your Larwoods and Govers can bowl a few overs
Of rollocking raspers and shakers,
And can even come through with a wicket or two,
If the ball has come straight from the makers:
That the lads, given 'shine', can deliver the dope:
That (conversely) without it they haven't a hope.

Yet one cannot recall that the state of the ball,
In the times that are gone, was so vital;
And one wonders if they of an earlier day
Needed 'shine' as an aid to their title.
Did Tom Richardson itch – or did (later) Bill Hitch –
For the ball that was chaste and unsmitten?
Did Spofforth and Kortright consider their sport right
If called on to bowl with a bit 'un?
Did they claim, like Aladdin, the new for the old?
Did the venomous Lockwood? Did Brearley or Mold?

Is the thing so essential, one wonders. In fine,
Is it *really* important – or is it all 'shine'?

*F. A. J. Godfrey*

### LORD'S

Lord's! What tender recollections
    Does that famous name suggest!
What a crowd of fond reflections
    Throng my antiquated breast,

As I lounge in the Pavilion
   And, from my exalted seat,
Watch the undistinguished million
   Surging at my feet!

Hither, with a 'Rover's Ticket',
   In the days of youth I came;
Glued my eye upon the wicket,
   Missed no moment of the game,
While to feminine relations
   Whom I happened to escort
I explained the complications
   Of this form of sport!

Here, like ocean breakers roaring,
   I would stamp my feet and yell,
When I watched my heroes scoring,
   Or opponents' wickets fell;
Here, when inningses were ended,
   To the tents I turned my gaze,
Where the hock-cup subtly blended
   With the mayonnaise!

Happy days! Like shadows flitting
   O'er my mind, those mem'ries pass!
Now, in the Pavilion sitting,
   I grow elderly, alas!
Though no tittle I am losing
   Of the zeal I felt of yore,
Now and then I can't help snoozing –
   Wake me if I snore!

*Harry Graham*

## ODE TO A CRICKETER—W. G. QUAIFE

The field is set; in silent skim, loop, dive,
   The idle ball travels from hand to hand,
Till now with quick, firm step, diminutive
   You cross the wide expanse; you take your stand.
Like a slim schoolboy in a Fathers' Match,
Tall elders hovering greedy for a catch,
   So do you look – but such is your disguise.
For you are Quaife, the bowler's last despair,
   Whose stern defence defies
Fury of fast, or wiliness of slow,
Gathering ones and twos with patient care
   From strokes in perfect flow.


Yet now and then your supple wrists lash out
   To cut a short one stinging to the rail
Past silly point or, too much tempted, clout
   A hanging long-hop, harmlessly to sail
Just out of reach. In faultless measure beat,
Back, forward or across those nimble feet,
   A clockwork faithful to the inward time
Of eyes that master flight and spin and pace.
   Oh, see the slow score climb!
An hour to go, you've ninety on the board;
Safe as a tortoise you will win the race,
   Another hundred scored.


One day, I well recall, of broiling sun
   You broke the heart of Lockwood, that great heart.
He from his strong, swift catapulting run
   Bowled good-length lightning. You with gentle art
Resisted, and the ball came trickling back
In glum defeat along the self-same track.

At last, he could no more; all patience lost
He thundered up again, but limp and high
    A lob unmannerly tossed –
In languid, long parabola to fall
Behind you, like a last protesting sigh
    From bowler and from ball.


Ah! gone the days when I, a Warwick boy,
    Paid you my homage. The sad sun is set
On you and on your comrades, yet the joy
    That once you gave I never can forget.
Backward I travel, many a long mile,
To watch the quiet rhythm, the sheer style,
    Of Lilley keeping wicket, or the hale
Rubicund Diver slamming a great six,
    A rustic with a flail.
On these and many more, good men and true,
The grateful eyes of memory I fix,
    But most of all on you.


Who could more fitly the initials share
    Of Cricket's mighty Doctor? Though your place,
Your rarer name, no zealot may compare
    With his, your nature had the more of grace.
In their own firmament, like men of rhyme,
To their appointed heights the players climb:
    Oh therefore may no dazzled sight allow
That flaming portent, that Great Bear, to screen
    The point minute where now,
Distinct amid the galaxy divine,
You on the hollies and the shaven green
    Of Shakespeare's county shine!

### CRICKET

Where else, you ask, can England's game be seen
Rooted so deep as on the village green?
Here, in the slum, where doubtful sunlight falls,
To gild three stumps chalked on decaying walls.

*G. Rostrevor Hamilton*

### NINTH WICKET

The bowling looks exceptionally sound,
 The wicket seems unusually worn,
The balls fly up or run along the ground;
 I rather wish that I had not been born.
I have been sitting here since two o'clock;
 My pads are both inelegant and hot;
I do not want what people call my 'knock',
 And this pavilion is a sultry spot.
I shall not win one clap or word of praise,
 I know that I shall bat like a baboon;
And I can think of many better ways
 In which to spend a summer afternoon.
I might be swimming in a crystal pool;
 I might be wooing some delicious dame;
I might be drinking something long and cool –
 *I can't imagine why I play this game.*

Why is the wicket seven miles away,
 And why have I to walk it all alone?
I hope that Bottle's bat will drive today –
 I ought to buy a weapon of my own.
I wonder if this walk will ever cease;
 They should provide a motor-car or crane
To drop the batsman on the popping-crease
 And, when he's out, convey him back again.

Is it a dream? Can this be truly me,
    Alone and friendless in a waste of grass?
The fielding side are sniggering, I see,
    And long-leg sort of shudders as I pass.
How very small and funny I must look!
    I only hope that no one knows my name.
I might be in a hammock with a book –
    *I can't imagine why I play this game.*

Well, here we are, We feel a little ill.
    What is this pedant of an umpire at?
Middle and off, or centre – what you will;
    It cannot matter where I park the bat.
I look around me in a knowing way
    To show that I am not to be cajoled;
I shall play forward gracefully and pray. . . .
    I have played forward and I am not bowled.
I do not like the wicket-keeper's face,
    And why are all these fielders crowding round?
The bowler makes an imbecile grimace,
    And mid-off makes a silly whistling sound.
These innuendoes I could do without;
    They mean to say the ball defied the bat.
They indicate that I was nearly out;
    Well, darn their impudence! I know all that.
Why am I standing in this comic pose,
    Hemmed in by men that I should like to maim?
I might be lying in a punt with Rose –
    *I can't imagine why I play this game.*

And there are people sitting over there
    Who fondly hope that I shall make a run;
They cannot guess how blinding is the glare;
    They do not know the ball is like a bun.
But, courage, heart! We have survived a ball;
    I pat the pitch to show that it is bad;

We are not such a rabbit, after all:
    Now we shall show them what is what, my lad!
The second ball is very, very swift;
    It breaks and stands up steeply in the air;
It looks at me, and I could swear it sniffed;
    I gesture at it, but it is not there.
Ah, what a ball! Mind you, I do not say
    That Bradman, Hobbs, and Ranji in his prime,
Rolled into one, and that one on his day,
    Might not have got a bat to it in time. . . .
But long-stop's looking for my middle-stump,
And I am walking in a world of shame;
My captain has addressed me as a chump –
    *I can't imagine why I play this game.*

*A. P. Herbert*

### SCORE BOOK

The Score book gives the outline of the match,
Who scored the runs, who bowled with due success,
But only mentions Jones's lyric catch
And Thompson's epic stand, with casualness.
*Caught Jones, bowled Smith,* so runs the level prose
Of Jones's running catch far in the deep.
*Thompson, bowled Johnson, nought,* the legend goes,
As though he made one ineffective sweep.
He was the last man in, and long he stayed,
And all the bowlers' onslaughts he defied.
He kept his end up while his partner made
The runs that won the victory for his side.
The book omits the poetry of Cricket,
How Brown superbly bowled, but took no wicket.

*W. A. G. Kemp*

## PAST AND PRESENT

Daisies are over Nyren, and Hambledon
Hardly remembers any summer gone:
And never again the Kentish elms shall see
Mynn, or Fuller Pilch, or Colin Blythe.
– Nor shall I see them, unless perhaps a ghost
Watching the elder ghosts beyond the moon.
But here in common sunshine I have seen
George Hirst, not yet a ghost, substantial,
His off-drives mellow as brown ale, and crisp
Merry late cuts and brave Chaucerian pulls;
Waddington's fury and the patience of Dipper;
And twenty easy artful overs of Rhodes,
So many stanzas of the Faerie Queen.

*William Kerr*

## THE HAYFIELDS

Their refuse tip increased. One day
A lorry shot down flattened tins,
The next half an old house. But play
Continues. Oil drums pitched, coin spins.
The skippers thumb the wicket, glance
Up at the sky, decide. All field,
Except the two men in, whose stance
Means business. Play. Wait, haven't peeled
Off yet (to quote the Gem), not stripped
Our jackets off. Bats dig their graves.
Dust, more dust, as more clinker's tipped
Before the first man swipes. He saves

His strength for bowling. Caught. He pouts,
Then bowls at both ends he's so big,
Bounces down like rubble bricks, shouts
To warn a nipper whose smart jig
Is chasing butterflies across
Cloud shadows, rushes, halts, hops, leaps –
What? Googly, yorker, wide, full toss?
Swinging, the bat flings dust up, heaps
Chalk white clouds. No one sees at first
The ball soaring away, sun high,
So close in line it seems to burst
Poles scaffolding a cold glass eye
(The new Tube station) in lark skies,
Then drops inside the refuse tip.
Lost ball. Fetch it. Six and out. Cries
The nipper, haven't batted. Slip
Across and ask. You. But the big
Star bat and bowler stirs the dust.
You go, you're fielding. And all dig
Toes harder in. You go. You. Trust
Him not to. Batsman fetches. Fists –
But ten a.m.'s too soon and hot
And he's too big to fight, his wrists
Hair covered. A fresh lorry's shot
Sticks, beams. Whose ball? It's buried now.
Not worth a tanner. Bob. Say please.
Who hit it? Who bowled? Hold your row.
A mutiny subdues to bees,
This endless August sun above,
That asphalt road, the cars close by,
Tipped water bottles fitting glove
Tight to red lips, and guzzled sigh
In nettles and tall thistles and
Unwanted hay. A driver yells
This yours? And throws it, huge paw hand
A friendly wave. The big boy tells

All he knew where to find it, but
Prefers to laze while play goes on.
Next year sign-board, contractors' hut;
Sand, barrows, mixers. Hayfields gone.

*R. D. Lancaster*

## PLAY!

Well, there's one word that moved me when a boy,
    That moves today:
It's when the Umpire, to the general joy,
    Pronounces 'PLAY!'

May I, ere time with all that he can bring
    Of sorrows serried,
Takes *that* delight from the delight of Spring,
    Be dead and buried

By some field path where cricketers may pass
    Along its mazes,
And over me the green short English grass,
    The English daisies!

## BALLADE OF DEAD CRICKETERS

Ah, where be Beldham now, and Brett,
    Barker, and Hogsflesh, where be they?
Brett, of all bowlers fleetest yet
    That drove the bails in disarray?
And Small that would, like Orpheus, play
    Till wild bulls followed his minstrelsy?
Booker, and Quiddington, and May?
    Beneath the daisies, there they lie!

And where is Lambert, that would get
   The stumps with balls that broke astray?
And Mann, whose balls would ricochet
   In almost an unholy way
(So do baseballers 'pitch' today);
   George Lear, that seldom let a bye,
And Richard Nyren, grave and gray?
   Beneath the daisies, there they lie!

Tom Sueter, too, the ladies' pet,
   Brown that would bravest hearts affray;
Walker, invincible when set,
   (Tom, of the spider limbs and splay);
Think ye that we could match them, pray,
   These heroes of Broad-halfpenny,
With Buck to hit, and Small to stay?
   Beneath the daises, there they lie!

*Envoy*

Prince, canst thou moralize the lay?
   How all things change below the sky?
Of Fry and Hirst shall mortals say,
   'Beneath the daisies, there they lie!'
                *Andrew Lang*

### GRACE AT GLOUCESTER

I saw the 'Old Man' once
When he was old as I
Was young. He did not score,
So far as I recall, a heap of runs,
Nor even hit a four.

But still he lives before my schoolboy eye
A giant among pygmies. In his hand
The bat looked like a toy. I saw him stand
Firm set on legs as massive as the piers
Of the Norman nave at Gloucester; and the cheers
Which greeted him on the 'Spa' were heard
As far as the Cathedral. When he stirred
The ground shook, and the crazy old
Pavilion creaked and groaned. I saw him field
– At point. When 'Father' Roberts bowled
And the batsman, now forgotten, from the group
Around the wicket cut a fast one square
Along the ground, the Doctor saw it there
A moment ere it was concealed
By his great bulk. He did not deign to stoop,
But let it pass. He bowled a few
Himself, slow lumbering to the crease. The
   batsmen knew
By then his simple bluff, and did not care.

Upon the Spa no county players pace;
The great ones of to-day it does not know.
I deem it better so,
Leaving the elm-girt field its dreams of Grace.

*Oscar Lloyd*


DRIVING TO THE MATCH

The linnets flit from hedge to hedge
   The lark exults on high,
The cattle, crowded at the brook,
Lift up their dripping heads to look
   As we go driving by.

The hoofs are on the road, boys,
    They sing a merry catch:
O the sun's at noon, and the year's at June,
    And we're driving to the match!

The brown-armed peasants in the hay
    Stand still with shaded eye,
The village children shout with glee,
And mothers leave their work to see
    As we go driving by.

The milkmaid flings a saucy smile,
    The farmer heaves a sigh,
Our horses' music floods the air.
And all the world is O so fair
    As we go driving by!

The hoofs are on the road, boys,
    Hark to their jocund catch;
O the sun's at noon and the year's at June,
    And we're driving to the match!

                                    *E. V. Lucas*

### TO CHARLES WORDSWORTH
*in reply to the present of a bat*

That bat that you were kind enough to send,
    Seems (for as yet I have not tried it) good:
And if there's anything on earth can mend
    My wretched play, it is that piece of wood.

                        *Henry Edward, Cardinal Manning*

## THE VILLAGE PITCH

They had no Grand Stand or Marquee,
 Down by the Quarry Farm:
There was a wealth of leafy tree
 Behind the bowler's arm.

There were no score cards to be had,
 Cushions for folk to hire;
Only we saw the butcher's lad
 Bowl out the Village Squire.

Lord's and the Oval truly mean
 Zenith of hard-won fame,
But it was just a village green
 Mothered and made the game.

## THE PITCH AT NIGHT

The sunset brings the twilight chill
 That steals, all noiseless, on the air.
The wind-freed world is standing still,
 The smoothed, worn ground looks strangely bare.

The bowler's run has blurred the crease,
 Which glints, a dim and spectral white,
Half sad, half comforting, this peace
 That settled o'er the ground at night.

Steps give a faintly eerie hiss
 On less tried turf towards the rough
(Was I too hard on Jones's miss,
 Or was I not quite hard enough?)

Here is an ancient, useless pad.
   The score-board stares, a square of ink.
Some of this outfield's rather bad. . . .
   It's colder now; to bed, I think.

             *G. D. Martineau*

### EPITAPH

As in life so in death lies a bat of renown,
   Slain by a lorry (three ton);
His innings is over, his bat is laid down:
   To the end a poor judge of a run.

             *George McWilliam*

### CLUB MATCH

Across green taffeta the bowler runs
With circling arm. The red ball magnified
Down to the clicking bat. The balls seem suns
Whose planets are the watchers' turning eyes!
The lazy lie with sweet grass in their lips;
The ladies twirl their Japanese sunshades.
All day the ball leaps down, the scratched bat clips;
All day the soft oppressive sun persuades.

The evening offers up the scent of grass
Scorched sweet; the light is little but dies long.
From the pavilion a man will sometimes pass,
Between his lips a drowsy butt of song.
As the moon rises, a great orange glass,
Crickets play on, with clicking sweet and strong.

             *George Moor*

## VICTORY CALYPSO, LORD'S 1950

Cricket, lovely cricket,
At Lord's where I saw it;
Cricket, lovely cricket,
At Lord's where I saw it;
Yardley tried his best
But Goddard won the test.
They gave the crowd plenty fun;
Second Test and West Indies won.

*Chorus:* With those two little pals of mine
Ramadhin and Valentine.

The King was there well attired,
So they started with Rae and Stollmeyer;
Stolly was hitting balls around the boundary,
But Wardle stopped him at twenty.
Rae had confidence,
So he put up a strong defence;
He saw the King was waiting to see,
So he gave him a century.

*Chorus:* With those two little pals of mine
Ramadhin and Valentine.

West Indies first innings total was three-twenty-six
Just as usual.
When Bedser bowled Christiani
The whole thing collapsed quite easily,
England then went on,
And made one-hundred-fifty-one;
West Indies then had two-twenty lead,
And Goddard said, 'That's nice indeed.'

*Chorus:* With those two little pals of mine
Ramadhin and Valentine.

Yardley wasn't broken-hearted
When the second innings started;
Jenkins was like a target
Getting the first five into his basket.
But Gomez broke him down,
While Walcott licked them around;
He was not out for one-hundred and sixty-eight,
Leaving Yardley to contemplate.

*Chorus:* The bowling was super-fine
Ramadhin and Valentine.


West Indies was feeling homely,
Their audience had them happy.
When Washbrook's century had ended,
West Indies' voices all blended.
Hats went in the air.
They jumped and shouted without fear;
So at Lord's was the scenery
Bound to go down in history.

*Chorus:* After all was said and done,
Second Test and West Indies won!

*Egbert Moore ('Lord Beginner')*


THE NAMES

There's music in the names I used to know,
And magic when I heard them, long ago.
'Is Tyldesley batting?' Ah, the wonder still!
. . . . The school clock crawled, but cricket-thoughts
would fill
The last slow lesson-hour deliciously.
(Drone on, O teacher: you can't trouble me.)

'Kent will be out by now.' . . . (Well, if you choose
To keep us here while cricket's in the air,
You must expect our minds to wander loose
Along the roads to Leicester, Lord's and Leeds,
Old Trafford and the Oval, and the Taunton
    meads. . . .)

And then, at last, we'd raid the laneway where
A man might pass, perchance, with latest news.
Grey-grown and grave, yet he would smile to hear
Our thirsty questions as we crowded near.
Greedily from the quenching page we'd drink –
How its white sun-glare made our young eyes wink!
'Yes, Tyldesley's batting still. He's ninety-four.
Barlow and Mold play well. Notts win once more.
Glo'ster (with Grace) have lost to Somerset –
Easy: ten wickets: Woods and Palairet. . . .'
So worked the magic in that summer lane.
The stranger beamed. Maybe he felt again
As I feel now to tell the linked names
Jewelling the loveliest of our English games.
Abel and Albert Trott, Lilley, Lillywhite,
Hirst, Hearne, and Tunnicliffe – they catch the light –
Lord Hawke and Hornby, Jessop, A. O. Jones –
Surely the glow they held was the high sun's!

Or did a young boy's worship think it so,
And is it but his heart that's aching now?

Thomas Moult

## THE FIELD

Let me first describe the field:
Its size, a double acre; walled
Along the north by a schoolyard,
West by a hedge and orchards; tarred
Wood railings on the east to fence
The grass from the station shunting lines,
That crook like a defensive ditch
Below the ramparts of the Church;
And south, the butter meadows, yellow
As fat and bumpy as a pillow,
Rumpling down the mile or more
That slopes to the wide Cumbrian shore,
With not a brick to lift a ban
Between the eye and the Isle of Man.
A common sort of field you'll say:
You'd find a dozen any day
In any northern town, a sour
Flat landscape shaped with weed and wire,
And nettle clump and ragwort thicket –
But this field is put by for cricket.
Here among the grass and plantains
Molehills matter more than mountains,
And generations watch the score
Closer than toss of peace and war.
Here, in matches won and lost,
The town hoards an heroic past,
And legendary bowlers tie
The child's dream in the father's lie.
This is no Wisden pitch; no place
For classic cuts and Newbolt's verse,
But the luck of the league, stiff and stark
With animosity of dark
In-grown village and mining town
When evening smoke-light drizzles down,

And the fist is tight in the trouser pocket,
And the heart turns black for the want of a wicket.

Or knock-out cricket, brisk as a bird,
Twenty overs and league men barred –
Heels in the popping crease, crouch and clout,
And the crowd half-codding the batsmen out.
Over the thorn and elder hedge
The sunlight floods, but leaves a ledge
Of shadow where the old men sit,
Dozing their pipes out. Frays of light
Seam a blue serge suit; gnats swarm,
And swallows dip round the bowler's arm.
Here in a small-town game is seen
The long-linked dance of the village green:
Wishing well and maypole ring,
Mumming and ritual of spring.

### OLD MAN AT A CRICKET MATCH

'It's mending worse,' he said,
Turning west his head,
Strands of anxiety ravelled like old rope,
Skitter of rain on the scorer's shed
His only hope.

Seven down for forty-five,
Catches like stings from a hive,
And every man on the boundary appealing –
An evening when it's bad to be alive,
And the swifts squealing.

Yet without boo or curse
He waits leg-break or hearse,
Obedient in each to lease and letter –
Life and the weather mending worse,
Or worsening better.

## MILLOM

The soft mouths of summer bite at the eyes,
Toothless as a rose and red as the ragged robin;
    Mouths on lip
    Rouse to sleep
And the green of the field reflected in the skies.

The elder-flower curls inward to a dream,
And memories swarm as a halo of midges;
    Children on the grass,
    Wicket-high, pass,
In blue sailor jackets and jerseys brown and cream.

Among the champion, legendary men
I see my childhood roll like a cricket-ball.
    To watch that boy
    Is now my joy –
That he could watch me not was *his* joy then.

*Norman Nicholson*

## AN ENGLISHMAN'S CREASE

I've been standin' 'ere at this wicket since yesterday, just
    arter tea;
My tally to date is eleven and the total's an 'undred an' three;
The crowd 'as been booin' an' bawlin'; it's booed and it's
    bawled itself 'oarse,
But barrackin', bawlin' an' booin' I takes as a matter of
    course.

'Oo am I to be put off my stroke, Mum, becos a few 'ooligans
    boos?
An Englishman's crease is 'is castle: I shall stay 'ere as long
    as I choose.

It's not when the wicket's plumb easy that a feller can give of 'is best;

It's not 'ittin' out like a blacksmith that wins any sort of a Test.

The crowd, they knows nuthink about it; they wants us to swipe at the ball;

But the feller 'oo does what the crowd wants, I reckon 'e's no use at all.

'Oo am I to be put off my stroke, Mum, becos a few 'ooligans boos?

An Englishman's crease is 'is castle, I shall stay 'ere as long as I choose.

*Hubert Phillips*

## IN MEMORIAM, ALFRED MYNN

Jackson's pace is very fearful; Willshire's hand is very high:

William Caffyn has good judgment, and an admirable eye:

Jemmy Grundy's cool and clever, almost always on the spot:

Tinsley's slows are often telling, though they sometimes catch it hot.

But however good their trundling – pitch, or pace, or break, or spin –

Still the monarch of all bowlers, to my mind, was Alfred Mynn.

Richard Daft is cool and cautious, with his safe and graceful play;

If George Griffith gets a loose one, he can send it far away.

You may bowl your best at Hayward's, and whatever style you try

Will be vanquished by the master's steady hand and certain eye.

But whatever fame and glory these and other bats may win,
Still the monarch of hard hitters, to my mind, was Alfred
Mynn.

You may praise the pluck of Burbidge, as he plays an uphill
match;
You may thunder cheers to Miller, for a wondrous running
catch;
You may join with me in wishing that the Oval once again
Shall resound with hearty plaudits to the praise of Mr Lane;
But the gentlemen of England the match will hardly win
Till they find another bowler, such as glorious Alfred Mynn.

When the great old Kent Eleven, full of pluck and hope
began
The grand battle with All England, single-handed, man to
man,
How the hop-men watched their hero, massive, muscular,
and tall,
As he mingled with the players, like a king among them all;
Till to some Old Kent enthusiasts it would almost seem a sin
To doubt their county's triumph when led on by Alfred Mynn.

Though Sir Frederick and 'The Veteran' bowled straight and
sure and well,
Though Box behind the wicket only Lockyer can excel;
Though Jemmy Dean, as long-stop, would but seldom grant
a bye;
Though no novices in batting were George Parr and Joseph
Guy
Said the fine old Kentish farmers, with a fine old Kentish
grin,
'Why, there ain't a man among them as can match our Alfred
Mynn.'

And whatever was the issue of the frank and friendly fray.
(Aye, and often has his bowling turned the fortunes of the
    day),
Still the Kentish men fought bravely, never losing hope or
    heart,
Every man of the Eleven glad and proud to play his part.
And with five such mighty cricketers, 'twas but natural to
    win,
As Felix, Wenman, Hillyer, Fuller Pilch, and Alfred Mynn.

With his tall and stately presence, with his nobly moulded
    form,
His broad hand was ever open, his brave heart was ever
    warm;
All were proud of him, all loved him. As the changing seasons
    pass,
As our champion lies a-sleeping underneath the Kentish
    grass,
Proudly, sadly will we name him – to forget him were a sin.
Lightly lie the turf upon thee, kind and manly Alfred Mynn!

*William Jeffrey Prowse*

### THE ONE-WAY CRITIC

Upon the groaning bench he took his seat –
    Sunlight and shadow on the dew-blessed grass –
He spread the *Daily Moan* beneath his feet,
    Hitched to his eye an astigmatic glass,
Then, like a corn-crake calling to an owl
    That knows no answer, he began to curse,
Remarking, with an unattractive scowl,
    'The state of cricket goes from bad to worse;
Where are the bowlers of my boyhood's prime?

Where are the batsmen of the pristine years?
Where are the fieldsmen of the former time?'
  And, as he spoke, my eyelids filled with tears;
For I perhaps alone, knew they were dead,
    Mynn an old myth, and Hambledon a name.
And it occurred to me that I had read
  (In classroom) 'All things always are the same';
So, comfort drawing from this maxim, turned
    To the myopic moaner on the seat;
A flame of rage, not pity, in me burned,
    Yet I replied in accents clear and sweet –
'There *were* no bowlers in your boyhood's prime,
    There *were* no batsmen in the pristine years,
There *were* no fieldsmen in that former time' –
  My voice grew firm, my eyes were dry of tears –
'*Your* fathers cursed the bowlers you adored,
    *Your* fathers damned the batsmen of your choice,
*Your* fine, ecstatic rapture they deplored,
    There was the *One-Way Critic*'s ageless voice,
And their immortal curse is yours today,
    The croak which kills all airy Cricket Dryads,
Withers the light on tree and grass and spray,
    The strangling fugue of senile jeremiads.'

I ceas'd; and turn'd to Larwood's bounding run,
And Woolley's rapier flashing in the sun.

### THE ONE-WAY BOY

When coaching boys the other day,
Recalling legs that legward stray,
Wearily pleading that it mars
The style, if bats are scimitars;

Persuading bowlers that their length
And rectitude are more than strength,
However jovially applied
If all it ends in is – a wide.
The father of some cricketer,
A heavy man, approach'd, said, 'Sir,
My boy is *always* caught at slip;
It gives me one gigantic pip:
Now can you give me any reason
Why this should happen *all* the season,
Instead of intermittently,
As it occurs with you or me?'
'Show me the boy,' quoth I, 'sir, please.'
Whereat, scorbutic, ill-at-ease,
Stole from behind his ample father
A boy, obscured till now, or rather
What might have passed for boy, by chance,
But for his cow-like countenance:
Never in any town or rank
Saw I a face so *wholly* blank:
No freckle, twinkle; nothing dimly;
It was a facial Sahara, simply.
'Put on those pads' his father said
As if conversing with the dead,
'And show the gentleman the stroke,
Concerning which I lately spoke.'
He donned them filially resign'd.
I gave him guard, to leg inclined,
I bowled him long-hops free from guile,
Full-pitchers you could hit a mile,
Half-volleys straight, half-volley's wide,
Swervers, delicious for the glide;
*He* never swerved, nor lost his grip,
But snicked the ruddy lot to slip.
Strange wonders have there been in Cricket –
Once, in a match, I took a wicket,

Shod in a heel-less evening shoe
(A confidence 'twixt me and you),
Jones bowled a ball through Grace's beard,
And Ranji only Lockwood feared,
But never, since the game began,
Since old men stood while young men ran,
Was such consummate batsmanship
As to hole out, each ball, at slip.
'Take off those pads,' his father said
(Resuming converse with the dead)
'You've shown the gentleman the stroke
By which my heart and mother's broke;
Good-day, sir!' and with footsteps slow
He took his tragedy in tow,
The parent first, the portent after,
Leaving me deep in awe and laughter.

R. C. Robertson-Glasgow

## ON AN ENGRAVING OF
### ALFRED MYNN ESQ (1852)

Grasped like a twig in his enormous hands,
The crude bat is a measure, as now his expanding
Frame places him in Time – a Victorian,
Whose engraved features yellow while a band
Plays in the distance, and a gulf of pleasure
Yawns. Now, as we watch his careful,
Studied posture, we imagine the bowler rolling up his
    sleeve.

Beneath the solemn black-quiffed forehead
The eyes, like cameras, study us – developments
Of their passive gaze; and what is said
Nobody knows, as all we see is part
Of our costumed Past – the stomach bellying like a sail,

Pale-blue sash, and narrow, faded flannels.
And what is hidden is the art
That made his name a byword in a social age,
The brilliant speed and swinging flight
No portrait can suggest, words recreate or disparage.

## J. M. PARKS AT TUNBRIDGE WELLS

Parks takes ten off two successive balls from Wright,
A cut to the rhododendrons and a hook for six.
And memory begins suddenly to play its tricks:
I see his father batting, as, if here, he might.

Now Tunbridge Wells, 1951; the hair far lighter,
The body boyish, flesh strung across thin bone,
And arms sinewy as the wrists are thrown
At the spinning ball, the stance much straighter.

Now it is June full of heaped petals
The day steamy, tropical; rain glistens
On the pavilion, shining on corrugated metal.
The closeness has an air that listens.

Then it was Eastbourne, 1935; a date
Phrased like a vintage, sea-fret on the windscreen.
And Parks, rubicund and squat, busily sedate,
Pushing Verity square, moving his score to nineteen.

Images of Then, so neatly parcelled and tied
By ribbons of war – but now through a chance
Resemblance re-opened; a son's stance
At the wicket opens the closed years wide.

And it is no good resisting the interior
Assessment, the fusion of memory and hope
That comes flooding to impose on inferior
Attainment – yesterday, today, twisted like a rope.

Parks drives Wright under dripping green trees,
The images compare and a father waves away
Applause, pale sea like a rug over the knees,
Covering him, the son burying his day

With charmed strokes. And abstractedly watching,
Drowning, I struggle to shake off the Past
Whose arms clasp like a mother, catching
Up with me, summer at half-mast.

The silent inquisitors subside. The crowd,
Curiously unreal in this regency spa, clap,
A confectionery line under bushes heavily bowed
In the damp. Then Parks pierces Wright's leg-trap.

And we come through, back to the present.
Sussex 300 for 2. Moss roses on the hill.
A dry taste in the mouth, but the moment
Sufficient, being what we are, ourselves still.

## CRICKET AT BRIGHTON

At night the Front like coloured barley-sugar; but now
Soft blue, all soda, the air goes flat over flower-beds,
Blue railings and beaches; below, half-painted boats, bow
Up, settle in sand, names like Moss-Rose and Dolphin
Drying in a breeze that flicks at the ribs of the ride.
The chalk coastline folds up its wings of Beachy Head
And Worthing, fluttering white over water like brides.
Regency Squares, the Pavilion, oysters and mussels and gin.

Piers like wading confectionery, esplanades of striped tulip.
Cricket began here yesterday, the air heavy, suitable
For medium-paced bowlers; but deck-chairs mostly were
    vacant,
Faces white over startling green. Later, trains will decant
People with baskets, litter and opinions, the seaside's staple
Ingredients. Today Langridge pushes the ball for unfussed
Singles; ladies clap from check rugs, talk to retired colonels;
On tomato-red verandas the scoring rate is discussed.

Sussex v. Lancashire, the air birded and fresh after rain,
Dew on syringa and cherry. Seaward the water
Is satin, pale emerald, fretted with lace at the edges,
The whole sky rinsed easy like nerves after pain.
May here is childhood, lost somewhere between and never
Recovered, but again moved nearer like a lever
Turned on the pier flickers the Past into pictures.
A time of immediacy, optimism, without stricture.

Post-cards and bathing machines and old prints.
Something comes back, the inkling and momentary hint
Of what we had wanted to be, though differently now
For the conditions are different, and what we had wanted
We wanted as we were then, without conscience, unhaunted,
And given the chance must refuse to want it again.
Only, occasionally, we escape, we return where we were:
Watching cricket at Brighton, Cornford bowling through
    sea-scented air.

## TEST MATCH AT LORD'S

Bailey bowling, McLean cuts him late for one.
I walk from the Long Room into slanting sun.
Two ancients halt as Statham starts his run.
Then, elbows linked, but straight as sailors
On a tilting deck, they move. One, square-shouldered as
    a tailor's
Model, leans over, whispering in the other's ear:
'Go easy. Steps here. This end bowling.'
Turning, I watch Barnes guide Rhodes into fresher air,
As if to continue an innings, though Rhodes may only
    play by ear.

## THE BLUES AT LORD'S

Near-neighboured by a blandly boisterous Dean
Who 'hasn't missed the match since '92',
Proposing to perpetuate the scene
I concentrate my eyesight on the cricket.
The game proceeds, as it is bound to do
Till tea-time or the fall of the next wicket.

Agreeable sunshine fosters greensward greener
Than College lawns in June. Tradition-true,
The stalwart teams, capped with contrasted blue,
Exert their skill; adorning the arena
With modest, manly, muscular demeanour –
Reviving memories in ex-athletes who
Are superannuated from agility –
And (while the five-ounce fetish they pursue)
Admired by gloved and virginal gentility.

My intellectual feet approach this function
With tolerance and Public-School compunction;
Aware that, whichsoever side bats best,
Their partisans are equally well-dressed.
For, though the Government has gone vermilion
And, as a whole, is weak in Greek and Latin,
The fogies harboured by the august Pavilion
Sit strangely similar to those who sat in
The edifice when first the Dean went pious –
For possible preferment sacrificed
His hedonistic and patrician bias,
And offered his complacency to Christ.

Meanwhile some Cantab slogs a fast half-volley
Against the ropes. 'Good shot, sir! O good shot!'
Ejaculates the Dean in accents jolly. . . . .
Will Oxford win? Perhaps. Perhaps they'll not.
Can Cambridge lose? Who knows? One fact seems
    sure;
That, while the Church approves, Lord's will endure.


### THE EXTRA INCH

O Batsman, rise and go and stop the rot,
And go and stop the rot.
(It was indeed a rot,
Six down for twenty-three).
The batsman thought how wretched was his lot,
And all alone went he.

The bowler bared his mighty, cunning arm,
His vengeance-wreaking arm,
His large yet wily arm,
With fearful powers endowed.
The batsman took his guard. (A deadly calm
Had fallen on the crowd.)

O is it a half-volley or long-hop,
A seventh-bounce long-hop,
A fast and fierce long-hop,
That the bowler letteth fly?
The ball was straight and bowled him neck and crop
He knew not how nor why.

Full sad and slow pavilionwards he walked.
The careless critics talked;
Some said that he was yorked;
A half-volley at a pinch.
The batsman murmured as he inward stalked,
'It was the extra inch.'

*Siegfried Sassoon*

## AT LORD'S

It is little I repair to the matches of the Southron folk,
  Though my own red roses there may blow;
It is little I repair to the matches of the Southron folk,
  Though the red roses crest the caps, I know.
For the field is full of shades as I near the shadowy coast,
And a ghostly batsman plays to the bowling of a ghost,
And I look through my tears on a soundless-clapping host
  As the run-stealers flicker to and fro,
    To and fro:
  O my Hornby and my Barlow long ago!

It is Glo'ster coming North, the irresistible,
  The Shire of the Graces, long ago!
It is Gloucestershire up North, the irresistible,
  And new-risen Lancashire the foe!
A Shire so young that has scarce impressed its traces,
Ah, how shall it stand before all-resistless Graces?
O, little red rose, their bats are as maces
  To beat thee down, this summer long ago!

This day of seventy-eight they are come up North against thee
   This day of seventy-eight, long ago!
The champion of the centuries, he cometh up against thee,
   With his brethren, every one a famous foe!
The long-whiskered Doctor, that laugheth rules to scorn,
While the bowler, pitched against him, bans the day that he
   was born;
And G.F. with his science makes the fairest length forlorn;
   They are come from the West to work thee woe!

It is little I repair to the matches of the Southron folk,
   Though my own red roses there may blow;
It is little I repair to the matches of the Southron folk,
   Though the red roses crest the caps, I know.
For the field is full of shades as I near the shadowy coast,
And a ghostly batsman plays to the bowling of a ghost,
And I look through my tears on a soundless-clapping host,
   As the run-stealers flicker to and fro,
     To and fro:
   O my Hornby and my Barlow long ago!

### 'RIME O' BAT OF O MY SKY-EM'

Wake! for the Ruddy Ball has taken flight
That scatters the slow Wicket of the Night;
   And the swift Batsman of the Dawn has driven
Against the Star-spiked Rails a fiery Smite.

Wake, my Beloved! take the Bat that clears
The sluggish Liver, and Dyspeptics cheers:
   Tomorrow? Why, tomorrow I may be
Myself with Hambledon and all its Peers.

Today a Score of Batsmen brings, you say?
Yes, but where leaves the Bats of yesterday?
   And this same summer day that brings a Knight
May take the Grace and Ranjitsinhji away.

Willsher the famed is gone with all his 'throws'.
And Alfred's Six-foot Reach where no man knows;
   And Hornby – the great hitter – his own Son
Plays in his place, yet recks not the Red Rose.

And Silver Billy, Fuller Pilch and Small,
Alike the pigmy Briggs and Ulyett tall,
   Have swung their Bats an hour or two before,
But none played out the last and silent Ball.

Well, let them Perish! What have we do to
With Gilbert Grace the Great, or that Hindu?
   Let Hirst and Spooner slog them as they list,
Or Warren bowl his 'snorter'; care not you!

With me along the Strip of Herbage strown,
That is not laid or watered, rolled or sown,
   Where name of Lord's and Oval is forgot,
And peace to Nicholas on his bomb-girt Throne.

A level Wicket, as the Ground allow,
A driving Bat, a lively Ball, and thou
   Before me bowling on the Cricket-pitch –
O Cricket-pitch were Paradise enow!

2

I listened where the Grass was shaven small,
And heard the Bat that groaned against the Ball:
   Thou pitchest Here and There, and Left and Right,
Nor deem I where the Spot thou next may'st Fall.

Forward I play, and Back, and Left and Right,
And overthrown at once, or stay till Night:
    But this I know, where nothing else I know,
The last is Thine, how so the Bat shall smite.

This thing is sure, where nothing else is sure,
The boldest Bat may but a Space endure;
    And he who One or who a Hundred hits
Falleth at ending to thy Force or Lure.

Wherefore am I allotted but a Day
To taste Delight, and make so brief a stay;
    For meed of all my labour laid aside,
Endeth alike the Player and the Play.

Behold, there is an Arm behind the Ball,
Nor the Bat's Stroke of its own Striking all;
    And who the Gamesters, to what end the Game,
I think thereof our witting is but small.

Against the Attack and Twist of Circumstance
Though I oppose Defence and Shifty Glance,
    What Power gives Nerve to me, and what Assaults, –
This is the Riddle. Let dull bats cry 'Chance'.

Is there a Foe that domineers the Ball?
And one that Shapes and wields us Willows all?
    Be patient if Thy Creature in Thy Hand
Break, and the so-long-guarded Wicket fall!

Thus spoke the Bat. Perchance a foolish Speech
And wooden, for a Bat has straitened Reach:
    Yet thought I, I had heard Philosophers
Prate much on this wise, and aspire to Teach.

Ah, let us take our Stand, and play the Game,
But rather for the cause than for the Fame;
     Albeit right evil is the Ground, and we
Know our Defence thereon will be but lame.

O Love, if thou and I could but Conspire
Against this Pitch of Life, so false with Mire,
     Would we not Doctor it afresh, and then
Roll it out smoother to the Bat's Desire?

                                        *Francis Thompson*

## CHANT ROYAL OF CRICKET

When earth awakes as from some dreadful night
And doffs her melancholy mourning state,
When May buds burst in blossom and requite
     Our weary eyes for Winter's tedious wait,
Then the pale bard takes down his dusty lyre
And strikes the thing with more than usual fire.
Myself, compacted of an earthier clay,
I oil my bats and greasy homage pay
     To Cricket, who, with emblems of his court,
Stumps, pads, bails, gloves, begins his summer sway.
     Cricket in sooth is Sovran King of Sport.

As yet no shadows blur the magic light,
     The glamour that surrounds the opening date
Illusions yet undashed my soul excite
     And of success in luring whispers prate.
I see myself in form: my thoughts aspire
To reach the giddy summit of desire.
Lovers and such may sing a roundelay,
What'er that be, to greet returning May;
     For me, not much – the season's all too short;
I hear the mower hum and scent the fray.
     Cricket in sooth is Sovran King of Sport.

A picture stands before my dazzled sight,
　　Wherein the hero, ruthlessly elate,
Defies all bowlers' concentrated spite.
　　That hero is myself, I need not state.
'Tis sweet to see the captain's growing ire
And his relief when I at last retire;
'Tis sweet to run pavilionwards and say,
'Yes, somehow I was seeing them today' –
　　Thus modesty demands that I retort
To murmured compliments upon my play.
　　Cricket in sooth is Sovran King of Sport.

The truth's resemblance is, I own, but slight
　　To these proud visions which my soul inflate.
This is the sort of thing: In abject fright
　　I totter down the steps and through the gate;
Somehow I reach the pitch and bleat, 'Umpire,
Is that one leg?' What boots it to enquire?
The impatient bowler takes one grim survey,
Speeds to the crease and whirls – a lightning ray?
　　No, a fast yorker. Bang! the stumps cavort.
Chastened, but not surprised, I go my way.
　　Cricket in sooth is Sovran King of Sport.

Lord of the Game, for whom these lines I write,
　　Fulfil my present hope, watch o'er my fate;
Defend me from the swerver's puzzling flight;
　　Let me not be run out, at any rate.
As one who's been for years a constant trier,
Reward me with an average slightly higher;
Let it be double figures. This I pray,
Humblest of boons, before my hair grows grey
　　And Time's flight bids me in the last resort
Try golf, or otherwise your cause betray.
　　Cricket in sooth is Sovran King of Sport.

King, what though Age's summons I obey,
Resigned to dull rheumatics and decay,
    Still on one text my hearers I'll exhort,
As long as hearers within range will stay:
    'Cricket in sooth is Sovran King of Sport'.

*H. S. Vere Hodge*

## BOY AT A CRICKET MATCH

Holding his hands like strange ivy,
He twines them round his mother's broad shadow;
She is his tree, only with her he grows.
For him she keeps her leaves, her first love,
All the year round. He does not know.

(The sun coming through branches, green,
And leaves, like warm water unseen.)

Turning horizon-smiling eyes around,
He sees the sky aghast with light
Between the trees, oppressive boughs, and sees
The bowler flex his arms like wings
And knows a real need for flight.

*Hugo Williams*

## MISSED!

The sun in the heavens was beaming;
The breeze bore an odour of hay,
My flannels were spotless and gleaming,
My heart was unclouded and gay;
The ladies, all gaily apparelled,
Sat round looking on at the match,
In the tree-tops the dicky-birds carolled,
All was peace till I bungled that catch.

My attention the magic of summer
Had lured from the game – which was wrong;
The bee (that inveterate hummer)
Was droning its favourite song.
I was tenderly dreaming of Clara
(On her not a girl is a patch);
When, ah horror! there soared through the air a
Decidedly possible catch.

I heard in a stupor the bowler
Emit a self-satisfied 'Ah!'
The small boys who sat on the roller
Set up an expectant 'Hurrah!'
The batsman with grief from the wicket
Himself had begun to detach –
And I uttered a groan and turned sick – It
Was over. I'd buttered the catch.

Oh ne'er, if I live to a million,
Shall I feel such a terrible pang.
From the seats in the far-off pavilion
A loud yell of ecstasy rang.
By the handful my hair (which is auburn)
I tore with a wrench from my thatch,
And my heart was seared deep with a raw burn
At the thought that I'd foozled that catch.

Ah, the bowler's low querulous mutter,
Point's loud, unforgettable scoff!
Oh, give me my driver and putter!
Henceforward my game shall be golf.
If I'm asked to play cricket hereafter,
I am wholly determined to scratch.
Life's void of all pleasure and laughter;
I bungled the easiest catch.

*P. G. Wodehouse*

## THE BAND AT PLAY

In Festivals or Cricket Weeks
Muffled or intermittent squeaks
Denote the presence of a band,
But what I fail to understand
Is why half-hearted use is made
Of local instrumental aid.
If you have music, I submit
That you should make the most of it.
The band might play the batsman in,
That stirring march from 'Lohengrin'
Would fill the bill; now how about
A tune to play the batsman out?
No difficulty here at all,
Handel's C Major 'March in Saul'.
'The Rosary', 'Lest we forget',
'Funeral March of Marionette',
'Goodbye for Ever' (this to be
A second innings threnody). . . .
Such melodies as these I think,
(Culled and arranged by Herman Finck),
As incidental to the action
Should merit general satisfaction.

*Ralph Wotherspoon*

## COUNTY CRICKET

The day's last ball is being bowled:
Here it is now in the air,
Harmless looking,
Lacking guile,
Even makes the batsman smile,

For he knows there's no more play
When he's got this one away.
With batsman set
The ball you'll bet
Will go for six,
And so it should.
But don't forget
In county cricket,
That a ball well off the wicket
Never should be hit for four;
So the batsman carefully plays it
Slowly back
Along the floor.

*Ron Yeomans*

# PART V

# New Poetry

'The hoofs are on the road, boys,
Hark to their jocund catch;
O the sun's at noon and the year's at June,
And we're driving to the match!'

*E. V. Lucas*
DRIVING TO THE MATCH

## CRICKET MASTER
### (*An Incident*)

My undergraduate eyes beholding,
    As I climbed your slope, Cat Hill:
Emerald chestnut fans unfolding,
    Symbols of my hope, Cat Hill.
What cared I for past disaster,
Applicant for cricket master,
Nothing much of cricket knowing,
Conscious but of money owing?
    Somehow I would cope, Cat Hill.

'The sort of man we want must be prepared
To take our first eleven. Many boys
From last year's team are with us. You will find
Their bowling's pretty good and they are keen.'
'And so am I, Sir, very keen indeed.'
Oh where's mid-on? And what is silly point?
Do six balls make an over? Help me, God!
'Of course you'll get some first-class cricket too;
The MCC send down an A team here.'
My bluff had worked. I sought the common-room,
Of last term's pipe-smoke faintly redolent.
It waited empty with its worn arm-chairs
For senior bums to mine, when in there came
A fierce old eagle in whose piercing eye
I saw that instant-registered dislike
Of all unhealthy aesthetes such as me.
'I'm Winters – you're our other new recruit
And here's another new man – Barnstaple.'
He introduced a thick Devonian.

'Let's go and have some practice in the nets.
You'd better go in first.' With but one pad,
No gloves, and knees that knocked in utter fright,
Vainly I tried to fend the hail of balls
Hurled at my head by brutal Barnstaple
And at my shins by Winters. Nasty quiet
Followed my poor performance. When the sun
Had sunk behind the fringe of Hadley Wood
And Barnstaple and I were left alone
Among the ash-trays of the common-room,
He murmured in his soft West-Country tones:
'D'you know what Winters told me, Betjeman?
*He didn't think you'd ever held a bat.*'
 The trusting boys returned. 'We're jolly glad
You're on our side, Sir, in the trial match.'
'But I'm no good at all.' 'Oh yes, you are.'
When I was out first ball, they said 'Bad luck!
You hadn't got your eye in.' Still I see
Barnstaple's smile of undisguised contempt,
Still feel the sting of Winters' silent sneer.
Disgraced, demoted to the seventh game,
Even the boys had lost their faith in me.
God guards his aesthetes. If by chance these lines
Are read by one who in some common-room
Has had his bluff called, let him now take heart:
In every school there is a sacred place
More holy than the chapel. Ours was yours:
I mean, of course, the first-eleven pitch.
Here in the welcome break from morning work,
The heavier boys, of milk and biscuits full,
Sat on the roller while we others pushed
Its weighty cargo slowly up and down.
We searched the grass for weeds, caressed the turf,
Lay on our stomachs squinting down its length
To see that all was absolutely smooth.
 The prize-day neared. And, on the eve before,

We masters hung our college blazers out
In readiness for tomorrow. Matron made
A final survey of the boys' best clothes –
Clean shirts. Clean collars. 'Rice, your jacket's torn.
Bring it to me this instant!' Supper done,
Barnstaple drove his round-nosed Morris out
And he and I and Vera Spencer-Clarke,
Our strong gymnasium mistress, squashed ourselves
Into the front and rattled to The Cock.

    Sweet bean-fields then were scenting Middlesex;
Narrow lanes led between the dairy farms
To ponds reflecting weather-boarded inns.
There on the wooden bench outside The Cock
Sat Barnstaple, Miss Spencer-Clarke and I,
At last forgetful of tomorrow's dread
And gazing into sky-blue Hertfordshire.
Three pints for Barnstaple, three halves for me,
Sherry of course for Vera Spencer-Clarke.

    Pre-prize-day nerves? Or too much bitter beer?
What had that evening done to Barnstaple?
I only know that singing we returned;
The more we sang, the faster Barnstaple
Drove his old Morris, swerving down the drive
And in and out the rhododendron clumps,
Over the very playing-field itself,
And then – oh horror! – right across the pitch
Not once, but twice or thrice. The mark of tyres
Next day was noticed at the Parents' Match.

                      *John Betjeman*

### RITES

Many a time I have seen him savin'
the side (the tailor was saying
as he sat and sewed in his shop).

You remember that tourney wid Brandon?
What-he-name-now
that big-able water policeman –

de one in charge o' de Harbour Patrol . . .
You mean Hop-
a-long Cass! Is because a cow

give he mother a kick before he did born
that he foot come out so.
Yes, I know

but is not what I talkin' about. Ol'
Hoppy was bowlin' that day
as if he was hurricane father.

Lambert went in, play-
in' he know all about it as us'al
an' *swoosh!* there he go fan-

nin' outside the off-stump an'
is *click!*
he snick

de ball straight into de slips.
'Well boys it look like we lossin'
this match', says the skipper,

writin' nought in the exercise book
he was keepin' the score in; 'you think
we could chance it an' sen' Gullstone in

before Charlie or Spooks?'
So Gullstone went in.
You could see he face whitenin'

under he tan an you know
that that saga-boy frighten: bat
tappin', feet walkin' 'bout like they talkin'

wid ants; had was to stop meself axin'
meself if he ever play cricket on Brown's beach before.
An' I tole him,

I tole him over an' over
agen: *watch de ball, man,* watch
de ball like it hook to you eye

when you first goes in an' you doan know de pitch.
Uh doan mean to *poke*
but you jes got to *watch what you doin'*;

this isn't no time for playin'
the fool nor makin' no sport; this is cricket!
But Gullstone too deaf:

mudder doan clean out de wax in 'e ear!
Firs' ball from Cass an' he fishin';
secon' ball an' he missin', swishin'

he bat like he wishin'
to catch butterfly; though the all Gullstone ever could catch
pun dis beach was a cole!

But is always the trouble wid we:
too fraid an' too frighten.
Is all very well when it rosy an' sweet,

but leh murder start an' *bruggalungdung!*
you cahn fine a man to hole up de side.

Look wha' happen las' week at de O-
val!

At de Oval?
Wha' happen las' week at de Oval?

You mean to say that you come
in here wid dat lime-skin cone

that you callin' a hat
pun you head, an' them slip slop shoe strap

on to you foot like a touris';
you sprawl you ass

all over my chair widdout ask-
in' me please leave nor licence,

wastin' muh time when you know very well that uh cahn fine
enough to finish these zoot suits

'fore Christmas' an' on top
o'all this, you could wine up de nerve to stop

me cool cool cool in de middle
o'all me needle

an' t'read; make me prick me hand in me haste;
an' tell me broad an' bole to me face

THAT YOU DOAN REALLY KNOW WHA' HAPPEN
at Kensington Oval?

We was *only* playin' de MCC, man;
M-C-C
who come all de way out from Inglan.

We was battin', you see;
score wasn't too bad; one
hurren an' ninety-

seven fuh three.
The openers out, Tae Worrell out,
Everton Weekes jus' glide two fuh fifty

an' jack is de GIANT to come!
Feller name Wardle
was bowlin'; tossin' it up

sweet sweet slow-medium syrup.
Firs' ball . . .
'No . . . o . . . o . . .'

back down de wicket to Wardle.
Secon' ball . . .
'N . . . o . . . o . . .'

back down de wicket to Wardle.
Third ball comin' up
an' we know wha' goin' happen to syrup:

Clyde back pun he back
foot an' *prax*!
is through extra cover an' four red runs all de way.

'You see dat shot?' the people was shoutin';
'Jesus Chrise, man, wunna see dat shot?'
All over de groun' fellers shakin' hands wid each other

as if was *they* wheelin' de willow
as if was *them* had the power;
one man run out pun de field wid a red fowl cock

goin' quawk quawk quawk in 'e han';
would'a give it to Clyde right then an' right there
if a police hadn't stop 'e!

An' in front o' where I was sittin',
one ball-headed sceptic snatch hat off he head
as if he did crazy

an' pointin' he finger at Wardle,
he jump up an' down
like a sun-shatter daisy an' bawl

out: 'B . . . L . . . O . . . O . . . D, B . . . I . . . G B . . . O . . . Y
bring me he B . . . L . . . O . . . O . . . D'
Who would'a think that for twenty-

five years he was standin' up there
in them Post Office cages, lickin' gloy
pun de Gover'ment stamps.

If uh wasn't there to see fuh meself,
I would'a never believe it,
I would'a never believe it.

But I say it once an' I say it agen:
when things goin' good, you cahn touch
we; but leh murder start an' you cahn fine a man to hole up de
side.

Like when Laker come on.
Goin' remember what happenin' then
for the rest o' me life.

This Laker a quiet tall heavy-face fellow
who before he start to do anything ser'ous
is hitch up he pànts round he belly.

He bowlin' off-breaks.
Int makin' no fuss
ius' toss up de firs'

one an' *bap!*
Clyde play forward firm
an' de ball hit he pad

an' fly up over de wicket.
Boy, *dis* is cricket!
Laker shift weight

an' toss up de secon';
it pitchin' off-stump an' comin' back sharp
wid de men in de leg trap shinin' like shark.

Clyde stretchin' right out like a man in de dark
an' he kill it.
'N . . . o . . . o . . . o', from de schoolboys, 'hit it, hit it'.

Boy, dis is *cricket*.
Then Laker come down wid he third
one. He wrap up de ball in de palm

o' he han' like a package
AN' MAKE CLYDE WALCOTT LOOK FOOLISH.
Mister man, could'a hear

all de flies that was buzzin' out there
round de bread carts; could'a hear
if de empire fart.

An' then blue murder start:
'Kill one o' dem, Clyde', some wise-
wun was shoutin', 'knock he skull off;

doan let them tangle you up in no leg trap;
use de feet dat God give you!'
Ev'ry blabber mout' talkin',

ev'ry man jack givin' advice;
but we so frighten now at what happenin' there
we could piss we pants if we doan have a care.

'*Swing de bat, man*', one feller was shoutin';
an' Clyde swing de bat but de bat miss
de ball an' de ball hit he pad

an' he pâd went *biff*
like you beatin' bed
an' de empire han' stick

in de air
like Francis who dead
an' de bess o' we batsmen out.

The crowd so surprise you int hearin' a shout.
Ev'ry mout' loss.
But I say it once an' I say it agen:

when things goan' good, you cahn touch
we; but leh murder start
an' ol man, you cahn fine a man to hole up de side . . .

*Edward Brathwaite*

### RAISING THE SCREEN

Like a capsized schooner the white sight-screen
drifts broken and buckled at the field's edge,
thrown over in a Westerly gale its snapped spars
and slats jetsam the tall pre-season grass.

Much talk decides the way to right her, damaging
least, tacking and bolting off jacks. The tractor.

fresh painted and tough as a tug, is roped up
and the slack drawn in, three of us guyed as weights
at the back to stop her somersaulting.

The first rope snaps but we try again, racing
the April evening in. Tension, the rope strains,
holds and the old screen rises like a galleon
from a trough of sea, ever so slowly it seems,
creaking, faltering at the balance

then suddenly righting herself with a crash onto
the iron keel. But it crumples, sags, the solid
ash beams folding as a yard and rigging
smashed by cannon shot, the splintered slats
spuming through darkness like seagulls.

They settle and so do we, all questions answered;
quickly we break away what's left of the screen,
gather the driftwood, and in ten minutes
only the iron hulk remains, rusting and pathetic

as all such skeletons abandoned at the land's edge.
We go home quietly without opening the bar.
I dream a storm and high seas, my gallant corsair
The White Lady buffeted and broken off Tredrea.

### AT SABINA PARK

Proudly wearing the rosette
of my skin I strut into Sabina,
England boycotting excitement
bravely, something badly amiss.

Cricket. Not the game they play
at Lord's, the crowd (whoever saw
a crowd at a cricket match?)
are caged, vociferous partisans

quick to take offence. England
sixty eight for none at lunch.
'What sort o battin dat man?
dem caan play cricket again, praps
dem should a borrow Lawrence Rowe!'

And on it goes, the wicket slow
as the batting and the crowd restless.
'Eh white bwoy, ow you brudders dem
does sen we sleep so? Me a pay monies

fe watch dis foolishness? Cho?'
So I try to explain in my Hampshire
drawl about conditions in Kent,
about sticky wickets and muggy days
and the monsoon season in Manchester

but fail to convince even myself.

*Stewart Brown*


### HUCKSTEP

Huckstep was the groundsman at my prep school.
He put the heavy roller over the pitch,
Dragged by a horse in large flat leather shoes,
In those long-vanished summers.
A handsome smiling man and sunburned; quiet;
The brownest man I'd ever seen,
Dark oily hair and powerful arms in shirtsleeves.

He played, somebody told me, for the Kent Second XI,
Certainly he bowled at us in the nets,
Left arm medium, round the wicket,
With a beautiful action, a back-tossed lock of hair.

Now that I've been 'literary' for so many years
I recognize him. He might have been
Lady Chatterley's lover, Ted in *The Go-Between*,
The natural man. A Kentish yeoman
Who even then charmed me with his grace –
So that for ever I shall see him bowling,
Picture the wheeling arm, the fluent action.
His name is one of those like 'Adlestrop'
That, once absorbed, can never be forgotten.
Huckstep. We all admired him.
And who, if he was as I think he was, would not?
There is a place in life for simple people.

## VALEDICTION: TO THE CRICKET SEASON

As a boy who has lost a girl so sadly
tears up a photograph or her early letters,
knowing that what has gone is gone for ever,
   a lustful bustful,

the exchange of confidences, the hours of cuddling,
the paraphernalia of what some call sharing,
so we mourn you; televisually prepare for
   their filthy football,

professional fouls and the late late tackle
breakaway forwards held back by a jersey,
the winning or losing almost equally nasty.
   The English summer

is never perfect, but you are a feature
as pleasing to us as a day of sunshine,
to spectators at least a calm, straw-hatted
    Edwardian dandy.

Not really a game of physical contact,
the batsman pardons the ungentlemanly bouncer,
the only foul would be leg theory,
    bodyline bowling;

as nostalgic as those old school stories
the plock of bat on ball penetrates outfields,
calming to the mind. Warm pints of bitter
    and county cricket

are long married in our friendly folklore
of white marquees, the spires of cathedrals,
pitch-wandering dogs, boys on the boundary,
    mystified girlfriends,

all of it as much a myth and a ritual
as the fairy stories written by learned
elf-haunted dons who invent a cosmos
    neat but escapist,

where the rules are forever, can never be broken,
and a dragon, as it were, can be l.b.w.
if he puts a foot the wrong side of the mountain.
    You are the bright one

that shines in the memory; as old-fashioned writers
say 'she was a maid of some seventeen summers',
we don't reckon age by the passing of winters,
    by happier seasons

we count up that final inescapable total,
remember huge sixes by maverick sloggers –
compensating, like love, for the field that's deserted,
    the padlocked pavilion.

## THE CRICKET OF MY FRIENDS

Ross in his days of youth
was quite a bowler,
energy rushed through his veins
like Coca Cola,

he could concentrate like an obsessive
loony from Rampton,
he certainly played for Oxford
and for Northampton.

Worsley was another natural
born for cricket –
in the Cambridge University team
he once kept wicket.

Clark, with a bat in his hand,
could show his talents,
his timing and footwork were good
and so was his balance.

Symons could play a bit,
though table tennis
was the game where he made his mark
as a national menace

and worked himself up to be
reserve for England –
though never as good as the Chinks
from ping-pong Ming land.

Romilly, Rycroft and Madge
couldn't play for toffee –
they were fonder of sitting and talking
and drinking coffee.

I can't imagine a century
being made by Spender.
Was Fuller ever more
than a good tail-ender?

(I may be doing him a real
savage injustice).
Connolly – an acquaintance –
was better at pastis.

At least this is my own piece
of intelligent guesswork.
There's a gap between bat and pad
and playing and press work.

You can't see Angus Wilson
driving firmly through the covers;
the literary ladies
prefer playing games with lovers.

It's sad to see how little
the literati
have really achieved at cricket –
though hale and hearty

they don't seem to have the *flair*.
The French are hopeless.
If clean cricket were next to godliness
they would be soapless.

So it's all a bad business –
like the murder of a Kennedy –
as for Literary Cricket
I offer up this threnody.

*Gavin Ewart*

## CRICKET PITCH: 1944

The field was ringed with elms and grown
most part knee-high. They loosed sometimes
the cows there, that made all day the noise
of forelegs thrusting through the silky
tangle, and the rip of lariat tongues.
Only the centre, where the strip
had been, was shorn repeatedly.
Jack Pullman came there Sundays
lugging his mower. Before the War
he'd been the groundsman, unpaid. Before
that, left-arm medium-pace. 'First change
for fifteen years. Now it's the least
I can do, seeing there's not one
cricketer left. Sometimes I drag
that roller over it. They'd thought
of carting it off with the railings
to make shells. I hid it in the trees.
They've melted down the cricketers
for soldiers, and enough's enough.
I make it here most Sundays. Only the rooks
in the elms there sound like what it was
before the War, but I remember
that clattering scoreboard, the ball thumped,
a boundary being clapped. Some say
"There's Jack, off to the cemetery
again, cutting the week's grass back."
But here's a grave I'm keeping primed
for resurrection. It'll return some day,
the cricket. The more I do now,
the quicker we'll be back to normal.'
While he was talking, he carried
cut grass in manageable handfuls
to the slow fire on the boundary.
They looked like last year's birds-nests.

Their smoke creamed white.
                         And so Jack worked
on his chosen spot among the elms.
It was there he'd 'picked up wickets',
not grossly 'taken' them; bowled a
'steady line' and 'always to his field'
as if otherwise were rudeness; probed
batsmen by 'doing a little bit'
'through the air and off the pitch'.
Never a front-line bowler. Never
front-line in the War. Nor in the peace
much later, when some relatives
assiduously on Sundays
cleared his grave, while on the pitch
he'd tended, cricket began again,
timeless between elms, with different men.

### CRICKET FOR CHRISTMAS

These players, like white legends of themselves,
step soundless on to May green. Leaves
come big as hands from buds. The numbers
flower from winter scoreboard zeros.
Cricket is always the memory of cricket.

We store all this away: scorebooks
preserve plump boundaries in runic hachures
as soon we will freeze strawberries for Christmas.
I am hoarding that catch by the tree, preparing
a boredom for grandchildren.

A play drops poignantly into its last night.
A novel needs those lapsing paragraphs
to tie the knots and bows
round the gone lives, the feelings we felt.
But never elsewhere as here the slow

white glide into a destiny of pastness.
What more alive than shelves of tomblike Wisdens?
Now we who have wintered well
sit back and in the sun smile,
altering into the crowd that was there that May.

*Brian Jones*


### THE CRICKETERS

From the woodland's edge I watched the cricketers,
Their casual dedication and their clear
Instinct of movement's boundaries. It was
The time of evening when the gnats appear.

Not far away, the bracken shrieked and moved:
The boy was asking if she really cared
When she got up to go; he watched, unloved.
Neither was beautiful nor, it seemed, prepared.

They left the wood. Then, hearing from behind
That curiously unresonant applause,
I turned towards the cricket-pitch to find
The cricketers had disappeared indoors.

It was no more than proof of finitude,
An artifice enclosed by space and time:
For game as well as poem must exclude
All but the chosen number, stress, or rhyme.

We seek these limits, ordered and controlled
Unlike the gracelessness of doubtful lovers:
A world confined within the poem's mould
Or circumscribed by boundaries and overs;

Though thinking this I find myself clean bowled.

*Neil Powell*

## A PHOTOGRAPH OF HAMMOND

Even at 1/500th you can't freeze him,
Make his image quite static.
He remains more mobile than diagrammatic.

Take compass, protractor. However
You dismantle him, the parts
Remain true, suggest velocity.

Leonardo would have made him fly,
This batsman so revving with power
He seems airborne.

Like some prototype birdman
Straining at silk moorings, he conveys
Ambiguity, both imprisonment and release.

Never mind the earthbound heaviness
Of hip, of shoulders, his cover-drive
Evokes airiness, an effortless take-off.

A study in anatomy, circa 1930. Anonymous.
But there, nonchalantly stuffed
In his pocket, that blue handkerchief signs it.

## A CRICKETER IN RETIREMENT: GEORGE COX

The marine and the regency, sea frets
And somewhere the Downs backing a station
Like a Victorian conservatory. I come upon
A scorecard yellow as old flannels and suddenly
I see him, smilingly prowling the covers
In soft shoes, shirt rolled to the forearm,

Light as a yacht swaying at its moorings,
Receptive to breezes. An element
Of silk, of ease, with none of the old dutiful
Sense of the regiment, the parade-ground
Posture that gave even the best of them the air of retainers.
Instead, a kind of compassion linking top hats
With turnips, the traditional turning to devilry.
One apart, yet part all the same,
Of that familiar pattern of families,
Parkses and Langridges, Tates and Oakes and Gilligans,
Griffiths and Busses, Sussex is rich in,
The soft air phrased by their fickleness.

Never one for half-measures, as generous
With ducks as half-centuries, he seemed
To calculate extravagance, waywardly spendthrift
With the cold calculators, Yorkshire, the Australians,
Hove and the Saffrons ablaze with his fireworks,
Dad wincing in his grave. With others,
Less challenging, he was often vulnerable,
Giving his wicket to those who were glad of it,
Indulgently negligent against parachuting spinners.
Now there are no scorecards, just pulled hamstrings
In village cricket and instead of fancy-free

Strokes in festival arenas the soothing
Of successors. The forearms make gardens,
And the journeys have lengthened, a sunset
Of orchards and vineyards, where reclining in a bath
Of imperial proportions he observes a wife
As delicate with pastry as he was at the wicket.

*Alan Ross*

## WICKET MAIDEN

It is a game for gentle men;
Entirely wrong that man's spare rib
Should learn the mysteries of spin.

Women should not be allowed
To study subtleties of flight;
They should bowl underarm and wide.

Or, better still, not bowl at all,
Sit elegant in summer chairs,
Flatter the quiet with pale applause.

It shouldn't happen, yet it did:
She bowled a wicked heartbreak – one,
That's all. God help the next man in.

*Vernon Scannell*

## PACKER'S CIRCUIT

Something about this game
eternally fades, to bring
the lost outfielders in,

those whited ruminants
under the layers of green
whom old men at the field-edge

dream, dead name by name,
that played the day with a weeping
willow for ashes, ashes,

till you could believe, by a thin
tide of shadow that washes
play to its close, the ball

swung most sharply in tear-gas,
the rotten grave took spin,
a ghost could make a hundred

with the board of a coffin lid
and Father Time himself
scythe off his balls and sing

for something about this game
eternally fades, to bring
the lost outfielders in.

## THE CAPTAIN

I liked the Captain, all the seams
He fell apart at, going mad

Because he thought the shivered elms
Would fall upon his ashen head

And swifts would peck his eyes. Bad dreams
Can't take the quickness that he had

Who flighted slow leg-breaks that swung
In from the off, then looped away,

Or, lolled on August vapours, hung
And came through flat and how was that?

I liked the Captain, all his schemes
For harassing the right hand bat.

I liked the Captain, all his themes
And each strange learned word he said

Who read solely Victoriana
And had by heart half *Silas Marner*

Along with odd tunes in his head:
He thought the swifts would peck his eyes.

They shall not cut him down to size
Nor seek to break his flighted mind

In institutions. Nothing dead
But he shall be restored again.

Elms shall respect unshaven brain
And birds his wisdom. World needs him.

*Kit Wright*

# PART VI

# *New Prose*

'These players, like white legends of themselves,
step soundless on to May green.'

*Brian Jones*
**CRICKET FOR CHRISTMAS**

# The M.C.C. Match

## SIMON RAVEN

When Harold arrived the evening before the M.C.C. match, he learnt that the Baron's Lodge team had so far won all its matches but two, both of these having been honourably drawn. James, who was particularly anxious that this unbeaten record should be maintained, was in a state of feverish excitement about the next day. At one point he had even spoken of not playing himself, in order to 'make room for young blood'; but he had been persuaded that it was proper and even mandatory that he himself should lead the side on this, the last match of all.

'Quite right,' said Harold. 'And anyhow they tell me you've been in good form.'

'Not too bad for an old man,' said James with modest pleasure. 'Fifteen not out against the Butterflies and twenty-two yesterday against some very decent Forester bowling.'

'So of course you must play,' said Harold: and then, leaving James deep in thought about the batting order, he went to look for Georgy.

'How's Hugo been behaving?' he said at once.

'Rather well. A bit distant, but nothing you could object to.'

'And will he go on coming to see your father?'

'I don't know,' said Georgy. 'He refused at first, then said he would because of Nigel Palairet. It could mean anything. I no longer understand him, you see. He's become . . . alien.'

'Perhaps he always was.'

Then Harold went to find Hugo.

'What do you think of your uncle?' Harold said.

'He seems very well.'

'You know why. All this cricket, and all his friends, and, not least, seeing you again. After this match, he'll be feeling rather flat. I suppose you wouldn't think of staying on for a day or two?'

'No.'

'But I thought you'd promised Georgy—'

'I've changed my mind. Because all the reward I've had for coming at all is to have people nagging at me like you're doing now.'

'Your trouble,' said Harold, 'is that you're a second rate man with certain minor capacities which you're too proud to settle for. You're too proud to do the little things you *could* do. You could have been a good schoolmaster, in a modest way, and a great help to James. Even now, you could give him a lot of happiness. But no, not you. You're too grand, too greedy, for such simple things. You must for ever be trying to catch up with some new and more inflated idea of your own importance.'

'I haven't done too badly, Harold. I've become quite rich, you know. I lead a pleasant and civilized life. I read books. I look at things. I think.'

'While you're being so smug about it all, perhaps you'd care to tell me where the money came from.'

'You might say,' said Hugo, 'that I did a lucky piece of business.'

'I might say that you're a bloody little crook.'

'Don't start trouble, Harold. For the moment at least everyone is happy here. You wouldn't want to spoil it?'

Harold grunted and stumped off, but for the rest of the evening he made himself agreeable to everybody, Hugo included. Not that he had to suffer Hugo for long. Although the refreshments were as lavish as ever, James, apologetic but firm, insisted that those who were to play in next day's match should be in bed by ten-thirty sharp. With James and Hugo out of the way, Harold approached Nigel (whom James had pronounced, with regret, to be too light-weight a player for so serious an occasion) and came straight to the point.

'Whatever it is you do in Chester Row,' he said, 'Hugo

has evidently reaped considerable benefit. He must be grateful to you.'

'I doubt it,' Nigel said. 'Gratitude is not his *forte*.'

'But you must have *some* influence with him.'

'Perhaps.'

'Then get him to stay here after the cricket's over. Or at least to promise to come again very soon.'

'I see,' Nigel smiled coolly. 'You too want to spare James Escome the truth about his precious nephew.'

'I'm an old friend of Lionel's, of them all.'

'You don't need to explain. I'm on your side.'

'Well then?'

'Hugo,' said Nigel, 'is determined to push off again for good. He is not in the mood to listen to polite requests.'

'So I've found out. It seems he was more docile with Georgiana and Bessie, though. He said he'd do what they asked, because of you. Why was that?'

'At that time he thought I had a hold over him. So I had, but it gets weaker every day. It follows that we must arrange something else. Perhaps you would care to assist me in this? I need someone with a logical and strictly objective turn of mind. I don't know you, of course, but I've read some of your books —'

'— Which?' said Harold, flattered.

'One on the pre-Socratics and another on primitive notions of godhead – a subject that particularly interests me. It seems to me that you may have the qualities needed. Bessie and Georgiana think so too.'

'Qualities needed for what?'

'For what is to be done. Let us go outside,' said Nigel, moving towards the French window, 'and get a little privacy and fresh air. First of all, you'd better hear exactly what our young friend has been up to since he left London. . . .'

The M.C.C. had gathered a side of amateurs, most of whom had played for County Second XIs at one time or another and three of whom had played full seasons in first class cricket, albeit some years ago. This was opposition of a calibre unlike anything yet seen during James's cricket week; there would be no room for error or laxity, as was plainly apparent from the very beginning of the match. The M.C.C., having won the toss and chosen to bat, sent in two grizzled left-handers, the more grizzled of whom, receiving as his first ball a high and fast full toss, hit it calmly over square leg and out of the ground, thus removing most of its shine and much of the bowler's self-esteem. There followed another full toss and two long hops, each of which was despatched, with an efficiency so spare as to be almost casual, for four runs. After this the play settled down a bit, but no one was left in any doubt how matters stood: the opposition was a tough and old-fashioned bunch of campaigners who would hit bad balls, stop good ones, and drop dead on the ground sooner than give away one run in a hundred.

By lunch time, the M.C.C. had made a hundred and ninety runs for the loss of two wickets. Since this was to be a two day match, there was no prospect of an early declaration, and the Baron's Lodge contingent faced a grim afternoon ahead. The only one who was quite undaunted was James, who remarked that three lucky balls, which could happen at any moment, would be quite enough to restore the balance. After lunch, in the hope of illustrating this principle, he tried a number of quick changes in the bowling; but the M.C.C. batsmen had been in the game too long to be caught out by this kind of trick, and the only wicket to fall before three o'clock went to a grotesque leg break bowled by James himself – a ball which seemed to come back almost square behind the batsman's legs to hit his stumps. This made the score two hundred and seventy for three. There followed another hour and a half of vigorous and unsparing batting, until at tea time, with three hundred and ninety runs on the board, the M.C.C. declared:

The first innings of Baron's Lodge opened with a series of

disasters. The first batsman fell inside five minutes to a vicious yorker; number three was out to the very next ball, which went away from him at the last moment, touching the edge of the bat (if he hadn't been a very good player he would have missed it altogether) and proceeding straight into the wicket-keeper's gloves with a dull plop: and two overs later number four called an eccentric run to cover point and was run out by six foot clear. Nor did matters mend when Hugo went in: having driven a couple of balls to the long off boundary and being apparently well set, he received the only shooter of the entire week (all the wickets had been immaculately prepared) and looked round to see the three stumps forming a perfect equilateral triangle on the ground. His scowl was visible from the marquee; and Bessie, who was taking a moment off from clearing up the tea things, laughed so loudly that several M.C.C. men in the field raised their eyebrows, the only facial movement they made during the entire day except to consume food and drink.

After this, however, with a score of only thirty runs for four wickets, Baron's Lodge began to settle down. Number two, a dull but extremely sound player, looked as if he were capable of staying there for life, and number six, who now joined him, was blessed with that quality against which even the dour authority of the M.C.C. must be powerless: he was in luck. He snicked his first ball through the slips for four, chopped the second between his legs for two, and then, having sent short leg the kind of catch one gives a five-year-old child at a picnic, saw it slide like soap through the unfortunate man's hands and drop to the ground with the deliberation of a freshly ejected cow-pat. This mistake cost the fielding side dear; for despite his erratic start, number six was a correct and cool-headed player, just the man for an emergency, and he now proceeded to play the bowling with an unhurried, almost intellectual competence which the M.C.C. players themselves could hardly have improved upon. The score went steadily up, from forty to sixty, from sixty to a hundred; and when stumps were drawn at half past six Baron's Lodge had made a hundred and fifty odd for five wickets (number two having played so far back to a ball that he had hit his own stumps). As James remarked, Baron's Lodge was by no means out of danger but was very definitely still in the match.

Partly because of the dedicated nature of the M.C̣.C. players, partly because this was the last night but one of the cricket week (the last night on which people could still look forward) dinner was a rather muted affair, more formal than usual and far less gay. Although the match was still a live concern, there was an air of anti-climax, almost of futility, to which most people responded by going early to bed. James, solicitous for the health of his team, was not displeased by this ('When we've won the match we can have a real booze-up'), but when he himself said goodnight he urged all the non-players to stay and drink as late as they wished.

'There are not many nights left,' he said wistfully, and waved his hand from the doorway in what might almost have been a total valediction.

'Now,' said Nigel to Harold when the old man had gone, 'you're absolutely clear about tomorrow?'

'Yes,' said Harold indifferently.

'No doubts?'

'After what you told me last night,' said Harold, 'it is too late for doubts.'

The next morning saw Baron's Lodge battling hard but on the whole successfully to make up ground. Number six continued to cash in on his early good luck with controlled and accurate batting: and by the time the seventh wicket had fallen and he was joined by James, the score had advanced to two hundred and forty. Another hundred runs, and Baron's Lodge would be out of trouble.

James had acquitted himself very decently when playing in earlier matches, but he was now up against a standard of bowling which he had not faced for many years. At first he seemed confused and alarmed: his strokes were played without heart and even without hope, scrappy, aimless strokes, bearing little relation to the balls bowled, like those of a sulky schoolboy who has been forced to play against his will. Then, when the spectators were beginning to feel sad and embarrassed for him, he received a fast, short ball outside the off stump. In the old days this had been his favourite of all things; and even now some reflex stirred from its long sleep and took him into action: over came his left foot, up and across went the bat, all wrist and balance, quick and inevitable as a striking snake, and almost before the shot was completed the ball had flashed past cover and was at the boundary. It was the classical square cut off the front foot, a stroke which had been old-fashioned even when it delighted the Kentish crowds in the 'twenties and which had not been seen in cricket of any consequence since the old Nawab of Pataudi died. It was so unexpected, so beautiful, so absolute in its kind, that for a moment there was complete silence. Then, for the first time since the match started, the M.C.C. players began to clap. Gravely and slowly, without exaggeration but without stint, they applauded what each of them recognized as the work of a master hand.

And now it was for James as if all the years had fallen away and he was back on the Canterbury green in the full pride of his youth and skill. There was no more fumbling and snatching, no more dithering and backing away. Now that he had played his square cut everything was come right. Each stroke was as sure as the one before, neat, essential and precise. Most of them, to be sure, were strokes which scored behind the wicket or not at all (for where should an old man find strength to drive and force?), but they were crisp and firm, models of seemliness and grace. He cut square, he cut late; he glanced the ball to leg off the back foot and off the front: he played back in defence with the calculated suavity of a matador; when he hooked, it was with a feather-light touch, a mere deflection, by which he stole for his own end the bowler's power. It was a captain's innings in time of need: he batted from a quarter past twelve to half past one; and when he came back to the marquee, having declared the Baron's Lodge innings closed for 401 runs of which he himself had made sixty-five, the spectators rose to greet him with a great shout of triumph, many of them turning away to hide the tears which were running down their cheeks.

'Circumstances quite helpful so far,' said Nigel to Harold during the lunch interval.

'I suppose so,' answered Harold, and went on eating his cold salmon with prudence and solemnity.

The M.C.C. batted from after lunch until tea at four forty-five. Swiftly and dispassionately, they made three hundred and thirty-two runs for the loss of seven wickets. By declaring when they did, they left Baron's Lodge with three hundred and twenty-two runs to make in two hours (between five and seven, for either captain could ask for an extra half hour after six thirty). It was, on the whole, a sporting declaration; it left Baron's Lodge with an outside but, given the state of the ground, quite feasible chance. Even so, many captains would have ordered their men to play out time for a draw. Not James. 'All or nothing,' he said as he led his side off the field. 'Never mind the wickets. We want *runs*.'

'Remember,' said Nigel to Harold during the tea interval, 'as soon as the umpires pull the stumps.'

In order to save time, James posted members and supporters of the Baron's Lodge side all round the field so that they might gather the ball the moment it reached the boundary and return it to the bowler. For the first quarter of an hour of the Baron's Lodge innings this precaution was otiose. True, the opening batsman hit a six off his second ball; but he was clean bowled by the ball which followed it, and numbers three and four fared much the same. Number two survived, but he had neither the temperament nor the aptitude for aggressive play; so that when Hugo came in at number five, with the score at twenty for three, it was up to him to take charge without delay.

His behaviour was cool and assured. The first three balls he received he treated with modest deference (time spent in reconnaissance is *never* wasted). The fourth ball, which was only just short of a length, he hooked nippily for four, and the fifth, which was well up to him, and the last of the over, he pushed away towards mid-wicket for a single. Then, facing the bowling at the other end, he once again played three cautious exploratory shots – only to follow them with two rangy drives through the covers and another quick single to mid-wicket off the last ball of the over.

It had been a long day, and tough as the M.C.C. bowlers were, they were beginning to fail in speed and accuracy. For some overs, Hugo cut, hooked and drove with evident ease; then, when the M.C.C. tried the sensible but obvious tactic of putting on slow spin bowlers to tempt him into indiscriminate hitting, he kept his head, refrained from trying to strike the ball half-volley, and scored a quick succession of twos and singles either off the back foot or by leaving his ground and playing the ball carefully yet firmly before it pitched. But although the runs were coming very nicely, the rate of scoring at five-thirty (sixty-seven runs in the first half hour) was still not quite high enough to bring the Baron's Lodge total to three hundred and twenty-two by seven o'clock.

At this stage number two, desperate to pay his way, played a pull shot of almost blasphemous ineptness and was succeeded by number six, who was very much more suited to play the kind of innings required. For ten minutes all went well: but at five-forty-five number six, wrought upon by the perennial temptation to hit a leg break at the half volley, mistimed his stroke and was caught by long off. Number seven and number eight both scored a few useful runs, but both got over-excited and before long picked the wrong balls to hit. When James joined Hugo at the wicket the time was ten minutes past six and the score was a hundred and seventy; if Baron's Lodge were to win now, they must score at the rate of three runs a minute.

'You can rely on me to stay here, dear boy,' said James, 'but you'll have to get the runs.'

It was now that Hugo started to put on real pressure. The ground, though of ample size for little boys, was rather on the small side for grown men. It followed that lofted shots, in time of emergency, were often good investments: even if improperly hit, they were liable to sag over the boundary line, immune from being caught, for unmerited sixes. From now on, therefore, and whenever possible, Hugo started to lift the ball. This policy was rewarded by five sixes (two of them at least rather gungy ones) in three overs, quite apart from the runs he scored along the ground. Every time the ball reached the boundary, it was instantly retrieved and returned by one of the onlookers stationed for the purpose; and by half past six the score had reached two hundred and thirty-eight.

James's part was unspectacular but demanding. Every time he was left with the bowling, he had to contrive to place the ball for a single so that Hugo might renew his efforts. It was a measure of his cunning that only twice in his first half hour at the crease did he receive two consecutive balls and that not once did he receive more than two. Hugo, in a foam of sweat, his face glowing red as a winter's sun, continued game; but he was flagging a little now and badly needed the respite which James could not give him.

'One last effort, dear boy,' James called up the pitch between the overs. 'One last effort. . . .'

For now the shadows were lengthening over the ground and the birds were failing in their song. There were forty runs to be got and twenty minutes in which to get them. The M.C.C. captain, knowing that Hugo must soon make a mistake if only from weariness, was continuing with the slow bowlers who were the more likely to elicit it. One last effort, thought Hugo; now or never. He faced up to a tall, stringy, left-handed bowler, who was giving the ball plenty of air and bringing it in, with pungency, from the leg. One last effort.

The first ball of the over was slightly overpitched and outside the off-stump. Left elbow well up, left foot well across, Hugo drove it into the air over extra cover's head and saw it land just over the boundary line. The next ball was also on the off, but shorter and quicker: this time he put his right foot across and cut it just backward of square; third man, running round the boundary, saved the four, but Hugo and James ran a comfortable two. That's eight of them, Hugo thought. As the bowler's arm came over for the third time, Hugo saw him cock his wrist to turn the ball, for a change, from the off. I'll teach him to bowl Chinamen, Hugo thought; *hit with the spin*. He smashed into the ball with a rancorous cross bat and for the second time that week holed out in the swimming pool. For the fourth ball of the over, the bowler adopted a precisely similar action – wrist cocked for the Chinaman that would come in from the off. But he's faking, Hugo thought; it's going to be a googly, it's going to come in from the leg, and if it's that much higher in the air I'll be certain. It was that much higher. Back over his head then, no time for refinements now, back over his head hard and high. Hugo jumped out of his crease, did not quite get his foot to the ball, and hit it ballooning into the air with a good deal of slice. On the boundary long off waited, shading his eyes with his hands; but Hugo's luck held, and what would have been a catch on seven grounds out of ten cleared the boundary by five yards. The fifth ball was well short on the leg side; his arms felt like lead, but he managed to scrabble it away for two. The sixth ball was straight and quickish; abandoning all thought, Hugo just swished; he caught the ball on the meat, and it sizzled away crutch high between the bowler and mid-on to the boundary. He had scored twenty-six runs in the one over, and he was utterly spent.

'That's it, dear boy,' called James as the fieldsmen crossed over. 'There's time for me to get the rest.'

This he now did, crisply and prettily, and had the honour, some five minutes before the time for close of play. Moving from the wicket half dazed with triumph and fatigue, neither he nor Hugo saw Harold, who, as the umpires pulled up the stumps, walked rapidly away towards the house.

*From* Close of Play

# *A Station at War*

## J. L. CARR

I had worked it out that, once the breeze began to blow in from the west – that is across the mangrove swamps from the sea – it would stay in that quarter and would win the game for us. Trader, with his high left-arm action, bowling from the Guard Room end would use it to float the ball towards the slips, and their batsmen would follow it round and tickle it into Slingsby's big hands. And Slingsby himself, from the Work Area end, with the palm trees masking the ball, would jerk his fast off-breaks into their bodies and I'd be waiting at silly-mid-on. It was a blessed breeze.

I borrowed a timber frame from Ground Defence [from which they used to hang a bag of straw to practise bayonet plunging] and I fitted this up across the popping crease. Then I chalked a cross chest high on the sack and, after work, set on Trader and Slingsby bowling short to lift the ball. And, out of the corner of my eye, I saw Maidstone and Fife stop to watch. I knew it would worry them, because find me the batsman who likes the ball up at him, especially when it's moving in or away. We packed it in then because it had been for their benefit, not Trader's nor Slingsby's, that I set the thing up.

The day before the game the breeze still blew. If anything, it had veered a couple of points and was coming in from forward short-leg towards gulley which was better than I'd dared hope, putting a sharper drag on off-breaks and carrying the outswingers with a keener nip from the matting. As I've said before, I like working to a plan: it gives you that extra confidence in a panic. Of course, you never can rule out luck in any game, cricket more than most, but it's plain madness to bank on it.

That week, most of the Catalinas were away on dispersal so that we were slack in the section and I was sitting under our mango tree getting the benefit of the breeze, feeling a bit weak at the knees thinking about this final game. I felt sure that the Station XI were so damned confident of winning that *their* only plan would be simplicity itself – get rid of me and then massacre the others. It was a great responsibility.

I was pondering the horrors of being out first ball or first over, and all my careful plans over the past months collapsing like a pack of cards into a ridiculous heap, when Slingsby came.

I could see he was blazing mad; he was so pale.

'Turton's made himself captain,' he said, his voice trembling.

I was staggered. Then I went cold and I began to shake in all my limbs: something I can never remember happening before. Outside old time history books, I couldn't even begin to imagine anything like this happening.

'He can't,' I said. 'It's our team. It isn't *his* team.'

'Not according to him. He's called it *The* 697 Squadron XI.'

He hurried me off to the board outside the squadron offices.

The full force of what he'd done didn't hit me until I saw his name heading the list and my own near the bottom, and a Squadron Ldr. Rumm I'd never heard of – a new flight commander it turned out – and saw that Henty and Cork had been pushed out, both only run-of-the-mill players who couldn't be relied on to score ten between them and only really able to stop the ball with their legs. But loyal lads who'd come all the way up with us.

'Ah, Flanders, looking over the Team?' Turton had come up behind us. I could think of nothing to say: I felt stunned. 'After the way you let things get out of hand in the Liberator Game, it was thought in the Mess that I'd better run things,' he said. 'Quite a strong side. If we all pull our weight we should give them a good game.'

I still could only stare stupidly at the board and Slingsby at his feet as he walked off. Oddly enough, in the middle of this horror, I thought what a tactical blunder he'd made putting Slingsby No. 8 and replacing Wood as vice-captain by one of the officers. There was always a chance they might have deserted me but, now he'd given them a back-hander apiece, they weren't likely to forgive him any more than I was.

But '*Ah, Flanders, it was thought in the Mess that I'd better run things* . . .' I'll hear it till my dying day and still feel the baffling heat of the squadron street and my own coldness. It was like a scene from a Western. He'd done it! Usurped our weeks of work and planning just like that! He had all the authority and power he could use, but he had to take over our little corner too! Damn and blast him!

By next morning, I'd settled into depression. There didn't seem to be a thing that I could do about this abominable business. In the day-to-day routine of service life, you had to suffer fools and put up with rations of inhumanity from N.C.O.s and officers without answering back. But interference with leisure – that was something new. I'll be frank: I didn't care now if we lost or won. This wasn't the Game we'd been planning and preparing for, the Game that made sense of all the other games we'd won. I've spoken of this before so I'll not labour it.

But, even so, I'd have gone on and played the game, shelving all responsibility of course, but played as I always played, if it hadn't been for the S.H.Q. Sergeant, Fife. I was sitting just inside the Section door, when he poked his head in and said, 'Ready for the thrashing we're going to give you Thursday, Flanders?'

'You'll not be giving *me* one,' I said. 'I'm not captain and it's not my team.' But he laughed and went off laughing. And you could tell from the attitude of his cronies that it was me they had it in for, to smash *my* side and put *me* in my place amongst the fragments. Little Wood put it into words. 'They're going to crucify us,' he said. That was pitching it a bit thick; I don't care for scriptural words taken from their setting.

I half-heartedly tried to persuade the temporary corporal to insist that I couldn't be spared from duty on Thursday, but he had his ear close to the ground and knew what was going on. Only a sharp bout of malaria could save me from the bitterest pill I'd ever had to swallow. One or two of the lads and Slingsby came round to the billet but, honestly, I couldn't bring myself to talk about it. I still felt numb.

And, when it came to the afternoon itself, I didn't know where to put myself. As skipper, there'd been so much to see to – last minute tactical arguments with Slingsby, jollying up the nervous ones, screwing up my own will to win as I took the over-elaborate pains with my kit I always indulged in (because you have to *think* the game before you play it). It was awful not going out to toss with Maidstone, just waiting to be told what it was to be, bat or field. As it turned out it was *field* – Turton had won the toss and put them in. (That showed how little confidence he had in us!)

Maidstone opened for them and, after he'd been missed by Turton in the slips (where Slingsby should have been) in Trader's first over, they never looked back. Trader and Slingsby were good bowlers; in fact very good. But on asphalt, accuracy wasn't enough. I don't want to appear immodest, but they needed me to direct their fire-power from mid-off and he'd stuck me third man and long-on so that the refinements of the game (if there were any) were lost to me.

About the tenth over, remembering his success against the Liberator Squadron, he put himself on at one end and the new officer, Rumm, at the other. But, as anybody who understood the game could see, Maidstone and Co. with their tails up were a very different kettle of fish, and they put the pair of them to the sword, Maidstone particularly taking anything over-pitched and thumping it like a cannonball through the covers and making massive pulls out of short balls. It was butchery.

I won't prolong the agonizing details – they hurt me still. It was enough to see Slingsby looking half crazy, furiously pushing his long forelock back over his brow, or to have to listen to their supporters making as much row as a cup-tie. The Station side really stuck it in deep and then twisted. At half-past five they declared at 217 for 3.

'Christ!' Stone said, and put his head in his hands and rocked to and fro in misery on the bench under the acacia trees.

'Well, chaps,' Turton said in his jerky way, 'it's a lot. But, if they got 'em, so can we.'

He pinned up the batting order. S/Ldr. Rumm and F/O Oates numbers one and two, then Stone, then myself, Wood, Turton himself, Slingsby and so on. We didn't talk much as we sat there waiting. As a matter of fact, I was feeling pretty normal up till then, nothing like as nervous as I usually was. It was Fife and what he said that sent the balloon up. The Station went out, tossing the ball around one to the other and laughing but *he* couldn't resist rubbing it in to pay off old scores. He paused by the bench where I was sitting with Wood and Slingsby. 'Take your beating like a man, Flanders,' he said. Only the three of us heard him. The man was a sadist.

I didn't say anything. This is important because of what

came afterwards. I didn't need to as I glimpsed the faces of the other two as they glared at his back.

But he could laugh all right; second ball of the first over down went Rumm's bailliwick. He'd missed one of Angus's and that usually was fatal. Oates didn't last much longer, and it was two wickets for three runs when I went in, and, then, when poor Stone had been caught at point, it was three for five. Wood came waddling in (he was slightly bowlegged) and began to drop his bat like a hen-house shutter, even though Fife, bowling really fast, soon nipped his fingers. It was no joke. Then the poor kid was hit again and his hands began to run blood. I'd tried to get him out of the habit but, this time. he forgot all I'd told him. Let's face it: he didn't know how to lift his bat *and* stay in. And Fife knew his limitations and bowled at them.

But Wood gritted his teeth (I heard him!) and stuck it out. And, watching him from the other end, I felt (as you might say) a sudden lightening of the spirit. I nearly laughed aloud. What it amounted to was that this backstreet London kid who'd learnt his cricket in an elementary school playground had swallowed my pep talks over the past two months and was carrying them out mechanically. It made me suddenly ashamed too. So when this awful over stopped and he was wringing his bloody fingers, I called gently, 'Good lad, Woody!' and winked at him and he must have got the message when I lowered my stance and then let everything more than three inches wide of the off stump go through to the wicket-keeper. After that, I only tried to score a single an over just to keep him from the chopping block.

You might say that this was the crisis of the match. In ten overs we scored but eight runs. And suddenly Turton stood up, cupped his hands and yelled, 'Get a move on, Flanders.' I didn't look directly at him, because I could see the other lads sitting up looking cheerful for the first time with Slingsby jumping up and down behind them. Next over, Wood missed one and was l.b.w. and in came Turton. He glared down the pitch at me and called sharply, 'We'll have some quick singles.' And, in fact, he glanced his very first ball gracefully to leg, his favourite shot I suppose, and came racing down at me. 'Come on, come on, man,' he shouted. I didn't move and he reached my end, stuck his face no more than a foot from mine and yelled like a maniac, 'What the hell are you playing at, Flanders!' But Maidstone had moved quietly round from the slips to short fine-leg and the ball had gone straight into his hands.

The silence was electric. Turton suddenly knew something had gone wrong. He looked round and saw the ball being tossed gently into the air. 'I'm afraid you're out, sir,' the umpire said.

The Station still kept at it. With five wickets down, I suppose they still thought they had a half chance of winning. But they must have seen the writing on the wall when Slingsby came in and began to smother everything. He more or less sat astride his bat as though he'd taken up permanent residence in the crease. It was growing dark by now and Fife had just about lost control of himself, so that I heard Maidstone say quietly to him, 'Steady on, man, you'll kill somebody.'

Then Turton intervened for the last time. He advanced a few yards on to the field of play and called, 'Flanders, you are to retire.'

I didn't shift and he called again. The game just stopped. But I know the rules. A captain can make an entire side declare, but he can't winkle out one player. It would have been fatal to have argued this out with him, though. So I didn't look at him and stayed put and took my guard.

'Play on,' said the umpire, and Maidstone gave me a shy grin. Slingsby got a glancing blow on his head and, after that, didn't know whether he was coming or going and just went through the motions as taught in Ossett and District. Ten minutes later, you could hardly see who was in the longfield or even at extra cover and every third ball I was being rattled in the ribs. But we wouldn't appeal against the light.

Then, all at once, the game stopped. The umpires looked at one another and lifted the bails. And that was an end to it. It was crazy and silly and funny. 217 for 3 them, 27 for 5 us. A draw!

*From* A Season in Sinjhi *1967*

# *Hutton and the Past*

## HAROLD PINTER

Hardstaff and Simpson at Lords. Notts versus Middlesex. 1946 or 1947. After lunch Keeton and Harris had opened for Notts. Keeton swift, exact, interested; Harris Harris. Harris stonewalled five balls in the over for no particular reason and hit the sixth for six, for no particular reason. Keeton and Harris gave Notts a fair start. Stott at number three, smacked the ball hard, was out in the early afternoon. Simpson joined Hardstaff. Both very upright in their stance. They surveyed the field, surveyed themselves, began to bat.

The sun was strong, but calm. They settled into the afternoon, no hurry, all in order. Hardstaff clipped to mid-wicket. They crossed. Simpson guided the ball between mid-off and the bowler. They crossed. Their cross was a trot, sometimes a walk, they didn't need to run. They placed their shots with precision, they knew where they were going. Bareheaded. Hardstaff golden. Simpson dark. Hardstaff offdrove, silently, Simpson to deep square leg. Simpson cut. Hardstaff cut, finer. Simpson finer. The slips, Robertson, Bennett, attentive. Hardstaff hooked, immaculate, no sound. They crossed, and back. Deep square leg in the heat after it. Jim Sims on at the pavilion end with leg breaks. Hardstaff wristed him into the covers. Simpson to fine leg. Two. Sims twisting. Hardstaff wristed him into the covers, through the covers, fielder wheeling, for four. Quite unhurried. Seventy in 90 minutes.

No explosions. Batsmanship. Hardstaff caught at slip, off Sims.

Worrell and Weekes at Kingston on Thames. 1950. The Festival. Headley had flicked, showed what had been and what remained of himself, from the Thirties. Worrell joined Weekes with an hour to play. Gladwin and Jackson bowling. Very tight, very crisp, just short of a length, jolting, difficult. Worrell and Weekes scored 90 before close of play. No sixes, nothing off the ground. Weekes smashed, red-eyed, past cover, smashed to long leg, at war, met Gladwin head on, split midwicket in two, steel. Worrell wanted to straight drive to reach his 50. Four men at the sight screen to stop him. He straight drove, pierced them, reached his 50. Gladwin bowled a stinging ball, only just short, on middle and leg. Only sensible course was to stop it. Worrell jumped up, both feet off, slashed it from his stomach, square cut for four, boundary first bounce.

M.C.C. versus Australians. Lords 1948. Monday. On the Saturday the Australians had plastered the M.C.C. bowling, Barnes 100, Bradman just short. On Monday morning Miller hit Laker for five sixes into the Tavern. The Australians passed 500 and declared. The weather darkened. M.C.C. 30 minutes batting before lunch. The Australians came into the field chucking the ball hard at each other, broad, tall, sure. Hutton and Robertson took guard against Lindwall and Miller. Robertson caught Tallon off Miller. Lindwall and Miller very fast. The sky black. Edrich caught Tallon off Miller. Last ball before lunch. M.C.C. 20 for 2.

After lunch the Australians, arrogant, jocular, muscular, larking down the pavilion steps. They waited, hurling the ball about, eight feet tall. Two shapes behind the pavilion glass. Frozen before emerging a split second. Hutton and Compton. We knew them to be the two greatest English batsmen. Down the steps together, out to the middle. They played. The Australians quieter, wary, tight. Bradman studied them. They stayed together for an hour before Compton was out, and

M. P. Donnelly, and Hutton, and the Australians walked home.

First Test at Trent Bridge. The first seven in the English batting order: Hutton, Washbrook, Edrich, Compton, Hardstaff, Barnett, Yardley. They'll never get them out, I said. At lunch on the first day, England 78 for 8.

Hutton.

England versus New Zealand 1949. Hutton opened quietly, within himself, setting his day in order. At the first hour England 40 for none. Hutton looking set for a score. Burtt, slow left hand, took the ball at the Nursery end, tossed it up. To his first ball Hutton played a superb square drive to Wallace at deep point. Wallace stopped it. The crowd leaned in. Burtt again. Hutton flowed into another superb square drive to Wallace's right hand. Wallace stopped it. Back to the bowler. Burtt again, up. Hutton, very hard a most brilliant square drive to Wallace's left hand. Wallace stopped it. Back to the bowler. The crowd. Burtt in, bowled. Hutton halfway up the pitch immediately, driving straight. Missed it. Clean bowled. On his heel back to the pavilion.

Hutton was never dull. His bat was part of his nervous system. His play was sculptured. His forward defensive stroke was a complete statement. The handle of his bat seemed electric. Always, for me, a sense of his vulnerability, of a very uncommon sensibility. He never just went through the motions, nothing was glibly arrived at. He was never, for me, as some have defined him, simply a 'master technician'. He attended to the particular but rarely lost sight of the context in which it took place. But one day in Sydney he hit 37 in 24 minutes and was out last ball before lunch when his bat slipped in hitting a further four, when England had nothing to play for but a hopeless draw, and he's never explained why he did *that*. I wasn't there to see it and probably regret that as much as anything. But I wasn't surprised to hear about it, because every stroke he made surprised me.

I heard about Hutton's 37 on the radio. 7 a.m. Listened to

every morning of the 1946/47 series. Alan McGilvray talking.
Always England six wickets down and Yardley 35 not out.
But it was in an Irish kitchen in County Galway that, alone, I
heard Edrich and Compton in 1953 clinch the Ashes for
England.

Those were the days of Bedser and Wright, Evans, Wash-
brook and Gimblett, M. P. Donnelly, Smailes and Bowes,
A. B. Sellars, Voce and Charley Barnett, S. M. Brown and
Jim Sims, Mankad, Mustaq Ali, Athol Rowan, even H. T.
Bartlett, even Hammond and certainly Bradman.

One morning at drama school I pretended illness and pale
and shaky walked into Gower St. Once round the corner I
jumped on a bus and ran into Lords at the Nursery end to see
through the terraces Washbrook late cutting for four, the ball
skidding towards me. That beautiful evening Compton made
70.

But it was 1950 when G. H. G. Doggart missed Walcott at
slip off Edrich and Walcott went on to score 165, Gomez with
him. Christiani was a very good fielder. Ramadhin and
Valentine had a good season. Hutton scored 202 not out
against them and against Goddard bowling breakbacks on a
bad wicket at the Oval.

It was 1949 when Bailey caught Wallace blindingly at silly
mid on. And when was it I watched Donnelly score 180 for
the Gents versus Players? He went down the afternoon with
his lightning pulls.

Constantine hitting a six over fine leg into the pavilion.
Talk of a schoolboy called May.

*1969*

# Leyton and the Commentary Box

## ALAN GIBSON

Sir Home Gordon once declared that his idea of bliss in
eternity would be to watch a perpetual series of finely con-
tested cricket matches. At the other extreme was a character
called John Clegg of the *Manchester Evening News*, who – Sir
Neville Cardus has told us – rejoiced openly when it rained.

Once I arrived late at Old Trafford, after a journey from
Lord's. It was the lunch interval, and the scoreboard announced that Lancashire against Northamptonshire had lost
five wickets for fifty on a dull morning threatening bad
weather. I met Clegg as soon as I had entered the ground
and realized the dismal situation of the Lancashire side.
'Looks very bad,' I said to Clegg; but after an inspection
of the clouds above he said, 'Too high, I'm afraid, too
high.'

There was a time in my youth, extending even to my twenties,
when I would have been inclined to agree with Sir Home
Gordon. Probably this condition was extended, and exacerbated, by the relatively cricketless war years. There have
been times in recent years, when I have been broadcasting or
writing about cricket regularly, when I have glanced at the
looming clouds, and my thoughts have turned with Clegg's
to the refreshment tent.

Cricket has changed, and I doubt if it has changed for the
better, but most of the change has been in me. I noticed this
very much in 1968, the season I began to write about the game
for *The Times* as often as five, six or even seven days a week.
For twenty years before that I had been broadcasting commentaries from time to time, with an occasional newspaper
report, but I found a world of difference between perhaps a
dozen matches a summer, thirty or forty days of cricket, and

the daily grind. By the end of that season I realized, what in my youth would have been incomprehensible, that county cricketers have reason to feel stale by the middle of August. Since then we have had the rapid development of one-day matches, which have certainly brought variety to the scene. They have occasionally brought farce as well, especially in the Sunday League, but something drastic had to be done if the game was to continue as a professional entertainment. Two three-day county matches a week, played in the modern style, so often grimly cautious, so supposedly scientific, had ceased to be the way to get the best out of the game. One-day matches were the price cricketers had to pay, if they wanted to be able to continue with their three-day championship, even in a curtailed form; and most of the professionals have recognized this, even if they are not enthusiastic about it. No doubt there will be further experiments yet, and it may be that despite them all the three-day county game cannot last very long. If so, I should be sorry (though I should be very glad to see the five-day test match reduced to three). But cricket, as such, is not in decline. More people are playing it, all over the world, than ever before, and that is the only sane way of judging the health of a game.

It is astonishing that cricket should have taken root in the English climate. It almost makes me believe that our summers have grown worse over the past few centuries, though people who have studied the evidence say it is not so. The weather has often made me rue a cricket reporter's life, as it might be in a May shower of snow at Derby, or when an autumn easterly at Scarborough almost rips you off your seat.

I have told how the Leyton ground introduced me to cricket. H. S. Altham and E. W. Swanton, in their *History of Cricket*, called it a 'somewhat grimy yet not wholly unattractive enclosure which had brought all the great cricketers, in their time, to the East Londoner's doorstep'. So it did, and in the early thirties I suppose I saw them all, except Bradman, who did not play when the 1930 Australians were there.

Whenever Yorkshire came I reminded my school friends of my northern origins. There was not much risk of Yorkshire failing to live up to my faith, and there was one unforgettable day in 1932, when Holmes and Sutcliffe opened the Yorkshire innings and put on 555 runs together. That was then the record for any wicket anywhere, and is still the record for the first wicket anywhere, and for any wicket in England. The previous record (Brown and Tunnicliffe's 554, also for Yorkshire, at Chesterfield in 1898) was passed shortly before lunch on the second day, so I was home from school in time to watch it from the balcony.

There was an odd incident at the end of the partnership, of which I have since read several contradictory accounts. When the scoreboard moved to 555 there was much cheering, and Holmes and Sutcliffe strode down the pitch towards one another and shook hands. Sutcliffe had a carefree swing at the next ball and was bowled. Yorkshire at once declared. Then the two scorers disagreed about the total: there was a no-ball in one book which could not be matched in the other. The scoreboard reversed to 554. Indeed, Holmes and Sutcliffe were photographed under it, at that figure. They had only equalled the record, not broken it.

By this time I was within the ground, nobody bothering in the excitement to keep out the small boys who thronged at the gates. Some of my schoolmates rejoiced evilly at the tragedy. Ultimately the no-ball was demonstrated to sufficiently general satisfaction, and the board went back to 555 for another photograph; but it was a bad moment. My schoolmates and Essex, however, had a notable revenge a few years later, when Essex got Yorkshire out for 31 and 99 and, scoring over 300 themselves, won by an innings. But by then Essex had left Leyton.

Since they returned there for a week or so a season, a few years ago, they have been well supported. It was at Leyton that an old friend of mine, Carter Dodds (inappropriately called 'Dicky' by cricketers, who have a gift for inappropriate nicknames) had a very successful benefit match. He had not insured against bad weather, believing the event to be within the providence of God. A bad spell cleared just in time. He gave all the proceeds to Moral Re-Armament, a movement of which I do not much approve, but one which he has served for many years with the utmost selflessness.

I did not have the chance to watch cricket at Leyton again myself until 1970, and it was then with some emotion that I walked round the ground. At a glance it was much the same except about half the size my imagination recalled. It is less grimy than it was, and the assorted smells – the soap-works at Stratford, the wire-works by the Marshes – no longer float pungently across. The pavilion is the same, at least from the outside (I had never been inside before), a very decent piece of cricketing architecture. There used to be some big three-stepped rough stone seating for the general public, solid as the rock of Gibraltar and trying to tender behinds. That too had gone, and it must have been a formidable job to shift it.

There is now a handsome new sports centre on the Leyton ground. When Essex left, the ground passed to the Metro-politan Police, and I was particularly cross about having to watch fat policemen run where O'Connor had batted and Farnes bowled. Now it is owned by the borough of Waltham Forest, and in constant use for a variety of sports by many young people. One must be thankful that this patch of green in east London has still survived, and still has the character more of a field than a stadium. But as a consequence the out-field, once renowned for its richness and regularity, is bumpy and bare in places, though the square itself still usually plays well.

Near the Leyton ground there had been a bat-maker's shop, *W. J. Breeden*, which supplied many of the Essex cricketers with bats. Mr Breeden's nephew Bobby lived with him, much of an age with me. I cherished his friendship because he was my nearest contact with the mighty. One day Bobby and I, with some others, had been to Wanstead Flats for a picnic, and on the way back Bobby, throwing my bat in the air, failed to catch it as it fell, and it dropped on the asphalt road. It broke in two, right across the middle. It was nearly new, a Marks & Spencer three-spring driver, 4s 11d ('Nothing Over 5/–' was their slogan), so the calamity was dreadful. The only hope was that Bobby's uncle would be able to mend it. We hurried to the shop, but uncle shook his head sadly and said, 'Sorry, it can't be done.'

In 1970 I saw the little shop again, unchanged, even to the picture of the Australian eleven of 1888. I went in, and there, bless me, was Bobby Breeden himself. After a variety of jobs and much travel he had come back to run the family business – 'I had to do it,' he said, 'I was the only Breeden left.' But before that he had said, as soon as I had introduced myself, 'Why, I remember you – I broke your bat!' It seems an inappropriate story to tell of a bat-maker. But beautiful bats are still made in the little shop, and it was moving to find it still there, and still in the family, under the shadow of the big railway arches of Leyton Midland station; only a few yards from what was once one of the most famous cricket grounds in the world.

It was a grief to me that I could not play games better. I was just about good enough to enjoy them, and at school and college acquired by assiduity a fair number of colours, but it became clear quite soon that I was never destined for more than average competence. It is a handicap, in reporting a game, not to have played it at a first-class level; but not an insuperable handicap, as many distinguished names witness. It is certainly desirable, and in nearly every case necessary, to have played the game you are reporting at *some* level, regularly and enthusiastically. But, given that requirement, the same considerations apply to making a sports journalist or broadcaster as to making any other kind of journalist or broadcaster.

From my first experience of cricket commentary at Taunton in 1948 I progressed to covering matches in the western counties, perhaps half a dozen, then a dozen times a season.

After about five years I was considered good enough to be invited by other regions sometimes, but it was fourteen years before I was awarded a test match. I suppose I have done more commentaries at Taunton than anywhere, which is no doubt why it is my favourite ground. It is not particularly beautiful, if only because of the huge hoardings put up to stop spectators in the road watching for nothing. But it is comfortable, friendly, compact without being poky. Often in recent years there has been talk that Somerset would leave it, and certainly support has been rather better at Bath. I should be sad if the day came. I should be sad no longer to watch cricket against the background of the Quantocks, of Cothelstone with its quiff of trees. There are not so many county grounds which remind you that cricket was a countryside game. All the same, I had an alarming experience on that first occasion. The commentary box at Taunton in those days was a precarious affair, which looked as though the first puff of a south-westerly would blow it over. To reach it you had to climb a ladder out of the ground, over a wall into the churchyard, and then climb another ladder to the roof of the stand. Keith Miller, when he went in, threatened to knock the whole lot of us down with one blow, and came within a couple of yards of doing it. So my career as a cricket commentator might have been ended before it began: but it would have been a noble ending, I would have thought at the time. To be knocked off the air and into the churchyard by Miller!

The principal problem of cricket commentary, I have found, is to provide an adequate supply of background information which is both interesting and relevant. If you are fortunate enough to have a scorer, such as Arthur Wrigley or Bill Frindall, in the box, that is an enormous help; but statistics, even if appropriate, are not in themselves enough. There are often long periods in cricket when not very much is happening. Suppose a fast bowler spends five or six minutes bowling to a batsman who is determined to attempt no stroke, and all balls go down the off side and are taken by the wicket-keeper.

It is the ability to keep the commentary going, without obvious padding, without making the listener feel bored, that is needed – it is perhaps this more than any other quality which distinguishes Arlott above all the rest of us. Television commentators do not have this particular problem: a picture of the fast bowler retreating thirty yards, and silence, is sufficient explanation of the situation.

Even so, mistaken identifications are a nightmare, and I am not allowed to forget that once I got Colin Cowdrey wrong. Indeed, I had him out before he had come in to bat, and this at the crisis of a Kent–Hampshire match. There were some extenuating circumstances, but I will not rehearse them. The episode is too painful to me.

Then there are odd, and often inexplicable, mix-ups of words. Once, during a cricket match at Taunton, I informed the public that the ball had gone for two interviews. The word I intended to employ was overthrows. I had no interviews on my mind at the time. I was unaware I had said it, and did not even believe I had said it, until the recording was played back. Another time, Robert Hudson at Lord's, when the teams were presented to the Queen, said, 'What a moment this is for the New Zealanders! A moment they will always want to forget . . .' I hope he will not mind my stealing his story, because I was in the commentary box at the time, and diffidently pointed out to him, afterwards, what he had said; and he did not believe it either, until he had listened to the tape. This story has been retold and elaborated, and attributed to various commentators. There is one charming addition, in which the commentator is made to correct himself: 'I beg your pardon, I mean a moment they will never want to remember . . .' But that is apocryphal, and I can vouch for the original.

Spoonerisms can produce horrifying effects. I notice, however, that they rarely recur in the same form. Once they have been committed an automatic warning signal shows itself. I was very relieved, a few years ago, to hear an announcer refer to the Channel Island of Jernsey. I had been dreading it for years, but now there was the sense that the gipsy's curse was expiated. 'Jernsey' is not strictly a spoonerism, but it illustrates the point. For years I have been hopefully listening for the Bules of Kite, Chank Fracksfield and his orchestra, the well-known sculptor Shamuel Seepshanks, the Society for the Reservation of Plural England, and the famous rugby international John Carnal-Crumpeter. Hugh Shirreff recounts with gusto the occasion when he introduced a concert of mad songs and partrigals. There was another West Regional announcer who took us over to the Bath Room Pump.

A spoonerism, a transposition of the initial consonants of two words, takes its name from the Rev. W. A. Spooner, Warden of New College, Oxford. He died at the age of eighty-six in 1930, and in my Oxford days there were many who remembered and relished him. It is true that he once announced in chapel the hymn, 'Kinquering congs their titles take.' I am less sure of the story that he became engaged to be married when intending to ask a lady if she would make tea, and she did not need asking twice. No doubt they spent the honeymoon in Jernsey.

It has been said that the best commentators make the worst mistakes. As a statement that is untrue, and has the ring of someone laughing off incompetence. But a true point labours within the clumsy excuse. The best commentators, in my experience (and obviously I would be lying if I pretended I did not think I was among them) are those who have most trouble in conquering their nerves. It is a good thing to be a little edgy, a little tense – even if you contrive not to show it – before a big occasion. Studio broadcasts I have usually found easier; but a commentary, or any sort of unscripted outside broadcast where you can never tell what will happen next, is always a strain. The tension builds up over the years; sleep is the first thing to go. This is when you begin to drink too much and reach for the barbiturates too often.

*From* A MINGLED YARN

# A Few Old Buffers

## E. W. SWANTON

In my earlier years as a club cricketer – I suppose I strictly mean until the outbreak of war in 1939 – variety and humour were added to the scene by a number of old fellows who seemed pretty ancient to us then – how they would appear on the club scene in these days of limited overs and everyone doing the hundred yards in even time is unthinkable. More's the pity. They did little harm in return for the labour of managing innumerable sides and clearly extracted vast pleasure from the game. Their cricket pedigrees were varied, ranging from some who had once been very good players to a few who never had been, and never could have been.

Of the former sort Hampstead was something of a repository, and my first recollection of the type takes me back to Bognor. We used to enjoy family holidays at Felpham near by propelled there by Dr Edwards aforesaid in his rather grand De Dion Bouton. Arthur Goodall used to run the Bognor side which at times would include a Gilligan or two, and in my later teens a place was sometimes found for me. The M.C.C. colours of red and yellow were then seldom worn round the neck but often round the middle, the flannels of this generation being thus kept up. The sash was maintained in place by loops and was knotted at the front.

Hampstead in August used to progress clockwise round the south coast, with Bognor near the end of the run. I can see behind the stumps 'Father' Beaton, a walrus moustache almost brushing the bails, and with his sash or 'square' spilling out so that it covered most of his bottom. Old Beaton was the ultra-respectable father of two beautiful daughters much in the news as Bright Young Things of the '20s, and a son, Cecil, making his way as a society photographer. There was also a much more orthodox son, Reggie, who played for Hampstead, was an R.A.F. officer and died young. George Hickson was of the Hampstead red-and-yellow company, a genial man who for the charitable purpose of endowing a hospital bed started a club, which he called the Purchasers, with a tie of verdant green, gin and tonic (i.e. white and very pale blue). To be elected you had to have 'bought it', so to speak, by doing something unusual, bizarre or ridiculous. Word went round the cricket world, for instance, that Tom Pearce had been elected as having been the only county captain in 1948 to bowl out the Australians in a day. Essex did so at Southend – for 721! Freddie Brown, a congenial chap after the founder's heart, now runs the Purchasers.

There were two Georges, Hickson and Hewetson, great friends who seemed always to be laughing. George Hewetson was one of the deafest men I ever met at cricket but was said never not to have heard when asked to have a drink. He must have had a radar system in his hearing-aid. An alternative version had it that when he saw anyone talking to him he simply said, 'Thanks very much, gin and tonic.' Count Hollender (also with two lovely daughters) was there chiefly on social grounds, and the side were strong enough to carry one or two such. For there were several class performers around, such as the Atkinson brothers, N. S. M. and B. G. W., both of whom played for Middlesex as also had Leonard Burtt, Arthur Tanner and, a little later, the current President of M.C.C., 'Tagge' Webster. 'B' Atkinson, by the way, is credited with one of the most extraordinary hits ever made at Lord's. In the Middlesex–Surrey match, which used to mark the climax of the county season, he executed an overhead tennis smash at a bouncer, sending it high over the head of Alf Gover, the astonished bowler, into the pavilion seats for six. 'B' was an institution as a master at Edinburgh Academy, a splendid bat who used to get 1000 runs for the Grange, and then 1000 more for Hampstead and others during the school holidays.

Before getting back to my old buffers – the word being

used, as will be appreciated, in a wholly respectful sense – let it be recorded that no club in England can have fielded so many distinguished players over the years as Hampstead. F. R. Spofforth ('The Demon'), A. E. Stoddart, who once made 485 for Hampstead in a day, though exactly why he committed such an enormity I never heard, and Gregor MacGregor, all of early Test Match fame, head the list. I am proud to have played in the '50s for Hampstead, as I had earlier done for the club of comparable lustre south of the river, Beckenham.

H. D. Swan and T. H. Carlton-Levick I wrote about in *SOCP*, both buffers of the first order and the former *comfortably* the worst cricketer I ever saw. There was also Stanley Colman, of the mustard family, who ran The Wanderers and whose portrait still hangs in the Long Room at the Oval. Whether he was ever much good I'm not sure, but my recollection is of seeing him in the changing-room being bound up from ankle to crutch by his Jeeves. Varicose veins, perhaps.

Then there was Lord Ebbisham, father of the present peer, who as Sir Rowland Blades managed to combine an active life in the city of London – and indeed the office of Lord Mayor – while playing a lot of cricket, much of it for Sutton. His great ambition – he was an exceptionally slow bowler – was to take 100 wickets in the season and it was said that matches were sometimes hurriedly arranged in September in order for this annual milestone to be reached. J. C. Masterman used to tell how, encountering 'Rowly' during the winter, he put the time-honoured question. Had he done it yet again? Once the old boy seemed less pleased than usual to have been asked, and after saying 'yes' added after a pause that he might have taken the last two or three on the beach.

Billy Williams was a robust and upright old fellow who sported an M.C.C. cap as well as a sash and also a clipped white moustache. He had bowled for Middlesex in his youth before reverting to leg-breaks, but his chief achievement was, as a moving spirit on the Rugby Union, to urge the purchase of

Twickenham. The ground was considered too remote from London to be suitable as the game's headquarters and was scathingly referred to in its early days (before the first war) as 'Billy Williams's cabbage-patch'. Very late in life Billy, who was something of an old buck, was cited as co-respondent in a divorce suit, and was said to be highly indignant when the case was dismissed.

But of these old fellows of my youth none stands out more clearly than E. Shirley Snell, a figure of great dignity scrupulously turned out, whether on the field or off, and indeed known by the somewhat dubious title of 'the best-dressed man in London'. It fitted him perfectly that he was in Rothschild's: one felt the most crucial secret of City or State would be safe behind that suave, grave demeanour. Shirley's life-long interest, however, was not banking but Incogniti, for which distinguished club he played first in 1910 and last, at the age of 71, in 1953! He was many years on the committee and match-manager for 22 – which, of course, was far too long seeing that he was 28 when he was elected. Nor, strictly speaking, had he ever been much good.

When I knew him the chief characteristic of his bowling was width, and in the early days of the Romany Club when he played for me I used sometimes, much to his pleasure, to get through the conventional three overs at least expense by giving him the new ball. By the time a couple of young batsmen had decided that the stuff was every bit as guileless as it seemed, with luck he would be putting on his immaculate sweater and the faded Incog cap of purple, yellow and black. The secret was to get him off quickly, which he never minded, even if by chance he had taken a wicket.

In his early days he was, it was said, something of a martinet as a match-manager, and woe betide the candidate who offended his strict sartorial sense, or who failed to mind his p's and q's either on the field or off. But at heart he was a kind man, of the sort that in any club is worth his weight in gold, happy to play anywhere at the last minute, carry his bag for miles, and arrive early, and *expect* to bat No. 11. At Lord's he always sat in the same seat, on the left beneath the Committee Room window, where I would seek him latterly each summer scarcely thinking he would have survived the winter, living alone in a bachelor service-flat in Hallam Street. He seemed to regard me in a way as his protégé, always flattering about my work on radio and TV and in the *Telegraph*. Frail as could be, he saw through the summer of 1965, and died in the autumn aged 83.

There was one venerable figure from the golden period of amateur cricket, 'Buns' Cartwright, who never lost touch with young cricketers and who would have echoed these last sentiments, I think, up to his death at 87 last year. From time immemorial, first as secretary and then as president, he was the guiding spirit of Eton Ramblers. Apart from all else he was a far from conventional figure himself. It is unusual, after all, to see emerging from White's or the Bath Club a man in a London suit, with carnation, umbrella, a cloth cap and blue 'sneakers'.

'Buffer' does not in any way fit the eccentric personality of Colonel Cartwright. Old other things will occur to those who knew him. There are several appellations of variable politeness beginning with 'b'! Buns was seldom known to withhold any remark that came into his mind. Often he hit the nail on the head with cruel accuracy. Often he said outrageous things, not seriously meant. Authority was anything but sacred to him, in any sphere.

Buns broke upon the cricket scene in the Eton XI of 1907, from which date comes his first recorded comment. The afternoon before the Eton–Winchester match the visiting Eton team were taking tea with the headmaster of Winchester's wife, sitting nervously on the edge of drawing-room chairs and waiting for someone to break the ice. Young Cartwright did so, pulling out a handkerchief, mopping his brow, and exclaiming, 'Gad, ma'am, I'm sweatin'.' Whether or not this brave sally put everyone at their ease Dick Twining, his contemporary and the narrator of this little story, did not record.

Buns, like others who fought in the first war and by the grace of heaven survived, never followed a profession or business career – though they were the first to the colours when the call came again in 1939. While not exactly rich they had enough, as bachelors, to scratch very comfortably along, swelling the profits of the London clubs, playing various games with the utmost spirit in their due season, watching them at Lord's, Queen's Club, Twickenham and elsewhere, and, of course, following the horses at Newmarket, Ascot and Newbury. A limited existence, to say the least, but one can see how it might be drifted into, after the horrors of war and how, once accepted, a man without special qualifications or aptitudes might continue to opt for the easy life.

But I malign Buns Cartwright, to the extent that he served at one time as a judge's marshal, and also between the wars did fulfil another definite function and a highly responsible one. For when F. E. Smith became Lord Chancellor he appointed the gallant major (his rank retained from service in the Coldstream Guards in World War One – the continued use of temporary rank being then a regular custom) as his Patronage secretary. Though scarcely noted for his interest in things ecclesiastical, all church livings of which the Lord Chancellor was patron thus became Buns's concern. With his beetling brow and fierce military moustache he was a formidable figure at the best of times. How he must have seemed from the other side of a desk in the palace of Westminster to nervous young curates under inspection for preferment is, at this range of time, a comical thought. No doubt Buns fulfilled his duty as conscientiously as might be – but it was, on the face of it, a peculiar appointment.

Picking up Buns in his flat one evening to go round the corner to the XL Club dinner at the Hilton – he never missed either this or the two M.C.C. dinners, the Anniversary and the dinner to the touring side – I counted 23 items of headgear

hanging in the hall. More than half of them were decorated
with hat-bands of various club colours. If on a hot day at
Lord's he took off his jacket one would expect to see that a
Panama hat with an M.C.C. hat-band and a Rambler tie was
complemented with I.Z. braces. The Australians, on his visits
down under following M.C.C., were intrigued, to say the least,
by his sartorial variations, which prompted illustrated interviews in such papers as the *Sydney Sun*. There was even a
picture of him shaving, braces and all. This reminds me that
*The Times* a few years ago took a photograph of him at Ascot
in full fig (the sneakers perhaps for once discarded), and
failed to identify him in the caption. They were surprised
by a brisk demand for prints of a splendid picture. He was a
man full of peculiarities, one of which was that he never
owned a car: so how many hundred thousand miles he
travelled in other people's is anyone's guess.

As a cricketer Buns got near enough to an Oxford Blue to
be elected a Harlequin. I recall him as a rugged competitor
both on the cricket field and the golf course. I doubt whether
he ever met Stephen Potter; if he had I'm sure that the pair of
them might have swapped experiences in the subtler fields of
Gamesmanship. Buns was always a good friend and a bad
enemy; a shrewd sporting judge and critic. He was at his best
in the long annual letters accompanying the Eton Rambler
fixture-card, which he used kindly to send me, with news and
gossip of the great company of Ramblers of his time – literally
thousands of them covering his 70 years of membership. If
Shirley Snell was the best-dressed man in the city, Buns was
just about the best-known man in the West End.

Needless to say, stories about him are endless: he was, as I
say, a bachelor, but far from unappreciative of feminine company. A young cricketer once returned from a holiday in the
South of France, saying: 'Who do you think was there but old
Buns. Yes, and Mrs Buns too. She was charming.'

Now to a sketch of an utterly different sort of person though
he had in common with Cartwright a deep affection for

cricket. Sir Home Gordon Bt was likewise an Etonian, though he was no cricketer of any sort or kind. Born in 1871 his memory went back to a visit to the old Prince's ground in Belgravia where he was taken, before his seventh birthday, to see the 1878 Australians – the very first to come here apart from the Aboriginals – play the Gentlemen of England. In 1880 at Lord's he was presented to W.G., and later that summer he was also taken to see the first of all Test Matches between England and Australia at the Oval. Thereafter until his death at the age of 84 the abiding passion of this extra-ordinary little man who never had the physique to be a player was watching cricket. These were unusual credentials for one who, in addition to being a publisher, from his schooldays on practised cricket journalism, and set himself up as a statistician. His *Cricket Form at a Glance* purported to give the batting, bowling and fielding figures plus details of teams played for, number of Tests and Blues, and hundreds scored, for all who appeared in first-class cricket over two seasons even though in only a couple of matches. The first edition began at 1878 and ended with 1902, a second took things on to 1923, and yet a third, in paperback, told the story from 1878 to 1937. A note on the cover announced that all royalties would be allocated to cricket charities by the Committee of M.C.C.

In his book of memoirs, *Background of Cricket*, Home Gordon quotes Lord Hawke who in his foreword to Herbert Sutcliffe's *For England and Yorkshire* described him as 'the greatest statistician of the day, nay of all time'. Hawke 'then declared that the brain reels at the incredible toil of my ency-clopaedic computations, but that they were a labour of love. That is true, and they were also comprehensive, for after publishing the life figures of 3687 cricketers, inclusive of every one who had played in any two of these seasons in first-class cricket, only a minute number of accurate omissions were forwarded to me by correspondents.' The book also contains lists of all the runs and wickets for and against every county in the championship over this 60-year period.

Others were distinctly less complimentary about Home Gordon's value as a statistician and I think Irving Rosenwater's judgement, as the leading present-day historical researcher, may be safely accepted. He says:

> Home Gordon's figures were always extremely impressive to behold, but too rarely stood up to careful examination. There was a lack of science, and he was much more clearly an able gossip than an able statistician. His figures today are virtually never quoted because his inaccuracies have been proven time and again. He does, however, occupy a genuine niche in the story of cricket if only for the remarkable span of his watching experience. And he did claim to have got Jack White into Percy Chapman's side for Australia!

All in all, and one way or another, the Bart claimed a good deal. Nevertheless he earned full marks for industry, and for tackling such a vast job at a time when the game was far less closely documented than it is today. There were not so many rivals looking over his shoulder, quick to pounce upon error.

He was, of course, what would now be called a 'cricket nut' of the first order, a busy, vivacious, garrulous, good-hearted midget of a man who was enormously friendly with everyone and loved to be in the know. By many he was held in affection; others were irritated that one so ludicrously ignorant of every technical aspect of the game should have so much to say and moreover find many in authority apparently prepared to listen to him. On the face of it, it was strange that Plum Warner gave him a weekly platform on page one of the *Cricketer* which he filled with an egregious mingling of fact and fancy under the title 'In the Pavilion'. But, after all, the *Cricketer*, which never had a penny to spare, got the stuff for nothing, and at least they had a willing, not to say eager, contributor.

Home latterly attached himself almost exclusively and almost permanently to Sussex, but with his trim, minute figure, short, thick moustache, invariable red carnation and unmistakable cackle he was a familiar figure wherever the game was played. His particular friend was Peter, or Percy, Perrin, a fine bat in his day for Essex, and throughout the '30s one of the Test selectors. For seven years running the job was done by a triumvirate of Warner, Perrin and another little man busy for cricket, the ruling spirit in Lancashire, Tommy Higson.

It was a strangely incongruous alliance, the 'squeaking Bart', as he was sometimes called from the high pitch of his voice, and this rich East-ender, a head and more taller than Home, who in a low growl scattered aitches all over the place, was at his ease in any company, and was, incidentally, by repute an outstanding shot. He was said to be invited to the Sandringham shoots and to be a favourite with King George V, for whom blunt, earthy characters such as Pete Perrin and the railwaymen's leader, J. H. Thomas, apparently had a fascination.

'Anyone got a fag?' Perrin would ask gruffly. If no one obliged he added, 'Then s'pose I'll have to smoke one of mine,' brought a tin of tobacco from his pocket and rolled his own cigarette.

Like Buns Cartwright, neither Perrin nor Home Gordon was known to own a car, but the deficiency was made up by another extraordinary character called Leslie Hindley, who drove the pair of them round England, from ground to ground, in a large open tourer. Hindley was a lugubrious-looking fellow who, whether in London or the country, always wore a bowler hat. Whether he knew anything about cricket I cannot remember, but his pursuit of the game was insatiable. On one day Home records they saw the finishes of three games, at Leyton, Lord's and the Oval, and after the last one drove to Vincent Square to see whether anything was going on there. Here now is 'a nut' to beat all comers, on the evidence of Home Gordon's book:

Never allowing a servant into his room, he cleans it himself. In it, apart from some pieces of carving he has collected and a complete series of every modern postage stamp, are the cards of every cricket match he has seen, the itinerary of every motor run he has taken, copious diaries, the programme of every play and concert he has attended – he was once a pupil and subsequently instructor at the Academy of Music – every crossword puzzle published in the *Daily Telegraph*, five barometers and innumerable notebooks compiled on any subject . . . Motoring, he takes a despatch-case in which there is the drum-stick of a fowl, chocolate, various cricket reference books, maps and his daily paper.

He had never drunk alcohol, tea or coffee, and the height of his ambition was, according to the Bart, to cut his (Home Gordon's) hair.

Yes, we had our eccentrics in the '30s all right.

Long prior to his peregrinations with Perrin – when indeed the latter was piling up runs for Essex – Home, as I have said, was very friendly with Lord Hawke, who chaired the very first Test selection committee, in 1899, and thereafter served until 1909 inclusive. Add the tie-up with Plum Warner, and I suppose it may not have been such a presumption as it seems at first glance – though it scarcely smacks of modesty – that he should declare: 'It would be affectation to pretend that I have not been in closer association with a majority of successive selectors than anyone else.'

Home Gordon was an institution, around whom all sorts of stories circulated, including, I suspect, many rumours whispered in his ear by people just for the fun of seeing how they progressed. Sussex on retirement became his home, and cricket and the county club the centre of his existence. He went almost everywhere with the side and indeed in an expansive moment was actually presented with his county cap by Arthur Gilligan. He was photographed wearing it, sitting in a team group, the expressions on the faces of the players being not all of unalloyed joy at the sight of the recruit to their ranks. In his obituary *Wisden* records this unusual award, adding that it was 'an old one belonging to A. E. R. Gilligan'.

One can see him at a remove of forty years promenading the boundaries, spruce, button-holed, high-pitched and more than a little absurd. At Horsham he was supposed to have gone into the ladies' loo by mistake, and to have been shooed out by a large, furious woman towering over him. Crusoe claimed to have been an eye-witness of the scene as Home backed nervously away, making nasal, placatory noises which only increased her indignation.

'Get out, you horrible little man.'

'Thaank you.'

'How dare you come in here?'

'Thaank you.'

'I shall report you to the police.'

'Thaank you.'

No doubt the story was fancifully embroidered as it went the rounds.

Once or twice in the first week of August I would see the Bank-holiday match between Sussex and Middlesex at Hove and then motor across for the second match of the Canterbury Week, giving a lift to Home Gordon. It was thus I was first introduced en route to the Dormy House at Rye where he was a member – as he also was of the Golf Club, of which indeed, though no sort of player, he was once captain. It may well be that it was on one of these journeys he told me a story illustrative of his publishing instinct. When he was the proprietor of Williams and Norgate he published Lord Hawke's memoirs, entitled *Recollections and Reminiscences*.

Though the book was as pedestrian as the title it did well enough to encourage Home to order a reprint. Then one fateful day he saw the evening paper headlines announcing Hawke's speech at the Yorkshire A.G.M. wherein he said he hoped to God the day would never come when a professional would captain England. 'At once,' said Home, 'I picked up the telephone, got on to the printers, and was just in time to cancel the new edition. It was as well I did, for after that speech we didn't sell another dozen copies.'

I suppose of all maladroit remarks in the cricket world this one of Hawke's just about takes the biscuit. It has often been claimed in explanation that since in those days sides were invariably led by amateurs all he was trying to put across was that he hoped the day would never come when there was no amateur good enough to play for England. A pity then that the noble lord did not say so, for the phrase has been used ever since as evidence of the crippling snobbery supposedly surrounding cricket.

So much for Home Gordon and his companions, except to add there is no one living to whom this sketch could give offence. Though married twice Home Gordon had no issue, and the twelfth Bart – the title dating back to Charles I in 1631 – was the last.

The nearest parallel I can think of to his place in cricket was that of another small man of Sussex in the world of Rugby football, Major R. V. Stanley, known as 'Uncle'. Though never in residence and never a player – he was the Magdalen College organist – 'Uncle' Stanley for a spell on either side of the Great War more or less ran Oxford rugger. He was elected to represent the University on the Rugby Union and from this actually gravitated to become, for just one season, an international selector.

Who remembers *The Lady Vanishes* and the conversation in the train between Basil Radford and Naunton Wayne when one of them talks rather slightingly of someone and is rebuked by the other?

'Steady on, old chap, he did play for the Gentlemen.'

'I know – but only once.'

My characters seem rather to have declined from buffers to butts. Ah, well, there used to be room on the games scene for oddities, though in these super-serious times they seem scarcely to have a place. Some of them did much good, and none much harm: and they were often a source of such humour as nowadays we have to look hard to find.

*From* FOLLOW ON, *1977*

# *Frank Woolley*

## IAN PEEBLES

There are a small number of cricketers who, apart from questions of records and efficiency, have a lasting place amongst the immortals of the game. Gilbert Jessop does not figure amongst the leading international averages, but, by a shrewd mixture of audacity and unorthodoxy, was not only a devastating opponent but the greatest public attraction of his day. Neither are Learie Constantine's figures startling, but the combination of tempestuous hitting and fast bowling, and astonishing fielding, made him something of a one-man exhibition. People would go to watch McDonald bowl as much for the pleasure of seeing the complete perfection of action as to enjoy the material results.

Of all such figures in the game of cricket Frank Woolley has ample claim to be the most eminent. In his case there is a prodigious record of material success, but no scale exists upon which to estimate the pleasure which its compilation gave to countless thousands. Were there such a scale it is difficult to think of any cricketer who could challenge his supremacy. It may be said that Woolley was the most graceful of the efficient, and the most efficient of the graceful.

Frank Woolley scored just under 60,000 runs in first-class cricket and took over 2000 wickets. He caught 913 catches. He played for England 64 times, and appeared in no fewer than 52 successive Test matches. He scored 145 centuries. It is a formidable record.

Although a great all-round cricketer, it is the batsman who will be chiefly remembered. Frank was in his active career, and is to this day, a yardstick against whom all left-handers are measured and to whom the aspiring are compared. No one has, as yet, quite equalled the standard.

It is naturally rather easier to acclaim the performance than to convey even a dim impression of it. Each innings was an event. There was always something almost dramatic about the appearance of this majestic figure. He walked unhurriedly but purposefully to the wicket amidst a buzz of anticipation on the part of the crowd and a well-founded apprehension on the part of most bowlers. On arrival at the crease there were no affectations or mannerisms, either of which would have been wholly alien to the scene. He would be given guard, glance down at the setting of the field and take stance. He stood upright, bending only so far as his height compelled him, feet slightly apart, hands high on the bat, the general effect being one of ease and simplicity which characterized the whole performance.

There was about him an air of detachment, so that occasionally one got the impression that he was a casual, almost careless, starter. This was obviously not so, but I would say that, always eager to attack, it took him an over or two to get the feel of things and become warmed up. It might be added that this impression of indifference could be somewhat disconcerting to the opposition, acutely conscious that if they did not succeed immediately awful retribution was liable to befall them.

As the bowler reached the crease he would pick the bat up in a long, smooth circular sweep, parting his feet with a short, forward step of the right foot. The bat came down straight and firmly controlled close to the line of the off stump. There was plenty of time to make the choice of stroke and whatever it might be it was never otherwise than a flowing, rounded gesture. Never did one see a hasty stab or unbalanced jerk. His defence, being based chiefly on attack, did not have the rock-like impregnability of his contemporary, Philip Mead, but it was enormously aided by the fact that he was a most difficult man to bowl at. Once he was going there was no area in which the bowler could seek shelter. He had all the strokes, and he lent to them an unequalled force and beauty. Thus, when one is asked what was his best shot, it is impossible to say, for whatever he did was enthralling. He was a beautiful off-side player off back and front foot, driving, cutting, slicing to all sectors. I have frequently quoted what I consider to be the prettiest compliment ever paid on the field of cricket. It was at Canterbury in 1930 that Frank took 60 undefeated off the Australians in double-quick time. The first burst came chiefly off Alan Fairfax, a very high-class quick-medium bowler, who was lathered against all sections of the off-side fence. Seeking reassurance, he asked that fine rumbustious character Vic Richardson if he thought it was 'all right bowling at his off stump'. 'All right,' said Vic enthusiastically, 'it's bloody marvellous – we're all enjoying it.'

Frank was the most exhilarating straight hitter. The action seldom appeared to be more than a free swinging forward stroke, but the ball would sail away to clear the longest boundary. He loved to treat fast bowlers so and when in frustration they dropped the ball short he would pull them square with the same unhurried venom. This was essentially a pull, made with the full long-armed swing of the bat as the striker lay back on his left leg. The hook was somehow too angular a movement ever to fit into this flowing repertoire.

It was a dominating as well as a graceful performance, the batsman sailing serenely on his chosen course in all circumstances, disrupting and ignoring opposing stratagems.

At Tonbridge, when Walter Robins and myself were young and cock-a-hoop at getting a couple of early wickets, Pat Hendren indicated Frank's dominating figure advancing on the scene. 'Here comes the lion-tamer,' said he. It proved an apt description and when we had been flogged out of sight Nigel Haig devised a somewhat desperate device. Harry Lee, at square-leg, was to keep dropping back until he was right on the boundary, and Nigel would then bowl the fifth ball of the over short. To a point the plan worked out. Nigel dropped the ball short and Frank slapped it away straight in the desired direction. However, it bisected the line of the fielder's upturned eyes about eight feet above his head and went 'thwup' into a tent behind, so that the structure tugged at its moorings and shimmered like a belly-dancer. All, especially the fielder, were rather relieved that the plan had not worked out in the final detail.

He *hit* the ball beautifully on the leg side with the same full rhythmical swing of the bat. One stroke particularly pleases the memory and seems to be a penchant of left-handers, as Graeme Pollock also plays it to perfection. It is the pull-drive played off the front foot to the good-length or overpitched ball in the region of the leg stump. Ideally, this is played to the faster bowling, when the rise of the ball aids the 'take-off' and it goes sweet and far between mid-wicket and long-on.

Like all true artists, he took a keen interest in the implements of his craft. He had very particular tastes in bats, and Gunn and Moore used to make him four bats each season which he calculated would cover his needs. These were produced exactly to his requirements. He liked a heavy bat, weighing about two pounds six ounces, but with the weight evenly distributed and not too low in the blade. Thus, although he had plenty of wood, the bat would come up easily and in good balance. Frank's bats were certain to come in for some hard treatment and when he had made an appreciable dent in the driving section he would rest the bat, for he thought at this stage it lost something of its resilience.

On his retirement in 1938 he had two of these specially made bats intact. He gave them to Charlie Barnett, who found them superb in every way and put them to very good use.

Frank never expressed any preference for, nor prejudice against, any particular type of bowling. One would surmise that he enjoyed himself to the utmost against the fast bowlers. It was against them that he produced his most startling effects, and it was inspiring and amusing to see him quell any ill-advised attempts at retaliation. He was not a man to be intimidated and, not unnaturally, he had a fine confidence in his own powers of counter-attack. If he was hit he considered that he was the party to blame, and he was never heard to complain or speak a rancorous word against anyone who bowled aggressively. Indeed, he had little reason to do so, for the bouncer was ever grist to his mill.

He considered McDonald and Larwood the fastest bowlers he had ever played, and thought the latter the fairest and best. To watch him opposed to either must have been to see the highest expression of the game of cricket. I never myself saw him tackle McDonald, but I played in a North *v.* South Trial match at Old Trafford where he opened the innings against Larwood and Voce at full blast. He got 50 out of 72 in less than an hour. Always having a slight flair for the anticlimax, he lathered this powerful combination into retirement with joy and ease, and was then caught at long-on off a full-toss from Tommy Mitchell.

At Folkestone in a 'Festival' match where feeling ran rather high the West Indies fast bowlers let go such a burst of pace that certain of the home batsmen were visibly relieved when soon out. Frank and Bob Wyatt then made centuries. They provided an interesting contrast. Bob, rock-like and the more stubborn and immovable at the evidence of hostility about him, battled grimly. Frank, detached and apparently unaware that the bowling was intended for anything other than his enjoyment, serenely carved it to every point of the compass.

This scene rather underlined a very particular quality of Frank's play. He had at all times a quiet and unruffled dignity. This had no hint of pomposity, which is a highly assailable attitude, but sprang from a quietly determined personality allied to a natural physical grace. Amongst the innumerable charms of cricket is its power to inflict indignities and farcical situations on its lovers and practitioners. To these Frank seemed largely immune. Even when run out, an accident which befell him 44 times in his career, he seemed unruffled and unhurrying, in a situation where batsmen are inclined to look a trifle dishevelled.

The only instance I have heard of his being disturbed out of his Olympian calm was recalled by Leslie Ames. When he had thrashed the regular Glamorgan bowlers all over the field Emrys Davies appeared to bowl his seldom-practised left-handed 'chinamen'. These for some reason caused Frank great perturbation, which, in its turn, caused the purveyor and all else present great astonishment. There is something rather touching about this scene, which smacks of the elephant's unaccountable fear of the mouse.

Frank was a very fine slow left-arm bowler, if not quite the equal of Blythe and Rhodes, to whom he differed in being rather quicker. He bowled slightly 'behind the back', a style no doubt derived from association with the first-named. In his case, however, the arm came from the hip pocket rather than the right armpit as in the case of his model. His great height gave him a steep flight which, combined with a good power of spin, got a lively degree of bounce on all pitches. These qualities caused a number of good judges to remark that in certain conditions he was more dangerous than either of these great rivals. He still bowled well on the cast-iron Australian wickets, when pressed into service at a time when he was bowling rather less for his county. That he did have to econo-mize his effort was due rather to the strenuous demands of batting in six-day-a-week cricket than to any deterioration in the quality of his attack, although an injury to his knee in Australia in 1924 adversely affected his run up from then on.

He was a versatile as well as a fine fielder. In his earlier days he revelled in chasing and throwing from the deep, and was one of the best slips in the country. Close to the wicket his lively reflexes enabled him to make full use of his great reach and, like other masters of close-range fielding, he was seldom caught off balance.

*From* WOOLLEY – THE PRIDE OF KENT, *1969*

# Crusoe

## A. P. SINGLETON

The cricket season of 1934, my first at Oxford, opened with bitterly cold weather and grey skies. It was also apparent to those of us who had any aspirations to get into the University team, that the cricket was going to be conducted on austere lines. The various authorities, resident and imported, who controlled the conduct of affairs on the field seemed to have a fixation for physical fitness, the cleaner, better life, early to bed and early to rise, and a general disregard for the more light-hearted and humorous side of cricket. I think that the majority of us felt that the whole thing was being conducted far too much like a Test match campaign.

Then, one day, the whole atmosphere changed. This was partly due to the retirement of our honorary coaches to other duties, but mostly to the arrival on the scene of one of the most remarkable characters I ever met. I was at the nets at the time, and so saw him at once, for the nets are beside the approach path to the pavilion. He approached with a swinging yet springy gait, and looked like a character, even from a distance. He was dressed, reading from south to north, in what looked like rather an elderly pair of dancing shoes, blue socks, one with a large potato in the heel, a pair of wide grey flannels, worn at half mast, a sports coat held open by his left hand, which was in his trousers pocket, the arm also supporting the *Morning Post*, a far from new shirt, and a tie which had blown back over his shoulder. Surmounting all this was a bronzed face, rather like that of a Red Indian, containing the most humorous and sparkling pair of grey eyes I have ever seen. I was amazed, and awed, to find that this was the famous Somerset bowler and cricket writer, R. C. Robertson-Glasgow, and this was the beginning of a close friendship which lasted for many years.

From the moment he arrived in the Parks, it was as if the sun had at last broken through. There were gales of laughter, led by his own stentorian bellow, amusing stories, and incidents by the dozen. Even the most serious minded could not help joining in and laughing. He joined with us in the nets, and reported our cricket on the field with a kindly humour totally lacking in today's cricket writings, and, best of all, he treated us, not much more than schoolboys, as equals.

This became an annual event, his arrival at the Parks, and we all looked forward to it. Officially he was there to report on the trials and the early matches, and he carried in a side pocket of his sports coat one of those 6d. red memo books from Woolworths. This he referred to as 'The washing book', and this he would put on the mantelpiece in the pavilion, with a stub of pencil, with the remark, 'I've put the washing book up there. If anything happens, shove it in. I'm off to the nets.' And away he would go, while we entered the relevant details of the match in progress. His report the following morning was always most accurate, and full of humour.

After the day's play we would repair to Vincent's club more often than not for a pint or two of beer, and this was when he was at his best, and he would regale us with stories and memories, and occasionally his poetry, which was brilliant but, unfortunately, unprintable. But he was never a bore and I never knew anyone who did not welcome him except, possibly, one local, rather stuffy headmaster who thought that he should not be allowed in the club during the term as he was bad for the undergraduates; this opinion, I need hardly say, was unsupported. The talk was mainly concerned with cricket and golf, for Crusoe, as we all knew him, was a great theorist, especially about bowling.

I remember one February when he came up to report a golf match and duly appeared in the club on the Saturday evening – we agreed to lunch on the Sunday in th 'George'. This was a good lunch, washed down by several pints of bitter attended by half a dozen or so of us in the warm and

friendly atmosphere of the 'George', while the snow drifted
down outside. There was a great deal of noise and laughter,
and the conversation inevitably turned to cricket and swing
bowling. Crusoe was laying down the law about field placing,
and we did not all agree. So he decided that the only solution
was a practical demonstration, and with that he ordered half
a dozen rolls and we all went down into the street outside,
which had lamp posts at intervals in the middle of the street.

Crusoe placed his field and himself opened the bowling
with a roll from the station end, with a lamp post as the
wicket, and Mitchell-Innes taking strike using an umbrella
as a bat. The game progressed for a while, possibly a little
informally but with a great deal of noise and laughter, with
the snow still falling, and then a policeman appeared on the
scene and asked what was going on. Glasgow at once approached him and in his charming and forthright way, pointed
out that we were doing harm to no one, and that there was
very little traffic anyway, and that the policeman could do us
a great service by acting as umpire, for which job he was
admirably suited. To our surprise, the policeman laughed and
took up this position and joined in the general fun. Such was
Crusoe's personality.

He had a disarming lack of formality which saw him
through almost any scrape. I remember one wonderful
evening. He asked me to dine as his guest at the Savage Club,
and assured me that it would be perfectly all right to leave the
car in Waterloo Place, just round the corner. This was a great
occasion in my life; the guests including Sir Jack Hobbs, Sir
Malcolm Campbell, and many other of my heroes. Also were
present the Western Brothers, Starr Wood, Billy Bennett and
others from the stage, all of whom did turns. I also remember
Vivian Jenkins and Arthur Rees of the Welsh Rugby team,
and men of colossal muscle and build, teaching Andy
Sandham the elementary principles of rugger in a marble hall
with pillars in it. Sandham was sober and nippy enough to
keep out of harm's way, but how the other two survived

serious injury, or even death, I never understood. This was at about 2 a.m., and we then went out to the car. A lone policeman was sitting on the running board, waiting for us. On arrival we asked him if there was anything wrong, and he pointed out that that was a 2-hour park, and drew out his notebook. Crusoe asked him how it would be if we sloshed him and then drove away. The policeman replied that it would not be advisable 'as I happen to be the heavyweight champion of the Metropolitan Police!' This made everyone laugh so much that the policeman laughed too, and forgot all about the summons.

Crusoe also lacked formality in his dress; in fact, looking back on it, I cannot remember seeing him really well dressed, even in formal evening attire; somehow he always looked as if he had just arrived from a previous party, and a pretty rough one at that. Mrs Chapman once told me of a weekend visit to their house by Crusoe. He came down for a golf weekend, and Percy met him at the station. His sole luggage was a bag of museum-type golf clubs and a large cabin trunk. This was in midwinter. With difficulty the trunk was manhandled on to the luggage carrier at the back of the car and later into the house. They then settled down to tea and hot buttered toast. During this, the maid knocked on the door and asked if she could speak to Madam. Mrs Chapman went out and asked the trouble, to which the maid replied that she was in a bit of a quandary as to what to do about Mr Glasgow's luggage, as the sole contents of the cabin trunk was a dirty pair of cricket boots.

Such, then, are some of my memories of Crusoe. He was very clever, but never heavy. It was impossible for people to be serious or morbid in his presence, and there was almost always a lot of noise where he was, with his own tremendous laugh dominating the scene. He was welcome wherever he went. I never met anyone who disliked him, and I do not remember him saying anything unpleasant about anyone. Above all, he was young at heart, and he had the ability to get

on with young people and to make them think that they
counted. As a cricket writer, the last thing he would have
considered was sensationalism; he became famous in this
sphere purely by the charm and humour of his writing.

*May 1965*

# Tom Graveney

## J. M. KILBURN

Tom Graveney has always looked a cricketer of the West
country, though he was born in Northumberland. His schooldays were passed in Bristol, and when they were over he chose
voluntary Army service before conscription, to reach com-
missioned rank. By the time he returned to Bristol in 1947 his
elder brother, Ken, had become a Gloucestershire player, and
Tom was introduced to the county club as 'a kid brother I
can't bowl out'.

Cricket was not a compulsion for Tom Graveney. He had
talent that encouraged him towards a career in professional
golf, and he had opportunity to train in accountancy. He
accepted cricket and satisfied anticipations as a batsman of
uncommon grace and authority. By 1951 he was playing for
England.

On appearance alone Graveney's place in England teams
could never have been questioned. His batting, founded on
the classical forward strokes, contained an elegance that distinguished him even in the highest company, and when
derivations were sought for his style, Hammond was invariably the quoted model.

In fact Graveney could have drawn inspiration only from
Hammond's name. The two players were not contemporary
and resemblance in the eye of beholders was beauty seen and
beauty remembered.

Graveney's early international career was unspectacular without being unsuccessful, but ironically his successes sowed doubts of his adequacy; he did enough to create assumptions that he should be doing more. By the most exacting standards he was found wanting in critical moments, lacking concentration at the crunch. He was discarded for the vital matches in the 1954–55 tour of Australia, and the modest performances in the Test rubbers immediately following brought depreciation, with regret but not injustice.

Whenever Graveney was out of the England side England cricket was not necessarily weakened but it seemed slightly unrepresentative, as a June garden without roses or a banquet without wine. Roses blossomed and wine was relished in innings of 258 and 164 against West Indies in 1957, but another tour of Australia was disappointing and Graveney left the Test match scene for three years.

They were years of disturbance in his county cricket. He left Gloucestershire to join Worcestershire, but immediate registration for his new county was not permitted and he had to endure the summer of 1961 without appearing in the Championship. Success for Worcestershire and against Pakistan earned a third tour of Australia, but the outcome was disappointing and again a cricketer of international quality passed into the international wilderness.

Graveney emerged from his experiences a harder, grimmer player. Worcestershire's Championship contention stiffened his sense of batting responsibility; advancing age in itself eliminated some of the batting frivolities. In 1966 England lost the first Test to West Indies, and they turned back to Graveney as ten years earlier they had turned back to Washbrook and to Compton. The parallels were remarkable. Washbrook scored 98 in his innings of recall, Compton scored 94, and Graveney scored 96. Washbrook and Compton met the needs of a specific hour; Graveney stayed to build a new international reputation.

He played Test innings of substance and dignity and charm at home and in West Indies, and he remained an unquestioned selection until he fell into contractual dispute during the Old Trafford Test of 1969.

Graveney may have disappointed some cricketers by playing in Graveney's way, but he has adorned cricket. In an age preoccupied with accountancy he has given the game warmth and colour and inspiration beyond the tally of the scorebook. He has been of the orchard rather than the forest, blossom susceptible to frost but breathtaking in the sunshine.

Figures give him too little credit and too much. They rate him among the most prolific of scorers with a hundred centuries achieved, and ignore the failures to command where command was expected in a critical hour. They obscure serenity and fragility alike. Figures cannot convey the splendour of an evening's innings or the anti-climax of first-over dismissal next morning.

Graveney's batting has always been open-handed and open-hearted, though not always open-eyed. He has tended to read Test match and festival in the same context, his cricket a medium for uncomplicated contest of talent with his own gifts offering an opportunity but not an obligation to succeed. Graveney has presented his ability without enforcing its acceptance. He has felt no guilt in edging a slip catch, because error is a human frailty and he has never sought to eliminate the humanity from cricket.

The difference between his earlier and later batting, indicated by more marked stability, represents not so much a change of heart or change of method as a restriction of adventurous activity through the insistence of advancing years. Graveney has not attempted to circumscribe himself: the swing of his bat has been reduced by the natural process of age, and he still counts cricket in all its forms a game to be enjoyed. Taking enjoyment as it came he has given enjoyment that will warm winters of memory.

# Colin Cowdrey

## ALAN ROSS

As I write this, it is 15 years to the day that Colin Cowdrey made his first, and possibly most remarkable, Test century; 102 out of 191 in the third Test, at Melbourne, in 1954. Hutton, Edrich, May and Compton had gone to Miller and Lindwall for 20, and only a batsman of superb technique and complete composure could have survived long on such a wicket against such bowling. Cowdrey was 22, playing in his first Test series. 'His century,' I wrote at the time, 'had the bloom of youth on it; but the soil from which it sprang had been tended lovingly and long . . . [it was] a blend of leisurely driving and secure back play, of power and propriety.' Two runs later Cowdrey was out, playing no stroke and being bowled off his pads. The glory and the indignity, through the years, came somehow to seem typical.

Among the great English batsmen of the post-war period – Hutton, Compton, Washbrook, May, Dexter, Graveney, Barrington – Cowdrey, I suppose, has looked about the best 'bred'. Yet with breeding – the inherited grace and effortlessness that combine to form the grand manner – and the assumption of authority without tokens of display that is another characteristic, there has gone mildness, indecision, a stubborn passivity. I cannot think of a great player harder to coax into awareness of his reserves, nor one who, in the mood, made the art of batsmanship seem more artless, more a mere extension of his own geniality. At his best he was a dolphin among minnows, gambolling between the green and the blue as if cares were not invented, almost patronizing. At his less good he seemed imprisoned by some interior gaoler, feet chained, arms pinioned, shuffling away a long sentence.

More than most he is a mood player, delicate in his responses to the invisible strings of memory and music. A false note and he is becalmed, devoid of will and wizardry. Lesser players create their own context, impose their wishes on unpropitious elements, defy luck and roughness of touch. John Edrich is one such. Others, like May and Dexter, had a savagery of stroke that, once achieved, meant business. Cowdrey, like Graveney, has preferred to succeed or fail on his own terms, narcissistically declining to disfigure his own reflection, never hurrying, never bringing brute strength to the caressive lullaby of his stroke-play. His refusal to hit himself into form, or in mid-innings to demolish an attack, has often been maddening; sweet words when one wanted to see the big stick, reason when one hungered for violence. He could not, I imagine, be otherwise. Sometimes it has paid off, sometimes not. As captain and batsman he has, through injury, ineffectiveness and inability to turn the screw that last fraction, missed chances galore; yet, in the final analysis, his accomplishments have been immense, his achievements legion, his consistency, chivalry and charm of character unique.

'In the final analysis?' It is, at the start of 1970, a dubious moment to pronounce such phrases. Is this longest of post-war Test careers already over, or is the most glittering prize, victory in Australia under his leadership, still ahead? They say they never come back, but Cowdrey has, more than once, and if I had to bet on it I would, on balance, just take him to do so again.

He has, over the years, changed surprisingly little, being of that outwardly heavy build and solid gait that announces itself and the maturity it represents almost from the outset. In his round, sallow features the jester and the monk share a gravity of vocation; in his behaviour at slip, his walk between overs and his running between wickets, the ferryboat and the racing yacht share aptitudes.

My first overseas tour as cricket correspondent of *The Observer* was also Cowdrey's first as a player, so that, uniquely, he has been a major part of all the Test cricket I have covered.

We share, too, a background of India and Oxford, not particularly relevant except that it meant I warmed to him early on and remember his hundred for Oxford at Lord's as clearly as if it was yesterday. I cherish it with his 1954 Melbourne hundred, his superb batting in West Indies in 1959–60, and countless other purple passages in his hundred Test matches, to say nothing of his marvellous virtuosity at slip, as among the most enhancing images in my cricket experience.

He has, as few do, elaborated his technique, added new strokes (such as the latest effective but hideous scoop to long leg), refined old ones. His driving between point and mid-off, with minimal movement of the feet and gentle dismissiveness of the bat, is tidal in its rhythmic inevitability, its oceanic break. He can hook, when roused, with affronted grandeur. He cuts with the kind of glee sadistic surgeons bring to complex incisions or a wild conductor to the resuscitation of anaemic arpeggios.

He has brought to the cricket of his time high ideals, impeccable manners, an engaging presence. He has blossomed and bumbled, conjured rare tunes out of stodgy skies, suggested the richest of ports, the lightest of soufflés. He would have made my life happier if he had played for Sussex instead of Kent, but, that apart, most of the regrets in his career fade into insignificance compared to the shining rewards. He has in his comfortable way had to accommodate himself to many uncomfortable experiences; but though he has never, in a material fashion, had to struggle, I believe he has a sense of values and enough insight, if pushed deeply into himself and able to come to terms with more astringent concepts, to offset some of the deader wood at the top of the cricket tree.

# Ray Illingworth

## TREVOR BAILEY

They say that it's a funny old game and there can be few better examples of the strange quirks that cricket can play than the remarkable transformation in the career of Ray Illingworth in the last two seasons. It really all started a couple of winters ago, when Tony Lock decided not to return to England the following summer and Leicestershire suddenly found themselves without their captain and leading spin bowler. About the same time Ray Illingworth told Yorkshire that he was not satisfied with their terms and asked to be released. They reluctantly agreed to his request and thus provided the Midland county with an ideal substitute.

The general view was that Leicester had made a very shrewd appointment. Ray was probably the most reliable English all-rounder in county cricket with a fine knowledge of the game and tactically very sound. It seemed probable that his international career was over, which certainly did not worry his new employers who wanted him to take them to the top of the Championship. After all he had represented England on 30 occasions without ever quite establishing himself an automatic choice. He had been rather unfortunate that three of his contemporaries, Titmus, Allen, and Mortimore, were off-spinners, who had all gained the reputation of being more effective bowlers abroad. Leicester felt that Ray's bowling would gain them a number of points, as on a helpful pitch he is a matchwinner, his batting would provide the solidity to a middle order which had a tendency to fold, and as a captain of the Foreign Legion he would (like Tony Lock) be able to rekindle the enthusiasm and confidence in themselves.

What nobody, including Ray himself, realized was the far-reaching effects this move was to have on English cricket and that, in his very first season with his new club, he would be chosen to lead England, and in the following one be awarded the supreme honour of taking the side to Australia.

Since Ray became captain of England, as a result of Colin Cowdrey's injury, many people have expressed considerable surprise at the effectiveness and authority of his batting, because they regarded him as a highly efficient, and, in certain circumstances, deadly bowler and merely a competent middle-order county batsman. This does not do his prowess with the willow justice, as I have discovered for myself on a number of occasions. Ray did in fact score his first century against Essex and has shown a marked partiality for our bowling ever since. I have lost count of the times, after my county had achieved a breakthrough with the new ball, that we have been unable to press home our advantage because of his arrival at the crease. He has always been exceptionally good against seam bowling and clearly relished leading a recovery. This is perhaps not surprising when one realizes that Ray began his adult cricket as an opening bat for Farsley and originally went to Yorkshire as a batsman-cum-medium-pace swing bowler.

The reason why Illingworth's batting ability has been underrated is that he has normally gone in at number six or seven for Yorkshire. As they were one of the strongest teams in the Championship while he was with them, this has automatically reduced his opportunities of playing a big innings on a good pitch, because the earlier batsmen had normally climbed aboard the run waggon before he arrived at the wicket. It is significant that he scored most runs when he was allowed to bat at number five, but with the northern county's batting line-up this was seldom possible and, remembering the amount of bowling he had to undertake, was possibly undesirable. Be that as it may, this was partially responsible for reducing his effectiveness, as runs always beget more runs.

At one time Ray, like so many Yorkshiremen, was unhappy against a good leg-spinner, particularly on fast pitches because he preferred to play from the confines of his crease (while Jim

Laker trapped him l.b.w. on the back foot on a number of occasions). Now he has blossomed into a fine player of all types of bowling with an excellent temperament, a sound defence, and an especially fine square cut.

Although Ray began with Yorkshire as a swing bowler, it was not long before he abandoned this for the far more lucrative trade of an off-spinner.

His apprenticeship as a seamer gave him – just as earlier it had done for Jim Laker – a powerful body action which helped him make the odd ball leave the bat – a valuable asset. Like all Yorkshire bowlers his outlook is essentially mean, begrudging every run. His length and line are excellent, while his trajectory, except when he deliberately tosses one up, is low. This means that a batsman has to take positive action against him, if he wishes to score runs, because he will have to wait a very long time for a loose delivery. A favourite Illingworth ploy against a new player is to bring his fieldsmen in to save the single and have no deep midwicket or square leg. He thus challenges the batsman to attempt a lofted stroke and is prepared to concede a boundary if the shot is successful. He is, of course, a complete craftsman in his chosen profession, equally at home over and round the wicket. On a 'turner' he can be devastating, while on good pitches his ability to release the ball close to the stumps from over the wicket is a distinct advantage.

Ray has a thoroughly professional, Yorkshire approach to cricket and his captaincy is rather like his bridge, conventional, sound, and essentially practical. He would never attempt a finesse for a possible over 'trick', if he knew by so doing it could cost him the game. Similarly his calls are based on assessed points, not tram tickets. His captaincy of the England team this summer and last has been admirable, while his personal contribution, as a player, has been both inspiring and considerable. He is not a flamboyant skipper and in fact is inclined towards caution, but he makes few mistakes and, as with his bridge, misses very few 'tricks'.

When Ray established himself in the Yorkshire team, he became a member of an attack which was distinctly volatile, individualistic and liable to explode at any time. Their bowlers reminded me of the Greek guerrillas in the war who were united against the Nazis, the common foe, but never harmonized among themselves. Since those days, Ray has matured and has acquired a more philosophical outlook, possibly aided by his position as unofficial shop steward of the Yorkshire side. Above all he has learned toleration, while still retaining the hardness which one would expect, and wish, from an England captain. He ought to, and I think he will, do a good job in Australia, where his quiet, dry, and slightly sardonic humour should prove very helpful.

# Clive Lloyd

## MIKE STEVENSON

Whoever it was that described Clive Lloyd as 'a great, gangling, begoggled supercat' must (temporarily at least) have been inspired; nevertheless, he has been in county cricket just long enough to invite our taking him for granted.

Equally readily can be forgotten the immense impact of overseas cricketers from 1968 onwards, after the strict laws governing their inclusion were relaxed. A seasoned professional of the school of 'ritual cricket', writing home thereafter, might have couched his epistle in the following terms:

Old Trafford,
Friday, 13th

Dear Mum,
 Tell Dad it's a b . . . . .
 We're playing Lancashire first go off and I'm wheeling away on a nice length when this great, bloody bespectacled

bully starts belting me over the top as if we was in club cricket. I bowls it a bit shorter and 'e 'ooks me. Then to cap it all, he digs me best yorker out and that goes for 4 an' all.

When we bat, I push to cover to get off the mark and blow me if the flaming idiot doesn't throw down the bowler's wicket before I've got halfway.

Eeh! I do wish I'd gone into the shop, like you said.

Love, Joe.

To his admirers, Lloyd must appear unique; yet he belongs to the West Indian tradition as clearly as Sobers whose influence is clearly written on the younger man (as Sobers, when bowling, transfers the ball from right to left hand before delivery, acknowledging an early debt to Sir Frank Worrell). Surely much of the West Indies' success results from this tendency for the heroes of one generation to be copied by their aspiring juniors.

By contrast, English batting is so cerebrally over-theoretical. 'Open up,' says the coach, 'and take the inswinger on the thigh-pad or let it pass down the leg side.'

'Rubbish!' says a Sobers or a Lloyd. 'I believe in the old-fashioned leg-hit. I may get a top edge every now and again but please note what has happened to a number of reputable bowlers in the meantime.' Clive Lloyd believes (sing Hallelujah!) that attack is almost always the best form of defence.

Should the batsman, subscribing to the Pauline theory that 'all things be done decently and in order', play each ball on its merits? Surely the length ball played with decorum breeds confidence and efficiency in the bowler, whereas the length ball hit on the rise leaves him wondering just where to bowl the next one.

Any bowler confronted with Clive Lloyd must know the terrifying fascination of Russian roulette. 'Will it be this one . . . or this one . . . or . . . that one nearly killed me and it's broken the sightscreen!'

One former England player described Lloyd as a 'mere

slogger'. Apart from taking exception to the 'mere' (sad that there are so few 'sloggers' among our nines, tens and elevens these days), it is palpably absurd to describe anyone possessing the variety and precision of strokeplay at Lloyd's disposal in such disparaging terms.

A more valid criticism is that (like virtually all players) he is not relatively as good a batsman when the ball is moving as on a plumb 'un. When facing Tom Cartwright on a seamer's wicket at Southport, his batting suggested desperation, if not death-wish; but, to his credit, he got runs.

Certainly he is less vulnerable to the bouncer than he once was and one only has to consider the methods employed by several of the present Australian batsmen, when facing the England attack, to realize that there is a vast difference between periodic uncertainty and impotent capitulation.

Whatever attack he fears, Clive Lloyd tends to get runs or get out; last season he found himself confronted by a couple of medium-pacers clearly intent upon demonstrating his much-publicized Achilles' heel. The first time a ball was bounced at him, its next bounce occurred around 40 yards over the long-leg boundary. You can't kill tigers with a toothpick.

However exciting Lloyd's batting, it is his fielding that has already earned him a place among the immortals. With the strings of the puppet slack, he slouches like a double-jointed gangster. (It amazes me that so fine a mover can sometime look so unathletic.) But seconds, it seems, before an average cover would have moved, the elastic, hunter's stride carries his huge frame to impossibly distant regions, where the telescopic arm will click out and the slick pick-up and shy nudge the poor David of a batsman into belief that Goliath has beaten him to the draw.

Perhaps Lloyd's salient cricketing quality is his unpre-dictability, something which appears to have spread from his cover-driving to his car-driving, which shares many of the more uninhibited characteristics of the Keystone Cops.

He has enjoyed his time in Lancashire and Lancashire has enjoyed him. His two years at Haslingden in the League made him many friends, among whom is John Ingham: 'We were batting together against Enfield on a freezing day just after Clive had landed. There was a gale too and we'd both been pushing up the line automatically. I thought Clive was in a stupor, when there was an explosion the other end. I'd just time to turn my back before the ball took me on the backside and felled me like an ox.'

A friend of mine said of him: 'I've never known anyone laugh longer or more helplessly': a different view of the man who has so often played the Demon King to Harry Pilling's inimitable Fairy Queen.

But the last word on Clive Lloyd, 26 years old, of Guyana, Lancashire and West Indies, demolition expert, Chan Canasta of covers, consistently under-rated bowler and shy but friendly individual, should be allowed to his county captain. Jack Bond said of him: 'We don't tolerate "stars" in the Lancashire team. Clive has fitted in excellently and he's a great team man.'

Lancashire must be delighted to have acquired a star of Clive Lloyd's brilliance; they must be equally relieved that he resolutely refuses to behave like one.

# Mike Procter

## ALAN GIBSON

I suppose that most cricketers would say that now M. J. Procter is the best all-rounder in the world, and I agree, so far as such vague and unprovable tributes can be said to mean anything. He *is* a marvellous cricketer, beyond denial, though his bowling action has caused a scratching of heads among the orthodox. Not that there has ever been any suggestion of unfairness, of throwing: it is just that the strain he imposes upon himself every time he bowls a really fast ball, or even a moderately fast ball, seems more than a human frame can possibly withstand for long.

When Procter joined the Gloucestershire side in 1968, David Green (also a recent arrival) said after the pre-season practices: 'This bloke bowls at a hundred miles an hour from extra cover off the wrong foot.'

'Off the wrong foot'; it is a phrase with a long cricket history, but nobody had examined what it meant, nor indeed could, until slow-motion film enabled us to see how bowlers actually delivered the ball. Racehorses, as you will see from old pictures, were usually drawn, when galloping, with all four legs stretched out at the same time. Slow-motion film of Procter shows that at the moment of delivery it is his left, or orthodox, foot which is in contact with the ground. But I dare say this would have been true of all the supposed 'wrong-foot' bowlers of the past. Certainly Procter is a wrong-footed bowler, as the term has customarily been used. Even on a soft pitch, he does not dig a pit. His pace comes from the last-second circular whip of his arm, his power is generated by his very strong shoulders. His long run is a stimulus to him, and an alarming sight for the batsmen. He does not believe he can bowl really fast without it. Much of cricket is played in the mind.

As for bowling 'from extra-cover', he often uses every inch of the bowling crease. To vary the angle of delivery has always been a good quality of a bowler, and in fact Procter not only bowls from extra-cover but, when he feels like it, from mid-on. When he switches to bowling 'round the wicket', batsmen are inclined to suspect a deep plot or some sudden treachery in the pitch, but I expect he usually does it because he likes a change, just as he varies the length of his run-up with no logic, except the logic of how he feels (the best of arguments, given only that you are a good enough bowler: *cf*. K. R. Miller).

Procter first came to England in 1965, along with Richards; two unknown South African youngsters wondering whether to go into the English county game. They played for Gloucestershire 2nd XI while qualifying for the county. I remember seeing them as spectators, watching a Somerset match at the Imperial Ground, Bristol: two slight, shy boys they seemed then, baffled by their surroundings. Their figures for Gloucestershire 2nd XI that season were:

| Batting | Ins | NO | R | HS | Av. |
|---|---|---|---|---|---|
| M. J. Procter | 24 | 7 | 527 | 80 | 31.00 |
| B. A. Richards | 26 | 5 | 632 | 81 | 30.09 |

| Bowling | O | M | R | W | Ave. |
|---|---|---|---|---|---|
| B. A. Richards | 158 | 46 | 392 | 29 | 13.51 |
| M. J. Procter | 393 | 114 | 731 | 53 | 13.79 |

Between them in the batting averages came D. Bevan, and closely after them in the bowling averages came M. Ashenden, and I do not remember anyone saying *at the time* that Procter and Richards were noticeably better prospects than Bevan and Ashenden.

At the end of the season, Procter and Richards decided to go home. It was the 'instant qualification' clause that later decided them to return to England (Richards to Hampshire), and though it is true that the increase of overseas players has deprived many young English cricketers of chances, it is also worth remembering what an amount of pleasure these two have given since they appeared regularly in English summers.

Procter's development as a cricketer has been much influenced by Gloucestershire, because Gloucestershire in his time have needed a hundred wickets from him more than two thousand runs. In South Africa, where he scored his six successive centuries in 1970–71 (equalling the record of Fry and Bradman, though possibly in less taxing circumstances), he has been able to do more justice to his batting. Even so, I have always felt that Gloucestershire put him in too high in the order. He has great strength, but he is mortal, and nobody can be expected to take all the wickets and score all the runs on seven days of a week. Of course, it is always tempting to put him in early, because he can win a match in an hour, and he is always prepared to try. But that bowling action must take a lot out of the strongest man, and he has suffered a good many strains and breaks in the last year or two.

Two of his innings recur to me: the more recent the one he played against Somerset in the Benson & Hedges competition in 1972. I forget how many he made, well over a hundred, and I remember that he was dropped when 40 or so, but he demolished Somerset, and the variety and power of his strokes in the latter part of that innings I have never seen equalled (think again? No, I have never seen them equalled, even if it *was* a one-day bun-fight).

The other innings was quite different. In the fourth match between England and the Rest of the World in 1970, the Rest needed 223 to win in the last innings, and were 75 for 5 overnight, with Richards and Kanhai unfit (though both did bat on the last day). Procter came in to join Richards with eight wickets down, and 40 still wanted. From the way he played the first ball, plumb in the middle, it was clear he intended to win the match, and so he did. He scored 22 not out, and it does not sound much, but there was an authority about the innings which forbade any suggestion that he would ever get out.

There are, on the other hand, times when he seems to take his cricket casually. The appearance can be deceptive, and anyway a man who does so much work is entitled to an occasional breather. He is inclined, perhaps, to present to the world a picture of himself as one of the flannelled fools. But he has a generous and flexible mind, and his reactions to the problems at present facing South African cricketers have been honest, brave and even liberal.

# Derek Underwood

## ROBIN MARLAR

Derek Underwood is one of the larger gold nuggets on the cricket scene. As a cricketer he fascinates me. He is a phenomenon among bowlers. There is seldom more than one of those in a cricketing generation.

Our story begins, as Frankie Howerd might say, on a summer's day in 1945. The young Underwood, sired by a keen right-handed fast bowler christened Leslie Underwood, was born in Bromley 367 days after D-day. Sociologists would immediately park this young Underwood in the opening phase of the post-war bulge. The cricket boom which reached its peak in 1947 was due to begin. At the right moment a concrete wicket appeared in the Underwood garden: there was one in the garden of the young Frank Hayes, too. Concrete wickets in gardens make better grounding for young batsmen and fast bowlers than for spinners – but more of that later.

Derek Underwood duly arrived at the Dulwich College Preparatory School. He took nine wickets in an innings before he was 10; there's no experience like that for making a young bowler realize what is *possible* in cricket. For, ever after, eight or nine wickets in an innings represents a key to a private Shangri-La. If he enjoys visits to that special place, a bowler needs no other motivation. He is a bowler who has *bowled a side out*. Different. Formidable. A bigger figure in the side. Soon after, Underwood, now at Beckenham Grammar School, made 96 against the staff. Perhaps it was as well that he stuck to hitting wickets and not runs. He had developed a pair of bowler's 'plates'. That's what I remember best about his first season in the Kent side. He was 17. His feet were enormous. Great splayed members encased in heavy boots. To a Sussex man they looked especially ominous. They were Maurice Tate's feet.

In that season, 1963, Underwood bowled 950 overs and took 100 wickets at 21 apiece. There will never be a debut like it. And this comet blazed on and on. He had taken 1000 wickets before he was 26: only Rhodes and Lohmann reached that mark earlier in life. The 1000-wicket men are giants each and every one. In 1966 he became a Test cricketer. In 1968 he won a match against Australia: 7 for 50 in 31 overs at The Oval. He took the last wicket six minutes from the end. It was John Inverarity's. The ball pitched outside the off stump and would have hit. Inverarity was the last of three leg-before decisions Underwood got that day.

It was at about this time that cricket was beginning to come out of its worst-ever decade. One of the principal activities of this dark age was law-meddling. Under the new leg-before law Inverarity would not have been out unless he had played no stroke. To get a leg-before decision Underwood – left-arm round – had to pitch on the wicket and hit it. On a good wicket this was nigh impossible. Claude Lewis, the Kent scorer, thought Underwood, England's best bowler, ruinously affected. Most law-meddlers think like batsmen and are unaware of the mental effect of change on bowlers: the new law restricted Underwood's target area and hence his effectiveness.

Up to that time he was comfortably averaging a wicket every ten overs. Since then he has been pushing towards eleven overs. But he has continued to be a star among bowlers, and though Norman Gifford edged him out of the England XI on numerous occasions during the Illingworth regime Underwood remained the favourite of most critics simply because of his *matchwinning* capability.

There are two other reasons for the clouding of his early glory. Batsmen, pressed by the needs of one-day cricket, are prone to lay back their ears at the sight of any bowler slower than fast-medium. A left-hander is fair game for the cross-bat swing to leg. No longer can he operate with a weakened leg side on a good wicket. Being swung to leg unhinges confidence. Underwood, who learned the steadiness any seamer must have on his concrete wicket, was uncannily accurate in his late teens and early twenties. Hardly anyone got after him. Recently batsmen have sought to and sometimes succeeded in hitting him out of the firing line.

The second reason that life has become harder is that people now understand Underwood. As a world-class bowler with ten years' exposure he is revealed as a slow-medium to medium-pace left-arm bowler, primarily round the wicket, who can vary his pace, swing the ball in to the right-hander, occasionally make it leave the bat either off the seam or by finger cut, and – on a helpful wet wicket – make the ball rear to the point of being unplayable. In such conditions many sides – perhaps most of all New Zealand – have been annihilated. He is *not* a spin bowler as the ancients would understand the term. Spin bowlers are best reared not on concrete but on grass where they can see what happens when the ball is spun. It pitches and leaps off in another direction. The spun ball is the fun ball. A luxury.

Derek Underwood has the action of a medium-pacer. It is a fine action. Rhythmic. Controlled. Plenty of body. It lends itself to accuracy. He also has stamina. He can bowl for hours. But now he knows that this is not enough. To be as great a bowler in cricketing annals and affections as Wilfred Rhodes or Jim Laker or even Bishan Bedi he has to be able to get wickets all over the world and not primarily in England, the seamer's paradise. What is he to do? Is he to change his action and become a spinner, pure and simple? Or is he to develop another action and operate in two distinct styles? Who will teach him to spin the ball? 'This is a tricky one,' said another admirer, Colin Cowdrey. 'At this level we're talking about John Jacobs putting Tony Jacklin right.' Could Jim Laker do it? Someone must. Underwood has at least eight more years in which to play a vital part in winning a series on hard wickets overseas where the only aids are bounce and dust.

It will not be easy. Unlike some of the great non-spinning

leg-spinners like O'Reilly, or the quicker off-break bowlers like Bob Appleyard – another fascinating operator – Derek Underwood has a slow arm action. Appleyard, like Laker, had a fast arm. So did Tom Goddard. So did Tony Lock, especially when he had the extra degree of devastation from a bent elbow. Lance Gibbs has a quick arm. From a fast arm all excellence in spin bowling derives: both the spin and the flight. Without a fast arm a spinner is plain. Batsmen can measure the minimal risk he is likely to pose and attack without fear or folly. At present Derek Underwood is trying to experiment but he has not yet achieved the breakthrough. I wish him well. If he were ever to succeed to the point of bowling a side out by flight and spin a second Shangri-La would be revealed. And that will be a priceless bonus for hours of work on the rebuilding of an action. The downside risk is enormous: suppose that he lost even that which he has in a fruitless search for something better. His character as well as his cricket is under test.

# Bishan Bedi

## TONY LEWIS

When you have seen Bishan Singh Bedi twirl down his left-arm spinners after 60 overs with the same gentle rhythm and control as he first settled into at the start of his spell, you understand why his is a great bowling action. Even more so in his own country, where the test of stamina is more severe in burning heat and on hard-baked grounds which tug on the muscles and jar all the joints.

I have always thought that a great clockmaker would have been proud to have set Bedi in motion – a mechanism finely balanced, cogs rolling silently and hands sweeping in smooth arcs across the face. Yet it would be wrong to portray him as something less than human – all hardware and no heart – because he bowls with a fiery aggression which belies his gentle and genial nature. His rhythm too has only come after countless hours of practice in the nets.

His captains, who for most of his Test career have been 'Tiger' Pataudi and Ajit Wadekar, often introduced him to the attack within the first half hour of a Test innings. Indeed when England fell prey to the pressures of spin and close catching last time out in India, the brightly turbaned, left-arm spinner was seen loosening up at third man while Solkar was only in his second over.

That is not such crazy logic. On many overseas surfaces the shine is often gone within a quarter of an hour. So, without having genuine pace at their disposal, these Indian captains offered their high-class spinners a fairly new firm ball which settled easily into the hand and, most important of all, produced bounce at the batsman's end. Bedi thrived, with close fieldsmen leaping around the bat as batsmen attempted to fight through their first few overs.

Bishan Bedi was never formally taught the bowling skills. He confesses: 'As a young boy in Amritsar I just happened to get hold of a ball and roll it around as it left my hand.' So it is not surprising to learn that as the instinct to spin grew quickly, his stamina developed alongside, and the young man who had taken up the game only at the late age of thirteen at St Francis High School was making his debut in first-class cricket two years later for Northern Punjab in the Ranji Trophy.

'I was lucky with my easy action,' he admits, inferring that it came naturally. 'It is smooth, I suppose, and I have spent hours developing the rhythm. So I am not like lots of other spinners who get sore fingers, you know, strains in the ankles and thighs. A good action spares you that. Do you know, I have never had finger trouble.'

The fine art of Bishan Bedi is based on his personal philosophy. He bowls to get wickets by deceiving batsmen, tricking them into false shots, crowding them initially, but carefully placing fielders to trap the one that looks like getting away. I once asked him if he bowled differently in attack than in defence. 'I have never bowled defensively,' he quickly came back at me. 'Some left-arm spinners in English cricket set their fields straight away, six on the off and three on the leg. I like a couple up close to start, especially with the new batsman – a slip, a gully and a square gully if I can, and then one on the leg side, because the batsman might fear the off trap and play outside the ball. I always bowl at the stumps. I have never bowled one side or the other just to contain.'

In an era when limited-overs cricket has pushed British spinners along the defensive road, blocking shots and waiting for the indiscriminate move by the batsman, Bedi's approach is becoming almost a treasure of the past. Or should we consider ourselves fortunate that the very best of the world's spinners like Bedi and Intikhab are playing in county cricket, and have flare-lit the way for young spinners and their coaches?

The skills he has acquired therefore are attacking skills. Apart from the orthodox spin which *leaves* the right-handed batsman, he also grips the ball less firmly and slides the wrist under it, genuinely under-cutting it, so that it goes straight on the other end, despite the appearance of genuine finger-spin. Another ball, seam up, with similar action, he floats down at rather quicker pace. It can dip into you through the air, though I must be honest, when I have faced him abroad, the ball that has intrigued me most is the seamer which appears to drift outwards towards the slips. It never seems to happen in England. Or is it just me? I must talk to Farokh Engineer and George Sharp, the men who keep wicket to him.

We return again to the personal qualities which have made Bedi exceptional even by the highest standards, because he is surely the best left-arm spinner in the world.

Running hopefully in pursuit of a ball along the boundary line he bounces along, one-paced, without ever being able to

summon the muscle strength to slip his solidly-made body
into third gear. His head rolls from side to side and a large
smile tells the crowd that here is a man prepared to joke at his
own limitations. They love him in India.

When the moment comes to bowl, the smile vanishes. A
frown joins the pleats of the turban (patka, strictly speaking),
a serious concentration. Classically, the eyes of aggression
appear over the right shoulder, behind the raised right arm as
he bowls. He beats the bat and he groans, does it twice and he
hates. Yet should the victim leap from the crease and crack a
six, the first applause will come from the bowler. Stoically
Bishan Bedi casts his bait, over after over, each ball looking
like the last, until the victim is drawn forward where the ball
no more is, and that is the dream for which he endlessly toils
for Northamptonshire and for India.

# Dennis Lillee

## DAVID FRITH

There have been faster bowlers than Dennis Lillee, but not
many. There have been more hostile fast bowlers, but not
many. Spofforth, Ernie Jones, Constantine, Heine, Charlie
Griffith, Andy Roberts, Jeff Thomson – all have brought
menace, even terror, to the bowling crease. Lillee concedes
nothing to any of them.

He is one of the great fast bowlers of the twentieth century,
possessing a full set of gear changes, a knowledge of aero-
dynamics equal to Lindwall's, an abundance of stamina and
determination, and more courage than is given to most.

He needed that courage in 1973 and '74 when he set about
achieving one of sport's most impressive comebacks. The
four stress fractures in the lower vertebrae would have

finished many a career. Lillee, having dramatically bowled his way to fame, was faced with six weeks in plaster and a long and gruelling fight to full fitness. He withstood the punishment and handsomely repaid those who had worked with him and believed in him. He played cricket again, though only as a batsman. Then he put himself on to bowl. No twinges. At the end of the 1973–74 season his hopes were at least as high as the highest of his notorious bouncers.

England arrived next season to defend the Ashes in six Test matches. Lillee pronounced himself fit and dismissed Ian Chappell two or three times in early-season interstate fixtures. Australia selected him again. And in the first Test a new extermination firm was formed: Lillee and Thomson. England's batsmen at Brisbane would just as happily have taken their chances in the company of Leopold and Loeb, or Browne and Kennedy, or, at the end of the day, Burke and Hare. It was devastating, still fresh in memory.

Australia's opening pair took 58 wickets in the series out of 108 that fell to bowlers – this despite Thomson's withdrawal through injury halfway through the fifth Test and Lillee's after six overs in the final match with a damaged foot.

The full force of this controlled cyclone was felt in the 1975 series, though England's sleeping pitches absorbed some of the energy. This was when Lillee's other bowling skills asserted themselves. As in the 1972 series, when he took a record 31 Test wickets, Lillee beat batsmen by change of pace and with his wicked awayswinger. Rod Marsh and the ever-expectant slips cordon did the rest. He had more support now: from the tireless Walker, from Gilmour (who would have strolled into any other Test team in the world), and from Thomson whenever he had his rhythm.

This winter, interrupted only by pleurisy, he has gone on to torment and punish the West Indians, taking his hundredth Test wicket in the process. Still that remade and wonderfully broad back held up against the pounding constantly dealt it by its owner.

Dennis Lillee's inspiration, when only a boy, came from a West Indian: Wes Hall, the genial fast-bowling giant. The young fellow from Perth, born on W. G. Grace's 101st birthday (July 18, 1949), clambered with all the fervour of a Beatles fan into the members' enclosure at the W.A.C.A. ground just to be near his idol. There was also Graham McKenzie, the pride of Perth, to fan the flames of his ambition. And Fred Trueman. And Alan Davidson.

Not that this was enough. There had to be an inherent talent. The tearaway with long sideburns, who stormed in over a long distance and hurled his wiry body into delivery with every ounce of his might, eventually played for Western Australia. By 1970–71 he was considered good enough to play for Australia – one of the hopes in a reshaping of the national eleven. He took 5 for 84 against England at Adelaide in his maiden Test, opening the attack with another young aspirant, Thomson – Alan ('Froggy'), not Jeff.

A season in Lancashire League cricket with Haslingden followed. Next he bowled against a conglomerate team billed as the Rest of the World. In Perth he decimated them with 8 for 29, including 6 for o in one red-hot spell (when he wasn't feeling too well). Gavaskar, Engineer, Clive Lloyd, Greig and Sobers were among the victims. The wider world at last took notice and wanted to know all about him.

He was learning all the time, especially when trying to bowl to Sobers during his indescribably brilliant 254 at Melbourne, when straight-drives came bouncing back from the boundary before the bowler had raised himself upright in the followthrough. Yet he continued to harass the tourists, not by any means now trying to bowl every ball at top speed, and if England in the spring of 1972 thought Australian claims of Lillee's bounce and penetration were exaggerated, the threat was soon a vivid reality.

He has sometimes attacked batsmen with his tongue – and been denounced for it. Brian Statham used to let the ball do all his talking. Fred Trueman's ripe language was somehow not the antithesis of geniality. Dennis Lillee's 'verbal aggression' has been something else in its spirit of near-hatred. One could name others in cricket history who have gone about their business in this way, only to be left with the feeling that in each case the bowler has failed in one respect to do himself justice. Lillee was a central figure in Australia's re-emergence as a formidable side, and a great deal has continued to be expected of him. The chanting of the crowds, the persistent publicity, the inescapable typecasting, the need to transpose celebrity into a real-world security – all this must take a man away from himself, at least in part.

A truth that will remain is that Perth has given to cricket a fast bowler of hawklike countenance and perfect physique for his purpose, whose flowing approach and superb athletic action have been a thrilling spectacle for young and old, male and female, pacifist and warrior.

# Acknowledgments

1. The following acknowledgments were made in respect of texts included in the first edition.

To the Executors of the late E. W. Hornung and John Murray Ltd. for 'Chrystal's Century' from *Old Offenders and A Few Old Scores*;
To Mr Edward Bucknell and Williams and Norgate Ltd. for a chapter from *Linden Lea*;
To Mr Siegfried Sassoon and Faber & Faber Ltd. for *The Flower Show Match* and for two poems;
To Sir J. C. Masterman and Penguin Books Ltd. for 'Fincham v. Besterton' from *Fate Cannot Harm Me*;
To Macmillan & Co. for an extract from 'England, their England' by A. G. Macdonell;
To Mrs de Selincourt for *Tillingfold Play Wilminghurst* by Hugh de Selincourt;
To Mrs Joan Farjeon and Macdonald & Co. Ltd. for 'Herecombe v. Therecombe; from *Cricket Bag* by Herbert Farjeon; also to Mrs Farjeon for *The Call of May*;
To Mr Ian Peebles and Souvenir Press Ltd. for 'A Question of Policy' from *Batter's Castle*;
To Mr Rex Warner and The Bodley Head for 'The Average Match' from *Escapade*;
To Mr L. P. Hartley and Hamish Hamilton Ltd. for 'A Norfolk Visit' from *The Go-Between*;
To Mr Gerald Brodribb and Sporting Handbooks for 'Cricket in Fiction' from *All Round the Wicket*;
To Mr H. S. Altham and Allen & Unwin Ltd. for extracts from *A History of Cricket*;
To Mr Neville Cardus for numerous extracts from *The Essential Neville Cardus* (Cape) and *Cricket All the Year* (Collins); also to Mr Cardus and to The Cricket Writers Club for 'George Gunn' from *Cricket Heroes*;
To Mr A. A. Thomson and to Museum Press and Robert Hale Ltd. respectively for extracts from *Cricket My Happiness* and *The Great Cricketer*;
To Mr Clifford Bax and Phoenix House Ltd. for an extract from *W. G. Grace*; also to Mr Bax for *Cricket Days*;
To Methuen & Co. Ltd. for an extract from *Cricket Memories*;
To Mr Denzil Batchelor and Phoenix House Ltd. for an extract from *C. B. Fry*;
To Allen & Unwin Ltd. for a chapter from *Cricket Highways and Byways* by F. S. Ashley-Cooper;
To Mr Jack Fingleton and William Collins Sons & Co. Ltd. for extracts from *Masters of Cricket*;

To Mr R. C. Robertson-Glasgow and Dennis Dobson Ltd. and T. Werner Laurie Ltd. respectively for chapters from *All in the Game* and *Cricket Prints*; also to Mr Robertson-Glasgow for two poems;

To Mr John Arlott and Phoenix House Ltd. for a chapter from *Tate*, as also to Mr Arlott for five poems;

To Mr E. W. Swanton and Playfair Books Ltd. for an extract from *Denis Compton: A Sketch*;

To Mr Ray Robinson and William Collins Sons & Co. Ltd. for an extract from *From the Boundary*;

To Mr Arthur Mailey and Phoenix Sports Books for a chapter from *10 for 66 and All That*;

To Mr Dudley Carew and Secker & Warburg Ltd. for a chapter from *England Over*;

To Mr Edmund Blunden and William Collins Sons & Co. Ltd. for a chapter from *Cricket Country*, and to Mr Blunden for two poems;

To Mr Ivor Brown for his poem *Brighter Cricket*;

To J. M. Dent & Sons Ltd. for *Village Cricket* by Gerald Bullett;

To Mr Gavin Ewart for his poem *The Cricketer's Arms*;

To Sir George Rostrevor Hamilton and William Heinemann Ltd. for two poems;

To Edward Arnold Ltd. for the poem by Harry Graham;

To Sir Alan Herbert and Methuen & Co. Ltd. for *Ninth Wicket*;

To Mr W. A. G. Kemp for *Scorebook*;

To Mr R. D. Lancaster for *The Hayfields*;

To Longmans, Green & Co. Ltd. and the Executors for *Play!* and *Ballade of Dead Cricketers* by Andrew Lang;

To Mr William Kerr for *Past and Present*;

To Mr Oscar Lloyd for *Grace at Gloucester*;

To the Executors and Methuen & Co. Ltd. for poems by E. V. Lucas and Norman Gale;

To Mr G. D. Martineau and Methuen & Co. Ltd. for two poems;

To Mr George McWilliam for *Epitaph*;

To Mr George Moor for *Club Match*;

To Mr Egbert Moore (Lord Beginner) and Melodisc Records Ltd. for *Victory Calypso*;

To Mr Thomas Moult for *The Names*;

To Mr Norman Nicholson and Faber & Faber Ltd. for three poems from *Rock Face*;

To Mr Hubert Phillips for *An Englishman's Lease*;

To Mr Hugo Williams for *Boy at a Cricket Match*;

To Mr P. G. Wodehouse for *Missed*;

To Mr Ralph Wotherspoon for *The Band at Play*;

To Mr Ron Yeomans for *County Cricket*.

Finally, I should like to thank my own publishers, Hamish Hamilton Ltd. for the poem from *To Whom It May Concern*.

2. Acknowledgments and thanks are due to the following in respect of matter included in this edition.

To Sir John Betjeman and John Murray Ltd. for *Cricket Master*;
To Edward Brathwaite and Oxford University Press for *Rites*;
To Stewart Brown for *Raising the Screen* and *At Sabina Park*;
To J. L. Carr and London Magazine Editions for *A Station at War*;
To Gavin Ewart and Victor Gollancz for *Huckstep, Valediction: To The Cricket Season* and *The Cricket of My Friends*;
To Alan Gibson and William Collins Sons & Co. Ltd. for *Leyton and the Commentary Box*;
To Brian Jones and London Magazine Editions for *Cricket Pitch: 1944* and *Cricket for Christmas*;
To Ian Peebles and Hutchinson & Co. Ltd. for *Frank Woolley*;
To Harold Pinter and Eyre Methuen Ltd. for *Hutton and the Past*;
To Neil Powell for *The Cricketers*;
To Simon Raven and Blond & Briggs for *The M.C.C. Match*;
To Alan Ross and Eyre Methuen Ltd. for *A Photograph of Hammond* and *A Cricketer in Retirement*;
To Vernon Scannell for *Wicket Maiden*;
To E. W. Swanton and William Collins Sons & Co. Ltd. for *A Few Old Buffers*;
To the authors and The Cricketer Ltd. for *Crusoe, Tom Graveney, Colin Cowdrey, Ray Illingworth, Clive Lloyd, Mike Procter, Derek Underwood, Bishan Bedi* and *Dennis Lillee*.

# Index of Authors

# More About Penguins
## and Pelicans

For further information about books available from
Penguins please write to Dept EP, Penguin Books Ltd,
Harmondsworth, Middlesex UB7 0DA.

*In the U.S.A.*: For a complete list of books
available from Penguins in the United States write
to Dept DG, Penguin Books, 299 Murray Hill
Parkway, East Rutherford, New Jersey 07073.

*In Canada*: For a complete list of books available from
Penguins in Canada write to Penguin Books Canada
Ltd, 2801 John Street, Markham, Ontario L3R 1B4.

*In Australia*: For a complete list of books available
from Penguins in Australia write to the Marketing
Department, Penguin Books Australia Ltd, P.O. Box
257, Ringwood, Victoria 3134.

*In New Zealand*: For a complete list of books available
from Penguins in New Zealand write to the
Marketing Department, Penguin Books (N.Z.) Ltd,
P.O. Box 4019, Auckland 10.

*Look out for these from Penguins!*

CARNIVAL IN ROMANS
*A People's Uprising at Romans 1579–1580*

Emmanuel Le Roy Ladurie

'In February 1580, Carnival in Romans was a time of masks and massacres for the divided citizenry.' Concentrating on two colourful and bloody weeks, Professor Ladurie vividly resurrects the social and political events that led to the tragedy of 1580.

'*Carnival* . . . is a dazzling psychodrama . . . brilliant analysis of social conflicts . . . intriguing interpretation of the parades, masquerades and feasts of carnival time' – Lawrence Stone in the *New York Review of Books*

'Professor Le Roy Ladurie is one of the greatest historians of our time . . . this is a book not to be missed' – Christopher Hill

BENINGFIELD'S BUTTERFLIES

'A painter devoted to capturing the spirit of the countryside which endows his pictures with a quality that evades the mere illustrator' – *Guardian*

'Jewel-like beauty' – *Field*

This edition features additional illustrations of Gordon Beningfield's beautiful stamp designs for the Post Office – an artist who has an 'extraordinary knack of combining the naturalist's eye for detail with the painter's feeling for patterns and textures' – *Sunday Times*

THE HISTORY OF MYDDLE

Richard Gough   Edited by David Hey

The Parish of Myddle in 1701 was as full of life, gossip, intrigues, births, marriages and deaths as any other small community in Stuart England.

What made Myddle different was that one of its parishioners, Richard Gough, decided to write down the family history of the occupants of each pew in the church. And, as he was gifted with a remarkable ear for anecdote, a sharp eye for foible and a pithy pen for a telling phrase, his history, brimming over with a delighted curiosity and enjoyment, gives us a quite incredible glimpse into the seventeenth-century family and parish, and into the characters of the men and women who seem to live and breathe on his pages today as they did then.

## THE COUNTRY RAILWAY

David St John Thomas

For those who regret the passing of Britain's country railways, this
loving portrayal will bring back the charm and nostalgic delight
of that halcyon time when rural branch lines were a necessary and
much appreciated lifeline for people living in country outposts.
Trim station platforms, colourful gardens, tank engines' shining
brasswork, daringly built viaducts, decorative bridges and
embankments carpeted with flowers – all these features are celebrated
in words and pictures in this unique labour of love.

## THE BOOK OF CATS

Edited by George MacBeth and Martin Booth

P. G. Wodehouse's Webster, Saki's Tobermory, Kipling's Cat
that Walked by Himself, Eliot's Macavity, Don Marquis's
mehitabel: short stories from Patricia Highsmith, Roy Fuller
and Giles Gordon: the classics of Walter de la Mare, W. W.
Jacobs and Edgar Allan Poe: the cats of Robert Southey,
Théophile Gautier and Theodore Roosevelt: the observations
of Aldous Huxley, Henry Fielding and Mark Twain: paintings
by Bonnard, Goya, Picasso, Chagall, Hockney and Douanier
Rousseau.

In all an affectionate medley of prose, poetry and pictures,
assembled by George MacBeth and Martin Booth in praise of
that most elusive and fascinating of creatures – the cat.

## THE PLEASURE GARDEN

Anne Scott-James and Osbert Lancaster

From Roman peristyle to 20th-century patio, Anne Scott-James
conducts us through 2,000 years of the English garden; to linger,
first in simple, enclosed courtyards of medieval days and the
formal showpieces of Jacobean England, and later, to wander
through sweeping, moody landscapes of the 18th century.
We learn of each age's distinguished botanists, designers and
architects, who employed the social conditions and the fads and
fashions of the time to shape the gardens of their day.

Anne Scott-James's witty and informative text and Osbert
Lancaster's delightful drawings are so evocative that we can almost
smell the flowers as we step from one bower of pleasure to another.

*Look out for these from Penguins!*

## THE WORKS
Beryl Cook

'Beryl Cook is the nicest thing to happen to British painting for
years . . . it makes me laugh out loud' – Edward Lucie-Smith

'Wildly funny and painted with the most loving detail . . . her way
with bottoms, hands, bottles, newsprint and local vegetation
is all her own' – Alan Ross

Introducing the world of Beryl Cook – Plymouth Argyle
footballers, drag artists, transvestites, sailors on the Hoe, fish-
and-chip shops, Teddy boys, fat barmaids, and all manner
of wickedly funny goings on.

## WEATHER FORECASTING
*The Country Way*

Robin Page

Would you like to be able to choose the best weather for
gardening, fishing or visits to the Test Match? Then read on.

Observation of animal behaviour, plant growth or the wind,
clouds, stars and moon is an ancient and well-tried method of
weather forecasting. You may, for example, know what happens
if it rains on St Swithin's Day or if there is a red sky at night,
but what if it snows at Easter or if spiders spin long webs?

In this delightful book, Robin Page demonstrates that, by
applying common sense to country lore, you need never have
your holidays 'rained off' again!

'Good light reading, it is spiced with amusing asides and
pretty pictures' – *New Scientist*

## LET'S PARLER FRANGLAIS
Miles Kington

Le Franglais est un doddle! Parlez Franglais, et le monde est
votre oyster. Après 10 secondes, vous serez un expert, Belt
Noir des languages – sans kidding. Ici Miles Kington présente
40 lessons hilarieux en des situations d'everyday. Dans le stately
home, chez le dentiste, eyeball-à-eyeball avec la traffic warden,
dans Soho après dark, toutes les phrases essentielles sont là. So,
prenez un glass de bon plonk, light up une Gauloise et
commencez l'aventure la plus exciting de votre existence!

## THE VILLAGE CRICKET MATCH

John Parker

As the last ball is bowled, the stumps drawn, and the shadows
lengthen over the field of play, spectators and players adjourn to
the village pub to relive the game over good, strong ale . . .

The same gentle, sun-drenched atmosphere is beautifully
evoked in *The Village Cricket Match*: the common rustic swing, the
rare and truly elegant late cut, the demon fast bowler and the
lucky six into the village pond, are all here.

Written with a deep affection and enthusiasm, this novel is a
unique tribute to the game: a book that will more than substitute
for a wet Saturday afternoon and a rained-off test match.

## THE GO-BETWEEN

L. P. Hartley

In one of the first and finest of the post-war studies of early
adolescence, an old man looks back on his boyhood and recalls
a summer visit to a Norfolk country house at the beginning of
the century.

Not yet equipped to understand the behaviour of adults, he
is guiltily involved in a tragic drama between three grown-up
people. The author forcefully conveys the intensity of an
emotional experience which breeds a lasting mistrust of life.

## A MONTH IN THE COUNTRY

J. L. Carr
Winner of the *Guardian* Fiction Prize

In the summer of 1920 two men meet in the quiet English
countryside. One is a war survivor, living in the church, intent
upon uncovering and restoring a historical wall-painting. The
other, too, is a war survivor, camping in the next field in search
of a lost grave.

And out of their physical meeting comes a deeper communion,
with the landscape, with history, and a catching up of the old
primeval rhythms of life – past and present – so cruelly
disorientated by the Great War.